BRITISH MISCALCULATIONS

The Rise of Muslim Nationalism, 1918-1925

Isaiah Friedman

Transaction Publishers
New Brunswick (U.S.A.) and London (U.K.)

Library of Congress Catalog Number: 2011038259
ISBN: 978-1-4128-4749-0 (hardcover); 978-1-4128-6300-1 (paperback)
eBook: 978-1-4128-4710-0
Printed in the United States of America

Library of Congress Cataloging-in-Publication Data

Friedman, Isaiah.
    British miscalculations: the rise of Muslim nationalism, 1918–1925 / Isaiah Friedman.
        p. cm.
    Includes index.
    ISBN 978-1-4128-4749-0
    1. Arab nationalism—Palestine—History.   2. Palestine—Foreign relations—Great Britain.   3. Great Britain—Foreign relations—Palestine.   4. Great Britain—Foreign relations—1910–1936.   I. Title.
    DS119.6.F75 2012
    320.54095694089'927409042—dc23
                                                                    2011038259

To Barbara,
My dear wife and friend

Contents

Acknowledgments

With the completion of this book, third in the series, I am happy to express my thanks and deep gratitude to the many people and institutions that helped me.

First, I should like to reiterate my tribute to my alma mater, the London School of Economics and Political Science, where I first acquired the craftsmanship of a historian, the respect for detail and for detached presentation, and, above all, the urge to search for truth. I endeavored to follow the wisdom of the School's motto: *Rerum Cognoscere Causa.*

I cherish the memory of Professor W. N. Medlicott, Stevenson, Professor of International History at the LSE., and his successor, Prof. James Joll. I was extremely fortunate to have the goodwill of Prof. Sir Isaiah Berlin, OM. His encouragement and wise counsel over a great number of years were of inestimable value and left an indelible impression upon me. I also had the great privilege of knowing Lord Beloff (Prof. Max Beloff) who read closely my previous book, and I had the benefit of his observations and insights.

Unfortunately, none of the above has survived to see my latest volumes in print. I lament their passing.

I am greatly indebted to the Ben-Gurion University for their interest and support. I am particularly grateful to all the administrative staff whose friendship and eagerness to help has warmed my heart. This is particularly true of the staff in the Zalman Aranne Library of the university.

It goes without saying that this study, as well as the previous ones, would never have been possible without the wealth of documents available at the Public Record Office, London. Transcripts and quotations of Crown Copyright material appear by permission of the controller of

H. M. Stationary Office. Other archives and libraries to which I would like to record my indebtedness are as follows:

The British Library of the London School of Economics and Political Science; the London University Library; the British Library; St. Antony's College, Oxford; the Bodleian Library, Oxford; The Imperial War Museum Library; the National Library of the Hebrew University, Jerusalem; the Israel State Archives, Jerusalem; the Central Zionist Archives, Jerusalem; the Hagana Archives, Tel Aviv; and the Weizmann Archives, Rehovot.

I had the benefit of the editorial assistance of Ms. Edna Oxman, whose punctiliousness and expertise won my admiration. I am deeply indebted to her. Mr. Pavel Yartsev too deserves some words of praise for prompt and faultless typing of my MS.

My debt to my wife, Barbara, remains the greatest of all. She has read all of my MS, and I treasure her advice and assistance. It gives me great pleasure to dedicate this book to her.

—Isaiah Friedman
Emeritus Professor of History
Ben-Gurion University of the Negev
Beer-Sheva
August 2011

Introduction

After all the bloodshed and destruction during World War I, it seemed that the Wilsonian principles would usher in a new era for ravaged Europe. It was also assumed that President Wilson's point number twelve, in conjunction with Lloyd George's commitment in his Trade Union speech on January 5, 1918, would offer a sound negotiating basis for an equitable peace with Turkey. However, it appears that the Allied powers overlooked the meaning of peace. The deeper meaning of this word entails forgiveness and reconciliation. The kind of "peace" that the Allies imposed on the Central powers was a dictated peace—peace of revenge—the one against Turkey was harshest of all. After the war, Turkey had reconciled herself to the loss of her Asiatic provinces; all she cared about was that the Allies respect her sovereignty and that the territories of Anatolia and Thrace not be infringed. Such an optimistic scenario did not happen.

The Allies, Britain in particular, were unaware of the transformation that had taken place in Turkey's domestic policy. Nor did they take advantage of Turkey's genuine desire to conclude a separate peace during the latter part of the war. Turkey was prepared to grant the non-Turkish minorities autonomy, the Jewish community in particular. Britain rejected all the overtures.

Efforts were renewed when a new cabinet was formed on October 14, 1918, by Izzet Pasha. His message was that it would be more beneficial for England "to have a friendly and obedient Turkey than to drive her to the necessity of desperate resistance by dictating impossible terms." Turkey's only request was that no Greek warship would land in Istanbul (Constantinople) or Izmir (Smyrna) and that Istanbul would not be occupied by the Allies. The British cabinet accepted these conditions. So the question that inescapably comes to mind is: what went wrong? And what set Britain on a collision course with

Turkey and, indeed, with the Muslim world at large? The answer to these questions is twofold:

1. Britain's disregard of Muslim sensitivities
2. The Greek invasion of Smyrna

Throughout Islam, there was furious agitation against the dismemberment of the Ottoman Empire. For centuries Turkey was looked upon as the bulwark of Islam, and Muslims could not reconcile themselves to its overthrow. A British intelligence officer suggested that unless Britain took measures to placate Muslim opinion, she might be confronted with emergence of "a very strong political Islam" in Egypt, India, and elsewhere. The idea, however, was not taken up.

Lloyd George's mind was cast in the Gladstonian mold, and from his childhood, he had grown up hating the Turks. He was convinced that the Turks were "the ruffians of Europe . . . and that they had put themselves irredeemably beyond the pale of civilized society." Foreign Minister Curzon was an imperialist par excellence. His views on Turkey were extreme. It was, therefore, not surprising that Greek territorial claims to Smyrna and other territories in Thrace and Asia Minor, made known by Venizelos, the Greek prime minister, made such a strong appeal to Lloyd George. He was also won over by the idea of a Greater Greece. It became a cornerstone of his foreign policy.

The Greek occupation of Smyrna, with Allied connivance, took on the aspect of conquest and of a crusade—it was far from a *mission civilisatrice*. It shocked the Turkish people. Heretofore submissive and lethargic, they now had a rude awakening. They felt that their very existence as a nation was at stake. That Britain had broken her word was particularly offensive. It stimulated Turkish patriotism. The Turkish national movement came into being.

The Turkish national movement was fortunate in having a leader like Mustafa Kemal, later known as Atatürk. He resolved to fight for Turkey's independence—free from foreign domination—a homogeneous Turkey that would shed the vast Asiatic provinces. This concept was later embodied in a manifesto issued by the first Turkish National Congress, which met at Erzerum in eastern Anatolia on July 23, 1919, and amplified at the congress at Sivas, which claimed to represent the whole country. "Provided Turkish independence was assured," the congress declared, "a Nationalist government will not prove anti-English." The plea for Turkish cooperation with the British fell on stony ground however.

The British remained hostile toward the Turkish Nationalists. Rather than engage the British openly, Kemal adopted an indirect strategy by arousing the Muslim world against Britain. First, on June 16, 1919, he concluded an agreement with Emir Feisal. It was a political and a military alliance. Its purpose was to emancipate the Arab countries from British domination and to create Mesopotamian, Syrian, and Palestine states under nominal Turkish suzerainty.

What conditioned Feisal's attitude toward the British was religion. He was not alone. In October 1919 Colonel Meinertzhagen reported that in Arab countries "a whole movement is Pan-Islamic, pro-Turk . . . Yasin Pasha is the moving spirit."

This situation played directly into the hands of the Bolsheviks whose primary aim was to turn the Muslim world against the British Empire. They used the principle of self-determination for all it was worth. It facilitated the growth of nationalism and the desire for independence. The slogan that was gaining currency in the East was this: "Be Nationalist because it is the only way to save Islam."

Winston Churchill, then secretary of state for war, was greatly concerned about Britain's standing in the Muslim world and was critical of his government's policy. He urged it to come to terms with Mustafa Kemal and abandon reliance on "the weak and fickle Greeks." He failed, however, to carry the cabinet with him.

The Middle, as well as the Near East, were in a state of turmoil. In March 1919, there were violent outbursts in Egypt, trouble in Afghanistan, an open rebellion in Mesopotamia, an uprising in Syria in July 1920 and prolonged hostilities with Mustafa Kemal from 1919 to 1923, and the rise of a determined nationalism in Afghanistan and Persia.

George Nathaniel Curzon, the foreign secretary, was ill-equipped to deal with this development. A late Victorian of upper middle class, he failed to understand the rising nationalism in the Islamic countries and to encounter the postwar complexities in the East. Nationalism was an anathema to him. He was guided by the so-called forward policy—a concept suited for the nineteenth century.

There was no love for the British, and both the Persians and the Afghans refused to serve as pawns for British imperialists, however enlightened they might have been. Besides, the dismemberment of the Ottoman Empire, the supposed violation of the holy places, and the Greek invasion of Smyrna and beyond aroused violent hatred throughout the Muslim world and a belief that the Christian powers were bent on the destruction of Islam.

Concerned primarily with achieving their own independence, the Persians, as well as other people in the Near East, viewed Bolshevik policy to be less dangerous than that of the British. Like Churchill, Meinertzhagen, and others, the General Staff advocated a complete reversal of policy. It proposed to make concessions to the Turks and so to wean them away from their alliance with the Bolsheviks. Turkey would be recreated thus as a buffer state between the Allies and Russia, and one of the principal causes of unrest in the East would be removed. The suggestion found only few takers in the cabinet. On February 26, 1921, a Soviet–Persian treaty was signed. Two days later, a similar treaty was concluded with Afghanistan.

The campaign in Mesopotamia was the brain child of local officers in the East for whom the lure of Baghdad was irresistible. The initiative was that of amateurs. The army was not prepared and was ill-equipped. Medical services were totally inadequate and operational planning was nonexistent. Nor was there intelligence network, which is a precondition to any military operation.

The greatest error in the officers' thinking was the expectation that one could wean the Arabs away from Turkey and harness them in a way of liberation from the "Turkish yoke." The Arabs of Mesopotamia, as elsewhere, would not raise their hand against the sultan-caliph and substitute the domination of an infidel for a Muslim Empire. The native population regarded the British army as intruders, rather than as liberators.

The defeat of the British contingent at Kut-al-Amara was inevitable. Its fall reverberated through the East and caused considerable damage to British prestige. When General Maude eventually captured Baghdad in March 1917, the army had already paid a heavy price in manpower and matériel. The administration in the occupied territories, from its inception, registered the "bitter experience of Arab hostility, Arab thefts, and rapacity." Arnold Wilson concluded that cooperation between British and Arab elements in Mesopotamia was "impossible."

In May 1919 General Haldane reported that propaganda from Syria was poisoning the minds of the inhabitants of Mesopotamia, while Ms. Bell confirmed that Feisal's army "was at the root of national agitation." Feisal's propaganda caused considerable concern both in London and in Baghdad. His aim was to free Syria, Palestine, and Mesopotamia from foreign rule and establish Arab states under nominal Turkish suzerainty.

An outbreak of violence became inevitable. The fall of Tal Afar in June 1920 was the signal for a general uprising of all the tribes in the north. It spread to the middle of the Euphrates, and the position became serious. British officers were murdered with impunity. Both the Turks and the Bolsheviks played a role in fanning anti-British sentiments. Nationalism, intertwined with religion, bore its bitter fruit. An armed insurrection was in the making. On June 30, 1920, a rebellion broke out. Numerically, and otherwise, the British were outnumbered. Their position was becoming precarious. General Haldane managed at last to subdue the rebellion, though at a cost. The total of British and Indian casualties amounted to 2,270. The total war in Mesopotamia, from its inception, cost the British hundred thousand casualties and approximately £350 million pounds. British public opinion was outraged.

In September 1922 Lloyd George agreed with Churchill's analysis that the campaign in Mesopotamia was a mistake. Sir George Buchanan referred to it as a "tragedy—a tragedy of . . . suffering, wasted lives, and efforts."

And yet, the tragedy of Mesopotamia paled in comparison to what followed in the Greco-Turkish war in Asia Minor. The occupation of Smyrna was a fatal mistake. This, however, was compounded by the aspiration of the Greek government to create a Hellenic Empire on the ruins of Turkey. Carried away by enthusiasm, the Greek government was oblivious of the many pitfalls: Anatolia's vast territories, long lines of communication, Angora's impregnable strategic position, the financial shortcomings of the Greek treasury, and above all, the toughness of the Turkish peasant/soldier who was fighting for the survival of his country against an invading enemy. It was for these reasons that General Metaxas, an outstanding Greek military commander, refused to accept the offer to lead an offensive in Anatolia in April 1921. In his estimate, a war against the Turks could not be won. The statement bordered on the prophetic. The Turks won a resounding victory. Non-Turkish parts of Smyrna went up in flames and the non-Muslim population was brutally ill-treated and expelled.

Finally, our study shows that in the aftermath of World War I, there was a fair chance of mutual coexistence and good neighborly relations between Arabs and Jews in Palestine. This, however, was nipped in the bud by the military administration (1918–1920), while Herbert Samuel, when high commissioner, by supporting the extremists, complicated the situation still further. The appointment of Hajj Amin al-Husseini to the exalted post of grand mufti of Jerusalem, and subsequently to the presidency of the Supreme Muslim Council of the Palestinians, proved fatal to Arab–Jewish relations and to the peace in general.

1

A Missed Opportunity

In February 1918, William Yale found out that CUP leaders had realized their mistake in trying to Turkify the Arab people and had changed their policy drastically. In an effort to persuade the Arabs that their only salvation lay within the Ottoman fold, they were prepared to offer them full-scale autonomy and even transformation of the empire into a dual Turkish–Arab state with a strong Islamic and anti-British bias. Dismemberment of the Ottoman Empire in the aftermath of the war, Yale warned, would give birth to a general national Turkish revival. Moreover, Turkey would endeavor to sow seeds of discord and incite the Arab-Muslim population in the occupied territories with the object of undermining British and French rule.[1]

A year later, M. Gauvain—a well-known French commentator on foreign affairs on the other side of the spectrum—wrote in the *Journal des débats*: "The British government with a singular imprudence has created a Pan-Arabism and a new Pan-Islamism of which England will be the first victim."[2] Both statements, though written from different perspectives, proved remarkably prescient. When Turkish nationalism, actively supported and aided by the Bolsheviks, allied itself with Pan-Islam and Arab nationalism, the British position became precarious. The irony was that the predicament into which the British had fallen was of their own making: the Arab card that Cairo officials had played so zealously proved ineffective and unreliable, while the Prime Minister's policy vis-à-vis Turkey in 1918–1922 had led to disastrous consequences for Britain's standing in the East, as well as for his own political future.

This outcome had not necessarily been inevitable. When President Wilson enunciated his celebrated Fourteen Points, it seemed that a page of a new World Order had opened. Point twelve postulated that

> [t]he Turkish portion of the present Ottoman Empire should be assured of their sovereignty, that the other nationalities which are

now under Turkish rule shall be assured of undoubted security of life and absolute unmolested opportunity of autonomous development, and that the Dardanelles should be permanently open as a free passage to the ships and commerce of all nationals, under international guarantees.[3]

Three days earlier, in an address to the Labor Union Congress (January 5), Lloyd George, unfolding the Allied war aims in the East, had declared thus:

> Nor are we fighting to deprive Turkey of its capital, or of the rich and renowned lands of Asia Minor and Thrace, which are predominantly Turkish in race ... while we do not challenge the maintenance of the Turkish Empire in the homelands of the Turkish race with its capital at Constantinople—the passage between the Mediterranean and the Black Sea being internationalized and neutralized—Arabia, Armenia, Mesopotamia, Syria, and Palestine are in our judgment entitled to a recognition of their separate national conditions.[4]

These principles of policy offered a sound negotiating basis for an equitable peace with Turkey. As events showed, Turkey reconciled herself to the loss of her Asiatic provinces; all she cared about was that the Allies respect her sovereignty and that the territories of Anatolia and Thrace not be infringed. Such an optimistic scenario, however, did not take place. On October 2, 1918, the day after the capture of Damascus, and following Bulgaria's withdrawal from the war (September 30, 1918), the cabinet decided to offer Turkey an armistice, not a separate peace. The terms were extremely severe: they were purely of a military and naval character, devoid of any political clauses; they ordered the immediate demobilization of the Ottoman army on all fronts and complete disarmament; the Allies could occupy any strategic territory they wished, and control the means of communication.[5] Following consultation with France and Italy, additional clauses were added that made the conditions even more severe. After approval by the cabinet, they were sent to Vice Admiral Sir Somerset Gough-Calthorpe, the British commander in chief in the Mediterranean, and to General Sir George F. Milne and General Allenby. President Wilson was also informed.[6]

The armistice was signed on October 30, 1918, on the British battle ship *Agamemnon* at Port Mudros on the Greek Island of Lemnos. All the twenty-five provisions were exceedingly harsh.[7] Turkey was rendered defenseless and, with Constantinople—its capital—occupied, it ceased to be an independent country. It was a far cry from the solemn declarations made by President Wilson and Prime Minister Lloyd George in January 1918 and showed cynical disregard of the proclaimed Allied principles. There was no generosity or magnanimity on the part of the victors. Turkey was treated, not as a vanquished adversary but as a hostile power against which one must be on guard, ready to forestall any revanchist designs in the future. This premise was mistaken, since, in the aftermath of the war, Turkey was no longer hostile, nor was it dangerous to British strategic interests. The British cabinet, however, was unaware of the transformation that had taken place in Turkey's domestic policy and did not take advantage of Turkey's genuine desire to conclude a separate peace during the latter part of the war.

Early in February 1917, Tala'at Bey, minister of the interior, succeeded Prince Said Halim as grand vizier and Djavid Bey reentered the cabinet as finance minister. Together they made a formidable combination. Tala'at had risen to an almost unassailable position in the cabinet, overshadowing his rivals Enver Bey, minister of war, and Djemal Pasha, minister of marine, then commander of the Fourth Ottoman army in Syria and Palestine. Although as ruthless as his colleagues, in character, Tala'at towered head and shoulders above them. He was gifted with a swift and penetrating intelligence and, among diplomats, behaved like a European. He was a real statesman. "If any statesman could have succeeded in reforming the old Ottoman Empire, it would have been Tala'at Pasha," Count Johan H. Bernstorff, the last German ambassador in Constantinople, recorded in his *Memoirs*. Tala'at was the only Turk whom Bernstorff learned to like and respect. "A statesman . . . in the truest sense of the word. There was not a sign of the parvenu in his behavior or ideas . . . and his political conceptions were unencumbered by any pettiness."[8]

Djavid was considered Tala'at's alter ego. At the outbreak of war, he was one of four ministers who resigned in protest against Turkey's joining the Central Powers. He was the least pro-German of the Turkish statesmen and, from 1917, persistently endeavored to win American friendship as a counterbalance to Germany. He agreed to accept the portfolio of finance on condition that Turkey modified her extreme nationalist policy and improve her treatment of non-Turkish and non-Muslim elements. Early in March, he came out with a courageous speech in the Ottoman Parliament, denouncing "the spirit of nationalist maliciousness." He maintained that Turkey's weakness and financial predicament called for an early conclusion of peace. In December 1917, a motion was laid before the parliament to reform the empire and to decentralize the system of government.[9]

Both Djavid and Tala'at assiduously courted Abram Elkus, the American ambassador, in the apparent hope that they might secure America's backing in case of emergency. On April 2, when America was about to declare war on Germany, Nessimy Bey, the foreign minister, told Elkus that his country's attitude toward the United States was friendlier than ever and wished to continue in that sentiment. Elkus reciprocated this approach. At this juncture, both Tala'at and Djavid were willing to grant far-reaching concessions for Jewish immigration and colonization in Palestine as a quid pro quo for assistance given by Jewish financial circles in America to the Ottoman Treasury.[10]

Though forced to sever diplomatic relations with Washington, the Porte managed, much to Elkus's satisfaction, to resist the Wilhelmstrasse's pressure to declare war on the United States. Turkey's goodwill was matched by that of America's; President Wilson firmly believed that all the evil stemmed from German militarism and that the peoples of Austria-Hungary, Bulgaria, and Turkey desired to assert their independence; the corollary being that, should some equitable proposition be made to them, they might opt out of the war, leaving Berlin isolated.

Balfour, at that time in the United States, agreed that, should Turkey and Austria be willing to break away from Germany, "certain concessions [by the Allies] should be made to them." Shortly thereafter, Secretary of State Lansing informed Balfour of conversations he had had with Henry Morgenthau, the former ambassador to Constantinople, as well as with the former consul-general in the Balkans, from whom he gathered that conditions in Turkey were deteriorating, that the Germans were detested, and that the Turkish authorities were ready to conclude peace. Balfour was also told that Morgenthau was willing to go unofficially to Switzerland to pursue the matter. Balfour saw no harm in having Morgenthau make an attempt, "while if matters took a favorable form, results might be of enormous advantage." In London, General Robertson, the chief of the Imperial General Staff, also supported the idea.[11]

In fact, the idea was not a new one. Secret pourparler through various go-betweens to bring about a separate peace with Turkey had been going on for some time.[12] Following the March 1917 Revolution, when the provisional government in Russia renounced any annexationist claims to Constantinople, the circumstances seemed to be favorable for fruitful negotiations. This was why the British government at first welcomed America's initiative.

Yet nothing came out of it. Both Chaim Weizmann and James Malcolm, leader of the Armenian community in England, were greatly perturbed. They feared that their respective interests might be gravely prejudiced and made strong representations to the Foreign Office. Consequently, Sir Ronald Graham, the assistant undersecretary for foreign affairs, as well as Lord Robert Cecil, the undersecretary for foreign affairs, became convinced that the proposed Morgenthau mission could no longer serve any useful purpose. Ormsby-Gore used even stronger language. For Britain to let the Turco-Teutonic combine survive in such a unique strategic area, he wrote, was unthinkable, and at this juncture, it was vital not to lose sight of two great world forces: Islam and Jewry. A solution that would leave the Arabs and Zionists under Turkish rule would sooner or later involve the British Empire in another struggle. "If our declared war aims mean anything, surely Armenia . . . Syria and Palestine . . . have the same claim to liberation as Belgium." Idealistic motives apart, the overriding concern for Ormsby-Gore was to secure a viable line of defense in order to prevent a German–Turkish hegemony in Southwestern Asia.[13]

Morgenthau failed to carry out his mission. Weizmann, who met him in Gibraltar, skillfully managed to talk him out of it.[14] The end of Morgenthau's mission, however, did not mean that the Foreign Office altogether dismissed the idea of peace with Turkey. On July 7, Sir Horace Rumbold, the British minister in Berne, reported that a number of leading Turkish politicians had arrived in Zurich with the object of making a peace proposal. The delegation included, Rifaat Effendi, president of the Ottoman Senate, Muchtar Bey, the secretary of the senate, Hadji Adil Bey, president of the chamber of deputies, and Fethi Bey, minister at Sofia. They were later joined by Fuad Selim Bey, Turkish minister at Berne, and his military attaché. Cecil lost no time in suggesting that any Turkish advances should be given a sympathetic hearing. Lord Milner, senior cabinet minister, was also interested, while Balfour made no objections. A fortnight later, Rumbold learned that Tala'at wished to instigate a military uprising in order to get rid of Enver and, in return for England's support, was ready to concede certain constitutional changes in Syria, Mesopotamia, and Armenia. The Turks in Zurich, acting on Tala'at's behalf, thought that the pro-German policy

5

should be superseded by an Anglo-Turkish understanding, provided that there was "no complete partition of Turkey."[15]

Lord Hardinge, the permanent undersecretary of state for foreign affairs, was elated. Whatever lay behind this conspiracy, anything concrete that could come out of it could only benefit Britain. Cecil thought that "it would be madness to let slip such a chance"; Sir Louis Mallet, a stalwart Turcophile, considered it "essential" to meet Turkish overtures, while Sir George Clerk, although skeptical of Tala'at's chance of success in view of the deteriorating conditions in Russia and the military impasse, insisted that the British should do everything in their power to detach Turkey. Cecil became impatient when, early in September, Ismail Muchtar Bey, the secretary of the Ottoman Senate, confided to a British agent in Geneva that the Turks would have liked to go over to the Allies—they were willing to open the Straits to Allied fleets to sink the German warships anchored in the Bosporus—but the indispensable prerequisite was that the Allies would grant Turkish independence. A separate message from Rahmi, vali of Smyrna, known for his integrity, sounded even more promising. Thereupon, Cecil advised Rumbold that the British government would be ready to offer any terms that would be consistent with British obligations to Arabs, Armenians, and Jews.[16]

The only dissenting voice was raised by Sir Mark Sykes. He thoroughly distrusted the Turks. Enjoying the prime minister's support, he delivered one of the most scathing attacks on what he termed "the Foreign Office pro-Turk gang." Their ideas were ill-advised and risky. The C.U.P. leaders were "masters in the old art of chicane . . . bounded by no moral scruple." A soft peace with Turkey would leave Germany as the dominant power in the East. This fact, taken together with Pan-Islam in Turco-German hands, left Britain's position in India and Egypt exposed to perpetual harassment. To forestall such an eventuality, it was essential, Sykes thought, that the friendship between England and France should be given a permanent foundation and that their respective imperialist leanings be transformed into patronage of the oppressed peoples: the Arabs, the Jews, and the Armenians. "We are pledged to Zionism, Armenian liberation, and Arabian independence. Zionism is the key to the lock." Turkish influence over her Asiatic provinces should be completely eliminated, to be superseded by an Arab–Zionist–Armenian Entente under Anglo-French aegis. It was to serve as an antidote to a soft peace with Turkey and would form the nucleus of a new order in the Middle East. At the same time, the

Allies should declare that they harbored no sinister designs against Turkey proper.[17]

Persuasively as both Sykes and Ormsby-Gore argued, the premise on which they had built their strategy was faulty. Turkey was war-weary and, since Tala'at's accession to premiership, wished to emancipate herself from Germany's embrace and conclude a separate peace. Enver was a notable exception. The so-called German–Turco combine that constituted a threat to British imperial interests was much in evidence early in the war, but after the capture of Beer-Sheva, it was no longer relevant. Germany, for her part, diverted her *Drang nach Osten* to more profitable objectives: the Ukraine in Eastern Europe and Persia in Central Asia.

At home, Turkey was prepared to decentralize the government of the empire and grant the non-Turkish minorities autonomy, the Jewish community in Palestine in particular. Tala'at was known to be a friend of the Jews and was favorably disposed toward Zionists. Before the war, when minister of the interior, he had lifted all former restrictions on Jewish immigration and colonization and during the war, did his best to curb Djemal Pasha's excesses against the Jewish community in Palestine. In January 1918, he met a Jewish delegation composed of Zionists and non-Zionists in Berlin and told them that he was willing to encourage the immigration of a large number of Jews to Palestine and to grant them autonomy. Turkey had long recognized Palestine as the "Jewish religious center," leaving, however, no doubt that the term "religious" was not necessarily synonymous with "spiritual." The delegation got the distinct impression that, although the word "national" was not used, it was nonetheless implied. At any rate, they could point out with confidence that the "most important Jewish national demands" were not rejected.[18]

Tala'at's statements belie the black image that Sykes had presented of him and show that a modus vivendi—at least as far as Zionism was concerned—between the British and the Turks could have been found. In October 1917, Lloyd George told the war cabinet that it was necessary first to deal the Turks "a heavy blow and then offer them terms designed to buy them out" of the war.[19] Such a move, however, was never made, either after the capture of Jerusalem, or after that of Damascus.

As for the Arabs, it will be recalled that the Allies were committed only to recognizing and support Arab independence won by the Arabs themselves.[20] Since, with the exception of King Hussein, the

Arabs, by and large, did not fight for their own liberation, the Allies were absolved from their commitment. In 1922, both Lloyd George and Churchill admitted that conquest of Syria and Mesopotamia was a wasted effort.[21]

Failing to elicit a response from the British to his overtures, Tala'at, during his visits to Vienna and Berlin in September 1918, tried to convince the Austrian and German governments to jointly approach the Allies and sue for peace. In Vienna he found a ready ear, but Berlin remained obdurate. Tala'at was frustrated and, during his meeting on September 20 with Matthias Erzberger, the leader of the Catholic Centrist Party, he bitterly complained about the ruinous policy of the German Generals. "If Germany wishes to get peace at all, she should transform her constitution to a parliamentary democracy,"[22] he stated.

Tala'at saw the writing on the wall. On August 8, Ludendorff suffered a disastrous defeat in France; it was a "black day" [*schwarze tag*] for the German army. The German guarantee for the integrity of the Ottoman Empire, as prescribed in the Turco-German Treaty of September 28, 1915 and ratified twice thereafter, became meaningless. On his return home, Tala'at witnessed the disintegration of the Bulgarian army; his Bulgarian opposite number told him about the decision of Sofia to opt out of the war. On September 30, 1918, Bulgaria signed an armistice with the Allies.[23] The territorial link between Germany and Turkey was disrupted. This opened the road for General Franchet d'Espèrey, the officer commanding the Entente army in Macedonia for an assault on Constantinople. The Turks panicked. On October 1 Damascus fell. It was, however, Bulgaria's collapse, not General Chauvel's victory in Syria, brilliant though it was, that prompted the Turkish government to seek peace at any cost. On September 22, Mustafa Kemal Pasha (about whom much will be said later) succeeded in withdrawing the Seventh Ottoman army under his command, as well as the remnants of the Eighth, to the east of the Jordan River. He made no attempt to defend Damascus and, on October 5, reached Aleppo unscathed. There he reorganized the surviving units from the Fourth and Eighth armies and headed toward the Taurus passes on the Syrian–Turkish border to build a new front.[24] The passes were well fortified in a mountainous terrain. The ANZAC cavalry reached Aleppo, exhausted and sick. There was no chance that they could have taken the passes. According to General Sir Charles Townshend, "the Turks could have gone on resisting [the British forces] fully four or five months, perhaps longer."[25] It was the fear of the danger of an imminent attack on Constantinople that made the Turkish cabinet anxious to conclude an armistice.[26]

Tala'at returned to Constantinople in a somber mood. His long-standing fear that the Central Powers would lose the war had come true. He offered to resign and recommended Ahmed Tewik Pasha and General Ahmed Izzet Pasha to form a new cabinet. Tewik had served during Abdul Hamid's reign as prime minister, while Izzet had made his name as an army commander in the Balkans and as war minister, representing the empire at the Brest-Litovsk peace talks. Neither of them was guilty of dragging Turkey into the hapless wars, nor were they tainted by the ill-treatment of the Armenians. Tala'at hoped that their untainted background would make them more acceptable to the victorious powers and spare Turkey harsh terms. This, however, was not to be. On October 11, learning that the British government would impose on Turkey an armistice, he resigned at once and two days later, the whole C.U.P. cabinet followed suit.

On October 14, a new cabinet was formed by Izzet Pasha as prime minister and minister of war, Djavid Bey, minister of finance, and Hussein Rauf Bey, as minister of marine. During World War I, Rauf Bey had served as chief of naval staff but resigned in protest against undue interference by his German counterparts. He was known to have harbored pro-Entente proclivities and participated in the peace negotiations at Brest-Litovsk where he displayed some diplomatic acumen.

The first act of the new cabinet was to send a message to President Wilson (through the good offices of the Spanish Embassy), asking him to undertake the task of "reestablishment of peace" on the basis of his Fourteen Points and subsequent messages. Wilson passed on the Turkish note to the Allies, who, ominously, did not respond.[27]

It was when all the avenues seemed to be closed that a likely savior from unexpected quarters appeared. This was General Sir Charles V. F. Townshend, who was captured during the siege of Kut-al-Amara in Mesopotamia in 1915–16. He had been kept on the island of Prinkipo off Constantinople in relative comfort and was allowed to socialize with leading Turkish politicians. Those with whom he was in touch told him that Turkey's only hope of salvation was to make peace with England, that they had enormous losses in the war and even greater losses from disease and malnutrition, that at least three hundred thousand deserters were roaming about the country, terrorizing the inhabitants, and that there was a move to divest Enver of his post.

Townshend was convinced that Turkey was too weak to cause Britain any harm and that the British should offer her lenient terms for peace. "[T]hey should be left on our road to India"[28] as a potential strategic asset. This thinking reflected the traditional British policy, which the Indian Office had habitually advocated.

On October 12, when he heard about the resignation of the Tala'at–Enver government and that Marshal Izzet Pasha had become grand vizier and minister of war, Townshend asked the Vizier for an urgent interview. He also sent a note to Rauf Bey, the newly appointed minister of marine, whom he had befriended, suggesting that, in return for the honorable way in which he had been treated during his captivity, he was willing to assist the Turkish government in its negotiations with the British. On the following day, October 16, he received an invitation from Izzet to meet him at the Sublime Porte. The latter greeted Townshend warmly and admitted that his only reason for accepting the post was his wish to save his country from ruin. He came from a family that had always respected England and remembered her support of Turkey during the Crimean war and thereafter. "It was a crime," he emphasized, "for Turkey to have made war on England and [he] referred bitterly to the Enver party that had done so." In an answer to Townshend's question, Izzet stated that he was ready to open the Dardanelles and the Bosphorus and to grant autonomy to Syria and Mesopotamia, though under the sovereignty of the sultan. All that Turkey wanted, he said, was the "protection" of England. Like Townshend, he thought it should be more advantageous for Britain to keep Turkey as a guardian on the road to the East instead of another entity that could become a thorn in her side. "But," he exclaimed,

> We could not accept dishonorable terms; we are not Bulgarians . . . we will put our backs to the wall and fight. You know what the Turks can do when driven to it, for you have fought against them. Do not drive us out of Constantinople or Turkey-in-Europe, where we have been settled for centuries, for this is impossible for us to accept.

To enable Townshend to fulfill his mission, Izzet granted him liberty.[29]

Rauf came to see Townshend on the same day in his house at Prinkipo and was even more cordial. During a lengthy conversation, he elucidated that Turkey wished to maintain friendly relations with England and was ready to give autonomy to the territories occupied by the Allies. He expected in return that Turkey's political, financial, and industrial independence be respected and that England would protect her and be generous in granting financial assistance in order to tide her over the crisis. "Treat us as gentlemen, and we will be loyal." He added that he was ready to concede a free port at Constantinople that would be of tremendous commercial advantage to Britain.

Townshend thought that such a concession, taken together with the control of the Straits and free access to the Black Sea, put "all Turkey at [Britain's] feet." He saw no advantage in occupying any of the towns in Turkey. "On the contrary, I see a great strategical error, for it means . . . a violation of the greatest of fundamental principles of war, namely, Economy of Force." For the same reason he thought that there was no justification for keeping the British army both in Syria and Mesopotamia; if it was found that the latter was important, he would recommend retention only of Basra, which should be made into a free port.[30] Significantly, Townshend did not mention Palestine; it was a sui generis.

On October 20, accompanied by a Turkish officer, Townshend arrived at Mudros, much to Admiral Calthorpe's surprise. From Mitylene he sent a cable to London in which he briefed the cabinet of Izzet's terms for peace and quoted Rauf's plea: Turkey trusted England; England in her part would find it more beneficial "to have a friendly and obedient Turkey than to drive [her] to the necessity of desperate resistance by dictating impossible terms."[31]

Townshend's message was discussed by the cabinet on the same day. Andrew Bonar Law, leader of the Conservative Party, which was a partner in Lloyd George's coalition government, stated that, as the new Turkish government was favorably disposed toward England, the terms should be ameliorated. "It would be worthwhile," he suggested, "to accord an armistice on the terms of free and secure passage of the straits alone, which would really give us all that we require." Lloyd George fully agreed. The most important thing in his opinion was "to obtain access to the Black Sea." On the other hand, Lord Curzon, an avowed imperialist, objected on grounds that the Turks were "a badly beaten enemy." Sir General Henry Wilson, the chief of the Imperial General Staff, supported Lloyd George and advocated soft terms; that is, an armistice based solely on freedom of passage through the straits to the Black Sea.[32]

Clemenceau and Orlando were consulted, but the French Premier objected to any alteration of the terms. Pichon, the French foreign minister, protested firmly that Admiral Calthrope had entered into direct negotiations with the Turkish representatives without authorization from the Allied powers. Lord Milner, the secretary of state for war, was dispatched to Paris to pacify the French. Eventually he gained Clemenceau's acquiescence, but the exclusion of Vice Admiral Amet, a senior French officer at Mudros, from negotiations with the Turks, was a slight, which the French did not forget.[33]

In consequence, the terms remained practically unaltered and, as mentioned above, they were extremely harsh. It was much to Admiral Calthorpe's diplomatic skill and tact that the Turkish delegation swallowed the bitter pills, one by one with good grace. Calthorpe impressed Rauf as being "an honest and open-minded man." Admiral Seymour, though more narrow-minded, also did not appear to be moved by the spirit of revenge. In short, the English delegation "had behaved not as the arrogant representatives . . . of victorious nations but [as though they were] two nations who had clashed under the influence of events but who now felt the need of ending the struggle."[34]

There was hard bargaining on the question of the straits. The Turks finally agreed that the Allies would occupy its fortifications but issued a stern warning: "the English can come and secure the guns," Rauf declared, "but if the Greeks or the Italians come, I tell you plainly that we had better see ourselves killed . . . than allow it." He hoped that, having satisfied Britain in this matter, they would not covet any other territory of Turkey proper. He calculated that, as before the war, the British would be concerned to keep Russia out of the straits and that, for this reason, "it would be in their own interest to ensure the survival and freedom of a strong and peaceful Turkey."[35] Before signing the armistice (October 30, 1918), Prime Minister Izzet showed the text to Mehmed Vahideddin VI, the new sultan, who commented, "However heavy the conditions are, I accept them so as not to lose England's friendship. Later on it will be possible to lighten the terms, thanks to this friendship." In his memoirs published in 1962, Rauf wrote the following:

> Since the Crimean War there was a general conviction in our country that England and France were countries faithful not only to their written pacts but also to their promises. And I had this conviction too.

On an aside, however, he recorded an admission: "What a shame that we were mistaken in our beliefs and convictions!"[36]

However humiliating the terms and whatever the scruples of the Turkish delegates, in fact they had no choice but to accept them; the alternative was prolongation of the war, which Turkey could ill afford. The nation was ruined financially. By 1918, its public debt of 1914 had quadrupled; the effect of war damage, general despoliation, widespread misery, and raging inflation were devastating. Turkey was obligated to sever relations with Germany, and all German industrial constructions, including the Taurus Tunnels, were left in ruins.

Turkey was now totally dependent on Allied goodwill for sheer sustenance. Food and fuel were in short supply,[37] and there was a breakdown of law and order and the total absence of rudimentary security.

After the signing of the armistice, Admiral Calthorpe gave Rauf Bey a letter promising that only the British and French would be allowed to use the straits in the presence of a very small number of Turkish soldiers. Calthorpe added that he had passed on the Turkish requests to London that no Greek warship would land in Istanbul or Izmir and that, unless the Turkish government failed to maintain order, Istanbul would not be occupied by the Allies.

The British cabinet, in its meeting on October 31, confirmed Calthorpe's recommendations. The cabinet was greatly pleased with Calthorpe's achievement and even Curzon, the hard-liner among his colleagues, admitted that the compliance of the Turkish delegation exceeded his expectations.[38]

Townshend was not privy to the negotiations. When invited by Rauf to come on board HMS *Agamemnon*, he found that all the delegates, British and Turkish, were delighted. Rauf welcomed him warmly, saying: "Turkey will never be able sufficiently to show her gratitude to you for making the peace possible." And privately he asked him to pass on a message to Lord Curzon and tell him that Turkey could be counted as "a faithful ally to England" and that the sultan had told him before leaving for Mudros that the Turkish delegation "must make peace with England . . . We can be trusted," he added, "to give equal rights to Greeks and Armenians . . . Turkey has no intention of interfering in any way with the Arabs. They can have autonomy but, you know as well as I do, that the Arabs are not capable of ruling themselves, and that this autonomy ought to be under the suzerainty of the sultan."[39]

It seems that, in 1917, the Tala'at–Djavid government, and now the new cabinet of Izzet and Rauf, aspired to reform the Ottoman Empire and to create a modus vivendi with the non-Turkish and non-Muslim nationalities. Izzet and Rauf, both Anglophiles, were making a serious effort to achieve a genuine reconciliation with the British and to open a new page in Turkish history. So the question that inescapably comes to mind is, what went wrong? And what set Britain on a collision course with Turkey and indeed with the Muslim world at large? The answer to these questions is twofold:

1. Britain's disregard of Muslim opinion.
2. The Greek invasion of Smyrna.

Before dealing with the first question, it would be useful to sketch the historical background of relations between Islam—with particular reference to Turkey—and the Western, non-Muslim powers. "Islam," wrote Sir Theodore Morison, in an article quoted already, "is more than a creed, it is a complete social system; it is a civilization with a philosophy, a culture . . . in its long struggle against the rival civilization of Christendom it has become an organic unit conscious of itself. To this civilization the Muhamadans are very deeply attached."[40]

The conflict with Christianity, as well as with other religions, is built in the very doctrine of Islam, which is both exclusionist and expansionist. According to the Koran, the only true religion is Islam, and those who follow other religions are losers.[41] The Muslims believe that the world is divided into two Houses: the House, or domain, of Islam [*Dar al-Islam*] and the House of War [*Dar al-Harb*], inhabited by non-Muslims. One of the duties of Muslims, the true believers, is to expand *Dar al-Islam* at the expense of *Dar al-Harb*. The term *jihad* was understood to mean "command for expansion of Islam" or "struggle for its defense." As Prof. Bernard Lewis points out, between the House of Islam and House of War (which was inhabited and ruled by the infidels), there was "a perpetual state of war until the entire world either embraced Islam or submitted to the rule of the Muslim State."[42]

During the Middle Ages, the Persian and Turkish Muslim Empires were the richest, the most powerful, and the most enlightened regions in the world, while Christendom was on the defensive. The year of 1683 was a watershed. The second Turkish siege of Vienna ended in total failure, followed by a steady retreat from occupied lands. Now the European powers in the West and Russia in the East went on the offensive, gradually building their empires and establishing a dominant role in world trade. The invasion of Napoleon Bonaparte in Egypt and Palestine caused a profound shock to Islam, only to be surpassed by even greater shock that the French departure was not caused by the Muslim state but by a naval squadron of another infidel country,

England. By the early twentieth century, huge Muslim territories were incorporated into four European empires of Britain, France, Russia, and the Netherlands.[43]

These reverses were doubly painful to the Muslims because loss of territories implied diminution of the sultan's temporal power. More to the point, the Muslims felt that once the temporal power of the caliphate disappeared, Islam would be doomed. In an address presented to Lord Chelmsford in January 1920, the All-India Caliphate Conference stated inter alia as follows:

> Temporal power is the very essence of the institution of the Khalifat, and Mussulmans can never agree to any change in its character, or to the dismemberment of its empire.

Two months later, the caliphate delegation declared that "[t]he Khalifa was not the Pope, and the moment he consented to be "Vaticanized," he would cease to be Khalifa."[44]

Resentment against territorial encroachment by the Christian powers was augmented by their unwarranted meddling in Turkey's internal affairs. The powers abused their privileges, which, based on the principle of extra territoriality, had been concluded in early treaties known as the capitulations. Originally, the system had proved a blessing to all concerned. It spared the Ottoman government the complicated task of administering the affairs of foreign visitors, increased the visitors' security, and stimulated trade. But with Turkey's decline, particularly during the nineteenth century, the system had degenerated into blatant abuse by the European powers. The privilege of extraterritoriality had been extended to a sizeable non-Muslim population who misused it, flouted local regulations, and did not hesitate to make capital out of their legal security. Foreign banks, post offices, and commercial houses mushroomed on Turkish soil and took full advantage of the country's feebleness, while the foreign consuls grew more insolent as they grew more powerful. Protégés of foreign powers, claiming partial immunity from the laws and exemption from local taxation, had become a scourge to the country.

It was not until the late 1850s that Turkey, becoming more conscious of her own sovereign rights, had begun to regard the capitulations as a humiliating encroachment. The turning point came in 1856, when Turkey first raised the question of abrogating the capitulatory rights, holding them to be both harmful and obsolete.

For decades, Turkish diplomats strove, albeit unsuccessfully, to nullify, or at least to restrict, the excessive prerogatives of the powers. The latter would not budge. On the contrary, the London Conference of January 7, 1871, reaffirmed and extended them, while the Treaty of Berlin of 1878 endorsed them yet again. The capitulations thus assumed a binding character and acquired a valid international status. Turkey remained, in fact, outside the pale of international law. This had a profound effect on her and determined her attitude toward the European powers and foreigners in general.[45]

As a consequence, everything that was foreign became suspect. Muslims opposed "Westernization," considering it dangerous and bordering on the heretical. Western values, although admired and imitated in certain circles, were rejected by the general population. Intensified Christian missionary activities were viewed as a challenge to the religio-cultural identity of Muslims. Islam was under threat; Europe was the enemy—this was the concept propagated passionately and vociferously by writers and preachers, such as Muhammad Abdu Jamal al-Din (commonly known as al-Afghani), Muhammad Rashid Rid'a, and others of the same ilk.[46] The Pan-Islamic propaganda of Abdul Hamid was also directed against the Christian West and aimed at awakening a sense of Muslim solidarity. Captain N. N. E. Bray pointed to the "extreme vitality" of the Pan-Islamic movement. During his stay in Damascus before the war, and later in Jeddah, he witnessed the intensity of the efforts to propagate the gospel of Pan-Islam; its ideals were being taught in schools and preached in mosques.[47] Pan-Islamic sentiment transcended geographical and ethnic boundaries and was particularly strong among the seventy million Muslims in India.

Foreign Minister Grey was fully aware of the very strong feelings of loyalty in the Muslim world toward Turkey—their political and religious center. Supported by Prime Minister Asquith, he advocated the policy of status quo. One of the reasons that made the de Bunsen Committee reject the partition of the Ottoman Empire in the aftermath of the war was that it would deeply offend Muslim opinion.[48]

It was the proposal of Muhammad al-Faruqi of an Arab revolt against Turkey in the whole of the Fertile Crescent that destroyed the good work of the de Bunsen Committee and changed drastically the direction of British policy. The British miscalculated badly. In fact, there was no general Arab revolt. Sharif Hussein's rebellion came as a shock to the whole Muslim world, particularly in India. There was, at the time, no real support for the idea of Arab nationalism, and the

British belief that their sponsorship of such an idea could be instrumental in overthrowing Turkish rule was based on a misconception. The Arabs regarded themselves primarily as Muslims and, as such, were reluctant to be ruled by non-Muslims. This reluctance stemmed from the very nature of Islam according to which, rule by non-Muslims was tantamount to blasphemy. Far from being welcomed as liberators from the Turkish "yoke," the native population looked upon the victorious British army as uninvited occupiers. Eventually, this basic misconception of Arab sensibilities sparked a flame of religio-nationalist feeling that finally drove the European powers out of the Middle East.

Soon after the armistice, attempts were made to win back Arab allegiance to Turkey while Pan-Islamic elements were fanning Arab hostility against the Entente powers.[49] The call for Arab independence was merely a euphemism for the elimination of a European presence. In fact, the entire East was in a tumultuous ferment. Leone Caetani, duke of Sermoneta, a leading Italian authority on Islam, expressed grave alarm. In the spring of 1919, speaking on the effect of the war against Turkey, he declared thus:

> The convulsion has shaken Islamic and Oriental civilization to its foundations. The entire Oriental world, from China to the Mediterranean, is in ferment. Everywhere the hidden fire of anti-European hatred is burning. Riots in Morocco, risings in Algiers, discontent in Tripoli, so-called Nationalist attempts in Egypt, Arabia, and Libya are all different manifestations of the same deep sentiment, and have as their object the rebellion of the Oriental world against European civilization.[50]

India was no exception. The Muslim community, which for decades had been quiescent, was becoming more militant than it had been even before the war. A prominent activist was Abul Kalam Azad, a noteworthy scholar of Islamic theology. Influenced by al-Afgani, he became a fervent advocate of Pan-Islam and endeavored to give it political substance. He was joined by one of the most energetic political leaders of Indian Muslims, Muhammad Ali. Ali's daily newspaper, *Comrade*, served as a platform for some unusually extreme views, such as those expressed by Zafar Ali Khan, himself an editor of the Lahore newspaper, *Zamindar* [Landholder]. In his article entitled, "Indian Muslims and Pan-Islam," Ali maintained that

> [t]o the man in the street Pan-Islamism was synonymous with a gigantic union of the Muslims of the world, having for its cherished

object the extermination of Christianity as a living political force . . . The bombardment of Meshed by the Russians, the descent of Italy on Tripoli, the onslaught of the Balkan Allies on Turkey, with all their attendant horrors, have made the Muslims of India a changed people. They are not what they were two years ago.[51]

Sir Theodore Morison also pointed out that the British erred in thinking that in the East there was no sympathy for Turkey. Quite the contrary. Throughout Islam there was a furious agitation against the dismemberment of the Ottoman Empire. For centuries Turkey was looked upon as the "bulwark of Islam," and Muslims could not reconcile themselves to its overthrow. There were outbreaks of violence in counties as remote as Afghanistan while the riots in Cairo were symptomatic of the widespread resentment. In India, in particular, the Muslim community was seething with passion. Not only the ordinary people but even the mediaeval Muslim clergy whose detachment from the modern world was proverbial came out from their cloisters to protest against "the destruction of Islam," and Muslim liberals were driven to join the camp of political Islam.

Morison, who had been in close touch with Indian Muslims for over forty years, warned that dismemberment of the Ottoman Empire would be "a disastrous blunder"—that it would provoke chronic unrest in the Muslim world and the tragic history of the Balkans would repeat itself under a different guise. The discontent would not blow over and would undermine world peace. The British Empire, with its eighty million Muslim subjects, would be particularly affected by the unrest emanating from the Turkish nerve-center. Out of plain self-interest, Morison appealed, "England should not destroy the Turkish Empire."[52]

Lieutenant Colonel H. F. Jacob, an intelligence officer, reported that the Indian Muslims objected to King Hussein serving as a guardian of the holy places and preferred that the suzerainty of the sultan-caliph be rehabilitated. He was of the opinion that, unless Britain took measures to placate Muslim opinion, she might be confronted with the danger of the emergence of "a very strong political Islam" in Egypt, India, and elsewhere. He suggested the establishment of a Muslim bureau in order to improve intelligence and promote the exchange of views.[53]

The idea was not taken up. The British government had more pressing priorities than the Eastern questions. Ignored also were reports from British intelligence officers in Switzerland about a revanchist trend among the Young Turk refugee politicians there. Thus, a speech made by Nedjmeddin Mollah, a former Ottoman Shaikh al-Islam, was particularly ominous. In a meeting of Young Turk activists on May 17, 1919, in Lausanne, he stated that the partition of Turkey had stimulated the awakening of the Muslim world. An entente cordiale had been created among the Turks, the Egyptians, the Afghans, and Indians with the purpose of fomenting riots and rebellions of such ferocity that the Allied armies of occupation would not be able to suppress them. He warned thus:

> The peacemakers in Paris are cudgeling their brains how best to prevent new wars; they little suspect that a greater menace than the German one, which hangs over Europe, comes from Muslim Asia and Africa. The Arabs too will eventually obey the call of Islam.

During the meeting, a committee was elected that consisted of eight members: Emir Bey, former chamberlain to Sultan Hamid; Mouktar Bey, the son of Sheikh al-Islam; Djemalleoline Effendi, a former ambassador in Berlin; Ahmed Djevid, a director of *Ikhdam*, a newspaper in Constantinople; Reshid Pasha, former governor of Broussa; Halil Zia Bey, former first secretary to Sultan Mehmed I and rector of the University of Constantinople; Shukri Pasha, son of Riza Pasha, former minister of war; and Munir Pasha, former ambassador in Paris. The executive committee was comprised of Mouktar Pasha, Rashid Bey, and Munir Pasha. Among other activists mentioned were Shakib Arslan, a Druze leader and a former deputy of Hauran. The committee was in close communication with Tala'at, Enver, and Djemal, who had found refuge in Munich.

Parallel with the Young Turk Committee was the Egyptian Nationalist Bureau, which was based in Berne, whose program was to achieve "the complete independence of Egypt" and remove the British protectorate. Ali Bey Zulfikiar, the secretary of the Egyptian revolutionary party, proclaimed that the Egyptians were firmly resolved to liberate themselves regardless of any measures the British might take to prevent them from doing so.

All these proceedings were reported by Hugh E. C. Whittal, who, in 1917–18, served as a chief intelligence agent in Switzerland. Whittal had a competent staff and benefited from friendships he had made with high-ranking Turkish officials before the war. He could therefore speak authoritatively when reporting on his special mission to Switzerland in the spring of 1919. He summarized his findings tersely thus:

1. The Eastern enemies of Great Britain have united with the avowed object of overthrowing British rule in the East.
2. They can rely upon the support of Germany and of the Russian Bolsheviks, whose interests coincide with their own.
3. They hope to gain the support of the Entente Socialist Parties as well.
4. The center of the movement is in Switzerland.

Germany, although defeated, still controlled the revolutionary Muslim organization she had created during the war. Bent on revenge, Germany, together with her Muslim friends, found new and powerful allies in the Russian Bolsheviks, "whose fear and hatred of England rivals their own and who likewise plan to undermine British power by rousing the East to rebellion." It was Germany that had combined all the Eastern revolutionists into one Pan-Islamic union, while German marks, Russian rubles, and Turkish liras infused new life into their activities. Whittal gained the distinct impression that a plot was afoot and that the fomenters were only waiting for the outcome of the Peace Conference in Paris. "Peace in Europe," he concluded, "might be anything but rest in the East."[54]

Information gathered by the British Legation at Berne, as well as by the India Office, tallied with that gathered by Whittall. The secretary of state for India summarized the data thus:

> Recent reports from agents in Switzerland about existence of strong Pan-Islamic organization at Berne [and elsewhere] based upon Egyptian National Committee which has transferred headquarters from Berlin. Organization has ample funds and enjoys active support of Turkish Minister at Berne, who is said to be playing definitely hostile role against ourselves. Movement which is stated to be still directed by Germany is not confined to Egypt but includes hostile propaganda in India and elsewhere among Mohammedan subjects of Entente powers . . .

One of the agents (signed S. J.) suggested that, in order to forestall the impending Muslim rebellion, Britain should deal "leniently with Turkey, who was only too anxious to be on friendly terms with England." In return, Turkey would be able to point out to all her coreligionists that England had resumed her traditional role as Turkey's protector.[55]

This line had been advocated by the India Office since the armistice. The general staff also favored it.[56] The direction of policy, however, rested in the hands of Lord Curzon, who had succeeded Balfour as foreign minister, and particularly with the prime minister, Lloyd George, who nourished a deep-seated dislike of the Turks. They took hardly any notice of the Indian Muslim sensitivities with regard to Turkey's future. This point was articulated with commendable skill by Ganga Singh Maharajah and Lord Singh, who headed an Indian Muslim delegation, in their memorandum, dated April 30, 1919, to the British delegation to the Peace Conference in Paris.

On behalf of an Indian Muslim delegation, they pointed to the contribution made by the Indian army to the conquest of Mesopotamia, Palestine, and Syria. Notwithstanding the strain of dual loyalty, the Muslim soldiers fought bravely. The seventy million Muslims, who constituted more than one-fifth of the entire population of India felt deeply about Turkey; while the Indian army was fighting the Turkish troops, prayers were being offered daily in the mosques of India for the sultan of Turkey, their caliph. India had demonstrated a remarkable loyalty to the British Empire, and it was thanks to the influence of Prince Nizam of Hyderabad, who ruled over thirteen million people, that, throughout the war, the Muslim population remained tranquil.

The delegation did not object to the straits being open to international navigation or to the destruction of the adjacent fortifications. They would also sorrowfully, but without rancor, accept the severance of Arabia, Mesopotamia, Armenia, and Kurdistan from the Turkish Empire, but justice "required" that European Turkey [Thrace] and Asia Minor [Anatolia] "should be maintained as a Turkish National State, subject to such guarantees as are necessary for the protection of subject nationalities." This was consonant with the principle of self-determination and proclamations made by President Wilson and Prime Minister Lloyd George. Under no circumstances should Turkey be deprived of Constantinople, as well as Smyrna, an important outlet for trade. It would offend millions of Muslims who loyally supported the Allied cause. "We have no hesitation in saying that the complete dismemberment of Turkey, coupled with ejection of the Turk from Constantinople, would produce in India disastrous and far-reaching effects."[57] This well-reasoned and statesmanlike memorandum elicited no response.

On May 29, 1919, when Colonel Cornwallis and Colonel Joyce met Feisal in Damascus, the Emir admitted that "by breaking up the Turkish Empire, England has caused alarm among all Muslims who look to the sultan as their caliph."[58] In June, Dajani Bey, an Arab official who, before the war, had served as the under-secretary of state in the Turkish ministry of the interior, appealed to the League of Nations, as well as to the Indian Muslims, "to prevent the calamity of dismemberment of the Ottoman Empire . . . and the abolition of the caliphate . . . The Muslims in India should intervene with the British government to avert the disaster."[59] There was hardly any need to prod the Indian Muslims. Earlier (May 17), a delegation had appeared before the supreme council, pleading against the partition of Turkey, as well as for the retention of the caliph-sultan, an institution that was venerated not only by the Turks but by the whole Muslim world.[60] Three months later (August 14), the delegation submitted a second memorandum, but their pleas fell on sterile ground.[61]

Independently a newly formed Central Caliphate Committee, led by Muhammad Ali, made yet another attempt to have a meeting with Lloyd George and other British ministers; however, their claims, although exceptionally moderate, were rejected in toto by the prime minister on the grounds that acceptance would imply recognition of Pan-Islamism. The British government was reluctant to acknowledge the right of Muslim Indians to speak on behalf of the Ottoman Empire.[62]

Edwin Montagu, the state secretary for India, was an exception. He was fully aware of the depth of pro-Turkish sentiment in India and, in December 1919, before his departure for India, he pleaded against the dismemberment of the Ottoman Empire.[63] In the meantime, Muhammad Ali persevered in his campaign and in his speeches, warning that, should Muslims be submitted to the rule of Christian minorities, whether Greek or Armenian, Indian Muslims would refuse to serve the Allies in their next war.

Mushir Hosain Kidwai, a writer, made another point. In 1919, he moved to London where he founded a number of weeklies: *Muslim Outlook*, *Islamic News*, and subsequently *The Muslim Standard*—all staffed by Indian journalists committed to the Caliphate movement. He tried to drive home a message that the British Empire was facing a new danger: a German–Bolshevik rapprochement that had already begun to take shape. In the East, he maintained, it was only the Islamic

Empire (i.e., Turkey) and Islam at large that could neutralize its harmful effects and serve as a bulwark for Britain.[64]

Branches of the Caliphate movement proliferated throughout India and became a religious-political force to be reckoned with. It achieved a notable feat when Mahatma Gandhi, himself a Hindu, decided to join it. In a series of articles in *Young India* (1921), Gandhi explained that his decision had been prompted by a sense of moral responsibility and deep sympathy for the case of Indian Muslims. Consequently, a Hindu–Muslim alliance, which the British tried in vain to frustrate, was formed. Against the Muslims' promise to support the Hindu policy of noncooperation with the British, the Hindus joined the Muslims in their campaign to prevent a total dismemberment of the Ottoman Empire and any infringement on the sovereignty of the sultan-caliph.[65]

The abolition of the caliphate by Mustafa Kemal Atatürk in 1924 was a severe blow to the Caliphate movement. Nonetheless, bitterness against England remained. Henceforth, the momentum toward independence, fueled by the principle of self-determination, became unstoppable. In the end, India—the jewel in the crown of the British Empire—was lost to Britain.

The new Turkish government was antagonistic to the Young Turks and steered clear of their activities in Switzerland. Nor is there any evidence of it being associated with, let alone lending support to, the campaign led by the Indian Muslims. Izzet Pasha, the prime minister, as well as Rauf Bey, the minister of the marine, who led the Turkish delegation to armistice negotiations, put their faith in Britain and relied on British fairness. Their expectations were misplaced. Lloyd George, as he revealed in his memoirs was determined not only to deprive Turkey of her Asiatic provinces but also to push the Turks out of Constantinople and even partition Anatolia.[66] This was in stark contradiction to his solemn declaration of January 5, 1918.[67]

Lloyd George's mind was cast in the Gladstonian mold, and from his childhood, as one of his biographers characterized him, had grown up hating the Turks. "He was convinced that they were the ruffians of Europe—a band of cutthroats who ought to be exterminated—and that they had put themselves irredeemably beyond the pale of civilized society."[68] He referred to the Turk as "an oppressor and a source of trouble"; Constantinople has been not only "the hot bed of every sort of Eastern vice, but it has been the source from which the poison of corruption and intrigue has spread far and wide into Europe itself."

He went so far as to state that Constantinople was "not Turk, and the majority of the population was not Turkish." Moreover, the sultan was "an alien monarch ruling over an alien population."[69]

This was obviously untrue, and yet these erroneous opinions, tainted with emotion and transparent prejudice, governed his policy. He adhered tenaciously to them, notwithstanding criticism leveled against him that endured until practically the end of his term of office. The only person who could have moderated his views was Sir Mark Sykes, whose influence over the prime minister during the war in shaping Middle Eastern policy had been profound. In fact, their views were identical: both of them were fiercely anti-Turk. Disillusioned, however, with the Arabs following his tour in Syria and Palestine at the end of 1918, Sykes's views were transformed, and he consequently veered closer to the stand taken by the general staff and the war office, who favored a soft peace with Turkey. Ormsby-Gore, his close associate, described him as "a knight errant for peace and justice. He hated intransigence, but he loved goodwill." Although he wished to dismantle the Ottoman Empire, "he bore no malice to the Turk."

> The Turkish armistice struck him as bad. A severe armistice followed by a generous treaty was his formula, and had he lived, the history of the near East since the war would have been different. When he was gone, no one emerged in government with the same energy or power to keep continuous watch over the whole area—to put before ministers, soldiers, and civil servants the vision that was so essential in handling situations that had far-reaching and often unexpected reactions. The disastrous delays that followed the armistice would never have been possible had Sykes been alive.[70]

On the final day of his activity in Paris (February 10, 1919), Sykes told a friend despondently that Turkey was in a very bad state. "The ridiculous armistice terms had been taken by the Turks as a great victory for themselves . . . ," adding that "'the little man', LG, had suddenly gone off at half cock and wired the admiral [Calthorpe] to make terms at once . . . [and] make them in such a way as to be first into Istanbul,"[71] in order to forestall the French.

Lord Curzon had entirely different ideas than Sykes. On November 18, 1918, he declared in the parliament that Lloyd George's statement of January 5 had not been intended "as a binding engagement" but merely a peace offer that became null and void when the Turks rejected it. By no means, he went on, should the "evil Turkish government" be allowed to remain in Constantinople. Moreover, England has remained true to her aim of liberating such oppressed nationalities as the Armenians, Kurds, Arabs Greeks, and Jews from the Turkish yoke.[72] This was a cynical and distorted interpretation of Lloyd George's statement.

An aspirant to premiership, Curzon was an imperialist par excellence. His views on Turkey were extreme. Thus, he thought that the Turks should be expelled from Constantinople. It would be "the crowning evidence of their defeat in the war."[73] Consistent with his policy, he proposed that Muslim control of Constantinople should end and that the city should be administered by European powers and placed under international administration, that both the spiritual and temporal powers of the sultan-caliph should be drastically reduced, and, that the former Byzantine Church of St. Sophia should revert to Christendom.[74]

Edwin Montagu was outraged by these ideas. Concerned with the effect on Muslim opinion in India, he warned the cabinet against imposing harsh terms on Turkey. "I cannot reconcile my conscience to be a party to a treaty which does a thing which . . . is going to be of infinite trouble to the British Empire and India."[75]

Winston Churchill, then secretary of state for war, steered a middle course. For identical reasons he, too, objected to the expulsion of the Turks from their capital and pointed out that, in the Middle East, Britain depended heavily upon Indian troops. Moreover, he feared that such a hostile act would force the Turks to make common cause with the Bolsheviks and that it would be immensely difficult for the depleted British army to impose a stable peace in that region.[76] Churchill's analysis proved remarkably prescient.

In June 1919, the Turkish delegation came to Paris to plead its case before the Allied powers at the Peace Conference. President Wilson was present, but the atmosphere was inauspicious. The delegation claimed that "Turkey was dragged into a fatal war . . . in spite of the manifest opposition of the national will," that she had acted as "the subservient tool of Germany," that the Turkish people should not be held responsible for the misdeeds of the Young Turk government, and that, as a result of the war, the Turkish people had suffered no less than other ethnic groups. About three million Muslims were "condemned to death," while Asia Minor had been turned into "a vast heap of ruins." The present Turkish government profoundly disapproved of the policy of its predecessors. It was entirely out of harmony with Turkish tradition of hospitality and tolerance toward non-Turkish nationalities.

Furthermore, the delegation stated, Turkey should be rehabilitated in the eyes of the civilized world; its mission henceforth would be to embark on intensive economic and cultural activity in order to become "a useful factor in the 'League of Nations'"; the maintenance of the Turkish Empire was necessary in order to maintain "the religious equilibrium of the world."[77]

The supreme council rejected these arguments on the grounds that "a nation must be judged by the government which rules it, which directs its foreign policy, [and] which controls its armies."[78] The council judged the Turks by the yardstick applicable to a democracy, which was not the case for Turkey. The Young Turk government was anything but an elected government and the decision to enter the war had been taken without consulting the people.

The Allies, themselves having sustained heavy losses in the war, both human and material, were bent on revenge rather than on reconciliation with their former adversaries. The latter part of the motto ". . . in victory—magnanimity; in peace—good will," coined by Edward Marsh and made famous later by Winston Churchill in his book, *The Second World War*, Vol. I (1948), had not yet been adopted. The peacemaking at Versailles was devoid of true statesmanship and oblivious to the sensitivities of the former enemies. Rather than win them over and build a constructive settlement, both in Europe and in the East, the Allied powers created bitterness and covert antagonism—a fertile ground for unrest and upheaval. The victorious powers won the war but lost the peace.

The Turkish nation, impoverished, depopulated, and demoralized was at its lowest ebb of fortunes and morale. With Constantinople under Allied control, it looked as if it had lost the very will for independent existence. In all likelihood, it would have accepted the imposed peace terms, however humiliating, had it not been for an unexpected event that was to have far-reaching consequences in the history of modern Turkey: the occupation of Smyrna by the Greek army. This event rekindled Turkish nationalism and made the Turks more determined than ever to get rid of foreign invaders and assert Turkish independence.

Greek territorial claims to Smyrna, among other territories in Thrace and Asia Minor, were made known first by Eleutherios Venizelos, the Greek prime minister, a talented and colorful personality and a gifted speaker. A Cretan by birth, he read law at the University of Athens and came into prominence as the leader of the Cretan insurrection against Turkey in 1896. He was noted as one of the most uncompromising of the Greek nationalists, and, in 1911, he became prime minister. In 1912 he entered into an alliance with Bulgaria and Serbia—during the Balkan Wars, their joint armies drove the Turks almost completely from the European continent, save for Constantinople and its immediate vicinity. His ambition, however, went far beyond his native Greece. His goal was to expand well into Anatolia and revive the ancient Hellenic entity, if not an empire. His slogan was "Hellas is where the Hellenes are," and the Hellenes were scattered over Western Anatolia.

His moment came during the Peace Conference in Paris. For two successive days, February 3–4, 1919, he presented his case with commendable skill and eloquence. He displayed maps, quoted abundant statistics, and made recourse to Greek historical roots in the region. Central to his exposition were the principles of self-determination and nationality.[79] In a memorandum, which he had presented earlier to Lloyd George (November 2, 1918), Venizelos asserted Greek territorial claims to Western Anatolia from the Sea of Marmora to Mugla on the coast facing the island of Rhodes.[80]

His strong appeal aroused the imagination of the members of the supreme council. Particularly impressed was Lloyd George, who had declared on a number of occasions that Venizelos was "the greatest statesman Greece has thrown up since the days of Pericles."[81] Lloyd George was also won over by the idea of a Greater Greece and made it a cornerstone of his foreign policy. Sentiment for the Hellenic civilizing mission apart, out of long-term strategic calculations, Lloyd George had come to regard Greece as an invaluable ally tied to Britain by bonds of friendship and common interests. He wrote later thus:

> We could not invariably rely upon the Dardanelles remaining closed to a future Russian fleet. It would thus be of direct British advantage to safeguard our communications with India by placing at a point of immense naval advantage [relying on] a country whose benevolent neutrality, or even alliance, would, in time of war, be certainly assured to us.[82]

And yet, for all his diplomatic adroitness and, in spite of the British prime minister's support, Venizelos appeared initially to have scored no practical results in Asia Minor. His claims there conflicted with those of Italy. In 1917, Italy agreed to join the Allied camp in return for promises made by Britain and France entitling Italy to share the spoils of war carved out of a western strip of land of Anatolia. The tripartite agreement, known as the Agreement of St. Jean de Maurienne, had been concluded in April 1917. Its terms, however, were made subject to Russia's concurrence.

Since the Petersburg provisional government renounced the Asia Minor Agreement that of St. Jean de Maurienne formally lapsed. Moreover Italy's military performance was disappointing. The Caporetto Campaign (October 24–December 26, 1917) ended disastrously during the Austro-German attack, and French and British troops had to be transferred to help hold the front; the Italians had lost almost three hundred thousand men as prisoners and even more than that in deserters.

Nonetheless, after the war, the Italian government had the audacity to ask for equal treatment in the distribution of territories in Western Anatolia. As a certain Italian member of senate stated, "If the others have nothing, we will demand nothing."[83] The Italian public was caught in a frenzy of nationalism and Prime Minister Emanuele Orlando, as well as Baron Sidney Sonino, the foreign minister, feared that, unless they satisfied the amour propre of their constituency, their political position would be seriously undermined. With no chance of the Allies agreeing to their territorial claims, the Italians threw diplomacy to the winds and resorted to action. In mid-March 1919, Italian troops landed at Adalia (nowadays Antalya) in southern Anatolia and subsequently on the coast of Marmaris. The Allies could not accept such a unilateral move and President Wilson, inspired by Lloyd George, appealed to Orlando for moderation. Orlando stormed out of the Peace Conference and, early in May 1919, Italian warships were spotted off the coast of Smyrna. President Wilson was outraged. He was ready to order the American Navy to block the Italian ships and was reported to be considering a declaration of war against Italian aggression.[84]

Lloyd George, too, lost patience, but, instead of supporting Wilson's suggestion for restraining the Italians, fell upon the ingenious idea of letting the Greeks occupy Smyrna under the pretext that the Turks were "threatening" their Greek neighbors. Surprisingly, Wilson gave his consent. It was a fatal mistake with unforeseen consequences. For Venizolos, however, it was a godsent opportunity, which he enthusiastically embraced.

On May 14, Venizelos dispatched a Greek division to "Ionia," as he called it, and appointed a high commissioner for Smyrna. Escorted by a sizable flotilla of British, French, and American warships, the Greek troops presented the Turkish citizens (who made up half of the one million inhabitants), with a virtual fait accompli. The Greek population of Smyrna was ecstatic. Their celebration, however, turned into pandemonium when some Turks began shooting at the crowd. Infuriated, the Greeks took revenge by looting in Turkish neighborhoods. Over four hundred Turkish civilians were killed and wounded and two thousand arrested. The Greeks gave vent to the subdued antagonism of a depressed minority in a most savage fashion. Venizelos did not try to restrain his unruly compatriots and, instead, dispatched seven additional battalions, which occupied Smyrna's neighborhood for strategic reasons (June 5, 1919). He knowingly exceeded his brief and the supreme council of the Peace Conference issued an urgent resolution prohibiting any further advances. An inter-Allied commission, which met in July, concluded that "the Greek occupation, far from presenting itself as the execution of a *mission civilisatrice*, immediately took [on] an aspect of a conquest and of a crusade."[85] In consequence, the whole vilayet was plunged into chaos and bloodshed, causing untold horrors that the Allied powers ought to have prevented.

The General Staff had repeatedly advised against letting the Greeks occupy Smyrna (as well as the Italians in Adalia), but to no avail. It was, however, Colonel Richard Meinertzhagen, then a member of the British military section of the British delegation to the Peace Conference, who argued the case from a broader perspective. Meinertzhagen was a man of outstanding ability, head and shoulders above his peers, and even superiors, both military and civilian. An unusually perceptive observer, he had the courage to face realities, however unpalatable, and to report his findings without fear. Above all he was a man of integrity and unquestionably loyal to his government. His loyalty, however, did not deter him from criticizing it whenever convinced that its policy was erroneous. This was particularly the case with regard to Turkey. He thought that by allowing the Greeks to occupy Smyrna and letting the Italians into the area around Adalia, Great Britain and her Allies had committed a grave error; the idea of dismembering Turkey proper in Asia Minor was, in his opinion, inexcusable. On May 17, 1919, he submitted a strongly worded memorandum to the Command of the Imperial General Staff:

> . . . Apart from the immoral principle of handing over to a foreign race what is Turkish on ethical, political and geographical grounds,

the idea of placing a Greek or Italian government as Mandatory Power over pieces of Turkey proper shows a terrible ignorance of the past and present administrative ability and political morality of these people. As previously pointed out, the results will be a hideous failure.

But apart from these considerations, the partitioning of Asia Minor will sound the death knell of the British Mohammedan Empire. Evidence on this point is overwhelming, and, from a military point of view, the situation is more than serious.

With Egypt in revolt, Afghanistan proclaiming a *Jihad*, trouble brewing in Mesopotamia, the not at all unlikely prospect of an Indian mutiny and general upheaval such as will eclipse all previous efforts to throw off the British yoke in India, and an almost certain prospect of an Arab-Jew conflict in Palestine—on top of all this, we are deliberately inciting Mohammedans all over the world to unite against the Christian, which is the British Empire, and do not let us deceive ourselves we are unable to meet it.

Very naturally, Greece, Italy, and France have no such fear of the result of a Pan-Mohammedan *Jihad*, for they are not Mohammedan Powers in the sense that we are . . . Therefore, do not let us sign our own death warrant just to satisfy the greed and grasp of Greece and Italy. Rather let us stand firm for the consolidation of Turkey in Asia Minor, and sooner let us have strife and trouble with the Greeks and the Italians than risk the odium of Islam.

It is doubtful whether our politicians realize that the military effort we may have to make during the next year or so, on account of this pandering to Latin races at the expense of Islam, is beyond our power, and they should be solemnly warned that by showing reasonable regard for Mohammedan feelings and by not destroying the Turk and morally wounding his pride, we secure ourselves in possessions which at the present moment we are unable to defend with success. It is the old story of policy outstripping military strength, and it is the soldier's duty to warn the politician of the danger he runs by ignoring such a principle.[86]

In subsequent memoranda written two days later, Meinertzhagen reinforced his warning of the disastrous effects that the policy would have on Muslim feelings throughout the world. Moreover,

with the inevitable result of the Turks fighting Greece and Italy in Asia Minor and the Arabs fighting France in Syria, we cannot hope to be free from turmoil in Palestine, one of the few countries in the Near East still in a peaceful state. Our present policy will plunge the whole of the Near East into renewed war and even Palestine cannot hope to escape infection.

Meinertzhagen pointed also to the adverse effects of Turkey's dismemberment on Indian troops, over 134,000 strong. Throughout the war, the loyalty of Indian Muslim soldiers had been torn between their religious convictions and their devotion to the British government. "On the whole, their behavior has been admirable amid a flood of poisonous propaganda which aimed at their defection." But now, he feared their sentiment might change and tip the balance against the British because, though hostilities in the main theatre of war have ceased, enemy effort at alienating our Mohammedan Troops and our Mohammedan subject races is stronger than ever. Egypt, though dominated by British bayonets, is in subdued revolt, Afghanistan has broken out into open hostility. Mesopotamia has an undercurrent of discontent which may burst forth as unexpectedly as it did in Egypt, and the Arabs of Syria and Palestine are by no means inclined to accept without bloodshed the mandate of a Christian Power.

> If a Pan-Islamic rebellion broke out it would engulf also the Arab East, Egypt, Persia and the Indian continent and, when combined with recrudescence of Turkish military operations, the British position would become precarious. It would be criminal in the interests of the British Empire to regard a reconsideration of our policy towards Turkey even at this eleventh hour, as too late, and, cost what it may, we cannot, from a military point of view, afford to see Turkey proper partitioned among the Latin races of Europe.

It would produce, he predicted, such an upheaval among the Muslims throughout the East that Britain, in her present military condition would not be able to cope with it. He therefore felt that it was his duty to protest most earnestly against a policy that outstripped by far the ability of the British Empire to suppress it and which "can only lead to a disaster of the first magnitude."[87]

There was a prophetic ring to Meinertzhagen's memoranda. Prophetic was also his analysis of Allied policy toward Germany. The terms of peace imposed on her were, to his mind, "too harsh, unworkable and containing the germs of future wars." There was "too much French violence in the Treaty and too much American dreaming." The Germans, in his opinion, were

> the most civilised, the most progressive, the most intelligent and the most aggressive of European Peoples. To keep them down perpetually is a hopeless and dangerous task. It is utterly impossible to keep Germany down unless force is used continually and even

then nationalism will assert itself and rebel. I therefore regard the Treaty as dangerously repressive. The German people . . . degraded, will react violently to what they regard as hopelessly unjust. They will clutch at any straw which gives them hope—perhaps to Russia and Communism—or to some violent little revolutionary of their own who offers them hope; the Germans cannot remain underdogs; they will surge to the top again somehow; that is inevitable and this wretched Treaty will make them long for revenge.[88]

Meinertzhagen was flabbergasted at the sluggish pace at which the Peace Conference was moving. The procedure was cumbersome and inefficient. The atmosphere had been poisoned by intrigue and material interests. The politicians were dishonest, all working for their own ends and not for the general good. "Never before," he noted, "have such vital decisions, which affect millions of persons, hung in the balance. Seldom have such intrigues and immoral principles had such fair ground on which to work . . . I feel that . . . even if we do get a Peace it will be of such a sort that it is no Peace at all." He submitted yet another memorandum outlining suggestions for a firm policy and avoiding any further delay. Impressed, General Sir Henry Wilson, Chief of the Imperial General Staff, passed it on to the Prime Minister.[89]

Meinertzhagen was appalled by the poor quality of the politicians unequal to their task. Thus, a glorious opportunity of making "a lasting and great Peace" was slipping away. "We soldiers and sailors," he noted with resentment, "feel that we gave the British government an enormous Political Balance at their Bank, which they are now frittering away with no results . . . It is a ghastly example of the old error, allowing Policy to outstrip strategy for[,] when the time comes, we shall be without means to enforce any terms whatsoever."[90]

He did not withhold his criticism from President Wilson either. Wilson's principles were premature and caused more harm than good, he argued. Since they had been announced, twenty-two minor wars had broken out. There was scarcely "a small race worthy of the name, from Morocco to Afghanistan, which is not warring with its neighbor, encouraged by the idealistic dreams of [an unrealistic] American Professor." The end result was that the ideal of self-determination, in practice, had become an exercise of "self-extermination," while the League of Nations from its birth had proved to be as "important as a still-born babe."[91]

One of the few statesmen who did impress Meinertzhagen was Chaim Weizmann:

> Seldom did I admire [a] man more. Never did I see such singleness of purpose, such determination, such far-sightedness and such a rich intellect, all embodied in one soul. Seldom has a man dealing in such large ideas been so honest and so sincere. So much is this the case, that it annoys me that Weizmann should be a Jew, it annoys me that he should be so far ahead of Christians in intelligence and general purity of mind.[92]

Naturally, Meinertzhagen's eyes were turned to Lloyd George. He regarded him as "a man of grit who could alone gain success with the whole British Nation behind him," and expected him to show courage and honesty.[93] It took him only a month to realize that the Prime Minister was blind to what lay in store, that he was hopelessly out of touch with political opinion outside England, and that he lacked the necessary qualities for which the situation called. "He cares but does not know. Balfour knows but does not care. The rest neither know, nor care." Meinertzhagen revealed his thoughts to General Sir Henry Wilson in the bluntest of terms.[94] Meinertzhagen spoke also with General Jan Smuts and Louis Botha of South Africa. They fully concurred and denounced unequivocally the proposed Peace Treaties with Germany as well as with Turkey, stating that they fostered the germs of new wars.[95]

Earlier (May 6, 1919) General Wilson approached the Prime Minister and asked him whether he realized that the Greek landing in Smyrna would begin another war, but Lloyd George disregarded the General's warning.[96] It was tragic that a Prime Minister, whose leadership during the War had been supreme, had embarked upon a policy of peacemaking that was ill-conceived and would prove disastrous for his own political future.

Predictably, the occupation of Smyrna shocked the Turkish people. Heretofore submissive and lethargic, they had now a rude awakening. They felt that their very existence as a nation was at stake. When the news reached Constantinople, the cabinet instantly submitted its resignation to the sultan. Mass demonstrations took place in the capital and elsewhere and black flags were displayed. Speeches proliferated bearing strong nationalistic and religious overtones. The Turks resigned themselves to the presence of British troops, which was expected to be temporary, but occupation by the Greeks, a subject people (*dhimmi*), who were despised, was intolerable. Unlike the British, the Greeks came to stay and nourished territorial ambitions on the ruins of the Turkish homeland. The Greeks' brutal behavior toward innocent Turkish civilians and the ensuing chaos in Smyrna alienated them still further. Even more disconcerting was the news that the Greek occupation was merely a prelude to the partition of Anatolia among other Powers: Italy and France. That Britain had broken her word was particularly offensive. During the armistice negotiations, Admiral Calthorpe solemnly promised the Turkish Delegation that neither the Greeks, nor the Italians would be allowed to invade Smyrna or Constantinople—a pledge that was later endorsed by the British cabinet.[97]

Relying on this pledge, the Turks, in their wildest imagination, had not expected that the Greeks would ever invade Smyrna. Even after its occupation the Turks remained relatively quiescent. Only when "the Greeks persisted in their cruelties, and continued to burn villages, massacre Turks, rape and murder their women folk, and kill their children" did resistance become apparent. "Now," a British Intelligence officer reported on September 3,

> the Turks say that their feelings of hatred against the Greeks have grown so intense that they can never submit to be controlled by them. Thinking little of their lives, they would sooner be exterminated fighting against the Greeks, than have the country a second Macedonia.[98]

Admiral Webb, who deputized for Calthorpe, pointed out with much prescience that Venizelos did a disservice to his country when he had persuaded the supreme council to allow the Greek troops into Smyrna "to 'pacify' the place." Apart from turning the whole district into a shambles, which never would have occurred if Allies had been left to control it, "it has sown the seed of still more bitter animosity between Greek and Turk than existed before—an animosity which has to be seen to be realized." So despondent was Webb that he saw "the only possible hope" for comparative peace and tranquility between the two races in the future was the withdrawal of Greek troops, as well as of the Italians from Asia Minor, and a return to the "*status quo ante.*"[99] J. B. Hohler, the political adviser to the high commissioner, expressed a similar opinion: "I see no hope of clearing up [this hideous mess] short of getting the Greeks and the Italians out of Asia Minor, and I guess there is no hope of that."[100]

Admiral Sir Francis de Robeck, who succeeded Calthorpe as high commissioner, admitted that occupation of Smyrna had damaged the reputation of the British for honesty of purpose "very considerably" in Turkish circles that had been potentially well disposed to the British.

"Rightly or wrongly, they attribute the decision to send Greek troops to Aidin principally to British influence; and they cannot reconcile that decision with our avowed principles as regard the rights of nationalities." The Turks felt that they had been betrayed and not treated in accordance with the principles that the Allied had proclaimed. In *sum toto*, the Greek occupation of Smyrna had stimulated "a Turkish patriotism probably more real than any which the war was able to evoke."[101] The Turkish national movement came into being. As a result, as Professor Bernard Lewis wrote, "the Turks were ready to rise against the invader—only the leader was awaited."[102] That leader was Mustafa Kemal, later known as Atatürk ("Father of the Turks").

Mustafa[103] was born in 1880 in Salonica, then part of the Ottoman Empire and was of Albanian and Thracian Turkish ancestry. He was an excellent student, particularly in mathematics, and in recognition, his teacher gave him a second name—Kemal—which in Arabic means "perfection." It was a most apposite characterization. Ambitious and aiming at perfection, Mustafa was endowed with a rational and calculating mind, and was always aware of the limit of the possible. An introvert who kept his thoughts to himself, he knew what he wanted. Once the objective became apparent, he endeavored to achieve it with relentless energy undeterred by obstacles.

He read French literature surreptitiously, which shaped his secular outlook and gave him a dislike of religious fanaticism. His primary love, however, was for the military. He spent six years at the Senior Military College at Monastir and thereafter was at the Staff College in Constantinople. In 1905 he graduated with the rank of captain. Henceforth his military promotion was rapid. An ardent Nationalist, like other young officers, Kemal joined the Young Turk movement and in 1908, and, when the Revolution broke out, was among those who marched on Constantinople. He acquired a reputation as an orator, preaching liberation from Abdul Hamid's despotism and undue interference by foreign Powers. His relations with the Young Turk leaders, however, were less than cordial; he particularly detested Enver, and was at variance with both his style and policy. Making little headway in politics, he returned with zest to a military career. He served in the Italo-Turkish war of 1911 and thereafter in the Balkan wars.

Kemal opposed Turkey's entry into the World War, considering it both unpolitic and risky. From the start, he was skeptical of an ultimate German victory. He feared that Germany's defeat would spell disaster for Turkey, whereas her victory would turn Turkey into a German satellite.

When the war broke out, he was placed under the command of Liman von Sanders, the head of the German Military Mission, who appointed him to command the Turkish forces in Southern Gallipoli. Kemal distinguished himself as a skillful tactician and, in a series of battles between April and August 1915, managed to repulse the Australian forces. These victories saved the Straits and Constantinople for the Turks.[104] Writing appreciatively of Kemal's military ability, Von Sanders described him as "a leader delighting in responsibility."[105]

Mustafa Kemal returned to Constantinople as a national hero, but his popularity made him too dangerous to the CUP government, which posted him far away to the Caucasus front. The outbreak of the Russian Revolution in March 1917 and the consequent withdrawal of the Russian forces rendered Kemal's presence on that front unnecessary and he was transferred to Syria—then the most dangerous front. Disagreements with General Erich von Falkenhayn, the newly appointed supreme commander of the combined Ottoman and German forces (the *Yildrim*), soon broke out and Kemal returned to the capital. When Liman von Sanders replaced Falkenhayn, Kemal returned to Palestine in August 1918, only to witness an impending catastrophe. He did not lose his nerve. Assisted by Generals Ismet and Ali Fuad (who later were to play an important part in the Kemalist movement), he led a successful, albeit desperate, rearguard battle, retreating to Damascus and thence to Aleppo. He vowed to make a stand at the gates of the Taurus passes and not let the galloping ANZAC Cavalry penetrate into Anatolia. They never did.

He was shocked by the terms of the Armistice; in his opinion they violated the Allies self-proclaimed principles. Unlike the Anglophiles Izzet Pasha and Rauf Bey, he harbored no illusions about Britain's fair play and did not take seriously even President Wilson's Fourteen Points. "Poor Wilson," he expressed himself rather contemptuously, "did not understand that no principle can protect a frontier defended neither by force nor by honor." Only the Turkish bayonets could ensure the existence of Turkey.[106]

He resolved to fight for Turkey's independence free from foreign domination—a homogeneous Turkey that would shed the vast Asiatic provinces, which, for long, had encumbered and hampered the development of the Turkish nation. His moment came following the Greek invasion of Smyrna. The news reached him on May 19, 1919 while he was landing at Samsun. The sultan had just appointed him inspector general of the Third Army in Anatolia (*irade*). He embarked on a course[107] that proved nothing short of momentous, in both his personal career and in the annals of Turkish modern history. It was clear to him, as he revealed in his speech to the congress of the People's Party in 1927, that a national struggle had to be carried out for "the sole purpose of delivering the country from foreign invasion . . . and establish principles and forms for government founded on national sovereignty."[108]

With this aim, Kemal contacted army generals, as well as district governors in Eastern Anatolia, asking them to reverse the central government's orders; i.e., to abandon disarmament and instead rearm in order to rebuild the national army. The provisos of the Armistice were to be disregarded and the British occupation seriously challenged.

A national struggle, however, called for popular support. To enlighten the farmers about the situation, Kemal toured villages and townlets extensively stirring up national sentiment. The response was overwhelming. So was, proportionately, the concern of the central government. Damad Ferid, the new English-educated grand vizier and the sultan's brother-in-law, ordered Kemal to return to Constantinople, but Kemal refused to obey.[109]

On July 2, Admiral Calthorpe drew the attention of the Turkish minister for foreign affairs to the "formation of armed bands . . . in the districts of Sivas and Konia . . . an action contrary to the interests of the Allies." He associated them mistakenly with the Committee of Union and Progress of the Young Turks, an error which was current also in London. On June 6, General Milne, the commander in chief of the British army of the Black Sea, requested the Turkish Minister of War to dismiss Mustafa Kemal. A month later, concerned by the "disastrous effects" of the rebellious movement, Calthorpe demanded Kemal's immediate recall to Constantinople "without conditions and without delay."[110]

On July8, Damad Ferid officially cancelled Kemal's commission. Kemal however, sensing what was afoot, had preempted the Porte and, on the previous day, had submitted his resignation from the army, declaring that he had resolved to continue the national struggle in the capacity of a private citizen unencumbered by any official restrictions. He could well afford to take such a daring step knowing that Ferid's government was weak and unpopular, whereas the newly awakened nationalism had struck a chord among the masses and was gathering momentum. He also gained the valuable support of Refet Pasha and Rauf Bey, whom he met in Amasia. Rauf, it will be recalled, signed the Armistice and was an avowed Anglophile.[111] He changed his mind, however, following his visit to Smyrna. What he saw and heard there shook him. Without hesitating, he joined Kemal's camp and, as an experienced politician, was able to render important and valuable service to him.

At Amasia on June 19, 1919, Mustafa Kemal, Ali Fuad, Colonel Refet and Rauf Bey signed a document known as the Amasia Protocol, which proclaimed that every effort should be made to unite the Turkish nation in the struggle for its independence, and that a provisional government should be situated in Anatolia.[112] Kemal emerged as the undisputed leader of the movement and triumphantly proclaimed: "Henceforth Stamboul does not govern Anatolia, but Anatolia Stamboul."[113] The rift with the central government was complete. He thoroughly despised it for its meekness and subservience to Britain, the occupying Power, to the detriment of Turkish interests and dignity. In a speech delivered to the Congress of the Turkish People's Party in 1927 (already quoted above), he recalled:

> He who occupied the position of sultan and caliph was a degenerate who, by infamous means, sought only to save his own person and throne. The cabinet, presided over by Damad Ferid Pasha, was composed of men both incapable and cowardly, utterly without dignity.

Nonetheless, in 1919 Kemal was careful not to challenge the sultan-caliph, since the position was still widely venerated by the Muslim world—and especially by the Turkish people. Ideologically, however, he felt that the sultanate had outlived its usefulness. Mehmed Vahideddin VI had become a willing tool of an infidel Power and a shadow of the once powerful sultans—the defenders of Islam against the encroachments of Christian Powers. Although, for tactical reasons, Kemal refrained from criticizing the sultan, the future of the sultan-caliph was doomed. It was ingrained in the phrase: the "sovereign will of the people," which Kemal used in his dialogue with Kiazim Karabekir, a gentle and respected figure, who owed his allegiance first and foremost to the sultan.[114]

The concept of the sovereignty of the people originated with British and French philosophers like Hobbes Locke, Rousseau, and others. It was enshrined in the French and American Revolutions; but in Turkey such an idea was totally novel and bore far-reaching implications. The concept was embodied in a manifesto issued by the first Turkish National Congress, which met at Erzerum in Eastern Anatolia on July 23, 1919. It indicated that the chief object of the movement was "to consolidate the national forces into a ruling factor and to establish the will of the nation as sovereign power."[115] To assuage the concern of dissenters, a special cable of homage was sent to the sultan by the congress stating that the sultanate and the caliphate would be safeguarded "by all methods and all means."[116]

In their Manifesto the delegates declared also that the entire country within its national frontiers was "an indivisible whole"; that the nation would resist any attempt at occupation or interference by foreigners; that, should the central government prove incapable of preserving the national independence and the integrity of the country, "a provisional government shall be formed, elected by the national congress"; and that the idea of a mandate or a protectorate by a foreign Power should be rejected.[117] The Congress reconciled itself to the idea that Asiatic provinces of the Ottoman Empire had to be relinquished and resolved that a new and homogeneous Turkish state should be built. It was an historic decision and signaled a finis to Ottomanism. The Erzerum Manifesto was the Magna Carta of the new Turkey and served as a blueprint for the subsequent congress that met at Sivas on September 4, 1919 for a week-long session.

The congress at Sivas was more representative than that of Erzerum. The latter, as Rear Admiral Sir Francis de Robeck reported, "professed to represent the Eastern *vilayets* only, [that] at Sivas . . . claimed to represent the whole country, including, very significantly, Turkey in Europe." The Congress at Sivas declared all the territory that had been demarcated by the Armistice to be "one indivisible" whole; that independent Greek or Armenian states would not be tolerated; and that non-Muslims would not be allowed to enjoy special privileges, though equality of rights irrespective of religion would be respected. Turkey's integrity and independence would be assured by "the national forces and the national will," to which the central government should submit. Moreover, the Congress urged that the National Assembly should be convoked without delay. The Powers were called upon to abandon any idea of partitioning the territory within the Armistice boundary and to desist from any encroachment on Turkey's independence. Lastly, it was decided to merge all the existing national associations into a single association under the chairmanship of Mustafa Kemal. Robeck summarized the fundamental aim of the Congress thus: "They want Turkey for the Turks. They want no foreign interference or foreign protection."[118]

One of those who was able to view the proceedings of the Conference was Robert Dunn. A Lieutenant in the U.S. Navy, he served on the staff of Admiral Bristol, the American high commissioner, and was traveling on intelligence missions in the interior of Asia Minor. He recorded his impressions:

> For days . . . I kept meeting delegates to the Erzerum Congress . . . I had the feeling that I was witnessing the birth of some far-reaching cause. Thus our forefathers converged upon Philadelphia in 1776 to sign the Declaration.[119]

This kind of feeling must have imbued the delegates themselves, as well as a great many Turks—a feeling that the Turkish nation was being reborn.

The phenomenal growth of the Kemalist movement, as Robeck reported, "has gone on steadily, day by day, week by week, until to-day the Allies are confronted with an entirely different Turkey to that which signed the Armistice." The Press glorified the Sivas Congress, while portraits of Mustafa Kemal, as well as of Rauf Bey, adorned the local papers. "The great majority of the intelligentsia and the officer class (the only ones which count in Turkish politics) is in sympathy with the Nationalists." Their leaders have become more reassured and aggressive. In consequence, Robeck warned, the Allies were confronted with "a new situation and . . . it would be more difficult to-day than it would have been eight months ago to impose on Turkey a distasteful Peace Treaty without fresh resort to force."

Well-informed, the Turkish national leaders were aware of Britain's domestic difficulties and that, because of budgetary restraints, she was compelled to withdraw large military contingents from Asia Minor, the Caucasus, and elsewhere. They were convinced therefore that an "exhibition of vitality" on their part would expose Britain's weakness and thus the British lion would eventually cower "on the first display of Mustapha Kemal's teeth."[120]

Territorially, too, the Nationalist forces were expanding their operations, and Ferid's government was left in control only of the capital and of its adjacent cities. He was losing the confidence of his people and his position was becoming "more desperate than he would admit. It was perhaps even more desperate than he realized,"

Robeck remarked with a glimmer of irony.[121] This was, in a way, the position of the British. Concomitant with the rise of Turkish nationalism, there was a noticeable surge of anti-British sentiment about which both Calthorpe and Robeck reported. What did escape them, however, was that, in spite of the widespread antagonism toward the British, Kemal and his aids tried to avoid a direct confrontation with them.

On September 30, Kemal Bey, a former ADC to the grand vizier and a member of the Armistice Commission, came to see Lt. Colonel Ian Smith, the military attaché to the high commissioner. He was familiar with the Nationalist movement and was on very good personal terms with Mustafa Kemal, whom he knew intimately. Colonel Smith got the impression that Kemal Bey came in the capacity of "the unofficial mouthpiece of the leaders of the [national] movement.

Kemal tried to correct the misconception that the Nationalists were in league with the CUP politicians. Mustapha Kemal had pointedly warned Enver Pasha that, if he came to the Erzerum Conference, he would be arrested. The Nationalists were led by "very intelligent men." Their confidence in England had been badly shaken by the events in Smyrna. Nonetheless, they knew "quite well that it . . . [would] be fatal for them to allow any hostilities to break out against the English." The Nationalists' leaders were not intransigent like Enver and Djemal. They were "reasonable in their aims and wanted a rapprochement," provided the British did not aim at destroying the integrity of the country and its sovereignty. The war with Turkey was over, and it was high time, Kemal Bey insisted, that England recognize the seriousness of the Nationalist movement and come to terms with it. It lay in Britain's own future interest, to deal with a well-disposed Turkish nation, not a hostile one.

By backing the Damad Ferid government, Kemal Bey went on, the British had alienated "reasonable patriotic Turkish opinion" and harmed their own standing. Hence, the British should prevail upon Ferid to be more forthcoming toward the Kemalists. He summed up: "A Nationalist government will not prove anti-English and is quite disposed to be reasonable and work with the British," provided Turkish independence was assured.[122]

The plea fell on stony ground. Nor was Curzon's opinion changed following reports by American observers. Brigadier-General McCoy, second in command to the American high commissioner, was very favorably impressed with Mustafa Kemal and gained the distinct impression that the Turkish people, although exhausted by the war, were solidly behind him.[123] Lieut. R. Dunn of U. S. Intelligence, thought that the Nationalists "represented the Turkish opinion and included the best brains of the country." The British were mistaken. They had made themselves "thoroughly unpopular all over the East . . . British policy in the East was a failure proved by the discontent shown by the recent rising in Egypt, which had been under her guardianship for so long a time."[124]

The Ferid government was deluding itself if it thought that it could crush the Nationalist movement. It appointed Ali Galib Bey, the vali of Kharput, as governor of Sivas and instructed him to arrest Mustafa Kemal and to break up the Congress at Sivas. For this purpose he was to raise the native Kurds; the latter were bribed and promised independence under British protection.[125]

Galib soon found himself in alliance with Major Noel, a British officer serving in northern Mesopotamia. Hohler described Noel as a "fanatic" and "the apostle of the Kurds" who was trying to play the role of "a Kurdish Col. Lawrence."[126] On September 27, 1919, Colonel Meinertzhagen, then Political Officer under General Allenby, warned Curzon that Noel was conducting a "dangerous form of anti-Turkish and pro-Kurd propaganda."[127] It is not clear what the attitude of the British government was, but the Galib–Noel misadventure fizzled out even before it really began. The Kemalists were in control of all telegraphic communications between Constantinople and the interior and succeeded in deciphering all the instructions. Consequently, Mustafa was fully apprised of the situation. In a surprise attack, the Nationalist forces easily defeated the Kurdish tribesmen and took Noel prisoner. From the intercepted correspondence, particularly from Noel's en clair telegram to the high commission, the Nationalist leaders were able to deduce that an "unholy compact" between Ferid and the British existed which aimed to liquidate them. "This belief," Robeck reported, "inflames the anti-British feeling" still further.[128]

Ferid did not concede defeat and implored the three high commissioners to launch an offensive against the Nationalist forces. By then, however, the Italians had abandoned their expansionist dreams, while the French remained lukewarm. The British, realizing that the task was beyond them, declined. This served as the coup de grâce to Ferid's government. On October 1 he resigned.[129]

Mustafa Kemal could thus rightly congratulate himself on achieving a double victory. Constantinople became thoroughly discredited in the eyes of the Turkish people, while Britain was exposed as a toothless lion. And yet, the danger was not over. After attempts to reach a rapprochement with the British proved fruitless, Britain, in Mustafa Kemal's eyes, emerged as the chief antagonist. Even Turkish circles formerly friendly to England felt deeply aggrieved by the alleged British responsibility for the Greek landing in Smyrna; they could not reconcile such a policy with Britain's "avowed principles as regards the rights of nationalities." In consequence, Robeck admitted, British reputation for honesty of purpose had been considerably damaged.[130]

Ruling out direct confrontation as imprudent, Kemal resorted to indirect strategies, which he pursued with great skill and determination. "They want to fight . . . England with the weapons of pan-Islam and Pan-Turanism . . ." but Turkey would "continue to foment trouble in the Muslim, particularly in the British[,] world." Moreover, Robeck remarked, Mustafa Kemal was seeking an understanding with the Arabs. "There have been quite lately disquieting reports from Syria, also from Egypt, where in present circumstances the Turkish national movement cannot fail to win sympathy."[131]

There was yet an additional factor that militated against British presence in the East. As Robeck pointed out:

> Throughout the Near and Middle East there is a growing tendency to react against European domination and control . . . The expression 'self-determination', though perhaps imperfectly understood forms the theme of every . . . leader of public opinion.

The principle of self-determination turned thus into a double-edged sword.

As we shall see in chapters 4 and 5, the Bolsheviks made most skillful use of it in order to incite the people in the East against the British Empire. During the early twenties, Britain had to face not only a determined Turkish nationalism, but also a menacing rebellion of the Arab and Islamic people—this at the time when the Allied coalition was falling apart; when the cabinet was split down the middle, and the country was hit by multiple crises: the budget, unemployment, and, on top of these, the Irish problem.

Notes

1. Reports of William Yale, No. 13, February 4, 1918, pp. 4, 13.
2. *Documents on British Foreign Policy 1919–1939*, E. L. Woodward and Rohan Butler (eds.), First Series, vol. IV (London, 1952) (henceforth *DBFP*)—referred to in Grahame (Paris) to Curzon, August 12, 1919, 350n4.

Ambassador Grahame pointed out that M. Gauvain put the blame on subordinate British agents and not on the British government itself.

3. Woodrow Wilson, *President Wilson's Great Speeches and Other History-Making Documents* (Chicago, 1919), 346.
4. *British War Aims. Statement Made by the Prime Minister, the Right Honourable David Lloyd George, on January 5, 1918* (London, 1918), 5, 9–10.
5. CAB 23/14, War cabinet meeting no. 481 A, October 2, 1918; also CAB 23/8, no. 480 (1) and (2).
6. CAB 23/8, no. 484(3) War cabinet meeting October 11, 1918, App. I, Annex I; Sir Henry Newbolt, *History of the Great War Based on Official Documents. Naval Operations*, vol. V (London, 1931), 351–2.
7. A full text of the Mudros Armistice Agreement can be found in J. C. Hurewitz, *Diplomacy in the Near and Middle East 1914–1956*, vol. II (Princeton, NJ, 1956), 37, and in Gwynee Dyer, "The Turkish Armistice of 1918: Part 2. A Lost Opportunity: The Armistice Negotiations of Moudros," App. II, 340–1, *Middle East Studies*, 8 (1972) 313–41.
8. Isaiah Friedman, *Germany, Turkey and Zionism, 1997–1918*, 2nd edition (New Brunswick, NJ: Transaction Publishers, 1998), 211, 431.
9. Ibid., 286–7, 398.
10. Ibid., 282–3, 286–7.
11. Isaiah Friedman, *The Question of Palestine, 1914–1918. British–Jewish–Arab Relations.* 2nd edition (New Brunswick, NJ: Transaction Publishers, 1992), 211–2.
12. F.O. 371/3057/104218, memorandum by Lord Drogheda, dated November 20, 1917, where various attempts are conveniently summarized (p.n. 222199); also ibid., file 4215.
13. Friedman, *The Question of Palestine*, 212–4.
14. Ibid., 214–8.
15. Ibid., 218–9.
16. Ibid., 219–20.
17. Ibid., 219–21.
18. Friedman, *Germany, Turkey and Zionism*, 144, 188, 209, 217, 294, 379–80, 386–9, 397–8, 404, 407, 411–2.
19. CAB 23/13, no. 247b, meeting held on October 11, 1917.
20. Isaiah Friedman, *Palestine: A Twice Promised Land?* vol. I. *The British, the Arabs, and Zionism, 1915–1920* (New Brunswick, NJ: Transaction Publishers, 2000), 47–59.
21. See pp. 100–1.
22. Matthias Erzberger, *Erlebnisse in Weltkreg* (Berlin, 1920), 307.
23. Sir Frederic Maurice, *The Armistices of 1918* (London, 1943), 12.
24. Cyril Falls, *Armageddon 1918* (London, 1964), 171–2.
25. Sir Charles V. F. Townshend, *My Campaign in Mesopotamia* (London, 1920), 385.
26. Ulrich Trumpener, *Germany and Ottoman Empire 1914–1918* (Princeton, NJ, 1968), 356, where the interview between Izzet and Nabi Bey with Ambassador Bernstorff on October 15, 1918 is quoted.
27. Laurence Evans, *United States Policy and the Partition of Turkey 1914–1924* (Baltimore, MD, 1965), 84.
28. Townshend, *My Campaign in Mesopotamia*, 374–5.

29. Ibid., 376–9, 382–3.
30. Ibid., 379–80. CAB 23/14, War cabinet meeting no. 489A, October 20, 1918, App. I.
31. CAB 23/14, War cabinet meeting, no. 489A, October 20, 1918, App. I.
32. Ibid., meeting, October 21, 1918.
33. Ibid.
34. Adolphe Laurens, *Le Commandement Naval en Méditerranée 1914–1918* (Paris, 1931), 330. Laurens analyzes the French point of view in their dispute with the British, pp. 321–5.
35. Ibid., 327, 335–6. Dyer describes the negotiations clause by clause in great detail, drawing both on British and Turkish sources, "The Turkish Armistice of 1918," 326–36.
36. Dyer, "The Turkish Armistice of 1918," 332, 345n42.
37. Howard M. Sachar, *The Emergence of the Middle East 1914–1924* (New York, 1969), 248, 291.
38. Dyer, "The Turkish Armistice of 1918," 336–7; CAB 23/14, War cabinet meeting no. 492A, October 31, 1918.
39. Townshend, *My Campaign in Mesopotamia*, 384–5.
40. Sir Theodore Morison, "England and Islam," *The Nineteenth Century and After* (July 1919), 117.
41. The *Koran*, Sura 3, Verses 19 and 85.
42. Bernard Lewis, "Revolt of Islam," *New Yorker*, November 19, 2001, 52.
43. Ibid., 53.
44. Cited in William Paton, "Indian Moslems and the Khalifate," *International Review of Missions*, 12 (1923) 86–7. The last statement belies Kedourie's assumption of a "spiritual headship of the Muslim world, a papacy of Islam," Elie Kedourie, *England and the Middle East: The Destruction of the Ottoman Empire 1914–1921* (London, 1987), 52–3. For a discussion, see Isaiah Friedman, *British Pan-Arab Policy 1915–1922: A Critical Appraisal* (New Brunswick, NJ: Transaction Publishers, 2010), 23–5.
45. On the system of Capitulations, see Friedman, *Germany, Turkey and Zionism*, 33–5.
46. Friedman, *British Pan-Arab Policy, 1915–1922*, 159–61.
47. F.O. 371/3057/103481, memorandum by Bray, March 25, 1917, encl. in Wilson (Jeddah) to Wingate 29/3/1917; a copy in F.O. 882/15, 95.
48. Friedman, *British Pan-Arab Policy, 1915–1922*, 15–9.
49. F.O. 882/24, A. Calthrope, British High Commissioner (Constantinople) to Clayton, April 30, 1919.
50. Special cable from Rome to the *New York Times*, May 28, 1918, cited in Lothrop Stoddard, *The New World of Islam* (New York, 1921), 76. Stoddard discusses at length the effect of World War I upon Asiatic and African peoples in his book, *The Rising Tide of Color Against White World Supremacy* (New York, London, 1920).
51. Jacob M. Landau, *The Politics of Pan-Islam* (Oxford, 1990), 190–1.
52. Morison, "England and Islam," 116–21.
53. F.O. 882/23, 183–4, "Plea for a Moslem Bureau," memorandum by Jacob, July 1, 1919, printed.
54. F.O. 882/23, 118–29, "The Near East and the British Empire," memorandum by Whittall, London, May 5, 1919. There is a biography on Shakib Arslan

by William L. Cleveland, *Islam Against the West. Shakib Arslan and the Campaign for Islamic Nationalism* (London, 1985).

55. I. O., L/PS/11/150, Rumbold (Berne), March 31, 1919, and enclosures; Secretary of State of India to Viceroy of India and to the Civil Commissioner, Baghdad, April 26, 1919.

56. CAB 24/107, "Turkey," memorandum, dated June 7, 1920.

57. F.O. 376/21, 203–5, "Memorandum by Maharajah of Bikaner and Lord Sinha on the Future of Constantinople and the Turkish Empire," Paris, April 30, 1919.

58. *DBFP*, I, IV, pp. 290–1, App. B to No. 199, encl. in Clayton to Curzon, June 23, 1919.

59. I.O., L/PS/11/154, p. 4323/1919, encl. in Calthorpe (Constantinople) to Curzon, June 18, 1919.

60. U.S. Department of State, *Papers Relating to the Foreign Relations of the United States, The Paris Peace Conference Series*, vol. V, 690–701.

61. F.O. 374/21, Pt. II, Peace Conference, Paris, 1919, 203–4.

62. Landau, *The Politics of Pan Islam*, 208.

63. F.O. 371/4239/151671, "The Turkish Peace," Memorandum by Montagu, December 18, 1919, secret; also ibid., January 1, 1920. On Montagu's views see Harold Armstrong, *Turkey in Travail: The Birth of a New Nation* (London, 1925), 136–7. In 1919, Armstrong was serving as the Acting Military Attaché at the British High Commission in Constantinople.

64. Landau, *The Politics of Pan-Islam*, 207–8.

65. Ibid., 205–6.

66. Lloyd George, *The War Memoirs*, vol. II (London, 1936), 549–58, where he discusses the Turkish treaty in detail.

67. Above, p. 2.

68. Peter Rowland, *Lloyd George* (London, 1974), 564.

69. George, *The War Memoirs*, 658.

70. Cited in Shane Leslie, *Mark Sykes: His Life and Letters* (London, 1923), 290.

71. Ibid., 291.

72. Cited in Richard Bigelow, *Turkey Reborn* (Scotch Plains, NJ, 1941), 28.

73. Harold Nicolson, *George Curzon. The Last Phase, 1919–1925. A Study in Postwar Diplomacy* (London, 1934), 80.

74. Earl of Ronaldshay, *The Life of Lord Curzon*, vol. III (London, 1928), 262–4.

75. S. D. Waley, *Edwin Montagu* (New York, 1964), 243.

76. Martin Gilbert (ed.), *Winston S. Churchill, The Stricken World 1916–1922* (Boston, 1975), 477–8.

77. *DBFP*, I, IV, pp. 645–51, App. IX and X, No. 426. "Ottoman Delegation to the Peace Conference," June 23, 1919; *Lloyd George, Memoirs*, II: 652–3.

78. Ibid., 645–7.

79. H. W. V. Temperley (ed), *A History of the Peace Conference of Paris*, vol. VI (London, 1920 and 1924), 25; David Lloyd George, *The Truth About the Peace Treaties*, vol. II (London, 1938), 1233, 1239–40, 1242; Howard M. Sachar, *The Emergence of the Middle East: 1914–1924* (New York, 1969 and London, 1970), 306–9.

80. George, *The Truth About the Peace Treaties*, II:1228.
81. Ibid., 1204.
82. Quoted in Nicolson, *Curzon: The Last Phase*, 96–7.
83. Paul C. Helmreich, *From Paris to Sèvres: The Partition of the Ottoman Empire at the Peace Conference of 1919–1920* (Columbus, OH, 1974), 18.
84. Ibid., 19–20, 94–5.
85. Sachar, *The Emergence of the Middle East*, 312–4.
86. Rhodes House Library, Oxford (Mss. Dept.) The Richard Meinertzhagen Papers, Meinertzhagen to the Command of the Imperial General Staff (C.I.G.S.), May 17, 1919.
87. Ibid., Meinertzhagen to C.I.G.S., May 20, 21, 1919, urgent.
88. Ibid., Diary, Paris, entries January, 30, May 8, 1919.
89. Ibid., entry February 20, March 1, 1919.
90. Ibid., entries February 20, March 26, and June 26, 1919.
91. Ibid., entry May 8, 1919.
92. Ibid., 126, "Some remarks on Zionism," n.d.
93. Ibid., entry February 20, 1919.
94. Ibid., entries March 19, 23, 1919.
95. Ibid., entry June 26, 1919.
96. Major-General Sir Charles E. Callwell, *Field Marshal Sir Henry Wilson*, vol. 2 (London, 1927), 190, entry May 6, 1919.
97. Above, pp. 9–19.
98. *DBFP*, I, IV, No. 509, Report on "feelings of the Turks," encl. in Webb to Curzon, Constantinople, September 10, 1919, 758–60.
99. Ibid., No. 487, Webb to Crowe (Paris), Constantinople, August 17, 1919, 733.
100. Ibid., note 3, letter dated August 15, 1919.
101. Ibid., No. 597, Robeck to Curzon, November 18, 1919, 895–6; also F.O. 608/89, Calthorpe to Balfour, July 1.
102. Bernard Lewis, *The Emergence of Modern Turkey* (London, 1961).
103. There are a number of biographies: H. E. Wortham, *Mustapha Kemal of Turkey* (Boston, 1931); Lord Kinross, *Atatürk: The Rebirth of the Nation* (London, 1964); Hans Froembgen, *Kemal Atatürk*, trans. Kenneth Kirkness (London, n.d.); Dagobert von Mikusch, *Mustapha Kemal Between Europe and Asia*, trans. John Linton (London, 1931); Greg Wolf, *Mustafa Kemal, An Intimate Study of a Dictator* (London, 1939). Kemal's career is aptly described by Bernard Lewis, as well as by other authors. But the most comprehensive and illuminating of these is by Andrew Mango, *Atatürk* (London, 1999).
104. Major-General Sir Charles E. Callwell, *The Dardanelles* (Boston, 1919), 94–105, 116–7, 206–7; Otto Karl Liman von Sanders, *Five Years in Turkey* (Baltimore, MD, 1928), 83, 91–2.
105. Liman von Sanders, *Five Years in Turkey*, 85.
106. Cited in Wortham, *Mustapha Kemal of Turkey*, 80.
107. The events were related by Atatürk in a six-day speech to the Congress of the People's Party in 1927. It is an important source, which, though subjective, is on the whole quite accurate. *A Speech Delivered by Ghazi Mustapha Kemal, President of the Turkish Republic, October 1927* (Leipzig, 1929); (hereafter referred to as *Kemal's Speech*). A supplement to this source is

Kemal Pasha, *Die Neue Türkei, 1919–1927*, vol. III, *Die Documente zur Rede* (Leipzig, 1929), which contains correspondence with army generals and officials, as well as with the Porte in French translation.

108. *Kemal's Speech*, 19–20.
109. Ibid., 14–5, 20–6.
110. *DBFP*, I, IV, No. 460. Calthorpe to Turkish Foreign Minister, July 2, 1919, encl. 1 to No. 460, 688–9.
111. Above, pp. 9–11.
112. *Kemal's Speech*, 31–4; *Die Dokumente zur Rede*, No. 26, p. 12; Salihi Ramsdan, *Turkish Diplomacy 1918–1921* (London, 1975), 15.
113. Cited in Wortham, *Mustapha Kemal of Turkey*, 97.
114. Ibid., 98–100.
115. *Kemal's Speech*, 59.
116. Wortham, *Mustapha Kemal of Turkey*, 103.
117. *Kemal's Speech*, 58–9.
118. *DBFP*, I, IV, No. 543, Robeck to Curzon, October 10, 1919, 802–10; *Kemal's Speech*, 77; *Die Dokumente zur Rede*, No. 27, 276.
119. Robert Dunn, "Kemal, the Key to India and Egypt," *The World's Work*, 44 (1922) 57–67.
120. See note 118, above.
121. Ibid.
122. Ibid., Encl. in No. 534, Robeck to Curzon, October 6, 1919; encl. "Report of Interview with Kemal Bey," by Ian Smith, September 30, 1919, 792–4.
123. Ibid., Encl. in No. 549, Robeck to Curzon, October 18, 1919; encl. "An Account of a Conversation Between Mr. Hohler and Brigadier-General McCoy," October 14, 1919, 821–3.
124. Ibid., Encl. 2, "An After-Dinner Conversation with an American Officer," 828–9.
125. *Kemal's Speech*, 111–3; *Die Documente zur Rede*, Nos. 62, 65, 42–4.
126. *DBFP*, I, IV, No. 464, Hohler to Tilley, July 21, 1919, 693–5.
127. Ibid., No. 523, Meinertzhagen to Curzon, September 27, 1919, 782.
128. Ibid., No. 543, Robeck to Curzon, October 10, 1919, 808.
129. Ibid., 805.
130. Ibid., No. 597, Robeck to Curzon, November 18, 1919, 895–6.
131. Ibid., No. 543, Robeck to Curzon, October, 10, November 18, 1919.

2

Turkish–Arabic–Pan-Islamic League versus the British

Sykes was the first British official to discover, during his visit to Syria/Palestine in November 1918, that Arab nationalism had assumed a Pan-Arab and a Pan-Islamic character; Islam at the core was anti-foreign and hostile toward the Allied powers. It was an eye-opening revelation. It destroyed his cherished doctrine that Arab nationalism—the "child of the Entente," as he referred to it—would constitute an effective antidote to Pan-Islam.[1] Sykes died too prematurely before he could reeducate his colleagues, both in London and the East, and warn them that the policy that Cairo had initiated—and to which he was a party—was erroneous. Events proved him right.

When accompanying the King-Crane Commission in July 1919, William Yale became convinced that what was generally considered to be an Arab national movement was, in fact, Pan-Arabism and Pan-Islamism and that it was a "very dangerous movement . . . it is almost certain," he emphasized, "that the present Arab movement or Syrian national movement will turn into fanatical Islamism."[2]

In October 1919, Major J. N. Clayton, the political officer in Damascus (not to be confused with Gen. Sir Gilbert Clayton who, in the meantime, had returned to England), ascertained that for "the vast majority of Moslems, Arab Nationalism and Islamism are synonymous terms." He did not discount the possibility of a *Jihad*, which the Baghdadi officers in the Sharifian army and other extremists were endeavoring to bring about. Their effort, "inevitably will lead to rapprochement with the Turks and with Mustafa Kemal. It is safe to say that the majority of the Muslims in Aleppo Vilayet, and a very large number in the vilayet of Damascus, are in sympathy with Turkish aspirations, and would prefer union with Turkey to being under an unpopular European Power."[3]

Clayton was unaware that, when he submitted his report, a formal agreement between Mustafa Kemal and Emir Feisal had already existed for three months. The agreement was signed at Aleppo on June 16, 1919, through the auspices of Essad Bey, the Mutessarif of Kerk in Trans-Jordan. Its purpose was to put an end to the "regrettable discord" between the Turkish and Arabic peoples, who have material, moral, and religious bonds, and whose duty is to help each other. Turkey and Arabia are united in their protest against partition of their respective countries. Should this come about in consequence of deliberations at the Peace Conference in Paris, the signatories would declare a holy war against the foreign powers (Articles 2 and 3).

Feisal was to advise all the Arabs in Syria, Mesopotamia, the Hedjaz, the Yemen, as well as those in North Africa (in Tripoli, Benghazi, Algeria, Morocco and Tunis), and even the Muslims in India, about this decision and was to invite them to join the holy war, the *Jihad* (Articles 2, 3, and 10).

With regard to the constitution, it was agreed (Articles 4 and 7) that Arabia would remain attached to Turkey and remain faithful to the caliphate whose title would be ratified and proclaimed afresh. The two governments, however, would remain separate. Arabia would be comprised of Syria, Palestine, Mesopotamia, and the Hedjaz. Thereafter, a military alliance would be concluded for offensive and defensive purposes. "In case of need, His Excellency, the sherif will assist the [Turkish] National Forces in Asia Minor." The signatories' seals were affixed above their signatures.[4]

On the face of it, the agreement appears to be too fantastic to be possible, since, at that very time, the two parties were too weak to assist each other materially and militarily. It should be taken, therefore, merely as a reflection of their respective national aspirations.

The scheme was not new. It was an expanded version of an idea that had been the brainchild of Aziz Bey Ali al-Misri, the founder of the Arab Secret Society, al-Ahd, a devout Muslim and loyal to the Ottoman Caliphate. Ali al-Misri moved to Constantinople, where, in 1891, he became an outspoken opponent of the British occupation of Egypt and, after the 1908 revolution, he was an influential member within the CUP ranks. Disturbed by their subsequent policy of Turkification, however, he became convinced that the only way to resolve a potential Turco-Arab conflict and ensure the territorial integrity of the empire was by decentralization. The program of the al-Ahd society advocated a broad federal scheme, modeled after the Austro-Hungarian *Ausgleich*.[5]

During his stay in Damascus, at the end of 1915, Feisal met members of the Arab Secret Societies and was sworn in as a member.[6] It could be safely assumed that this was when he became aware of al-Misri's scheme. In April–June 1918, when Djemal Pasha tried to induce Feisal to defect from the Allied camp and join the Ottoman army, among the conditions that Feisal put forth was that the Ottoman Empire should be reformed according to the Austro-Hungarian model, the *Ausgleich*, and would become a Turco-Arab Empire. This was a replica of al-Ahd's scheme. Such a demand, however, was too radical for the centralistic politicians in Constantinople. Neither the Porte, nor the sultan, could entertain it.[7]

What Feisal failed to elicit from the Young Turk government, he now obtained generously from Mustafa Kemal. Politically, it was a triumph for Feisal. As for Kemal, he gave up nothing and gained quite a lot. He gave up a priori the idea of repossessing the former Asiatic provinces and therefore, from his perspective, made no territorial concessions. On the other hand, he secured the constitutional attachment of the Arab state to Turkey and its loyalty to the sultan. Although now self-proclaimed brothers-in-arms, the military value of the Arabs was marginal. They could, however—as they did in Mesopotamia several months later—cause a great deal of harm to Britain. Moreover, the alliance with Arabs provided the basis for launching an all-out Muslim rebellion against the foreign powers, particularly if and when a call was issued from the holy places in the Hedjaz. In July 1919, the intelligence officers at Constantinople learned from a "very reliable source" that Feisal had approached the sultan as well and that the intermediary for the negotiations for the creation of a Turkish–Arabic–Pan-Islamic League between the emir and the sultan was Essad Bey, the Mutessarif of Kerak. Essad had been in secret communication with General Kutchuk Jemal Pasha (not to be confused with his namesake, Ahmed Djemal Pasha, the former commander of the Fourth Ottoman army) when the latter was at Konia. Jemal brought a handwritten letter from Emir Feisal and delivered it personally to the sultan. In it, Feisal assured the sultan of his "devotion and fidelity." Jemal Pasha was to convey a reply as well as some secret instructions. Another report from a different and independent agent was almost identical.[8]

It was later learned that General Kutchuk Jemal Pasha had given the sultan a copy of the original treaty between Feisal and Kemal and that a copy of this copy was obtained through a clerk at the ministry of interior and bought, for the French authorities in Constantinople by Dr. Topjian, an Armenian, for the sum of 150 Turkish Liras.[9]

Another copy was given by Boghos Pasha, the head of the Armenian delegation, to Robert Wansittart in Paris. Vansittart, then a member of the British delegation to the Peace Conference, thought that the document was a forgery (presumably by the Turks), but Balfour suggested that Constantinople, London, and Cairo should be consulted in order to verify its authenticity.[10]

At the Foreign Office, Hubert Young suggested that "the encouragement of the Arab movement would have been the surest way of weakening political Pan-Islamism in Syria and Mesopotamia." This was the essence of the doctrine that had been propounded by Sir Mark Sykes. Contrary to Sykes, however, Young failed to realize that the doctrine was bankrupt because Arab nationalism was also Islamic. On examination of the treaty, however, Young had some second thoughts. He minuted thus:

> Even if this treaty is a forgery, which is more than likely, as Feisal would not be such a fool as to sign anything of the kind, it would, I think, be a mistake for us to underestimate the risk of his taking some such action. What line are the Allies to take if as an immediate result of the treaty with Turkey, the Muslims of the Middle East combine on religious grounds to drive out the infidel invader? We can hardly suppress them by force. . .

Sir Ronald Graham, assistant under-secretary for foreign affairs remarked that he had heard about the treaty from James Malcolm, a respected Armenian politician domiciled in England. "It all goes to show the pernicious effects of the delay in the settlement at Paris. We squabble with the French and Feisal muddles his future with intrigues."[11]

In Cairo, General Allenby suggested that the Turks were endeavoring to tempt Feisal into taking advantage of his displeasure with the proposed French Mandate for Syria and the British for Mesopotamia. "But," he emphasized, "I do not believe that he would be disloyal . . . but that he is very perturbed at the prospect of a French mandate, there is no doubt . . . If he intends to oppose the French openly, which is what I believe he will do, it is obvious that better than anything else an alliance with the Turks will give him a chance."

Colonel French at the General Headquarters in Cairo thought the same. "There is no evidence of such a treaty as you mention." French recalled that a few days earlier the political officer at Damascus had tried to dissuade Feisal from issuing his people a call to arms, warning him that such a course would at once cause an open breach with the British. Undeterred, Feisal blamed the British for not fulfilling their obligations and warned that "he would make such a war a religious one against both [the British] and the French." This was a bad omen, but curiously, the political officer (his name was not given) thought that the crisis "can generally be smoothed over . . . At the same time, I do not believe that such a treaty exists though C.U.P. would no doubt like to conclude it."[12]

The officer misread Feisal's mind as he erred in dismissing the existence of the treaty. Two weeks earlier (August 16, 1919), the director of military intelligence had reported that a Turkish–Arabic–Pan-Islamic League had been created by Emir Feisal and Kutchuk Jemal Pasha, who was acting on behalf of Mustafa Kemal Pasha. The purpose of the league was to liberate the Arabic-speaking provinces from Christian domination, with Feisal being appointed as the overlord.[13]

That the British officers demonstrated such a complete trust in Feisal is not surprising. They were possessed by the idea of which Sykes and Lawrence were the chief exponents—that by liberating the Arabs from the Turkish "yoke," they were winning eternal friends for Britain, with Emir Feisal as the prince of an Anglo-Arab alliance. The possibility of disloyalty, let alone betrayal, was not even considered. Nobody was aware of Feisal's secret negotiations with Djemal Pasha, during the summer of 1918, (and subsequently with Kutchuk, his namesake). The plan amounted to Feisal's complete defection from the Allied camp, turning Arab arms against their British patrons. When Lawrence discovered by chance, through a secret agent, how far Feisal had ventured in his *pourparlers* with Djemal, he became alarmed. And yet, with the exception of David Hogarth, who was unable to imagine that Feisal could be so treacherous,[14] Lawrence did not find it necessary to officially report this extraordinary piece of Intelligence—an unforgivable breach of discipline.

Lawrence failed also to note that Feisal and he were at cross-purposes: Lawrence's ultimate goal was to create an Arab Dominion—a "Brown Dominion" as he called it—whereas Feisal's aimed at an association with Turkey. Rather than face reality, Lawrence conceived an idea, which Clayton articulated in an official memorandum (April 2, 1918) in which he wrote as follows:

> The attitude of Sherif Feisal does not necessarily mean disloyalty to us, nor does it show any intention of making terms prematurely with enemy. He has already expressed to Major Lawrence opinion that it will be necessary for Arabs to make terms with Turks as soon as they have secured their aims in Arab territories. A hostile Turkey immediately north of Arab territory would be a perpetual menace to Arab independence, and seeing that Arabs would naturally turn to us for protection, it would prove a source of anxiety to us. It does not follow, therefore, that Feisal is doing more than attempt to ascertain attitude of Turkey towards an eventual rapprochement . . . A [British oriented] friendly Moslem Arab State or Confederation of States would be counterpoise to hostile Pan-Islamism . . .
>
> At the same time, it must be remembered that Feisal may not regard the destruction of Turkey, a great Moslem power, with complete equanimity, since he is a strong Moslem.[15]

Was Clayton's memorandum a clever attempt to whitewash Feisal or a product of imperfect knowledge of what really passed between Feisal and Djemal Pasha? Since Lawrence's brief in this matter was selective, if not tendentious, the end result was that both Cairo and London continued to regard Feisal as a loyal ally.

Gradually, however, the truth unfolded. Thus, Arnold Wilson, the civil commissioner in Baghdad, was nearer the truth when he assessed that information about the Feisal–Kemal agreement was "accurate in substance, even though formal treaty may not yet exist . . . Alleged treaty has clearly been drafted in Turkey, and its acceptance by Feisal, if such is the case, is probably in theory realization by him of growing unpopularity of Sharifian party in Arabia."[16]

Several days later, a report about Mustafa Kemal's speech at Aleppo (October 9, 1919) made all the skeptics about the treaty pause. In his proclamation, Kemal appealed to the Syrians to put all their mutual misunderstandings behind them and not trust the promises made by the enemies of Islam. The Turks had decided to fight them and all those who wished to save their country and Islam should join them. "The *Mujahidis* [fighters for a religious cause] . . . will soon be visiting their Arab brothers and will scatter away the enemy."[17]

Several months later, it was learned that, during Feisal's second visit to Paris in the autumn of 1919, the Turks made yet another effort to tighten their relations with the Arabs. They had managed to convince the Syrians, as well as the king of the Hedjaz, that—promises for Arab independence notwithstanding—the Allies intended to divide Syria and Mesopotamia and reduce them to the status of French and British colonies respectively. It was the emir Ali Haidar Pasha, Hussein's younger brother, who lived in Constantinople, as well as Hilmi Pasha, the ex-Khedive, who were chiefly instrumental in facilitating the unification with the result that a pro-Turkish party was founded in Aleppo with branches in other Syrian towns. Its objective was to achieve independence with Turkish assistance. King Hussein consented and appointed Emir Zeid, his son, as one of the delegates to the negotiations.[18]

On his return to Damascus, Feisal concluded a second agreement with Mustafa Kemal, signing it on his father's behalf. Two new paragraphs appear in this document. Paragraph 4 reads thus:

> In order to guarantee mutual assistance . . . the Turks will be allowed to organize the Arab Army and furnish officers to supervise the training of the Arab and Syrian troops. The Turks will also supply the Arab and Syrian Armies with arms and ammunition as far as it is in their power to do so.

In return (paragraph 5), the Arab-Syrian government agreed not to enter into any military agreement with any other power without the consent of the Turkish government.[19]

Early in 1920, the Arab Bureau reproduced verbatim the June 16, 1919 Feisal–Kemal Agreement in the original French version.[20] The authenticity of this document could no longer be questioned. Late in September 1920, the Foreign Office confirmed that there was some evidence that Feisal had entered into an understanding with Mustafa Kemal and even with the Bolsheviks.[21]

The reference to Bolsheviks is rather strange. The Foreign Office, however, had some solid grounds for suspecting that Feisal had communicated with the Bolsheviks as well, perhaps indirectly. On May 31, 1920, Feisal published in Arabic a Bolshevik Manifesto issued by the commissariat of the Soviet government. The manifesto announced the defeat of the White Russian army, led by General Anton Denikin. The British, who were supporting him, suffered a serious blow. The manifesto appealed to the people in the East—the Turks, the Arabs, the Indians, and the Persians—to aid the Bolsheviks in their campaign against the Allies: "The time of revolt and to drive away those who wish to steal your country and rob your freedom has come . . . Russia is ready to aid you . . . Please communicate this to all the people in Syria and Mesopotamia."[22]

By 1921, the existence of the Turco-Arab agreement became almost axiomatic. "The Sherifians are known to be in alliance with the Turkish Nationalists," wrote Captain C. D. Brunton of the General Staff Intelligence in Palestine to his superiors in Cairo. The agreement aimed at creating Arab States in Mesopotamia, Syria, and Palestine under nominal Turkish suzerainty.

The Turkish Nationalists, Brunton went on, had seized the psychological moment to bring about a reconciliation with the Arabs by showing them how "badly they have been treated by their Christian Allies," and that their only hope was in combined Muslim action against the "injustice and imperialism of France and Britain." The powerful bond of Islam and the hatred and distrust of Christian Powers and policies had lubricated the Turco-Arab alliance. "We are therefore now confronted by a Pan-Islamic movement," Brunton concluded, "which would foment insurrections resorting to the avowed tactics of guerilla and *cemitadji* warfare."

Brunton rejected the notion that Feisal was "a true friend" of the British. Such an opinion had been aired in the British Parliament and elsewhere, but "all evidence available," Brunton insisted, "does not bear out these theories. Moreover, during the War Arab friendship for the British has hardly been proved." At the height of the insurrection in Mesopotamia in 1920, the hostility was all-pervasive, while "no one who is in touch with Arab opinion in Palestine would venture to state that the Arabs there entertain any warm sentiments or regard for us."

As for King Hussein—and this was borne out by reports of the British agents in Jeddah—he "is by no means unlikely to pursue a policy hostile to British interests if the occasion arose."[23]

What conditioned Feisal's attitude toward the British and the Allies in general was religion. On April 11, 1921, whilst in a steamer heading for Port Said, he was interviewed by M. T. Kaderbhoy, an Indian caliphate official. The emir, Kaderbhoy noted, was deeply disturbed by the unrelenting hostility of the Muslim world against his father and himself.

Nervous and in a tense voice, Feisal declared that he wished to restore peace and concord in the Islamic world, adding that "he had no faith whatsoever in England . . . England was lying all along," and, as if to emphasize his resentment, he used the French expression *Anglais Menteurs*. France, too, was an "enemy," but England preferred to support her rather than her "Beduin Arab." He was anxious to make peace with Turkey and spoke in this vein with Bekri Sami Bey, who was with him in London. Should Turkey be attacked at any time in the future, he declared, "the Arabs, as brothers in faith, would volunteer to fight even their ally England."[24]

This statement throws light on Feisal's true mental disposition. He was not a genuine friend of the British as Lawrence wished him to be. Whenever it suited him, he protested his friendship for Britain, but, as Sir Ronald Graham, the assistant under-secretary for foreign affairs, characterized him correctly in April 1918, "Feisal's natural instinct is pro-Turk . . . We should discourage Feisal from making any arrangements for 'after the war' . . . with the Turks."[25] In this, the British were not successful nor were they fully aware of Feisal's conduct during the War.

Brunton's characterization of Feisal is fully borne out by Feisal's conduct during the war and thereafter. In 1914, when Turkey's participation was imminent, two courses seemed to be open to the Sharifian family: "[T]o stand by Turkey in her hour of trial and earn her grateful recognition, or to rise against her and seek their freedom at the point of sword. Which of those alternatives to take?" In sharp contrast to the British-oriented Abdullah, Feisal favored the first course.[26]

In March 1915, when meeting the leaders of the Secret Societies in Damascus, Feisal confessed that "his preference for the Turks came from his fear of Europe." An identity of views between himself and his questioners was thus established. At a meeting of the al-Fatat Committee, which had taken place earlier, it had been resolved that "in the event of European designs appearing to materialize, the society shall be bound to work on the side of Turkey in order to resist foreign penetration of whatever kind or form."[27]

Feisal was soon sworn in as a member of al-Fatat and thereafter proceeded to Constantinople on a mission on his father's behalf; Hussein sought to realize his ambitions within the framework of the Ottoman Empire. In Constantinople, Feisal met the sultan, the grand vizier, as well as Tala'at Pasha and Enver Pasha. He assured them, as well as Baron von Oppenheim, that his father's loyalty to the Ottoman realm was solid and unshakable, and that he would "not dream of defecting to the enemy." Moreover, on his father's behalf, Feisal offered to use the Hedjaz as a base for propaganda to all Islamic countries to instigate subversive anti-British activities. Both Baron Oppenheim, as well as Sheikh Saleh el-Tunisi, a confidant of the deposed Khedive

Abbas Hilmi, who questioned Feisal separately, concluded that the emir was sincere.

This was also the distinct impression of Djemal Pasha, whom Feisal met in Jerusalem on his return journey. In a speech to the staff at headquarters of the Fourth Ottoman army, he swore by the soul of the prophet to return at an early date at the head of his warriors—a camel corps of fifteen hundred men—to help the Ottoman army and "to fight the foes of the faith to the death."

It was only after the discovery of a secret squad dispatched by Enver to assassinate Hussein that Hussein decided to burn his bridges with the Turks and throw in his lot with the British. Perforce Feisal was drawn into the rebellion, but his performance as a leader was disappointing. He shied away from military encounters; nor did he guide, let alone inspire, his fellow Arabs to fight the Turkish army. It was not until September 1918, when the offensive toward Damascus was unfolding, that Lawrence grasped the anomaly that, although officially commander of the Arab army, Feisal had remained in the background. Lawrence thought that it was crucial at this stage of the war to build Feisal's image, noting that, without him, any serious venture "would be in vain." Feisal must be "present with us in a fighting line . . . ready to take over and exploit the political value of what our bodies conquered for him."

There is no evidence to show that Feisal followed Lawrence's advice. Since April, his mind had been diverted elsewhere. With his confidence in the Allied victory badly shaken, he was engaged in negotiations with Djemal Pasha with the object of defecting to the Ottoman army and joining the battle for "the defense of Islam." When Lawrence discovered through a secret agent some of the correspondence between the emir and the Turkish commander, he must have realized that Feisal's ambition was at cross-purposes with his own. As it had been pointed out already in our study, Lawrence's ultimate aim was to create a "Brown [Arab] Dominion" associated with the British Empire. Feisal's ideal, however, was the emergence of a Turco-Arab Empire in the Austro-Hungarian model, or alternatively, Arab autonomy within the Ottoman framework.[28]

In a rare emotional outburst, Abdullah charged that it was he who was mainly responsible for bringing the Arabs to the side of the British during the war, and that in 1918, he had dissuaded Feisal from accepting an offer from the Turks to defect to their camp.[29] Neither Abdullah nor Lawrence, however, were aware that Feisal had continued his pourparlers with the Turks even up until the end of the war;[30] still worse, he had passed on a military secret to the enemy. General Liman von Sanders, who, in 1918, served as a supreme commander of the German–Ottoman army in the East, disclosed that, during the latter part of August 1918, Feisal had informed the Turkish Command that the British were about to launch an offensive along the Mediterranean coast.[31]

Apparently the Turks took Feisal's information seriously. This transpires from Liman von Sanders's affirmative statement, "It was clear that we had to expect a big attack in the coast sector."[32] Such an attack, however, did not materialize. On September 19 it was reported to the Fourth Ottoman army Headquarters at Nazareth that "no trace of the enemy was observable at Haifa." The bitter surprise came on the following day at 5:30 a.m., when Nazareth was captured by the British; von Sanders and his crew only just managed to escape to Tiberias.[33] Feisal was totally unaware of General Chauvel's plan to make a dash at the head of his cavalry through the Wadi Ara to the Tel of Meggido and hence making a direct assault on Nazareth. He thus unwittingly deceived the Turco-German Command and indirectly contributed to Chauvel's victory.

Though at heart pro-Turk, Feisal habitually played a double game. This emerges clearly from a conversation between himself and General Alan Dawney about which Lawrence gave us a remarkably frank account. Thus, Feisal boasted to Dawney that he would try the coming autumn to take Damascus, but if the British would "not be able to carry their share of the attack, he would save his own people by making separate peace with Turkey."[34] Against this background, Lawrence's endeavor to stage a "victorious entry" into Damascus for Feisal[35] looks rather tragicomic.

It was also Lawrence who had elevated Feisal's status by bringing him to the Peace Conference in Paris to plead the Arab cause. However, as high as Feisal's expectations were, so his disappointment was shattering. He was stunned at the meeting of the Council of Ten on February 6, 1919, when President Wilson, responding to his demand to recognize the Arabs as "independent and sovereign peoples," asked whether he "would prefer for his people a single mandatory or several." Nor did he receive any encouragement from William Yale, then a member of the American delegation. Yale was not convinced that Syria was ripe for independence, nor did he believe that an Arab Confederation was a feasible idea.[36]

But the biggest blow to Feisal came when Lawrence advised him to reconcile himself to a French mandate for Syria. During the Peace Conference, Lawrence realized that under no circumstances would the British government accept a mandate over Syria and that it would be counter-productive to pit Feisal against the Quai d'Orsay. It also dawned upon him that the Pan-Arab scheme, which Feisal had advocated before the Council of Ten on January 1, 1919, was unrealistic. "The movement for Arab unity possesses no serious political value for the present or, indeed, for the future," he declared to the Anglo-French committee of Middle-East experts.[37] To Feisal, Lawrence's turnabout must have come as a shock, particularly since it was Lawrence himself who, throughout the war, had been inculcating in him an anti-French animus with the object of dislodging the French from Syria.

During the war, Feisal received yet another piece of advice from Lawrence. "I begged him," Lawrence recorded, "to trust not in our promises, like his father, but in his own strong performance."[38] Lawrence meant that Feisal's military performance should be demonstrated against the Turks. In his wildest imagination, Lawrence did not expect that Feisal would ever apply his counsel against the British. Disappointed, Feisal, back in Damascus, returned to his old love—Turkey. He signed an agreement with Mustafa Kemal, but it was Yasin al-Hashimi with whom the idea of rapprochement with Turkey originated.

Before the war, Yasin assumed the overall leadership of the Arab secret societies, al-Ahd and al-Fatat, and when the war broke out, was appointed chief of staff of the Twelfth Ottoman Division. Djemal, however, mistakenly suspected him of treason and deported him to Constantinople. There, jointly with his friends, Yasin engineered the defection of al-Faruqi to the British in order to win them over. As we know, al-Faruqi was eminently successful in misleading his British interlocutors and extracting a commitment for "Arab independence" in McMahon's hapless letter of October 24, 1915. Yasin himself, however, rejoined the Ottoman army. At the recommendation of Kaiser Wilhelm II, he was promoted to the rank of major-general in recognition of his gallantry. In the spring of 1918, he commanded the Ottoman troops at Es Salt and Amman and was largely responsible for the defeat of the Australian cavalry unit that General Allenby had ordered to establish a bridgehead east of the River Jordan. When the Turks retreated from Damascus, al-Hashimi, like other prisoners of war, changed his allegiance and joined Feisal. The latter appointed him as chief of staff. The new Arab army in Syria was largely Yasin al-Hashimi's creation. He exerted a tremendous influence on Emir Zeid and on Feisal himself. During Feisal's absence in Europe, he became the virtual ruler of Syria.[39]

Yasin al-Hashimi impressed Gertrude Bell as "the most forcible personality" she had ever met. He was one of the most extreme exponents of Arab independence from a French mandate in Syria or any other form of foreign control. Subsequently he also became the standard bearer for the liberation of Mesopotamia from British tutelage. He was in touch both with leaders of the Committee of Union and Progress as well as Mustafa Kemal. His sympathies were pro-Turkish. "If the Arab State collapses," Miss Bell surmised, "he would seek and find his fortunes with the Ottoman government . . . There is no room for his ambitions in any Arab province unless . . . it were to remain an integral part of the Ottoman Empire."[40]

The British Intelligence characterized him thus: "Capable, good soldier, intelligent, ambitious, fanatical. Supporter of complete independence, potentially dangerous."[41] Among Arab officers who seconded Yasin was Ja'far al-Askari: a Baghdadi of humble origin. In 1916, Ja'far was taken prisoner by the British. He joined Feisal and became commander of the Arab army. Intoxicated by the capture of Damascus, he, like other officers in the Sharifian army, seized power and were, in Miss Bell's words, "in a fierce pursuit of an exaggerated political ideal for the attainment of which. . . they were prepared to set the Syrian province in a blaze."[42]

Yasin revealed to Miss Bell that, under his command, there were seventy-five hundred soldiers, manned by four hundred officers, mostly Baghdadis and that they were being trained for guerrilla warfare. They were drawn from the Arab Legion, which had been founded by the British in 1917 and which was incorporated into the Arab army. As a fighting force against the Turks, they were useless. They were ill-disciplined and imbued with an unusual love of politics. The legion became a hotbed of radical Arab nationalism that asserted itself during Feisal's regime in Damascus between 1918 and 1920. Throughout the war, British officers complained bitterly about the ingratitude and antagonism shown by the Arab Legionnaires.[43] Now, though still equipped and maintained by British tax-payers' money (amounting to £150,000 monthly), they were bracing themselves to fight the French in Syria and, particularly, the British in Mesopotamia.

Yasin and his crew were not the only ones to aim at reinstating Turkish rule in the former Ottoman Asiatic provinces. The Young

Arab Societies nourished an identical ambition. The most prominent were *al-Muntada al-Arabi* (the literary club) and *al-Nadi al-Arabi* (the Arab club). The former was led by the al-Nashashibis and the latter by the al-Husseini family, both of them of Palestine. The number of members was small—no more than five hundred in each club—but their influence by far exceeded their numerical inferiority. They, as well as al-Ahd and *al-Fatat*, dominated local political life in Syria, and no major policy decisions could be taken without prior consultation with them. Although ridden by feuds, ideologically there was little difference between them. The moving spirit of the *al-Nadi al-Arabi* was Hajj Amin al-Husseini, who served as its president, whereas among the *al-Muntada al-Arabi* ranks, the most prominent member was Izzat Darwaza, its secretary. The head of the *al-Muntada al-Arabi* branch in Damascus was Abd al-Qadir al-Muzaffar, who was fanatically hostile toward the British and Jews alike.[44]

Major Garland, now the head of The Arab Bureau, told his colleague in Cairo that *al-Nadi al-Arabi* was founded immediately after Turkey's defeat and, though ostensibly a social and literary club, it had soon shown its political colors. It established branches throughout Syria, Palestine, and Mesopotamia and had an office in Constantinople. Garland described them as "Young hotheads of Damascus," and accused them of interfering with the administration of the country and of being partly responsible for the massacre of Armenians in Aleppo. He was not in a position to ascertain the extent of their association with the Turkish national movement or with the Bolsheviks, but since they had become definitely anti-European, it was only natural to suppose that they turned in this direction for additional help.[45]

The India Office enjoyed far better sources of information than the Arab Bureau did. Their Intelligence summarized the position thus:

> Nationalist elements in Syria and Mesopotamia were systematically organized for a considerable period until they obtained such cohesion among themselves as enabled them to exercise a powerful influence on local feeling in both countries, and on Arab government at Damascus. This having been achieved, their union with Turkish Nationalists was brought about. This was considerably facilitated by Feisal's failure to control extremists at the beginning of November 1919. Since that date active co-operation has been obtained between Syria and Anatolia, whilst both used their influence with the tribes. To obtain latter's co-operation a violent and well-organized Pan-Islamic policy has been instituted both in Syria and Angora.[46]

At this juncture it would be worthwhile to recall the observation made by David Hogarth after his visit to Syria in December 1918. He concluded despondently that, contrary to the view presented in the European press, the Syrian Arabs did not consider at all their "liberation" from Turkey as a "boon"; they regarded it merely as a means to achieve their independence. If they failed to achieve this, "they would rather have the Turk back and will scheme to get him."[47]

Colonel Meinertzhagen, during his term as chief political officer in Syria and Palestine (1919–1920), was able to witness how prescient Hogarth's analysis was. Shortly after his appointment, he cabled to Lord Curzon, now foreign secretary thus:

> Report from Damascus indicates that all Syrian, Palestinian, and Mesopotamian independent parties are now working in conjunction. The whole movement is Pan-Islamic, pro-Turk, and Anti-Sherifian. Yasin Pasha is believed to be the moving spirit.[48]

Several days later, he reported on intensification of Turkish propaganda in Syria and that the headquarters of the Arab army, as well as other elements (such as *al-Nadi al-Arabi*), were in communication with Mustafa Kemal. "General situation, delicate."[49]

How precarious the situation was transpires from the report of Major J. N. Clayton, who had pointed out that, throughout November, regular meetings were taking place at Damascus with the avowed object of coordinating plans for "a general rising over the whole of Arabistan, in conjunction with . . . the army under Mustafa Pasha Kemal." In addition to Yasin Pasha and Emir Zeid's adviser, Maulud Pasha, those who participated in the meetings were: Ja'far al-Askari, the governor of Aleppo, Rushdi Safadi, divisional commander at Aleppo, and Rashid al-Madfai, the military governor of Amman. "The movement," Clayton emphasized, "is definitely anti-European and is directed equally against the British and French. A most important point is that, while the whole plan is Pan-Islamic and the essence of it is religion, it is strongly anti-Sherifian." Should Feisal, then in Paris, accept an arrangement favorable to the French, the Sharifian family "will be thrown off." They would be accused not only of "selling Syria to the French but also of having betrayed Islam to the British by siding against Turkey during the war."[50]

The upper-classes in Syria, as well as a large section of the middle- and lower-classes, Clayton remarked, wished to settle down under a strong government—even a French one—and "to carry on trade or agriculture and do not want any more war!" They were powerless, however, against "a strong and determined body of men, who absolutely control the army and . . . [are] preparing to declare a holy war should circumstances permit." Moreover, public opinion had veered very strongly in favor of the Turks.[51]

The headquarters at Cairo also reported that Arab inhabitants of the vilayets of Aleppo and Damascus were sympathetic to Turkish aspirations. The same applied to Mosul and Baghdad, where rapprochement with Mustafa Kemal and Turkey in general was much in evidence as was a resurgence of the Islamic movement.[52] This tallied with Ayub Khan's advice to the Foreign Office.[53] Thus, Arnold Wilson told the secretary of state of India that "the Arab public at large would actively favor the return of the Turks over the continuance of an amateur Arab Government . . . Nor can the Sharifian family reckon on popular support."[54] Even in 1921, when Feisal was appointed by the British government as king of Iraq, the American Consul in Baghdad observed that there was a very large part of the population that "would welcome with open arms the return of the Turks . . . Feisal has never been popular."[55]

In the territory east of the River Jordan, the anti-Sharifian feeling was strong. In October 1918, the inhabitants of Es Salt, Kerak, Madeba, and elsewhere were agitated at the prospect of coming under Sharifian government; they had absolutely no confidence in it. Some of the inhabitants were "still hoping that the Turks will return," and this accounted, in Lieutenant J. P. K. Groves's opinion, for their reluctance to cooperate with the British.[56] During his tour of Trans-Jordania, Mendel Schneerson, an agent of the Zionist Commission, reported that the pro-Turkish movement was gathering momentum and that the leading sheiks had decided to renew contact with Turkey.[57] Jameel Lufti Muhammad, Yasin al-Hashimi's cousin and the governor of Kerak, was a very influential person who actively participated in the onslaught on the British garrison at Dair al-Zor and maintained close relations with Turkish Nationalists. Like most of the Beduins, he was highly dissatisfied with Feisal's regime.[58]

In December 1918, Yale reported that the Palestinians, though recently freed from Turkish rule, were "seething with discontent" and were "very much opposed to British rule."[59] The Muslims, he commented, "prefer the tyranny and despotism of a Mohammedan government to the benevolent and just rule of a Christian power."[60]

The Palin Committee, which had been appointed by General Allenby to investigate the anti-Jewish riots in Jerusalem in April 1920, admitted that the Jews were not the only objects of Arab antagonism and that "almost ninety percent of the Palestinians were bitterly hostile to the British administration." They were supported and played upon by every element in the Near East of an anti-British character; they were ready to follow any leader who would rise in revolt against the Allied powers; "elaborate plans are being discussed and dates fixed for an insurrection which may involve the whole of Islam in the Near East."[61]

Characteristic was a statement made by Hafes Ara Tukan, a Muslim notable, during a meeting on April 16 held at the house of Musa Kazim al-Husseini, the mayor of Jerusalem: ". . . Now is the time to declare our freedom . . . We must make it appear that our action is against the Jews," Tukan said, "but on the day of the revolution we shall destroy the British Administration and with it the Zionists." Several days later, Musa al-Husseini, though prohibited by the military governor form engaging in politics, sent a circular to a number of notables in various towns in Palestine, advising them about "great preparations for a revolution" and asking them to be ready for the day when Palestine would be liberated.[62]

In March, rumors were rampant that Kemal Atatürk, after retaking Smyrna, would turn against the British in Mesopotamia and against the French in Syria.[63] Impressed by Atatürk's military exploits, the Palestinian leaders were confident that they would be able to achieve their objectives. They counted as much on Turkish national leaders as they did on the Egyptians, who were in open rebellion against the British. Abd al-Quadir al-Muzaffar went on a special mission to Anatolia to forge an alliance with Turkey. Turkey, for her part, obligated herself to supply arms and instructors to organize and train the Arab army. The alliance bore both a military and a religious character, and its ultimate aim was to liberate all the Muslim countries from the control of the Christian powers and undermine Christian supremacy. Herbert Samuel, during a tour in Palestine before his appointment as high commissioner, warned Curzon that Arab supremacy would pave the way for a return of Turkey.[64]

In 1920, the Palestinians allied themselves with the Pan-Islamic movement, which was directed against Britain and the entente as a whole. This movement originated in Turkey and bore a distinct revanchist character.[65]

On January 15, 1919, Col. McMahon Sadik Bey Yahya, DSO, reported to Colonel C. E. Wilson in Jeddah how much the inhabitants of Medina missed the Turks. Under Turkish administration they enjoyed security and equality, and justice was meted out. During the long siege, no wanton destruction had been committed by Fakri Bey and his entourage; and, "on the contrary, all private property was scrupulously protected." On January 15, 1919, however, when the Beduin entered Medina, following the surrender of the Turkish garrison, "all sealed houses, about 4,850, were broken open, and the Arabs looted the contents indiscriminately. The pillage went on for twelve days under the eyes of Emir Abdullah. Not only the Beduins but also about 80 percent of the Baghdadi and Syrian officers participated in the orgy."[66] In 1921, during his visit to Jeddah, Lawrence was surprised to discover that, with the exception of Fuad al-Khatib, the foreign secretary, King Hussein's entourage entertained pro-Turkish leanings.[67]

This was the mood that prevailed among Arabs in the aftermath of the war—entirely different from that which the British had expected when launching their Arabian policy during 1915–16. Then the British were confident that they would be received as liberators from the Turkish "yoke" while simultaneously serving their own strategic interests. The Arabs, however, would have none of this. Their loyalty to Turkey throughout the war and thereafter remained undiminished. The conquest of the former Turkish Asiatic provinces touched a raw nerve, while the British were viewed as alien occupiers. There was thus a basic incompatibility between the British and Arab aspirations.

In the meantime, during his second visit to Paris in the autumn of 1919, Feisal realized that, without foreign help, Syria would not be able to survive. Moreover, the offer made by Clemençeau, the French premier, was extremely liberal and too tempting to dismiss out of hand. Consequently, Feisal decided to accept it, however distasteful it might be. At home, however, the effect was devastating. Violent demonstrations against Feisal took place in the streets of Damascus, undermining his tenuous position still further.[68] Emir Zeid briefed his father, King Hussein, that the news that England and France had decided on two separate mandates for Syria and Palestine had caused considerable consternation among the population, which demanded fulfillment of Allied promises "for complete independence . . . for which they shed their blood during the war. Revolutionary movements have begun."[69] Thereupon, Hussein, in a fit of anger, sent a cable to Feisal implying that England had reneged on her obligation. This obligation, according to Hussein, was embodied in MacMahon's letter dated March 10, 1916, in which the high commissioner had written, "His Majesty's government approved all your demands." Hussein warned that, if the Syrians would decide to fight for their liberty and independence, he would not hesitate to join them "so that they may know that I did not betray them."[70]

Pressed by his father on the one hand and facing, on the other, fierce opposition from the national extremists at home, Feisal had little choice but to fall into line. He did not disrupt his negotiations with France (the agreement was concluded finally in December 1919) but directed all his arrows against the British.

Before leaving Paris, Feisal met Zaghlul Pasha, the Egyptian leader. The latter found him even more bitter against England than he himself had been. In a subsequent letter to Zaghlul, Feisal complained that he had been deceived by the British, whose ultimate aim was "to divide and dominate the whole Arabia, sharing the proceeds with France. This," he emphasized, "would be opposed by all possible ways." Feisal proposed that all the chiefs of Arabia should unite on a Pan-Islamic basis, and that his father, King Hussein, be asked to take the lead, forgoing all rivalry and personal jealousy for the common cause. The Arabs feel that "they fought loyally against Turkey in the firm conviction that they would ultimately secure independence." They were deeply disappointed. Zaghlul sent a copy of this letter to Fuad Selim Bey, a leading personality in the Young Turk movement who was then in Geneva. It was seen by a British Intelligence Agent. The Intelligence Department considered the letter "important and from most reliable sources." It warranted distribution to the India Office, to Colonel Gribbon of the war office, to Arnold Wilson, the civil commissioner at Baghdad, as well as to Hubert Young at the Foreign Office.[71]

Ten days later, British Intelligence confirmed that there was an intensified anti-British feeling among the Syrians and Arabs in general and that Feisal and his entourage were "actively hostile and engaged in anti-British propaganda." It was also reported that a meeting between Tala'at Pasha, Fuad Selim Bey, as well as Feisal's emissary, among others, had taken place at which a campaign to secure the independence of all Muslim countries had been discussed. At another very secret meeting of Turks, Egyptians, and Syrians that was held in Montreaux under Tala'at's chairmanship, it was decided to depose Mehmed Vahideddin VI, the present British-oriented sultan and appoint Fuad Salim Bey in his place. Moreover, a holy war would be declared under the leadership of the king of the Hedjaz that would include not only Arabians, Syrians, and Egyptians but also Russian Mohammedans and Afghanis. This war would decide once and for all the fate of Islam and of the Orient. It was expected that the Muslims in India, as well as the Indian Nationalists, would be "ready for action." The intelligence officer confirmed that all the information emanated from very reliable sources."[72]

Feisal did not lose time. He immediately dispatched Zaki Pasha Khersa, his right-hand man, to assure Tala'at that he fully concurred with the decisions taken at the Montreaux Conference. Thereafter, Zaki made his way to Constantinople and Syria in order to further the plan of campaign and subsequently to secure the consent of the king of the Hedjaz and to invite him to head the movement.[73]

Feisal spread his wings still further. Emir Shakib Arslan, a Druze leader, then in Switzerland, wrote to Maxim Litvinov, the Soviet deputy commissar for foreign affairs, then at Copenhagen, assuring him that "all hatred against the Turks had dissipated and that he was looking for mutual trust and combination [with the Bolsheviks] in support of the common cause."[74] The phrase "common cause" was a euphemism for emancipation from British rule. That Feisal tried to enlist support even from the Bolsheviks is rather surprising though, as we shall see later, not accidental; nor was his contact with Zaghlul Pasha accidental. In Egypt, as elsewhere in Islamic countries, there was a deep resentment against Hussein for his rebellion against Turkey.[75] In consequence, Feisal was making frantic efforts to rehabilitate his own name, as well as that of his father. But what impressed him most was the struggle of the Egyptian people for their own independence. The riots, which broke out in March 1919, were unprecedented both in scope and vehemence, and their effects reverberated throughout the Middle East. The lesson that Feisal was able to learn from events in Egypt was that only by violence one could wring larger concessions from the British.

Notes

1. Isaiah Friedman, *Palestine: A Twice Promised Land?* (New Brunswick, NJ: Transaction Publishers, 2000), 240–2.
2. Ibid., 265, 276–7.
3. *DBFP, I IV*, encl. to No. 391, Report by J. N. Clayton, Damascus, October 15, 1919, pp. 565–7, encl. in Meinertzhagen to Curzon, Cairo, December 2, 1919.
4. A copy of this Agreement (in French) is found in F.O. 371/4233/115573, 463–5, and in the English translation, 473–4, encl. in Calthorpe, Constantinople, to Curzon, August 1, 1919. Reproduced in appendices.

5. Friedman, *Palestine: A Twice Promised Land?* 26–7.
6. George Antonius, *The Arab Awakening* (New York: Capricorn Books, 1965, originally published 1938), 152–3.
7. Isaiah Friedman, *British Pan-Arab Policy, 1915–1922: A Critical Appraisal* (New Brunswick, NJ: Transaction Publishers, 2010), 77–8.
8. F.O. 371/4233/115573, 450, 456, Intelligence Report by Major H.A.D. Hoyland of the India Office, July 22, 1919, encl. in Calthorpe to Curzon, August 1, 1919.
9. Ibid., 471, Intelligence Report, August 3, 1919.
10. Ibid., 462, A Note, British Delegation, Paris, August 20, 1919.
11. Ibid., Minutes by Young, and Graham, August 21 and 22, 1919.
12. Ibid., Allenby to W.O., August 28, 1919, Secret; French to F.O., September 3, 1919, Political; also F.O. 141/130/5411.
13. F.O. 371/4182/2117, 370–4, W.O. to F.O., September 5, 1919 and Appendix on "Turkish-Arab Pan-Islamic Activities."
14. Friedman, *British Pan-Arab Policy, 1915–1922*, 78.
15. W.O. 33/946, No. 9319, Clayton to W.O., for the F.O., April 2, 1918.
16. F.O. 371/4233/211, 496, a cable by Wilson, Baghdad, September 25.
17. Ibid., "Mustapha Kemal's Proclamation to the Syrians," Aleppo, October 9, 1919, encl. in Robeck, Constantinople, to Curzon, November 16, 1919; Robeck minuted: "This proclamation is interesting in view of the alleged treaty to have been concluded between Emir Feisal and Mustapha Kemal Pasha." The proclamation is printed also in *DBFP*, I, IV, 478, encl. in Meinertzhagen to Curzon, October 18, 1919.
18. F.O. 882/24, Arbour, 209–10, a note signed by G.S.I. (Courtney) 25/5/20, names of the delegates and of the founders of the so-called "Democratic Party" are listed.
19. Ibid.
20. F.O. 882/24, Arbour, 350–2.
21. F.O. 371/5040, E 115/2/44, Minutes dated September 20, 1920. The signature could not be deciphered.
22. F.O. 882/24, Arbour, 220–1, May 13, 1920.
23. Israel State Archives (hereafter ISA), 2nd Group, M/5/163, Brunton (Jerusalem) to General Staff Intelligence, G.H.Q., Cairo, February 28, 1921.
24. Friedman, *British Pan-Arab Policy, 1915–1922*, 310–1.
25. F.O. 371/3403/52131, Draft of Graham's cable to Clayton, April 2, 1918, Secret. Confirmed by Lord Hardinge.
26. George Antonius, *The Arab Awakening* (New York: Capricorn Books, 1965), 131–2.
27. Ibid., 152–3.
28. Friedman, *British Pan-Arab Policy, 1915–1922*, 43–4, 47–9, 53, 55, 61, 66, 77–8, 106.
29. Ibid., 335.
30. W.O. 158/634, Pt. 3, p. 136, Djemal Kutchuk Pasha (the "small") to Feisal, June 2, 1918.
31. Liman von Sanders, *Five Years in Turkey* (Annapolis, MD, 1927), 262; originally published in German, *Fünf Jahre Türkei*, 330.
32. Ibid., 261.
33. Ibid., 281–3.

34. T.E. Lawrence, *Seven Pillars of Wisdom* (Penguin, 1965), 571.
35. On which see: Friedman, *Palestine: A Twice Promised Land?* 201–8.
36. Ibid., 225–6.
37. Ibid., 245.
38. Lawrence, *Seven Pillars*, 572.
39. Friedman, *Palestine: A Twice Promised Land?* 18–9, 27, 255.
40. F.O. 882/24, "Syria in October 1919," memorandum by Gertrude Bell, November 15, 1919, 146–69.
41. Ibid., 135, "Who is who in Damascus Government Officials."
42. Friedman, *Palestine: A Twice Promised Land?*, 215.
43. Friedman, *British Pan-Arab Policy, 1915–1922*, 66–7; Général Ed. Brémond, *Le Hedjaz dans la Guerre Mondiale* (Payot, France, 1931), 229.
44. Friedman, *Palestine: A Twice Promised Land?*, 240–1, 254–5.
45. F.O. 882/24, pp. 204–205, Garland to Courtnay, May 11, 1920.
46. W.O. 106/200/82472, Secretary of State to Civil Commissioner, Baghdad, September 23, 1920 (a copy).
47. Friedman, *Palestine: A Twice Promised Land?*, 213.
48. *DBFP*, I, IV, No. 339, Meinertzhagen to Curzon, October 21, 1919.
49. F.O. 371/4184/2117, G.H.Q (Egypt) to D.M.I., November 8, 1919.
50. *DBFP*, I, IV, App. 3 to No. 391, "Meetings at Damascus," by Clayton, encl. in Meinertzhagen to Curzon, December 2, 1919, 568–9.
51. Ibid.
52. F.O. 371/4184/2157, G.H.Q, (Cairo) to D.M.I., October 20, 1919. Secret; also F.O. 371/4152/144, "Syria in October 1919," memorandum by Gertrude Bell, November 15, 1919, enc. in Arnold Wilson to Secretary of State for India Office, November 15, 1919.
53. Friedman, *British Pan-Arab Policy, 1915–1922*, 223.
54. India Office Archives, L/PS/11/165, Wilson to Montagu, November 15, 1919.
55. Friedman, *British Pan-Arab Policy, 1915–1922*, 308.
56. F.O. 882/17, 125–6, Groves to Arab Bureau, October 19, 1918.
57. Ha'agana Archives, Tel Aviv, Papers of Mendel Shne'ersohn, file 80/145/15, Rep. No. 18, January 26, 1920.
58. Ibid., Rep. no. 19; also May 13 and 25, 1920, Report nos. 27, 28.
59. Report by William Yale, "Present Situation in Syria and Palestine," December 18, 1918.
60. Ibid., "Great Britain, France, and the Near East," December 16, 1918.
61. Friedman, *British Pan-Arab Policy, 1915–1922*, 275–7.
62. Ibid., 277–8.
63. W.O. 106/199, "Pan-Islamic Conspiracy," Note, dated March 1920, signature blurred.
64. Friedman, *British Pan-Arab Policy, 1915–1922*, 278–9.
65. Ibid., 359.
66. I.O., L/PS/11/154, Sadik Bey Yahiya to Wilson, January 15, 1919, encl. in Residency in Cairo to Curzon, June 26, 1919.
67. Friedman, *British Pan-Arab Policy, 1915–1922*, 338.
68. Ibid., 258–9, 265–8.

69. I.O., L/PS/11/158, Intercepted cable from Zeid (Damascus) to Hussein (Jeddah), September 20, 1919; encl. in Cheetham to Curzon, October 8, 1919.

70. Ibid., L/PS/11/161, Hussein to Feisal (Paris), November 1, 1919.

71. Ibid., L/PS/11/161, a note, dated November 27, 1919, signed by A.W.

72. Ibid., "Pan-Islam," A.W. to Col. C. Kaye, November 25, 1919.

73. Ibid., L/PS/11/155, A.W. to Hose, December 6, 1919.

74. Ibid., A.W. to J. W. Hose (India Office), January 13, 1920.

75. William Yale Reports; "Arabia and the Hedjaz Situation," Report, dated November 5, 1917, 10.

3

Egypt's Struggle for Independence

Egypt's national movement, aiming at its liberation, took the British by surprise. The March riots erupted unexpectedly. Throughout the war the Egyptians—albeit per force—cooperated with the British and showed no sign of visible discontent. The British, on their part, fondly believing that the "golden age" of the Cromer era would continue indefinitely, were oblivious to the consequences of their policy and unaware of the profound changes that had been taking place in the Egyptian society during the war.

On December 18, 1914, the Asquith government proclaimed that Egypt had become a British protectorate. It changed the legal status of Egypt and detached the country from Turkey permanently. The move was done unilaterally without prior consultation, let alone the consent of the people concerned. It was a move of dubious legal validity as well as political imprudence for, though Ottoman suzerainty was only nominal, the Egyptians qua Muslims would not tolerate a Christian overlord for long. It was also superfluous, since, by virtue of the martial law imposed by the British army, they did control the administration of the country anyway. To sweeten the pill, however, the Asquith government announced in the same breath that Egypt's freedom and independence were among the goals for which Britain was fighting.

The Egyptians had therefore reason to believe that the Protectorate was only temporary—a wartime measure of sorts.[1] When they realized after the war that the British showed no enthusiasm for implementing their publicly pronounced obligation, a crisis in Anglo-Egyptian relations was bound to come. In a cable to the Foreign Office on December 11, 1921, Allenby admitted that "nothing is more resented in Egypt today than this backward step [i.e., Protectorate] on the part of Great Britain."[2] Historian P. J. Vatikiotis concluded that the "imposition of a

Protectorate . . . made a post-war clash between Egyptian nationalist aspirants to power on the one hand and the protecting power on the other inevitable."[3]

Additional reasons exacerbated the antagonism against the British. The civilian population was very much inconvenienced by the massive pressure of the imperial troops. Moreover, inflation had become rampant; profiteers exploited the situation, and the heaviest burden fell on the unemployed, the lower-salaried classes, and the peasants. Early in 1916, to assist in the construction of a railway in the Sinai, the British authorities formed an Egyptian Labour Corps and a Camel Transport Corps. In the beginning, the recruitment was voluntary and well-paid, but, during the following year, the project was delegated to the Egyptian government, which, in turn, passed it on to local authorities. This led to abuse and many of the *fellaheen* were forcibly recruited and taken away from their land and families. Their anger, however, was turned against the British. By the end of the war, over one and a half million Egyptians had served in the Labour Corps.[4] The Egyptians were thus involved in a war that was not theirs and which was directed against the sultan-caliph. It touched the raw nerve of every Muslim and produced a feeling of alienation from Britain among the ordinary population.

Strangely, the British were oblivious to these undercurrents within Egyptian society, but the Turco-German propaganda machine was not slow to take advantage of this atmosphere and persistently endeavored to instigate an insurrection against the "infidel army."[5] This propaganda did not produce immediate results, but by July 1917, no lesser authority than David Hogarth, the director of the Arab Bureau in Cairo, pointed out that "at present [Egypt] is potentially an enemy country."[6] Moreover, the Egyptians could not stomach the idea that the Arabs, whom they saw as so inferior to themselves economically, culturally, and sociopolitically, were being promised independence while Egypt was being denied the same privilege. President Wilson's Fourteen Points and reassuring Allied declarations reverberated throughout the Middle East and aroused hopes that a new era was dawning. The Allies denied that they were fighting a war of conquest and aimed only at upholding the rights of small and oppressed nationalities. Some politicians with whom William Yale was in touch, however, were skeptical of whether Britain and France would carry out their declarations to letter and the spirit.[7] Events were to prove them right.

One of the politicians who did take these declarations seriously—particularly the one made by the Asquith government in 1914—was Muhammad Saad Zaghlul.[8] Before the war, Lord Cromer, impressed by Zaghlul's administrative competence, as well as by his pro-British proclivities, prevailed upon Khedive Abbas to appoint him minister of education and subsequently a minister of justice. Zaghlul aspired, however, to a political career and, after the war until his death in 1927, he dominated the national political scene as the "Father of the Egyptians" and as the founder of the *Wafd*, the best organized popular party in the annals of modern Egyptian history.[9] On November 13, 1918, two weeks after the Turkish government officially surrendered aboard HMS *Agamemnon*, Zaghlul led a delegation to Sir Reginald Wingate, the high commissioner of Egypt, and demanded that the Protectorate and martial law be abolished. He expected that Britain would live up to her declaration of 1914 and grant Egypt independence. Moreover, the delegation expressed its desire to be heard at the council of the forthcoming Peace Conference in Paris. Wingate refused categorically on the pretext that the delegation was not representative.[10]

The Foreign Office, under Curzon's control while Balfour was in Paris, rejected out of hand the idea of an Egyptian delegation coming to London or Paris. This incensed the Egyptians even more, since the Hedjazi delegation, under Emir Feisal, were given a favorable hearing at the Peace Conference. To force the issue, Zaghlul doubled his efforts to broaden the base of his newly founded party, *Al-Wafd al-Misri*, and launched a countrywide operation of petition signing. The Wafd's motto was to seek complete independence of Egypt by peaceful means. The British authorities, however, considered the Wafd's activities to be dangerous to public security and tried to suppress the movement. This infuriated the Egyptians still further.

Wingate, foreseeing trouble, tried to prevail upon the British government to moderate its policy. On his arrival in London, he argued that it would be politic to allow both the Egyptian ministers, as well as the Zaghlul's delegation, to come and present their grievances; otherwise, he feared it would be difficult to form an Egyptian government willing to cooperate with the British authorities. Wingate's advice was rejected. The view of the Foreign Office, as expressed in a memorandum dated February 20, 1919, was that "the national leaders, who have placed themselves at the head of a disloyal movement to expel the British from Egypt, have no claim to be allowed to come here, and to accede to the demands of the ministers on this head would only be regarded throughout Egypt as a sign of weakness." A cable in this tenor was sent to Sir Milne Cheetham, who, in Wingate's absence, remained in change of the residency in Cairo. He was instructed to refuse permission to any Egyptian of consequence to leave Egypt for any reason whatever. On March 1, 1919, Husein Rushdi's Pasha's government resigned in protest.[11]

It is true that Britain required a base in Egypt—a necessity that had become only too apparent during the war. But it was also true that Britain had solemnly promised independence for Egypt after the successful conclusion of the war, and, further, had committed herself to uphold the principle of self-determination. These contradictory imperatives posed a serious dilemma.

Only a statesman of Sir Mark Sykes's caliber could have resolved the difficulty and worked out a compromise between Britain's strategic requirements and respect for Egyptian national aspirations. His untimely death left a void in Middle Eastern policymaking. In consequence, the course taken by the British government was rigid, counterproductive and, as we shall see later, harmful to imperial interests. Maintaining a military base in a hostile human environment negates much of its value.

Wingate's advice to Curzon might have gone a long way to mollify, even temporarily, the angry Egyptians, but his arguments made no impression on the acting foreign minister. It was also Wingate who, on September 15, 1918, envisaged the ill-effects of the arbitrary system of drafting Egyptians to the Labour Corps. He found no support in London and was eased out of his office. Sir Ronald Wingate told me how much his father had been aggrieved by the shabby treatment meted out to him by his superiors. Sir Reginald retired from public life making no statements and wrote no memoirs.[12]

The control of the residency remained in the hands of Sir Milne Cheetham, a counselor since 1911; a colorless and unimaginative official who, in spite of his long service, remained totally out of touch with the situation. Erroneously assuming that the disorder in the country was a product of a handful of agitators, he embarked, without prior approval of the Foreign Office, on a step that had far-reaching consequences. On March 9, 1919, he ordered the arrest of Zaghlul and three of his companions and deported them to Malta.

Cheetham was unaware of the wide support that Zaghlul enjoyed throughout the country. Among his secret supporters was Sultan (later king) Fuad. The arrest turned Zaghlul into a national hero and sparked off violent riots in Cairo, Alexandria, and other cities. Pent-up feelings of frustration and resentment that had accumulated throughout the war exploded in an unprecedented way. Public properties were destroyed, while foreigners and British military personnel were attacked. On March 18, eight officers and soldiers were brutally murdered on a train from Aswan to Cairo. The Residency reported that the army had lost control of Upper Egypt and that the upheaval was likely to lead to "a revolt in scale unparalleled in the Eastern Empire since the Indian Mutiny."[13] Cheetham, formerly complacent, now panicked. It finally dawned upon him, so he briefed to London that "the present movement in Egypt is national in the full sense of the word. It has now the sympathy of all classes and creeds, including the Copts."[14]

This was also Sir Gilbert Clayton's opinion. "I cannot disguise from myself," he wrote to Wingate, "that the principles of Nationalism and the desire for independence have bitten deep into all classes, and I am convinced that our policy in Egypt must be very carefully reconsidered on lines of increased sympathy with national aspirations so far as they keep within legitimate limits."[15]

Clayton, who, since his hapless encounter with al-Faruqi in 1915, had matured politically, saw only too clearly the dramatic change that had taken place within Egyptian society. In March 1919, the Egyptians were united as never before. The intelligentsia in towns rubbed shoulders with the *fellaheen* in a common cause. The division between the Copts and Muslims had almost evaporated. Copts were members of the Wafd and were among Zaghlul's closest associates. For the first time, Copt priests preached in mosques and Muslim clerics called upon men in churches to join the national struggle. During the demonstrations, banners of cross and crescent intermingled. The aristocracy also joined the national movement, while, for the first time, women marched in the streets with their male counterparts.[16]

Nationalism, formerly limited to the intelligentsia, now became a mass movement that was impossible to ignore. London seemed to be myopic, however; the British ministers did not evince any sympathy for Egyptian national aspirations. Lloyd George and Curzon, by appointing Allenby on March 20 as a special high commissioner, expected him to follow a policy exactly opposite to that which had been advocated by Cheetham and Clayton. The prime minister imagined him to be a strong man who would restore law and order and keep the Nationalists in check. In this he, as well as Curzon, was mistaken.

Allenby, though a distinguished general, was anything but the skillful diplomat that these particular circumstances required. Moreover, he proved to be a recalcitrant official who habitually disregarded his superior's instructions.[17]

The position of the British government was made clear in Curzon's speech in the House of Lords on March 24: Britain would not object to receiving Rushdi Pasha, the prime minister, as well as Adli Yakan, the minister of the interior, but would strenuously object to Saad Zaghlul Pasha and his colleagues coming to London. "They have organized the present movement . . . they are the self-appointed and irresponsible leaders of an agitation for the avowed purpose of expelling the British from Egypt."[18]

Curzon also indicated that the Protectorate would remain unchanged. This aroused the ire of the Egyptians, but rather than resort to violence, this time they turned to passive resistance: lawyers, officials, and students struck. The leaders of the strike presented new demands—recognition of the *Wafd* and the repudiation of the infamous Protectorate, among others. Moreover, Rushdi's cabinet resigned.

Thus, when Allenby arrived in Cairo on March 25, he found the country ungovernable. Strikes and demonstrations were daily occurrences, and it appeared that it would be counterproductive to resort to strong military measures. Thereupon, Allenby suddenly reversed his policy. Without prior consultations with London, he ordered the release of Zaghlul and other deportees from Malta and removed former travel restrictions (April 7). Allenby hoped thereby to appease the angry crowds and inaugurate a policy of conciliation with the Egyptian national movement. The Egyptians, however, saw in Allenby's move, not a gesture of goodwill, but capitulation. It made them even more truculent and wedded to the idea that only by violence would they be able to wring larger concessions from the British.

London was shocked. Curzon considered Allenby's policy "a disaster," whose consequences would be catastrophic in Egypt and elsewhere, while Sir Ronald Graham, the adviser to the Egyptian Ministry of the Interior, thought that this step, taken so precipitously, represented "a complete surrender."[19]

Allenby, for his part, hoped that, by this bold move, he would succeed in eliminating the chief source of grievance and pave the way toward reconciliation and settlement. Although in principle he was correct, his actions, taken without prior negotiations with the Nationalists, resulted in the opposite effect to what he had intended.

The Egyptians saw in Allenby's move, not an act of clemency but a sign of weakness bordering on submission. Rather that mollifying the Egyptians, it emboldened them.

Zaghlul and his colleagues went to Paris to plead their case before the Peace Conference. Their hopes, however, were dashed. The Peace Conference recognized the British Protectorate over Egypt and, surprisingly, even President Wilson endorsed it. It was at that time that Feisal established contact with Zaghlul and vented his frustration concerning the British.

Although rebuffed in Paris, Zaghlul's popularity at home grew by leaps and bounds. There was also a marked increase in donations. A new phenomenon crept in—organized terror. It had a destabilizing effect on the administration. The country became even less governable. Premier Rushdi and Adli, the minister of the interior, resigned on April 21, 1919. The position became so critical that the British government decided in May 1919 to send a special commission under Lord Milner, the colonial secretary, to inquire into the cause of the recent disturbances in Egypt and propose ways and means of ameliorating the situation. The terms of reference, however, indicate that the purpose of the commission was to buttress the Protectorate rather than relax it.[20] Indicative was Balfour's speech in the House of Commons. He declared, "British supremacy [in Egypt] exists, British supremacy is going to be maintained, and let nobody either in Egypt or out of Egypt make any mistake upon that cardinal principle of His Majesty's Government."[21]

The Milner Mission arrived in Egypt on December 7 and remained there until the following March. It interviewed British officials and businessmen, but the Egyptians, practically to a man, boycotted it. During its stay, a radical transformation took place in Milner's outlook. As his colleague on the mission, J. A. Spender, recorded, Milner became convinced that "if the Egyptians did not want us to govern them and could keep order and maintain solvency without us, we were under no obligation to undertake the invidious, difficult, and very expensive task of governing them against their will." Spender himself believed that undoubtedly the Egyptian national movement was "deep and genuine" and that this fact should govern all future British policy. It is probable that Milner also interviewed, among other British officers, Sir Gilbert Clayton. Clayton had been in favor of a policy of concessions as early as April 1919. In September of the same year, he told Ms. Gertrude Bell that the British should control the Suez Canal, the Nile waters, the army, and the police but that the administration should be left to the Egyptians themselves. Such concessions, he thought, would win the majority of the country to the British side.[22]

On November 4, 1920, in a debate in the House of Lords, Milner expressed his belief that it would be possible for Britain to maintain order and progress in Egypt without incurring the permanent hostility of the Egyptian people. "My intimate conviction," he declared, "is that, while there is undoubtedly an element of Egyptian nationalism, which is anti-British, the better and stronger elements of it are not anti-British but simply pro-Egyptian."[23]

This conclusion was overly sanguine since even the so-called pro-Egyptians were guided by the motto "Egypt for the Egyptians," which by implication meant that the majority of the Egyptians expected the British to clear out of their country. Moreover, in Egypt, as in the East in general, the extremists were habitually calling the shots.

This, Milner was able to experience for himself. In the end, he realized that it was not the Egyptian government but Muhammad Zaghlul who had the final say. Zaghlul, wily politician as he was, knew how to intimidate his rivals and take advantage of the mistakes committed by them as well as by the British. On June 23, 1920, Milner wrote to Yakan Yadli, the prime minister, that the object of his mission was to reconcile Egyptian aspirations with special interests of Great Britain, which included also control of Egyptian foreign affairs. Zaghlul, however, vetoed this, maintaining that it was "a question of capital importance that foreign affairs remained in the hands of the Egyptians"; otherwise, no agreement would be possible. He demanded "complete independence." On this issue he was absolutely adamant.[24] Per force, step-by-step, Milner had to give in. What the British could have achieved in November 1918, when Zaghlul approached Wingate, was now next to impossible.

Milner hoped to be able to conclude a treaty that would solve the Egyptian problem once and for all. It was a vain hope. Zaghlul, though an eminently influential politician, had no formal authority that would enable him to sign such a treaty. Milner thereupon crafted a document that he termed "an agreement." It became, however, a nonagreement. Zaghlul played an evasive game, careful not to commit himself to anything. He could well-afford it, since now it was the British who were doing the courtship. Milner was duped by this cunning politician and was unable to register any tangible achievement. Abolition of the Protectorate fell short of satisfying Zaghlul; he demanded complete autonomy in internal, as well as in external, affairs. This Milner was not in a position to grant. His mission thus ended in failure.

After negotiations with Zaghlul had reached a deadlock, Milner tried his hand with Adli; however, the latter—though representing the Egyptian government—lacked any following among the general public.

Competition between the Wafdists and the government ministers complicated matters still further. Zaghlul was a formidable rival and Adli was in no position to endorse an agreement with the British that Zaghlul had already denounced. These limitations escaped the British government when they invited Adli to come to London to hammer out the much sought-after agreement. Adli proved to be no less extremist in his demands than Zaghlul. Failure was inevitable. In desperation, the Foreign Office empowered Allenby and his advisers in Cairo to take up the challenge.

Mutual distrust was at the root of the difficulty. As a noted Egyptian historian characterized it aptly, "The Egyptian public distrusted the intentions of the British Government, and the British distrusted the goodwill of Egypt towards them."[25] It was Allenby's thoughtlessness that gave the Egyptians ample proof of Britain's unreliability. Allenby, on his return to Egypt, had embarked on a double-barreled policy. On one hand, he facilitated the appointment of Abd al-Khaliq Tharwat, Adli's deputy, to the premiership and, on the other, ordered Zaghlul's deportation to Aden and later to the Seychelles. Both Adli and Tharwat were Zaghlul's enemies. Since Zaghlul's followers persisted in their practice of rioting and disturbing public order, it was thought that his removal from the public scene would calm the situation. In this matter, Allenby found in Tharwat a useful collaborator, and the decision to expel Zaghlul won his approval.

The move, however, misfired. Zaghlul was a popular leader, whereas Tharwat was not. The rioting continued with even greater intensity. The conspiracy did not remain secret and harmed Britain's standing. Allenby's policy was seen as a gross interference in Egyptian internal affairs and a clear negation of the spirit and letter of his unilateral declaration of February 22, 1922. This declaration offered to recognize Egypt as an independent state on condition that vital British interests were safeguarded. These included security of Imperial communications, such as The Suez Canal, the defense of Egypt against all foreign aggression, and protection of minorities and of foreign interests, as well as of the Sudan.

Tharwat, although exhilarated by his unexpected achievement, did not endorse Allenby's declaration. From the Egyptian perspective, the conditions appended to it were not binding. The February 22, 1922 proclamation of independence was a gratuitous gift without Britain getting anything in return. Zaghlul, on his part, had no compunction in denouncing it as a "national disaster." At any rate, Tharwat's government was short-lived, whereas Zaghlul could not be kept indefinitely in exile. In an undisguised affront to Tharwat, Sultan Fuad, who now became king, allied himself with Zaghlul and supported him politically and financially. At the end of 1923, Zaghlul returned home as a hero and soon after was elected to the Parliament with a sweeping majority. He became prime minister for the following three decades, whereas Allenby suffered a resounding defeat. His gamble had not paid off and his policy, or rather impolicy, was now in ruins.

Zaghlul ascribed the achievement of Egypt's independence to himself and to his violent campaign. Britain, on the other hand, continued to maintain its military bases in strategic locations, such as the Suez Canal—not as a result of Egyptian consent but in spite of Egypt's refusal. This was not a sound basis for a friendly relationship. Britain's prestige was seriously undermined and repercussions were soon felt throughout the Middle East. Her good faith was now questioned. During the war, Britain had appeared as a champion of small nationalities, but, in its aftermath, all promises were disregarded and the old image of an imperialist power was resurrected. Thus, it came to be believed that, only by resorting to violence was it possible to bend Britain to local national aspirations.

Allenby, too, had to pay the price. The new government in London was less supportive than the previous one under Lloyd George. Allenby was censured in a rather brusque manner, at which he took offence and resigned without much ado.

The setback in Egypt opened the eyes of British officials anew to the strategic importance of Palestine. On this point, it is useful to quote Clayton's statement to Chaim Weizmann on November 7, 1922. Clayton noted that, following Egyptian independence, which had been granted early in that year, the strategic importance of Palestine had correspondingly increased. Britain was strongly bound up with the Zionist policy because only a thriving and prosperous Palestine could provide an effective base from which to protect the Suez Canal. Thereupon Weizmann, with a glimmer of irony, remarked that some Englishmen might suggest keeping Palestine, but dropping the Zionist policy; to which Sir Gilbert replied that "although such an attitude may afford a temporary relief and may quieten the Arabs for a short time, it will certainly not settle the question, as the Arabs don't want the British in Palestine, and after having their way with the Jews, they would attack the British position, as the Muslims are doing in the Mesopotamia, Egypt, and India."[26]

Clayton's statement tallies with that made by Lawrence eighteen months earlier to Shmuel Tolkowsky, a member of the Zionist Commission. On his arrival in London, Tolkowsky reported to Weizmann, as well as to Lord Melchett, on the 1921 riots in Jaffa. The latter was a member of the British cabinet and introduced him to Hubert Young, head of the Middle East Department at the Foreign Office. Young invited Lawrence to be present. Lawrence vehemently rejected the idea that the 1921 riots bore exclusively an anti-Zionist and anti-Jewish character. In his opinion they were directed primarily against the British: "Zionism served merely as a useful stick to beat the British." He added that those who expected any gratitude from the Arabs for being delivered from the Turks were under a misapprehension. "The Arabs are a fickle race and will stab us in our back as soon as they find a suitable opportunity."[27]

A Note: Professor Kedourie, in his illuminating article, quoted in our chapter, is critical of liberal-minded British officials who advocated being more forthcoming toward Egyptian national aspirations. He castigates Milner for his "failure of nerve," Spender for his "liberal fanaticism," and Hurst for his "low and misguided common-sense." In his opinion their policy destroyed "whatever loyalty and respect the British had managed to inspire in Egypt and [made] their position meaningless and untenable."[28] Kedourie went on that "British unpopularity in the country at large increased in proportion to the magnitude of British concessions."[29] Milner's speech in the House of Lords was noted, Kedourie points out, for its "fanciful character and sentimental tone," which indicated "loss of contact with reality," the outcome of which was

> [w]eakening of the will to rule, which became manifest among the British ruling classes in the aftermath of the First World War and which was to make the dissolution of the British empire so ugly and ruinous, to subjects and rulers alike.[30]

Whether concessions did indeed contribute to Britain's unpopularity among the Egyptians is a moot point. There were a host of other reasons—which have been pointed out in our study here—that intensified grievances. But the cardinal question is, what was the alternative—was it possible to go back to the prewar policy in the age of nationalism? One should bear in mind that Britain was a war-weary nation, the treasury was depleted, and the army was in the process demobilization. The British bayonets were getting somewhat rusty. A policy of coercion, which would have meant maintenance of a costly army for an indefinite period, was out of the question. The Parliament would not have supported it. Besides, as Kedourie himself admitted, if Egypt were held down by force, relations with the United States and with the Muslim world would have deteriorated.[31]

If the British Empire disintegrated, it was not necessarily because of the "weakening of the will to rule," but because of forces that were beyond Britain's control. They were: the principle of self-determination and nationalism—the twentieth century *Zeitgeist*. They were responsible for the destruction of the Austro-Hungarian Empire, just as these forces set a seal on the British Empire. British statesmen failed to come to terms with Egyptian nationalism at the right time, just as they were too myopic to appreciate the force of Turkish nationalism of the Kemalist brand. In consequence, although Britain emerged victorious at the end of the war, she lost the peace.

Notes

1. P. J. Vatikiotis, *The Modern History of Egypt* (London: Weidenfeld & Nicolson, 1969), 243.
2. Quoted in Elie Kedourie, *The Chatham House Version and Other Middle-Eastern Studies* (London, 1984, new edition), 151.
3. Vatikiotis, *The Modern History of Egypt*, 248.
4. Ibid., 244–5.
5. Egmont Zechlin, "Friedensbestrebungen und Revolutionierungs versuche im Eresten Weltkrieg," *Aus Politik und Zeitgeschichte. Beilage Zur Wochenzeitung. Das Parlament* (June 21, 1961); Fritz Fischer, *Griff nach der Weltmacht. Die Kriegszielpolitik des Kaiserlichen Deutschland: 1914–1918* (Düsseldorf, 1961), 146–54.
6. University of Durham. Sir Reginald Wingate Papers, file 470/7, memorandum by David Hogarth, July 22, 1917.
7. Yale Reports, Rep. No. 3, "The British Policy in the Near East," November 12, 1917, 7.
8. On Zaghlul, see an enlightening article by Elie Kedourie, "Saad Zaghlul and the British," in *The Chatham House Version and other Middle-Eastern Studies* (Hanover and London, 1984), 82–159.
9. Vatikiotis, *The Modern History of Egypt*, 248–54.
10. The above and what follows are based on works by Kedourie, Vatikiotis, and Darwin. The conclusions, however, are my own.

11. Kedourie, *Chatham House Version*, 99–100.
12. Letter to the author, dated September 20, 1961.
13. John Darwin, *Britain, Egypt, and the Middle-East: Imperial Policy in the Aftermath of War, 1918–1922* (New York, 1981), 72, 74.
14. Kedourie, *Chatham House Version*, 104; Darwin, *Britain, Egypt, and the Middle-East*, 74.
15. Cited in Kedourie, *Chatham House Version*, 113.
16. Hans Kohn, *A History of Nationalism in the East* (New York, 1929), 206.
17. Cf. Allenby's conduct with regard to the future of Syria, Isaiah Friedman, *British Pan-Arab Policy, 1915–1922: A Critical Appraisal* (New Brunswick, NJ: Transaction Publishers, 2010), 268–71.
18. *Hansard*, House of Lords, March 24, 1919.
19. Cited in Kedourie, *Chatham House Version*, 115–6.
20. *Hansard*, House of Lords, August 18, 1919, col. 1897.
21. Ibid., November 17, 1919, col. 771.
22. Cited in Kedourie, *Chatham House Version*, 120, 122, 147. On Clayton's views, see p. 77 and note 15.
23. Lords, Debates, 5s, November 4, 1920, col. 213.
24. Kedourie, *Chatham House Version*, 127, 129, 132–3.
25. Cited in Vatikiotis, *The Modern History of Egypt*, 266.
26. Central Zionist Archives (C.Z.A.), file Z4/16112, "Notes on Conversation Between Sir Gilbert Clayton and Dr. Ch. Weizmann on the Policy and Situation in Palestine," November 7, 1922 (a copy in Weizmann Archives).
27. The Ha'agana Archives, Tel Aviv, Tolkowsky Papers, file 80/82/2F, Tolkowsky to Samuel, May 14, 1921, cited in Tolkowsky to Avigur, October 27, 1953.
28. Kedourie, *Chatham House Version*, 123.
29. Ibid., 147.
30. Ibid., 121.
31. Ibid., 122.

4

Pan-Islamic–Bolshevik–Turkish Assault on Britain

James Jankowski in his article, "Egypt and Early Arab Nationalism, 1908–1922," ascertained that the overall Egyptian attitude during World War I had been "one of sympathy towards the Ottoman–German, rather than the Allied cause," and that contemporary records speak of "a considerable anticipation within Egypt of an Ottoman–German victory that would entail Egyptian liberation from British occupation."[1] Beth Baron aired a similar opinion stating that throughout the early 1900s, the Egyptians showed anti-British and pro-Ottoman sentiments.[2]

This anti-British disposition was almost a truism in the East. The negative attitude toward the West, England in particular, was deeply rooted in Arab and Muslim culture. The defeat of Turkey by an infidel army inflamed ill-feeling still further. The dismemberment of the Ottoman Empire had a traumatic effect on the Islamic people and gave rise to a Pan-Islamic movement, which was intertwined with fierce nationalism.

Mustafa Kemal, though himself a secularist, capitalized on the rising force of nationalist Islam and used it to further his cause whilst simultaneously undermining British standing in the East. With this purpose in mind he convened a conference at Sivas on September 4, 1919, at which delegates from Muslim countries such as Persia, Egypt, India, and the Arab world participated. Admiral de Robeck observed that throughout the Muslim countries of the Near and Middle East, there was a growing tendency to resist European domination and control. Pan-Islamism formed a framework for a community of religions and political interests as well as ideas "with the object of making a stand against European intervention and exploitation . . . The expression of self-determination has echoed throughout the Near East, and though perhaps naturally imperfectly understood, it yet forms the theme of every political scribbler and leader of public opinion." This trend, Robeck warned, had an important bearing upon the general political situation in the Near and the Middle East and the British government would be well-advised to take serious heed of it.[3]

Commander H. C. Luke, RNVR, the political officer on the staff of the naval commander in chief, analyzed the effects of Bolshevism on the security of the British Empire. One of the most important aims of the Bolsheviks, he pointed out, was to turn the Muslim world against the British Empire. No Allied power, however, had incurred so deep a hatred as Great Britain. To inflict injury on the British Empire, the Bolsheviks would not shy away from any instrument and any device and even disavow their own principles if it inhibited their anti-British campaign. Thus, for example, no principles were more fundamentally incompatible than those of Bolshevism and Islam. No two systems have less in common, and yet the Bolsheviks were making a determined effort to delude the Muslims into believing that the Muslim world would benefit from an alliance with Bolshevism in a war against the British Empire. These attempts were being made—not without some success—in Turkey, Transcaucasia, Persia, Turkestan, Afghanistan, India, Syria, Arabia, and Egypt. By making skilful use of British mistakes, such as the dispatch of the Greek army of occupation into Smyrna, as well as to the Muslim province of Aidin, by calculated misinterpretation and distortion of facts, the Bolsheviks had succeeded in making a large number of Muslims in the East believe that Britain was "the enemy of Islam."

The Bolsheviks, Commander Luke went on, had contrived very skillfully to turn the amorphous and somewhat vague aims of the Pan-Islamic movement into anti-British channels. Britain, who, before the World War, had been regarded by the Muslims at large as "their principal protector," had recently been made to appear in the contrary role, while Mustafa Kemal took full advantage of this trend.[4]

Mr. Ryan, a member on the staff of the high commissioner, fully concurred with Luke's premises, emphasizing that every evidence pointed to the converging activities of the Bolsheviks with political Pan-Islamism. The former's object "is to weld all Muslims into one-whole to be used as an instrument against the West . . . especially against Great Britain." Ryan pointed to an additional threatening factor, which might destroy the cohesion of the empire: nationalism. It is, closely intertwined with religion and encapsulated in a dual formula: "Be nationalist because it is the only way to save Islam," and "Be loyal to Islam because it is the only way to save our national inheritance." Ryan concluded on a pessimistic note, "We cannot crush Pan-Islamism any more than we can crush the nationalisms" and one should bear in mind that Muslim dislike the idea of being ruled by non-Muslims.[5]

Christian rulers were always regarded in the East as adversaries of Islam. Mustafa Kemal, although himself not an Islamist, was fully aware that Islam was a deeply-rooted component of Turkish identity and was scrupulous in respecting Islamic institutions such as the sultanate. He was skilful in using religion for political purposes. When endeavoring to rally the peasants in Anatolia to his flag, he invoked the name of the caliph in order to defend him and the country. He used the same tactics in the proclamation of holy war against the infidel Greeks.[6]

In November 1919, Mustafa Kemal sponsored the foundation of a Pan-Islamic association[7] jointly with Rauf Bey, his faithful lieutenant; he was cofounder of the *Mouvahidin* Association. Its purpose was to achieve "the complete and immediate emancipation of all Muslim countries at present under foreign protection or domination and to unite them all in a kind of worldwide Islamic confederacy under the presidency of the Ottoman Khalifate." The Association was still in its infancy but, as the intelligence officers observed, "It might eventually constitute a serious embarrassment to British imperial interests."[8]

Kemal was also on friendly terms with the Indian Khalifate Movement.[9] The Inter-Departmental Committee, having examined all the intelligence data, concluded that the Angora government had to take up the Pan-Islamic campaign enthusiastically and, once the Turkish National Assembly sanctified it, it became "an integral part of Turkish National policy." Moreover, serious efforts were made to establish connections with all other Muslim countries and encourage them in their struggle for "complete independence" and to become "self-contained units in a Federation of Union in Muslim communities under the religious and political leadership of Turkey." Representatives of all communities were invited to Anatolia to harmonize their activities and launch a concerted action.[10] The Kemalist Angora government aspired to assume the leading role in the Pan-Islamic Movement and become its fountainhead of ideas and its engine for political activity.

The Pan-Islamic Movement made great strides in Palestine and the *Mouvahidin* Association found numerous adherents there.[11] Turkey was popular during the war, and so in its aftermath, Turkish Nationalists were using every available avenue to infiltrate agents into Egypt,

Palestine, and India in order to incite the Muslim population against England and provoke hostilities.[12] Chaim Weizmann, drawing on reliable information, warned the General Assembly, as well as General Bols and Col. Waters-Taylor, that Emir Feisal was cooperating with "the dark forces radiating from Constantinople and Konia [which were] challenging Europe—constantly [evoking] the specter of Pan-Islamism, Bolshevism, and similar phenomena."[13] The warning fell on deaf ears. Soon afterwards, the Palin Committee submitted its report in which it stated categorically that the Pan-Islamic agitation was endeavoring to unite the Muslims from India to the Mediterranean and was linked to the Pan-Turanism upheld by Turkish Nationalists. "All these movements are definitely anti-British and anti-Allies."[14]

On May 28, 1920, Allenby finally admitted that there existed "considerable evidence to show that a determined effort is being made to unite Islam against all European powers." In the same dispatch he confessed that the Arab revolt had not been regarded with sympathy in India and elsewhere in the Muslim countries. "This feeling still exists today."[15] Allenby thus obliquely admitted that the policy of Cairo's officials during the war to sway the Arab and Muslim population at large to the British side had failed abysmally.

The nature of Turkish nationalism too was not fully understood by the Foreign Office officials. "It must be remembered that the Turks' aim at freeing Mesopotamia, Syria, Egypt, etc., and at asserting their influence on other Muslim countries . . ."—reads an unsigned minute on the Luke and Ryan memoranda.[16] This view was expounded more forcefully by Eric G. Forbes Adam in a memorandum addressed to Curzon for the prime minister's consumption. He wrote that the Turkish Nationalists policy

> is imperialistic both at home and abroad; it is definitely against any form of foreign interference (whether British or French). At home their policy is that of centralized bureaucracy and Turkification, so far as subject races of Turkey are concerned. As regards foreign policy they employ two weapons, (a) Pan-Islamism (religions); (b) Pan-Turanianism (secular and nationalist) . . .
>
> Both are employed according to the circumstances against Christian rulers of Mohammedan countries and all who threatens Turkish independence.[17]

While it was true that Turkish Nationalists (like other officials, Forbes Adam mistook them for members of Committee of Union and Progress) were determined to protect Turkey's independence and integrity, he was totally mistaken in regarding them as "imperialists both at home and abroad." Atatürk gave up the idea of reconstituting the Ottoman Empire and his policy was Turco-centrist. He controlled his forces by sheer force of his personality and conviction in his ideas. At that time, it should be recalled, he was a civilian, and those served under him were volunteers. The major decisions were taken by the National Assembly in a democratic way.

There was a tendency to belittle the strength of the Turkish National Movement. Admiral Webb felt duty bound to correct this misconception. While it was true that they were in a minority, they were nonetheless an "energetic and unscrupulous minority," which commanded the sympathy of the silent majority. An announcement by the Allies of harsh peace terms could automatically throw the Turkish population into the arms of the Nationalists and, unless the Allies were prepared to employ sufficient force, it would be impossible to suppress the Turkish National Movement.[18] Atatürk was fully aware that in the aftermath of the war the British did not command such a force, while the British, as we shall see later, miscalculated.

The Turkish national movement was not an isolated phenomenon. A memorandum by Major Bray, the political intelligence officer of the India Office, is illuminating. He wrote as follows:

> The national sentiment in the East created and bolstered by anti-Christian forces has grown to be a living reality in the hearts of even the moderate Moslem elements throughout the East. National independence is being striven to an unreasoned intensity unparalleled in politics. Regardless of cost, impervious to reason, its extremist adherents press forward as result, attainment of which, should throw the whole Eastern world into an inextricable chaos.
>
> Britain, in their eyes, is the chief impediment to the realization of these hopes and furnishes adverse material for universal hostile propaganda.[19]

It was Bolshevism, Bray asserted in another memorandum, that was largely responsible for the disruptive activities against the British, using the national card for all it was worth. And yet the alliance between the national movements in the East with Bolshevism was "a matter of expediency, not of sentiment." Nonetheless, Britain should have taken the matter seriously because nationalism had become a universal phenomenon and had infected countries as disparate as Egypt,

Anatolia, Mesopotamia, and Persia with British world predominance, providing a convenient target for "hostile propaganda." To counter this dangerous trend, Bray suggested, Britain should come to terms with the nascent nationalism in the East and declare boldly that she supports the principle of self-determination and self-government, whenever circumstances permitted.[20]

This was a prudent comment. There is no indication, however, that the Foreign Office had taken note of it.

Like other European powers, Tsarist Russia was animated by a drive to empire building. The greatest territorial expansion in the South, in the Caucasus and especially in the Central Asia, took place during the Romanov dynasty (1613–1917). Peter the Great (1682–1725), Catherine the Great (1762–1796), Nicholas I (1825–1855), and Alexander II (1855–1881) were especially noted for their aggressive policy in this respect. Expansion took place particularly eastwards; before World War I it had reached as far as Vladivostok.

Russia's cherished goal, however, was the straits and Constantinople—the gateway to the warm waters of the Mediterranean. F. M. Dostoyevsky, the celebrated author and thinker, gave sentimental expression to the yearnings of the majority of the Slavophiles as well as of the ambition of the government of Alexander II. In an article published in March 1877 he wrote thus:

> Yes, the Golden Horn and Constantinople—all this will be ours . . . It must be ours, not only because it is a famous port, because of the straits, 'the center of the universe', 'the navel of the earth' [which will enable the] giant Russia to emerge at last from his locked room . . . into the open spaces where he may breathe the free air of the seas and oceans . . . sooner or later, *Constantinople must be ours*, even if it should take another century.[21]

For Dostoyevsky this was Russia's historical mission. So deeply-rooted was this sentiment that in 1915, Sir Edward Grey, the British foreign secretary had to accede to Russia's desideratum to annex Constantinople, the straits, and a sizeable hinterland—"the prize of the entire war," not as a proof of friendship to Russia but in fear of losing her to Germany. The concession marked a complete reversal of the traditional British policy. Russia, however, claimed that in the early days of the war she had saved the Allies from defeat, and it was therefore essential for the successful prosecution of the war that she should be reassured about Constantinople.[22]

In 1917, however, the Russians no longer cared about the fulfillment of their "historic mission"; the Byzantine mirage faded away in the prevailing mood of war-weariness and apathy. Prince Lvov, the prime minister of the provisional government, declared on April 10 that Russia's aim was "not dominion over other nations . . . not seizure by force of foreign territory." The principle of self-determination was the only basis on which the provisional government was prepared to continue the war.[23] The annexationist claim of Constantinople and the straits had been shelved. On November 7, 1917, when the Bolsheviks came to power, they lost no time in declaring their policy. On the following day, they issued a call to all belligerent governments and people to conclude peace—a peace without annexations or indemnities based in the right of self-determination. Shortly thereafter, Leon Trotsky published in the official paper, *Isvestia,* the Turkey-in-Asia Agreement of 1916 (known commonly as the Sykes-Picot Agreement) in a distorted form, with the obvious intent of blacking the Allies' record and undermining their credibility, as in fact, it did.

On December 5 the Council of People's Commissars of the Bolshevik government issued an appeal to the Muslim population in Russia and in the East. It declared among other things that

> the secret treaties . . . regarding the seizure of Constantinople, which was confirmed by the deposed Kerensky, were now null and void. The Russian Republic and its government, the Council of People's Commissars, are against the seizure of foreign territories[;] Constantinople must remain in the hands of the Muslims.[24]

The charge against the former Prime Minister Alexander Kerensky, Prince Lvov's successor, was a blatant lie. This however was characteristic of the Bolshevik's propaganda; they blamed the other party in an attempt to project an image quite different from that of the "old Russia." Formerly Tsarist Russia appeared in the eyes of the downtrodden peasants and particularly the alien oppressed Nationalists as a symbol of oppression. Now, the Bolsheviks succeeded in convincing the masses that socialism was synonymous with freedom from serfdom at home and liberation from colonial imperialism abroad. As Richard Pipes summed up:

> The slogan of self-determination in Lenin's interpretation was to prove enormously successful. The outbreak of the Russian Revolution allowed the Bolsheviks to put it to considerable demagogic use as a

means of winning the support of the national movements which the revolutionary period developed in all their magnitude.[25]

A step further was made at the congress of Baku in September 1920. The idea of convening a Muslim Congress originated with A. Zeki Validov Togan, a prominent Bashkir from Muslim Central Asia, a collaborator with Karl Radek, a leading Bolshevik intellectual. Its purpose was to arouse the Muslim world against the West, England in particular. Zinoviev, the president of the executive committee of the Communist International, in his keynote speech declared a jihad— holy war against British imperialism, to which the Arabs, the Turks, and other Muslim delegates responded enthusiastically. Zinoviev's attack on Islam and Islamic institutions did not go down well with the audience and aroused suspicions. Yet, in spite of this error, the congress marked a turning point in Soviet-Muslim relations by creating the impression that only the Third International was capable of liberating the Orient. *Krasnaya Gazeta*, the Red Army mouth piece (December 10, 1920), with fiery rhetoric commented, "Now Baku is on our side . . . instead of oil the gentlemen imperialists will feel the flame of a revolutionary conflagration in the East."[26] A certain social democrat opined that at Baku the Bolsheviks had given up Socialism in favor of power politics.[27] This was particularly true with regard to the East. For, unlike in industrialized Europe where the Bolsheviks were propagating the socialist program, in the East, they cultivated the idea of nationality and emancipation from the colonial powers. This policy was not necessarily motivated by abstract altruism. The ultimate aim of the Bolsheviks was to destroy, or at least to emasculate, the British Empire in Asia and substitute it with Soviet influence.

The primary target was Turkey. "The situation in Anatolia," wrote Major Bray, "is of paramount importance to the Bolsheviks, both from an offensive and defensive point of view. From the offensive standpoint Anatolia provides the right flank on any advance on India," either militarily or politically. Ideally, Turkey should become a Soviet satellite; failing that, it was essential that both Anatolia and Georgia maintain "absolute neutrality." Under no circumstances, however, should they be allowed to enter into an alliance with European powers.

Major Bray warned that, contrary to Bolsheviks' proclamations, *"the Russian army has not been demobilized . . . in fact, it is stronger than before."* This was indicative of the intentions of the Russian government, all the more so since they were perfectly aware of Britain's inability to wage war against themselves and were well informed of the financial woes besetting Britain.[28]

In the event, the Bolsheviks adopted a double-barreled policy. On the one hand, they supported the newly-founded Turkish Communist party, and on the other, provided financial aid and arms and ammunition to Kemal's Nationalist army. The Bolsheviks hoped thus to win a dominating influence in Turkey. What their ultimate aim was had been revealed by Y. Steklov in an article "The Turkish Revolution," published in an official organ *Izvestia* on April 23, 1919. He pointed out that since the Turkish Revolution the question of the Dardanelles had assumed a different complexion; the straits had returned to "Turkish masses and through them to the world proletariat, which includes also the Russian. Thus, what Russian imperialism failed to realize by virtue of centuries of intrigue, now, as a ripe plum, will fall to the Russian working class."

In 1921 M. Pavlovitch, the editor of *Novyi Vostok*, reiterated the theme. He wrote as follows:

> Not until the entire Black Sea is in Soviet hands, and over Constantinople is raised the red Turkish banner or the banner of the Soviet Federations of the Black Sea States—the Ukraine, the Caucasus, Turkish Anatolia—will these states begin to lead a peaceful life and be able to devote themselves to creative and constructive work.[29]

The Bolsheviks posed as "liberators from a foreign yoke" and as "champions of peoples liberty." And yet their imperial ambitions were not different from those of the Tsars, though under a different guise.

The overture for rapprochement with the Soviets was made by Turkish Nationalists. The occupation of Constantinople by British troops on March 16, 1920, humiliated every Muslim. In response, Kemal decided to forge an alliance with the Bolsheviks. He called for the election of a National Assembly which met first in Ankara on April 23, 1920. Armed with its endorsement, Kemal dispatched a note to Lenin, asking him to establish diplomatic relations and appealing for help against foreign invaders.[30] G. Chicherin welcomed the idea in warmest terms. The date of June 2, 1920, could be regarded as commencement of diplomatic relations. It was, however, not before March 16, 1921 that a treaty of friendship and fraternity was signed by the two parties.[31] This agreement provided for Turkey's independence, as well as for the independence of Arabia and Syria. It recognized also

Turkey's right to the vilayet of Batoum and the whole of Thrace. The minorities were to be accorded the same rights and privileges as in other countries in Europe.

The question of the straits would be referred to a conference attended by the states on the Black Sea. The system of capitulations would be abolished, as well as the zones of influence of the foreign powers. The Turkish National Army would reject the terms of peace imposed by foreign powers. The Soviet government obligated itself to supply the Turkish Nationalists with "all kinds of necessary war material." In return, "the Turkish nation agrees to accept, for Turkey, the system of Soviet Government."[32] The last item was a bitter pill for Kemal's government to swallow, but he had no choice. The Greek army had just invaded the Turkish heartland with an aim of crushing the rebellious Nationalists, and the Allies imposed their Treaty of Sèvres on August 10, 1920. As Howard M. Sachar described it, the treaty was a "humiliating instrument of dubious legality, for Turkey was neither consulted nor asked to sign it; she was simply ignored."[33]

The Turkish-Soviet Treaty was designed to undo the Sèvres agreement. The latter agreement obliged Turkey to renounce permanently their entire empire, including eastern Thrace, all the Asiatic provinces, their islands in the Aegean, and the territory of Armenia; Smyrna and environs were allotted to the Greeks, and Constantinople was almost isolated from both Europe and Asia. In contrast, the Turco-Soviet agreement provided for Turkey's independence, as well as for the independence of Arabia and Syria which, was understood, were to be linked with Turkey. The powers parceled out Turkey proper to zones of influence. These the Turkish-Soviet agreement declared null and void. Abolished also was the system of capitulations and other restrictions and servitudes imposed on the country. The authors of the Sèvres Treaty decided on internationalization of the straits; its administration was to be controlled by a commission of ten powers, while the British navy was to patrol the waterway. This was a remarkable victory for the British.

Britain's domination of the strategic territory was greeted with dismay by both the Bolsheviks and the Kemalists, and they were determined to nullify it at all cost. The proviso that only the states "bordering on the Black Sea" were entitled to attend the conference indicated that Russia and Turkey would have a commanding voice in the administration of the straits. England, France, and Italy, who did not have a coterminous border with the Black Sea shores, were eliminated. Moreover, the objection of the Kemalists to the proviso entitling the foreign powers to impose peace terms shows how determined the Kemalists were in their struggle for independence. The Bolsheviks, on the other hand, embraced the cause of their newly found ally and obligated themselves to provide them with necessary tools and matériel.

Kemal Pasha was rather reticent about Soviet military assistance, but from a variety of sources we know that it was substantial. Soviet Russia provided the beleaguered Turks with thirty thousand rifles, one thousand rounds of ammunition for each rifle, about three hundred machine guns, twenty-five mountain cannons, and a large number of hand grenades sufficient to equip three divisions. Moreover, the Soviet government deposited in Berlin one million Russian rubles to the credit of the Kemalists. All this and other gifts served as a tremendous boost, both material and psychological, to Turkish revolutionaries, and it enabled them to defeat the invading Greek army. Moreover, by their treaty signed in Moscow on March 16, 1921, Soviet Russia and the Turkish Nationalists were emancipated from their international isolation and gained in prestige and influence. The Turkish newspaper *Istikba* of September 1, 1920, articulated the motives and the advantages of the Soviet-Turkish alliance thus:

> The most vital question of the day is the alliance between revolutionary Russia and Turkey, which strives for independence . . . but it must be said that in the past we could never have thought of a rapprochement with Russia, for the distinguishing feature of the Russian Tsarist government was its antipopular character and its determination to destroy Turkey. . . . After the overthrow of Tsardom, truth triumphed and a Russo-Turkish rapprochement has become a reality. The Turks, like the Russians, understood the benefit to be derived from a rapprochement of the two peoples.
>
> Events have helped even more to bring us closer. If the Allies had not forced the Turks to take up arms to defend their independence, a Russo-Turkish rapprochement would not have developed so rapidly. The Russo-Turkish rapprochement came into being as a result of the threat to both states.[34]

The alliance was a marriage of convenience or, rather, an unavoidable necessity. Both the Russians and the Turks felt threatened by the Allies, and it could safely be said that had the Allied powers, England in particular, treated Turkey with more consideration, in the spirit of forgiveness and reconciliation, the Turkish-Soviet rapprochement would never have come into being. The terms of the Sèvres Treaty were more severe than those imposed on Germany at Versailles. They wounded Turkish dignity. The most disastrous effect on Turkish psyche was the capture of Smyrna by the Greeks and their subsequent invasion of the Anatolian heartland.

And yet, in spite of mutual exchanges of "friendship and fraternity," Kemal was wary of the becoming subservient to, let alone a vassal state, his big neighbor in the North. Per force, he tolerated the Communist propaganda, but Turkish Communist activities were muzzled and incarcerated.

Winston Churchill, then secretary of state for war, expressed increasing concern about the Turkish situation. It had a bearing on Britain's standing as the greatest Muslim power. Moreover, in India, Egypt, Mesopotamia, and Palestine, Britain was forced to keep a military establishment at disproportionate cost. In Constantinople and the straits she was obliged to keep a strong force for an indefinite period—all this at the time when, owing to financial stringency, England was in the process of demobilization. "I am reluctantly drawn to the conclusion," Churchill insisted, "that the policy of the partition of the Turkish Empire among the European powers is a mistake. It will involve us in abetting a crime against freedom . . . and in immense expense for military establishment and development work far exceeding any possibility of return."

He thought it would be more prudent for the European powers, primarily the Greeks, to quit Smyrna—renounce their territorial ambitions and

> instead of dividing up the Empire into separate territorial spheres of exploitation, we should combine to preserve the integrity of the Turkish Empire as it existed before the War but should subject that Empire to a strict form of international control, breaking it as a whole and directing it from Constantinople . . . The Turkish Empire would be placed under the guardianship of the League of Nations.

Churchill was aware that for Britain, in particular, it would be difficult to relinquish "dreams of conquest and aggrandizement." However, Britain possessed more territory in her empire than she would be able to develop for many generations. "We ought to endeavor to concentrate our resources on developing our existing empire instead of dissipating them in her enlargements." The British should set an example to other powers.[35]

This sounded like an echo of Prime Minister Herbert Asquith's comment on Kitchener's proposal to create a large Arab state on the ruins of the Ottoman Empire. "It is very difficult to convince the ignorant or the foolish that swollen boundaries mean, or may mean, anything else that greater wealth [and] . . . authority," Asquith wrote on April 22, 1915 to Admiral Fisher. Moreover,

> New territories require the expenditure of more money, and even more important, the expenditure of more men. We shall be short of both at the end of this war. . . New territories will require new armies, new navies, new civil servants, new expenses . . . Where are these to come from? . . . And if we try . . . we shall arrest progress at home . . . and shall saddle the British taxpayer with huge liabilities for defence.[36]

This was an extremely prescient analysis. So was Churchill's; with the exception of Palestine, the acquisition of which, for strategic consideration, had been regarded unanimously by the cabinet (1917) as "the irreducible minimum."[37]

Churchill failed to carry the cabinet with him; there was no way of turning the clock back. He did not give in, however. In Mesopotamia, he argued, the military forces there were out of all proportion to any advantages that Britain could ever expect to reap from that country. In addition, militarily, the Bolshevik and Turkish Nationalist "menace," coupled with Arab disturbances, "will," he predicted, "expose all [British] troops in Mesopotamia to continued and increasing danger."[38] The campaign in Mesopotamia was a thankless task.[39]

By November 1920, Churchill reached the sorry conclusion that the burden of carrying out the British Middle Eastern policy was beyond the strength of the British army. Moreover, the policy was producing an adverse effect on the Indian troops upon whom the British were compelled to rely. Financial difficulties were another insuperable impediment and, unless the British government came to terms with the Turks and won the cooperation of the Muslim world, he saw little hope of assuring British control in the foreseeable future.[40] He asserted clearly and forcefully thus:

> We ought to come to terms with Mustapha Kemal and arrive at a good peace with Turkey, which will secure our position and interests at Constantinople and ease the position in Egypt, Mesopotamia, Persia and India.

Now is the time to abandon the policy of relying on the weak and fickle Greeks and by so doing estranging the far more powerful, durable and necessary Turkish and Mohammedan forces. We should thus recreate the Turkish barrier to Russian ambitions which has always been of utmost importance to us.[41]

During the cabinet meeting, which took place on March 19, 1915, Lord Haldane, the Lord Chancellor, agreed that the total destruction of Germany and Turkey was not "in the interests of a lasting peace." This provoked the fury of Winston Churchill, First Lord of Admiralty: "Surely, we do not intend to leave this . . . inefficient and out-of-date [Turkish] nation, which has long misruled one of the most fertile countries in the world, still in possession? . . . it is time for us to make a clean sweep."[42]

Now, in 1919, Churchill subscribed to a variant of recommendation made by the de-Bunsen Committee.[43] It was clear to him that a new Turkey had been born: no longer inefficient and corrupt but a vibrant nation, fiercely nationalistic, struggling for independence. With Germany's collapse, Turkey ceased to endanger British interests. It would therefore be more profitable for the British to have Kemal as a friend, rather than as an enemy. Bolshevism was the menace, not Turkey, and it was essential to separate the two. He was greatly aggrieved when his ideas were not taken up. During a cabinet meeting on March 20, 1922, he crossed swords with his critics and commented sarcastically thus:

> Our policy in regard of Turkey had resulted in achieving the impossible, namely the marriage of the Bolsheviks and the Turks in spite of the entire conflict of principles between them. This greatly increased our difficulties.

When Lord Curzon responded that the Bolshevik-Turkish union was "inevitable," Churchill disagreed, stating that it would have been more proper to adopt "an easy policy towards Turkey and a stiff policy towards Bolshevism. We had adopted exactly the contrary course, with results which were now visible . . ." He added thus:

> The Turks recognised the British Empire as their great enemy. At one time they would have taken anything from us, but we had rejected them and now they had in their hands an easy means to inflict humiliation upon us and to complete the destruction of our policy in Mesopotamia.[44]

Churchill maintained that the Treaty of Sèvres had been "one of the most unfortunate events in the history of the world." The signatories had no means to enforce it. The consequent result was that they had aroused in Turkey, which had been at the Allies feet, a spirit which they had no means to combat. "We had no leverage with the Turks, whereas the Turks . . . had the means of wrecking our policy without any great effort."[45]

A year earlier, Colonel Meinertzhagen wrote in a similar vein thus:

> We cannot blockade Mustafa. In the Bolsheviks he finds a ready source of war material, but for many reasons he would be glad to rid himself of obligations towards the Bolsheviks. He is able to support his policy by successful strategy. [In contrast] we have allowed our policy to outrun our strategy and our bluff is now transparent . . . We cannot afford to remain in Mesopotamia without the good will of Mustafa. It is an ugly and degrading state of affairs . . .
>
> Failing to come to terms with Mustafa will mean an armed clash, and we could never hope to reduce a single man in Mesopotamia as long as we remain there without his good will.[46]

Churchill was seconded by the India Office, which traditionally was pro-Turk, and particularly by the General Staff. He had, however, an uphill battle with Curzon and especially with the philo-Hellenic prime minister. "Curzon's mood," Edwin Montagu, the state secretary for India, wrote to Churchill, "is violently anti-Turk, and he is dreaming in *Greek*."[47] Several months earlier, General Sir Henry Wilson, the chief of the imperial general staff, noted in his diary as follows:

> L[oyd] G[eorge] is persuaded that the Greeks are [the] coming power in the Mediterranean both on land and on sea and wants to befriend them. The whole of LG's foreign policy is chaotic and based on totally fallacious values of men and affairs. I am pro-Turk and therefore I am suspect and my opinion not worth having just as it is not worth having about Ireland—and so I am no longer consulted . . ..[48]

Churchill was fighting a losing battle.

Notes

1. James Jankowski, "Egypt and Early Arab Nationalism," in *The Origins of Arab Nationalism*, ed. Rashid Khalidi, Lisa Anderson, Muhammad Muslih, and Reeva S. Simon (New York, 1991), 253–4.
2. Beth Baron, "Mothers, Mortality and Nationalism in Pre-1919 Egypt," in *The Origins of Arab Nationalism*, eds. Khalidi, Anderson, Muslih, and Simon, 274.

3. *DBFP*, I, IV, Robeck (Constantinople) to Curzon, December 26, 1919, 974–5.
4. Ibid., Luke to Webb, December 25, 1919, Encl. I to No. 647, 1001–3.
5. Ibid., "Memorandum by Mr. Ryan," Encl. 2 to No. 647, 1003–4.
6. Paul Gentizon, *Mustapha Kemal ou l'Orient en Marche* (Paris, 1929), 18.
7. Martin Kramer, *Islam Assembled: The Advent of Muslim Congresses* (New York, 1986), 73.
8. *DBFP*, I, IV, Intelligence report, dated September 30, 1919, encl. in Webb to Curzon, January 16, 1920, pp. 1029–30. On *Mouvahidin* Association see Isaiah Friedman, *British Pan-Arab Policy, 1915–1922: A Critical Appraisal* (New Brunswick, NJ: Transaction Publishers, 2010), 359.
9. Jacob Landau, *Politics of Pan-Islam*, rev. ed. (Oxford, UK, 1992), 208.
10. F.O. 371/7790/5336, Interim report of the Inter-Departmental Committee on Eastern Unrest, May 24, 1922, 5–6, "Most Secret."
11. Friedman, *British Pan-Arab Policy, 1915–1922*, 359.
12. F.O. 371/4238/45584, Intelligence Rep. December 26, 1919, encl. in ADM. to F.O., January 16, 1920.
13. Friedman, *British Pan-Arab Policy, 1915–1922*, 271.
14. Ibid., 275–7.
15. *DBFP*, Vol. XIII, Chap. 2, No. 253, Allenby (Cairo) to Curzon, May 28, 1920, 275–6.
16. *DBFP*, I, IV, 1004–5.
17. Ibid., Forbes Adam (Paris) to Kidston, January 13, 1920, 1026–7.
18. Ibid., Webb to Curzon, January 18, 1920, No. 664, 1035–6.
19. The British Library, The India Office Archives (hereafter I.O.A.), L/PS/11/194, 1114, "Memorandum on the Present Situation in the Middle East," by Major Bray, undated (1921), circulated to the war cabinet.
20. F.O. 371/6342, 31–2, "National Sentiment," a note by Bray, December 1920.
21. Ivar Spector, *The Soviet Union and the Muslim World, 1917–1958* (Seattle, WA, 1959), 16–7.
22. Isaiah Friedman, *The Question of Palestine, 1914–1918. British–Jewish–Arab Relations* (London, 1973), 14–5. Second edition by Transaction Publishers (USA and London, 1992), same pages.
23. Ibid., 186.
24. Cited in Spector, *The Soviet Union and the Muslim World*, 33–5.
25. Richard Pipes, *The Formation of the Soviet Union* (Cambridge, MA, 1954), 49.
26. Spector, *The Soviet Union and the Muslim World*, 44–61. On the Congress at Baku, see also Edward J. Carr, *The Bolshevik Revolution 1917–1929* (Harmondsworth, UK, 1966), 263–8.
27. Carr, *The Bolshevik Revolution*, 268n3.
28. F.O. 371/6342, "Russia. Appreciation of the Situation in the Middle East" by Major Bray, December 1920, 19–22.
29. Cited in Spector, *The Soviet Union and the Muslim World*, 64–5.
30. "A Speech Delivered by Ghazi Mustapha Kemal in October 1927" (Leibzig, 1929) transcribed from his speech over the course of seven days in the Turkish Parliament; see chapter 1 note 107.
31. Spector, *The Soviet Union and the Muslim World*, 69–75.

32. F.O. 371/6342, App. I, p. 33, "Russo-Turkish-Nationalist Agreement."
33. Howard M. Sachar, *The Emergence of the Middle East 1914–1924* (New York, 1969, 1970), 327. The terms are quoted in J.C. Hurewitz, *Diplomacy in the Near and the Middle East: A Documentary Record*, vol. II (Princeton, 1956), 82–7. A summary can be found in Sachar, *The Emergence of the Middle East*, 325–7.
34. Cited in Spector, *The Soviet Union and the Muslim World*, 72.
35. *Winston S. Churchill* by Martin Gilbert, Companion. Documents, vol. IV, Pt. 1, Churchill, memorandum, War Office, October 25, 1919 (London, 1973), 937–8.
36. Friedman, *The Question of Palestine*, 18–9.
37. Ibid., 164–75, particularly 172.
38. Churchill, Companion, IV, Pt. 2, ed. Gilbert, Churchill, Cabinet memorandum, February 7, 1920, 1032–3.
39. Ibid., Churchill to Lloyd George, August 31, 1920, 1199. The letter was not sent.
40. Ibid., Cabinet memorandum, November 23, 1920, 1250.
41. Ibid., 1249.
42. Friedman, *The Question of Palestine*, 17–8.
43. Ibid., 19–21.
44. Churchill, Companion, IV, Pt. 2, ed. Gilbert, minutes of the cabinet meeting, March 20, 1922, 1812–3.
45. Ibid.
46. Ibid., Meinertzhagen to Churchill, Colonial Office, May 31, 1921, 1480–2.
47. Ibid., Montagu to Churchill, January 18, 1921, 1315.
48. Ibid., Sir Henry Wilson: diary, June 13, 1920, 1123.

5

Anglo-Soviet Rivalry and the Rise of Nationalism in Afghanistan and in Persia

In our previous chapter, we have described Soviet ambitions in the East. Their deeds met their proclamations. Indeed, they were going from strength to strength in Central Asia. In January 1920, E. W. Birse, a member of the Foreign Office, reported that the Bolsheviks had established a protectorate over Khanates of Bokhara and Khiva and, subsequently, having secured their position in Tashkent, an area of considerable strategic importance, they continued their advance south-eastward securing the cotton fields of Ferghana and to the rest of Oxus, hence pushing onto Krasnovodsk.

Birse feared that once the Bolsheviks reached the Caspian Sea, they would also try to form close relations with the republic of Azerbaijan, famous for its Baku oilfields. From here they would be poised to attack the forces of General Denikin, the commander in chief of the White Russian forces in South Russia, and thereafter ". . . to form a coalition of Mohammedan States for the overthrow of British rule in India, Mesopotamia, and Egypt." Birse opined that, since the Bolshevik's drive westward into Europe had been stemmed, they had found an outlet in the East, making full use of the Pan-Islamic movement.[1]

Birse's assessment was not far off the mark. The Communist revolutions in Europe had failed miserably, that in Berlin (January 1919) ended disastrously with Rosa Luxenburg and Karl Liebknecht executed; the Hungarian Soviet government (1919) disintegrated soon after its creation, while the drive of the Polish army under the skilful command of Josef Pilsudski deep into Russian territory frustrated any hope of successful revolutions in Central Europe.[2]

In sharp contrast, Central Asia was in a state of national effervescence and deep discontent. Vladimir Lenin, with his unerring political instinct, was quick to detect that not only Turkey but also Afghanistan and Persia would be receptive to the Bolsheviks' assistance in their struggle for national liberation. Thus, in his speech to the All-Russian Congress, which took place in March 1920, he pointed with glee to the awakening of political consciousness in Asia and that the revolutionary movements were growing "from day to day." Lenin realized that the people in Asia, even more than in Europe, were not yet ready for absorbing the Communist ideology, since there was no social infrastructure enabling the so-called class-struggle, while Islam militated against the Communist doctrine. Therefore, he played the Nationalist card for all it was worth, targeting British imperialism as the main impediment to the national emancipation of the people of Asia. In this matter Stalin saw eye to eye with Lenin.[3]

The diplomatic pressure, as well as supplies of military matériel, however, was not possible before the defeat of the Kolchak and Denikin's White Russian army, as well as the conquest of Transcaucasia.[4] Azerbaijan was taken over at the end of April 1920 practically without resistance and on twenty-eighth of the month Red Army units were in Baku. Thereafter, they took over Armenia and subsequently overcame the stiff resistance of Georgia. Batum was occupied on March 19, 1921, thereby putting an end to the short-lived independence of Transcaucasia. It gave the lie to the Soviet proclaimed doctrine of liberation of small nationalities. On the other hand, strategically it wrought a dramatic change. Now Soviet Russia had a contiguous border with Turkey, Afghanistan, and Persia.

H. C. Norman, the British minister in Teheran, was alarmed. In a very urgent cable to Curzon, he assessed that the Soviet invasion

> would be disastrous both to Persia and to ourselves. Persia already deprived of revenues of Azerbaijan, Gilan and Mazanderan . . . financial rehabilitation of country would become impossible. Bolshevik propaganda would be stimulated everywhere and Bolsheviks would be in a position to threaten from the East as well as from the North . . .
>
> Our prestige would be shattered not only in Persia but throughout the East and we should have Bolshevism on our Indian frontiers . . . there can be no doubt that Afghans will eventually range themselves on the winning side.[5]

The Foreign Office was well aware of the danger indicated by Norman. Three months earlier Lord Hardinge, the permanent undersecretary for foreign affairs, in a long minute to Curzon, warned that "once the British forces evacuated northern Persia, the fall of Teheran would be inevitable . . . The Anglo-Persian Agreement will become a scrap of paper . . . and anarchy and destruction will prevail." Moreover, the flanks of both India and Mesopotamia would be exposed, and the Bolsheviks would be in a position to attack in whatever direction they choose, with the probable result of creating an Afghan-Bolshevik alliance directed against India. Hardinge concluded thus:

> I hardly need to say . . . how disastrous the effect of our evacuation and betrayal of Persia will be on our subjects in India, both Mohammedan [sic] and Hindu, and the loss of prestige that we shall suffer throughout the whole of the East.[6]

Lancelot Oliphant, of the Persia Department of the Foreign Office, was even more pessimistic. In a memorandum dated June 14, 1919, he feared that, should Bolshevism overrun Persia, the country would sink into chaos and the British position would become untenable; maintenance of even Baghdad "would be a matter for earnest consideration . . ." Moreover, the state of disorder and troubles in Persia would gravitate toward the East in general, "beginning with Afghanistan and the Baluchistan border with a consequent risk of spreading to India."[7]

Through the nineteenth and early twentieth centuries, the mainspring of Britain's policy in the East was to safeguard both the sea and land routes to India.[8] Now this vital interest seemed to be jeopardized. Persia, or more precisely southern Persia, was regarded as an essential link in the chain of strategic outposts ensuring the safe passage to India. G. P. Churchill, a senior official at the Foreign Office, envisaged a dismal picture. He predicted that with the likely withdrawal of British forces from northern Persia, the Bolsheviks would seize the opportunity and, with their allies in Ghilan, would fill the vacuum. The British position and that of the Shah and his government at Teheran would become untenable.

"This will be done, not necessarily by an advance of armed Bolsheviks . . . on the capital, but by means of propaganda, agents and sympathisers at Teheran. The government is likely to collapse and the Shah to fly to Europe."[9]

The Middle as well as the Near East were in a state of turmoil. From March 1919 there were violent outbursts in Egypt, trouble in Afghanistan (May 1919), open rebellion in Iraq, a rising in Syria in

July 1920, prolonged hostilities with Mustafa Kemal from 1919 to 1923, and the rise of a determined nationalism in Afghanistan and Persia.

With Lloyd George and Balfour away in Paris, all these unforeseen problems lay at the door of George Nathaniel Curzon, from January 1919 serving as the acting foreign minister. From 1898 to 1905, when serving as the viceroy of India, he had developed a strong sentimental attachment to that country. He took also a keen interest in Persia and published a book titled, *Persia and the Persian Question* (2 vols., rev. ed. London, 1966). On the strength of this study he was considered an expert on this particular region. His self-confidence was enhanced by his sense of mission. "His philosophy and faith," Harold Nicolson, his biographer, tells us, "was founded on the belief that God had personally selected the British upper classes as an instrument of the Divine Will." Such a belief called for unsparing self-sacrifice, a religious ideal of duty combined with an efficient conduct of public service. Nicolson goes on to list his virtues: Curzon possessed

> a superb memory, an unequalled power of assimilation, great intellectual curiosity, a genius for lucid exposition, abundant humour and oratorical capacity of high order. His will-power [and] his energy superhuman; his industry redoubtable . . .

"And yet," Nicolson remarked with a glimmer of irony, "the gods, in assigning to him these advantages, imposed their penalty." First and foremost he lacked a sense of proportion.[10] By nature egocentric, he demonstrated a palpable inability to delegate functions to others. Self-righteous and opinionated as he was, he underestimated the complexity of the problems that he confronted. Although lucid in exposition, he suffered from some intellectual rigidity.

An even more serious defect, as we shall see later, was his inability to understand the postwar developments, the rising nationalism in the Islamic countries in particular. Nicolson thought that essentially, Curzon was "an administrator. He was not a politician."[11] Nor was he a statesman. Sir Valentine Chirol commented that Curzon seldom, if ever, showed that he possessed "the spiritual vision, which is of the essence of real statesmanship."[12] He was a late Victorian of the upper middle class. Lord D'Abernon, in his brilliant analysis of Curzon's personality (in his book, *Ambassador of Peace*, Vol. I, p. 48), wrote that Curzon "was born and died in the faith of an aristocrat of the English eighteenth century."[13] Considering that by nature Curzon was not an adaptable man, one can appreciate why he courted failure when he had to encounter the postwar complexities of the East. His tragedy was that he was born too late.

To stem the Bolsheviks' advance Curzon advocated the "forward policy." This policy was the brainchild of Sir Henry Rawlinson, who served with distinction in the First Afghanistan War and afterward in Persia. Rawlinson's forward policy, which he elaborated in a memorandum dated July 1868, consisted of maintaining military outposts and support of a chain of states that were to serve as buffers against Russian invasion. By 1881 the forward policy had become an established British strategy and held the field for forty years, i.e., until 1921, with little or no regard for the wishes of the native population.[14]

What was feasible, however, during the period before World War I became counterproductive in its aftermath. Times had changed. This was pointed out with great clarity by Major Hubert Young in his eye-opening memorandum as follows:

> The time has gone when an Oriental people will be content to be nursed into self-government by a European Power. The spread of Western education, increased facilities of communication, and above all . . . the emergence of Wilsonian principle of self-determination, have combined to breed in the minds of Eastern agitators a distrust for, and impatience of Western control. We cannot ignore this universal phenomenon without endangering, and possibly, losing beyond recall, our position in the East . . .

Young went on,

> This national sentiment is again awake in those Eastern countries where it has slumbered so long. It is the Western nations who have evoked it, and it is for the Western nations to direct it into healthy channels . . .[15]

Curzon had regularly relied on Young's advice and benefited from his wise counsel. In this case, however, he ignored Young's memorandum. Nor did he take into account emerging nationalism in Islamic countries. As mentioned already, nationalism was an anathema to him. In the prewar period, from Palmerston onward, Turkey served as a staunch bulwark against encroachments of foreign powers, Russia in particular. Now, reduced to the status of a pariah, a strategic cornerstone had been removed and the framework of the forward policy was severely cracked. Like Lloyd George, Curzon hated and despised Turkey. He wrote thus:

> For nearly five centuries the presence of the Turk in Europe has been a source of intrigue and corruption in European politics; of oppression and misrule to the subject nationalities; and an incentive to undue and overweening ambitions in the Moslem world. It encouraged the Turk to regard himself as a Great Power, and has enabled him to impose upon others the same illusion. It has placed him in a position to play off one Power against another . . .[16]

The Kemalist Nationalistic Turkey responded in kind and launched vigorous anti-British propaganda among the Muslim people in Central Asia, as well as among the Arabs. This was a serious blow to Curzon's strategy since it was imperative that military bases be surrounded by a friendly and supportive population. However, in Central Asia this was wanting. There was no love for the British in Afghanistan. Two Anglo-Afghan wars "had made Britain Afghan's national enemy."[17] The Anglo-Russian Convention of 1907 caused considerable resentment among the Afghans and was regarded as gross interference by foreign powers. The state council maintained that the convention destroyed Afghanistan's independence, and the Amir refused to sign it.[18] It would be useful to point out that this convention divided Afghanistan, as well as Persia, into three zones: the north under Russian influence, the south under British, and the middle—no man's land of sorts.

Resentment made the Afghans even more susceptible to Pan-Islamic propaganda, and during World War I, Afghanistan sided with the Central Powers. Although Habibullah, the Amir, formally remained neutral, the people at large showed pro-Turkish and pro-German sentiments. German missions acted freely, and finally on January 24, 1916, Habibullah broke his neutrality and initiated a treaty of friendship with Germany, which was confirmed the following day. Accordingly, Germany and the Central Powers promised to recognize Afghanistan's independence and undertook to assist economically and supply military hardware. Afghanistan was almost drawn into the war.[19]

On December 22, 1918, Amir Habibullah expressed his "ardent wish" that Afghanistan participate in the Peace Conference and that Britain recognize Afghanistan's independence, as well as its freedom to conduct its own foreign policy. London, however, rejected these demands brusquely. Such an offensive attitude weakened

Habibullah's internal position and on the night of February 19–20 he was assassinated.

He was succeeded by his son Amanullah, popular among his people, an ardent Nationalist, and anti-British. With his accession to the throne, the political climate in Kabul had changed. Ideas of nationalism, Islamic solidarity, and self-determination took hold among the educated class. Sirdar Mahmud Tarzi, the editor of the influential newspaper, *Siraj al-Akhbar*, was a leading voice in propagating these ideas.[20]

Amanullah's first act was to declare Afghanistan's independence. On April 13, 1919, he announced as follows:

> I have declared myself and my country entirely free, autonomous and independent both internally and externally . . . No foreign power will be allowed to have the right to interfere internally or externally with the affairs of Afghanistan, and if any ever does, I am ready to cut its throat with this sword.

The second act was to attack India, assuming that an anti-British rebellion was about to break out. Amanullah miscalculated, however. Rumors about an uprising proved to be false, and the British forces, composed primarily of Indian troops, had no difficulty in repulsing the invaders. Lord Chelmsford, the viceroy of India, deliberately avoided administering a decisive victory. The fall of Amanullah would have resulted in chaos and anarchy. Moreover, like Young, Chelmsford realized that a new spirit was sweeping the East and that awakened Nationalist aspirations, and the impact of the Wilsonian principles coupled with Bolshevik propaganda were at the root of the unrest. Hence, a complete subjugation of Afghanistan would be counterproductive. The altered atmosphere militated against turning the clock back. Chelmsford's purpose was to establish mutual trust and friendly relations. It was imperative, therefore, he thought, to recognize Afghanistan's independence.[21]

During the peace negotiations that followed, the Afghani delegation pretended that they had won a great military victory and argued that the viceroy's generosity was not an act of charity but dictated by necessity. The Amir cold-shouldered a British proposal to sign a treaty of friendship and instead initiated diplomatic talks with the Soviet government. There were reports that Bolshevik emissaries were about to arrive in Kabul.[22]

It was a blatant act of ingratitude. On the other hand, it was further proof of the depth of antagonism and mistrust against the British. As mentioned already, the dismemberment of the Ottoman Empire, the supposed violation of the holy places, and the Greek invasion of Smyrna and beyond aroused violent hatred throughout the Muslim world and belief that the Christian powers were bent on the destruction of Islam. The Afghans were particularly sensitive because they had hoped that the caliphate would be transferred to Kabul. In these circumstances to indulge in the idea of "forward policy," as Curzon did, was most unrealistic.

Nor for the same reasons was there any chance that the Persians would welcome British military presence under the guise of the so-called forward policy. The budding Persian Nationalist movement viewed the Anglo-Russian Agreement as a "gross interference and unprincipled betrayal" by the Persian rulers. The vast majority of the Persians—peasants, tribesmen, and urban laborers—were illiterate and politically inarticulate; three groups, however, were violently opposed to foreign interference. They were the clerics, the merchants, and the intellectuals. They wanted the influence of the foreigners to be reduced and social reforms to be inaugurated. These groups, the intellectuals in particular, "exercised a dynamic quality"[23] which gathered momentum.

The clerics were under the strong influence of the teaching of Jamal al-Din, commonly known as Al-Afghani, whose aim was to eliminate Western imperialism from Asia and to combat the cultural, economic, and political inroads of the West. The tribes were "almost unanimous in their wish to be free of British control. During World War I, the German agents, who infiltrated the tribes, met with 'spectacular success in their anti-British recruitment.'" Those in central Persia harassed the British troops and joined the Turks and the Germans in their campaign against both the Russians and the British.[24]

To Britain Persia was far more important strategically and economically than Afghanistan. It lay astride the lifeline to India and, after the discovery of oil deposits, became a veritable source of wealth. There was no British statesman who valued the region more than Curzon. In a memorandum, dated December 21, 1919, he outlined his policy. He admitted that in the early stages of the war, the sympathies of the country were "unmistakably on the side of the Central Powers. Though Persia remained neutral, she lent what aid she could to enemy activity and intrigue." The situation became so acute that Britain was compelled to treat Persia as a hostile country. After the war the Shah adopted a pro-British policy. He appointed Vussug-ed-Dowleh, who was friendly to Britain, as prime minister, and Curzon considered the moment ripe to dispatch Sir Percy Cox, formerly resident in the Persian Gulf and later chief political officer in Mesopotamia, to Teheran to negotiate an agreement with the Persian government. Curzon felt that Persia was "incurably feeble" and that Britain ought to give her support until she could become an independent nation. In his magisterial style, he elucidated thus:

> If it be asked why we should undertake the task at all, and why Persia should not be left to herself and allowed to rot into picturesque decay, the answer is that her geographical position, the magnitude of our interests in the country, and the future safety of our Eastern Empire render it impossible for us now to disinterest ourselves from what is happening in Persia. Moreover, now that we are about to assume the mandate for Mesopotamia, which will make us coterminous [sic] with the western frontiers of Persia, we cannot permit the existence, [close to] the frontiers of our Indian Empire . . . of a hotbed of misrule, enemy intrigue, financial chaos, and political disorder. Further, if Persia were to be left alone, there is every reason to fear that she would be overrun by Bolshevik influences from the north. Lastly, we possess in the southern-western corner of Persia great assets in the shape of the oilfields, which are worked for the British Navy and which give us a commanding interest in that part of the world.

The desire of both the Foreign Office and the India Office was not necessarily to assume direct control over Persian administration, nor to undertake financial responsibility on a large scale; their purpose was to provide Persia with some expert assistance and advice, which "will enable the state to be rebuilt." The agreement, if satisfactorily carried out, "will be a valuable guarantee for the future peace of the Eastern World."[25]

This was the rationale of the Anglo-Persian Agreement which was announced on August 9, 1919.[26] In the first article, the British government reiterated its undertaking "to respect absolutely the independence and integrity of Persia." The other articles provided for appointment of British advisers to the Persian treasury, for reorganization of the Persian army, for assistance in the constitution of Persian railways and for a loan of two million pounds.

Curzon regarded it as the crowning achievement of his diplomacy. Though patronizing with undertones of an enlightened imperialism, on the whole it was a generous agreement, which in the prewar period would have been welcomed with much acclaim. Persia was an underdeveloped and disorganized country, which needed the guidance and assistance of a benevolent power. On the other hand, Britain would have gained a predominant influence. Times, however, had changed. The Nationalists denounced the agreement and regarded it as the thin end of a wedge to convert the country into an appendage of the British Empire. The National Legislative Assembly—the *majlis*—refused to ratify it, and Prime Minister Vossug-ed-Dowleh and the Anglophile ministers were accused of taking bribes. Consequently, Dowleh's government resigned, as did two successive Persian governments. The end result was that, much to Curzon's chagrin, the Anglo-Persian Agreement never went into effect. The Nationalists prided themselves on having frustrated it.

There was yet another serious impediment that made Curzon's "forward policy" impractical. This was pointed out by the General Staff in a memorandum submitted on June 9, 1920, to the cabinet by Churchill. It admitted clearly that "at the present moment we have absolutely no reserves whatever . . . with which to reinforce our garrisons in any part of the world." The British army was "weak everywhere" and incapable of meeting sudden exigencies. Hence, it was imperative to withdraw and concentrate the units thinly spread over the country.[27]

Maj. Gen. Sir Edmund Ironside, who commanded the North Persia Force during the period September 1920 till February 1921, disapproved of the Foreign Office policy. On December 14, 1920, he noted in his diary, "India should be defended behind her own frontiers and not in advance of them . . . It is fantastic to think of Russian armies invading India. Gradual penetration of Persia and Afghanistan, certainly, but that is another thing to an invasion of India." The mountainous frontiers of India are virtually impassable and therefore, the "forward policy" was unnecessary. Earlier he pointed out furiously, "I personally cannot see that we shall gain very much from controlling Persia . . . We do not want an extension of our military commitments but rather reduction if possible . . . The [Bolshevik] menace will grow, but it will not be a military menace."[28]

The General Staff went even further and, in November 1920, proposed a complete reversal of British policy. It advocated making

gracious concessions to the Turks, and so wean them from their alliance with the Russian Bolsheviks, by this means recreating Turkey as a buffer state between the Entente Powers and Russia, and removing some of the principal underlying causes of unrest throughout the British dominions in Egypt, Mesopotamia and India.[29]

The General Staff had put its finger on the heart of the matter. Had their advice been adopted, the course of British Middle Eastern policy would have been radically altered. Churchill advocated it time and again, and Meinertzhagen articulated it most forcefully, while the India Office adhered to it traditionally.

On November 6, 1920, Colonel Stokes, the British commissioner in Transcaucasia, residing in Tiflis, Persia, feared lest the present policy would turn the whole of Islam against Britain. He proposed to renew the friendship with Turkey, more precisely with Kemalist Turkey. "It will bring to our side whole of Islam, and it is vital to continuance of our Eastern Empire that Islam should be on our side." Stokes thought that this was perfectly feasible. He suggested that contact from Tiflis with Mustafa Kemal Pasha be established.[30] The prime minister, however, as well as Curzon, would not hear of it. For this mistake, they paid dearly in their respective careers.

Edwin Montagu, the secretary of state for India, did not have much love for Curzon. In a note, dated January 5, 1920, he accused him bluntly of being responsible for the Bolshevik menace. "The danger of the Bolsheviks to Persia and to India seems to me," he wrote, "to be so largely the fault of the Home government in their anti-Mohammedan policy that I really don't know how far we shall be able to rely upon Indian troops to assist in any fighting in Persia . . . We could have made Pan-Islamism friendly to Great Britain. We are making them hostile."[31]

This statement should be read together with that made by General Ironside quoted above, who pointed out that the Bolshevik menace was not necessarily a military one but political.

In this matter, the Soviets demonstrated greater astuteness than the British did, and by making friends in Afghanistan, Persia, and elsewhere, easily gained the upper hand. Thus, as early as January 1918 the Soviet government repudiated the 1907 Anglo-Russian Convention and renounced all Russian rights that infringed on Persian sovereignty. Moreover, it promised to expel all British and foreign troops from Persia. On June 26, 1919, the Soviets sent another note to Teheran, announcing the annulment of all Persian debts to Tsarist Russia, renunciation of all Russian concessions in Persia, and handing over to Persia all Russian properties, including banks, railroads, port installations, and other enterprises.[32] This was an expansion of the policy initiated by Prince Lvov and Alexander Kerensky, the successive prime ministers of the Russian provisional government in 1917, who were the standard-bearers of antiannexationism.

The British interpreted the Soviet move as weakness, and Curzon, in particular, hoped that an opportunity had been created to become the dominant influence using the Anglo-Persian Agreement of August 1919 as a vehicle. Events confounded Curzon's expectations. The Soviets projected an image of a benevolent and disinterested power. This, coupled with the promise to eject the British, made a strong appeal to the Oriental mind. Richard Cottam, the historian, recorded that there was a "tremendous emotional release" in Persia; there was dancing in the streets of Tabriz, and Russians joined the Persians in celebrations.[33]

The first manifestation of Soviet interest in countering that of the British was to send Karl Bravin, a veteran Russian diplomat, in January 1918 to serve as an envoy in Teheran. He handed over a message from Lenin and, soon after, embarked on anti-British propaganda. He associated himself with Persian Nationalist aspirations, participated in numerous anti-British meetings, and promised to assist our "Asian brothers in delivering themselves from the foreign yoke." In June 1919 the Soviet government sent a note appealing to the Persian people "to throw away . . . the burden of oppression and tyranny of the English and other allied colonial governments whose object is to strangle helpless Persia." G. V. Chicherin, the Soviet foreign minister, in an appeal to Persian workers and peasants, denounced the Anglo-Persian treaty of August 1919 as an "illegal and shameful" document and accused the Persian rulers of selling themselves to the "British robbers."[34]

Sir Percy Cox, the British minister in Teheran, reported that a large meeting under Bolshevik auspices took place in Ashkabat in mid-September; during the debate, "the tyranny and outrage of the British" in Persia were denounced. All Persians were asked "to combine . . . with the Bolsheviks to drive the British out and prevent defilement of holy places . . . Bolsheviks alone can bring relief to the poor; with their aid alone can Islam be free."[35] A month later, he observed rather ominously: "all Russian elements with which we are dealing here live in hope that Russia will regain her old footing in Northern Persia."[36]

The Soviet policy, however, was not bent on acquisition of new territories. This, from their perspective, would have been counterproductive and a negation of their proclaimed principles. Their overriding purpose was, if not to completely liquidate British influence, at least to neutralize it. They were obsessed by the fear that at any time Britain might initiate yet another military intervention into their country; it was imperative, therefore, for them to create a "security belt" of friendly countries on their southern borders. It was a "forward policy" of sorts in reverse, though with a difference. Unlike the British, Curzon in particular, who considered a military presence to be crucial to propping up his scheme, the Soviets resorted mainly to political means. Their propaganda fell on fertile ground in the Middle and Near East among the Nationalist elements. On the other hand, Curzon and his like-minded aides were too myopic to realize that it was the presence of British troops that provoked antagonism among the native populations.

Concerned primarily with achieving their own independence, the Persians, as well as other peoples in the Near East, viewed Bolshevik policy to be less dangerous than that of the British. Not only the ruler of Afghanistan, as mentioned above, but also the government of Persia turned now to Russia. Moshir al-Dowleh, who replaced Vossug-ed-Dowleh as prime minister, was more sensitive to Nationalist opinion than his predecessor. He told Norman, the new British minister in Teheran, that the British-Persian Treaty of August 1919 would be temporarily suspended. He also disclosed that he intended to send a delegation to Moscow in order to reach a modus vivendi and conclude a treaty of friendship with the Soviet government, provided the latter abstained from interfering in Persia's internal affairs.[37] Mushir el-Dowleh tried to explain that the dispatch of the mission to Moscow was "insistently demanded by public opinion."[38]

Eventually, the Soviet-Persian treaty was signed on February 26, 1921. Two days later, a similar treaty was concluded with Afghanistan, and another followed with Turkey on March 1, 1921.[39] They signaled a triumph of Soviet diplomacy. Particularly important were the provisions in the Soviet-Afghan and Soviet-Persian Treaties, under which the contracting parties agreed to refrain from entering into any political or military agreement with a third party, which was directed against the other. Moscow was also instrumental in achieving a successful conclusion to a treaty between Turkey and Afghanistan on March 1, 1921, which provided that the contracting parties would assist each other if attacked by another power. An identical treaty under Soviet inspiration was signed between Persia and Afghanistan on June 2, 1921.[40]

Thus, by concluding interlinking treaties among Muslim national states with herself, Moscow was successful in creating a friendly zone, which practically eliminated British political influence and removed the fear of British military aggression.

The Soviets fortified their position among their southern neighbors by encouraging commercial cooperation with the avowed purpose of making them economically more viable and of emancipating them from dependence on Western economies. Illuminating in this respect was the article by G. V. Chicherin, which appeared during the summer of 1923. Chicherin maintained that in order to support States in the East in their struggle against the imperialists, Soviet Russia should pay greater heed to the economic factor and to its social dynamics. "We must acknowledge that only an economically developed country led by a strong national bourgeoisie [!] can force foreign imperialism to retreat. A strong bourgeoisie actually means a victory over feudal tenants and over absolutism."[41]

For the Soviets, Persia was of prime importance. Konstantin Troyanovsky, in his book, *Vostok i Revolutsiya* (1918), considered it a gateway to India and "the citadel of revolution in the East." Just as Egypt and the Suez Canal serve as a key to British domination in the Orient, so is Persia for Soviet Russia. "By shifting the political center of gravity of the revolution to Persia, the entire strategic value of the Suez Canal is lost."[42] L. Levin, another writer, summed up the achievement of Soviet diplomacy thus:

> The Soviet-Persian Treaty of 1921, not only annulled all the successes achieved by England, 1917–1919, but it brought about a serious shift in the balance of power between English imperialism and Persia. After the Soviet-Persian Treaty of 1921 there could be no talk of ratifying the Anglo-Persian Treaty of 1919.[43]

Karl Radek, a leading communist ideologue, sensing that promotion of the Red Revolution, in the East in particular, was not feasible, threw overboard his dogmatism in favor of *realpolitik*. Writing in 1923, he pointed out that for the Soviet government it was unnecessary to create an "artificial" Soviet republic in Persia. "Its real interest in Persia consists in the fact that Persia should not become a base for an attack on Baku."[44] In a nutshell, Soviet policy boiled down to security. A similar policy pari passu applied to Afghanistan.

The capture of Enzeli on the Caspian coast of Persia too was motivated by security considerations. Enzeli (nowadays called Pahlavi) after the war served as a base for British and Indian forces. In 1918 Major General Dunsterville considered this base to be essential for an assault on Baku, and Commander Norris of the British navy inflicted heavy losses on the Red Naval fleet.

The Soviets for their part did not stand idle. On April 28, 1920, they advanced into the Caucasus and captured Baku, which was rich in oil deposits. They defeated the forces of the White Russian army led by Gen. Anton Denikin and consequently the White Russian ships took refuge in the port of Enzeli under British protection. The Bolsheviks were not certain whether the British would launch yet another military intervention threatening their newly won territories. They embarked, therefore, on a preemptive assault, capturing Enzeli on May 18, 1920, and took possession of the White Russian ships. They were a worthy prize.

Major General H. B. Champaign, the commander of the Northern Force, faced with a surprise attack and greatly outnumbered by the Soviet troops, realized that it would be useless to confront them. He sent an emissary to F. F. Raskolnikov, the commander of the Soviet Caspian flotilla, suggesting a compromise. The latter, however, was adamant in his demands. They were: surrender of all Denikin's ships, all the guns and large stores of ammunition, and other military matériel. Champaign had no choice but to comply. British evacuation of Enzeli took place the same night.[45] It was a humiliating capitulation and a serious blow to British prestige, which reverberated throughout the East. The Soviets, on the other hand, gained mastery of the Caspian Sea and improved their strategic position.

The Bolsheviks were astute enough to try and soothe Persia's wrath for having infringed on their sovereign territory. The local Russian diplomat invited the Persian governor of Astara and told him that his government "had no quarrel with Persians whom they regarded with friendly eyes but that British were their enemies and they intended to attack them."[46] This was a transparent maneuver to drive a wedge between the Persians and the British. Shrewdly, Raskolnikov advised General Champaign that the Soviet army had no intention of fighting the British nor the Persians; their sole aim was to defeat the White Russian troops and capture their fleet; the White Russians, he added, were provoking internal disorders in Russia.[47]

The Persian government was not mollified. They protested strongly to the Soviets at their unprovoked invasion and bombardment. They also filed a complaint with the League of Nations and appealed to the

British government. The league adopted a policy of "wait and see," whereas the British tried to wash their hands of it.[48] Andrew Bonar Law, the leader of the Conservative party, declared in the House of Commons that, under the Anglo-Persian treaty, the British government was under no obligation to defend Persia. Curzon, for his part, perforce admitted that "HMG are not in a position to augment their forces in Persia."[49]

The French Press tried to make capital out of British impotence. Thus, Auguste Gauvain, in an article in the *Journal des débats*, asserted that the Anglo-Persian Agreement of August 31, 1919, "has no way succeeded in protecting Persia against Bolshevik invasion." The *Gaulois* too, in an article titled, "Persia threatened," regretted that England had been incapable of protecting Persia against the Russian invasion, while Pertinax in the *Écho de Paris* painted the Allied position in the Near East in dark hues; the Turco-Bolshevik combine constituted a threat to British interests everywhere; the Persian Nationalists were irritated by the agreement with London, while the Amir of Kabul and his warlike tribes were getting restive. The British minister had miscalculated by assuming that they could "purchase peace . . . in raising in the Caucasus a fragile barricade of half-formed republics." Moreover,

> the precipitate evacuation of Enzeli coming after our bitter defeats in Cilicia teaches us a lesson; no more scattering of military forces, no more dispatching of troops in small bodies, no more isolated garrisons.

The *Temps*, one of the most prestigious papers in France and in Europe at large, was critical of the misguided British attempt to crush the Turkish Nationalists led by Atatürk and commented thus:

> In the East, as elsewhere, no lasting policy can only be based except on justice. In the East, as elsewhere, patriotism is the best rampart against Bolshevism. But, if we wish that the national sentiment of the Turks and the Persians should bar the way to Bolshevists, we must first of all know how to act ourselves.[50]

The ideas of Lord Chelmsford, the viceroy of India, conformed to those expressed in the *Temps*, though he elaborated them with much greater sophistication. The greatest obstacle to friendly relations with Teheran, he wrote, was "the universal misconception of the motive underlying the Anglo-Persian Agreement." Hence, he urged that it be disavowed publicly and it be made certain that the disavowal published throughout Persia. This, in his opinion, would reverse the public opinion in Persia in Britain's favor and create a proper antidote to the Bolsheviks who were posing as "deliverers of Persia and Islam, generally, from British domination." Britain, Chelmsford insisted, should endeavor to retrieve her old role of "champions of Islam against the Russian Ogre." Currently the roles were reversed, and Britain's position not only in Persia but throughout the Middle East was one of greatest difficulty in consequence. The remedy which Chelmsford advocated was to scrap the Anglo-Persian Agreement combined with "drastic readjustment of Turkish Treaty," known as the Treaty of Sèvres (1923). This would cut the ground from under Bolshevism. Currently, Chelmsford lamented, British policy in Persia "is regarded in Muslim Asia, especially in Afghanistan and in Muslim India, as another example of Britain crushing Islam, thus providing Bolshevik propaganda with arguments ready made."[51]

This was a very able exposition. On Curzon, however, it made no impression. Two days later, he commented thus:

> Considering that the Govt. of India decline to take the slightest interest in Persia, have steadily opposed the Anglo-Persian agreement from the start . . . and wash their hands of all responsibility. I regard the advice with which they so liberally regale us as an impertinence and would not pay it the compliment of a reply.[52]

Such disregard toward a respected and high-ranking official—in fact Curzon's successor as viceroy of India—was rare in British administration; it reflected badly on Curzon himself.

Curzon failed to appreciate that it was the very presence of the British troops that provoked antagonism; that imperialism, however benign, was repugnant to the people in Asia; and that the only way of regaining their confidence was to adhere genuinely to the principle of self-determination, which the Allies had so fervently advocated during the latter part of the war.

Curzon had no scruples and believed that his policy was the correct one and that the Persians were to lose the blessings emanating from the Anglo-Persian Agreement. The Persians, however, thought differently. The agreement acquired a bad name and what mattered for them was not necessarily economic benefits but national pride, i.e., to emancipate themselves from the real or assumed dependence on Britain and all that it entailed.

Norman, the British minister in Teheran, had sufficient courage to dissent from the secretary of state. The Anglo-Persian Agreement, he wrote, "will never be genuinely accepted . . . in our lifetime. . . . Persian nationalism has proved too strong for Persia to accept this willingly." The state secretary's proposals "are devoid of attractiveness. . . . We have failed because we have tried to do too much." He pointed out bluntly that in the native national spirit lies, in the long run, "our real defence against incursion of Bolshevism." He suggested that Persia be left "to work out her own salvation" and to provide her solely with assistance which she badly needed, e.g., financial and administrative advice. He went on, "Our own disappearance into the background will rob Bolshevism of her only valid excuse, and possibly remove temptation for open aggression."[53]

Such a drastic reversal of policy was not to Curzon's liking. From his perspective, it amounted to capitulation and abandonment of his cherished plan. He was, however, soon overtaken by events. On February 25, the new prime minister, Seyyid Zia ed-Din, disclosed to Norman that the Anglo-Persian Agreement must be denounced on grounds that "without such denunciation, the new government cannot get to work." This was not accidental since the new government had been supported by the Nationalist Party. Zia ed-Din added that denunciation would be accompanied by a declaration to the effect that this step implied "no hostility to Great Britain."[54] Three days later, the prime minister issued a long declaration, which could well be taken as a prelude to declaration of independence. It contained the following:

1. Denunciation of the Anglo-Persian Agreement, qualifying it by an acknowledgement of help rendered by Great Britain to Persia in the past (clause 12).
2. Freedom to seek help from any Power (clause 11).
3. Establishment of friendly relations with Russia (clause 13).[55]

As mentioned, on February 26, 1921, a Soviet-Persian Treaty was signed.[56] In spite of a polite acknowledgement for some unspecified services by Britain in the past, the new Persian government's move constituted a serious blow for Curzon and a finis for his pet scheme.

Save for a secret clause that, if Russia were to be attacked through Persia, she would have the right to send an army there, Russia respected Persian sovereignty scrupulously. With Denikin's army crushed and Britain abandoning her dream of renewed military intervention, the clause was never put into operation.

Persia was now tilting toward the Soviet Union; this, however, did not help toward solving her internal problems of disunity, maladministration, and financial woes. Seyyid Zia ed-Din was a weak leader and the Shah, though respected, was merely a figurehead. A savior appeared from unexpected quarters. It was General Ironside, mentioned previously. His impressive physique was matched by his healthy common sense. He arrived in Persia early in October and soon realized that the best solution for Persia would be a simultaneous withdrawal of both Britain and Russia and "to enable the Persians to work out their own destiny." Moreover, Professor Ullman, who draws on Ironside's diary, which he discovered, tells us that in order to counter the confused and anarchic state of Persian politics, it was essential to install a military dictatorship; a dictator would also create an army to prevent a Soviet invasion.[57] As we know, a Soviet invasion did not take place, but Reza Khan, a Persian colonel whom Ironside chose as candidate, laid the foundation for a new Persia.

Reza Khan was described by Norman as "an honest and capable officer without political ambitions."[58] He was the right man for the job. On February 12, 1921, Ironside told him that he would not oppose an attempt to take over the reigns of power provided that the Shah would not be deposed. Reza Khan promised to abide by Ironside's advice.[59]

Khan acted swiftly. He declared that his purpose in coming to Teheran was to establish strong government. He professed loyalty to the Shah but was determined to remove "the evil counselors by whom he had been surrounded . . . no foreigners had anything to fear." There was hardly any opposition to his entry into the town and his troops—the Cossacks, three thousand strong—encountered practically no resistance. The government ceased to exist. Soon afterward, some of the rich men of the town were arrested, and their money was confiscated in order to replenish the empty Persian treasury.[60]

It was a bloodless coup. Ironside, then in Baghdad on his way to the Cairo Conference convened by Churchill, was not surprised when the news of the coup reached him. He commented in his diary, "So far so good"; adding, "I fancy that all the people think that I engineered the *coup d'état*. I suppose I did, strictly speaking."[61]

Reza's second step was to dismiss all the British civilian and military officers, even those who had played a role in bringing him to power. It seems that he had no love for Britain. His accession marked the beginning of the rapid decline of British influence in Persia, a decline which reached its nadir in 1951 during Dr. Mussadiq's reign. Nor did Reza

Khan exhibit much love for the Russians. He was quite concerned about the danger posed by his Soviet neighbor in the north. He distrusted the British and feared the Soviets.[62]

Ullman compares Reza to Kemal Atatürk thus: "Reza Khan was to Persia what Kemal was to Turkey."[63] This may be so. There was, however, a world of difference between these two leaders. Kemal was a national hero who earned his fame in battlefields during World War I. In contrast, Reza had no military experience. Kemal ruled over his followers (even as a civilian) by sheer force of his personality; he was a democrat by conviction, though an autocrat when implementing Turkish national ambitions. Reza, by comparison, was a typical dictator. Kemal won Turkey's independence by a political confrontation with the British and bloody battles against the invading Greek army. To Reza, Persian independence came as manna from heaven as a consequence of interpower rivalry. Kemal essentially was European-oriented; Reza was an Easterner. Kemal was a man of vision: a leader beloved by his people—the father of modern Turkey who made a gigantic effort to transform his country—an Asiatic entity—into a secular European-ized polity. Reza was none of these. He was fortunate when rich oil deposits were discovered, which propelled Persia—renamed Iran on March 21, 1935—to prosperity. The common denominator between these two men was that they were fierce Nationalists jealous of the independence of their respective countries.

On October 28, 1923, Reza Khan took over the premiership. The Shah, unable to approve the dictatorship, left for Europe, from which he never returned (he died in 1930). In February 1925 the *majlis* (parliament) invested Reza with dictatorial powers. Thereafter (October 31), the absent Shah was deposed, and on December 13, Reza Khan was proclaimed Shah by Iran's assembly. On April 25, 1926, he was crowned with the title, Reza Shah Pahlavi (1925–41).

Afghanistan's road to independence was different. It was largely achieved by playing one power against the other. The negotiations with the British, which the government of India was so keen to conduct, could be described as a cat-and-mouse game.[64] The negotiations were strewn with endless crises, ups-and-downs, and recriminations, which only Sir Henry Dobbs, the head of the British Mission and endowed with extraordinary patience, could endure.

The arrival of F. Raskolnikov, the new Russian ambassador, in Kabul on July 6, 1920, coupled with the news about Kemalist's victories over the Greek army stiffened the Afghans' attitude and made them even more dubious about "the honesty and intentions of Britain." They were to announce to the world that their country had become independent and that they intended to establish diplomatic relations with various countries. When the British learned that Afghanistan was about to sign a treaty of commercial and consular relationship with Italy, they demurred on grounds that they still considered Afghanistan "to lie within the sphere of British political influence." This aroused the ire of the Afghanis and, on July 17 at a banquet, in presence of representatives of Russia, Kemalist Turkey and Revolutionary Bukhara gave vent to their anti-British sentiments. On August 13, Kabul announced the ratification of a treaty with Russia.

Curzon was furious and when the Afghan mission met him in London in the hope of resuming negotiations, he curtly directed them to Delhi. The Afghans asked Curzon to be introduced to the king of Great Britain, but Curzon rejected their request brusquely.[65]

Whether the Afghans deserved such an honor or not, no doubt a reception by the British monarch would have massaged their ego and perhaps would have contributed to a friendlier atmosphere.

Slighted, the mission returned to Kabul empty-handed. Negotiations reached a standstill. To break the deadlock, the Amir invited Dobbs to his residence and declared ready to break relations with the Russians against a promise of substantial aid from Britain and continuation of negotiations with the British Foreign Office, not with the India Office. London responded that the Afghan-Soviet Treaty precluded the conclusion of a treaty of friendship with Britain. Thereupon, the Amir asked Dobbs to leave.

The setback notwithstanding, a treaty with the British was signed on November 22, 1921. Dobbs, on his part, announced that the government of India was willing to grant Afghanistan some gifts and concessions as specified in the *aide-mémoire*. On December 1, 1921, however, when the Amir announced the conclusion of the treaty in the presence of the British delegation, he took pains to emphasize that the document was not "a friendship treaty, but merely one for neighbourly relations." Moreover, it was made contingent on British generosity toward Turkey and some frontier tribes. Adamec summed up, "The Anglo-Afghan Treaty of 1921 freed Afghanistan from British suzerainty and marked the beginning of a new era in the history of Afghanistan."[66]

On April 22, 1926, the Persian-Turkish-Afghan Treaty of mutual security was concluded under Russian auspices. The ruler of

Afghanistan followed the example set by Reza Shah Pahlavi and devoted his energies to rebuilding his country, abandoning all ambitions for territorial expansion.

The "forward policy" vanished forever. Curzon died in January 1924, bitter, disgruntled, and disappointed. The debacle was partly of his own making.

Notes

1. *DBFP*, Vol. XIII, Chap. III, No. 364, "Memorandum on Central Asia" by E. W. Birse, F.O., January 6, 1920, 429–32.
2. M. T. Florinsky, *World Revolution and the U.S.S.R.* (New York, 1933), 75–8.
3. V.I. Lenin, *The National Liberation Movement in the East* (Moscow, 1957), 244, 238–40.
4. On which see Richard Pipes, *The Formation of the Soviet Union: Communism and Nationalism 1917–1923*, 2nd ed. (Cambridge, MA, 1964), 225–41.
5. *DBFP*, XIII, Chap. III, No. 511, Norman (Teheran) to Curzon, July 13, 1920, very urgent, 565–6.
6. Ibid., Minute by Hardinge to Curzon, May 20, 1920, 487–8n4, 433.
7. Ibid., No. 464, "Memorandum on the Persian Question" by L.O. Oliphant, F.O., June 14, 1919, 517–9.
8. Max Beloff, *Britain's Liberal Empire 1897–1921*. Vol. 1, *Imperial Sunset* (London, 1967), passim; Elizabeth Monroe, *Britain's Moment in the Middle East 1914–1956* (London, 1963), 18.
9. *DBFP* XIII, Chap. III, No. 616, Memorandum by G.P. Churchill, December 20, 1920.
10. Harold Nicolson, *Curzon: The Last Phase 1919–1925* (London, 1934), 16–7.
11. Ibid., 7.
12. Sir Valentine Chirol, *Fifty Years of a Changing World* (London, 1927), 228.
13. Cited in Nicolson, *Curzon: The Last Phase 1919–1925*, 8n1, 9–10.
14. W.K. Fraser-Tytler, *Afghanistan. A Study of Political Developments in Central Asia* (Oxford, 1950), 133, 138, 143, 157.
15. *DBFP*, XIII, Chap. III, No. 250, Memorandum on the Future Control of the Middle East by Major H. W. Young, F.O., May 17, 1920, 260–9, 264–5.
16. Cited in Nicolson, *Curzon: The Last Phase 1919–1925*, 76–7.
17. Ludwig W. Adamec, *Afghanistan, 1919–1923. A Diplomatic History* (Berkeley, CA, 1967), 134.
18. Ibid., 72–5.
19. Ibid., 83–8, 93–7, 100–1.
20. Ibid., 104–9; On Siraj al-Akhbar see ibid., 8, 81–2, 100–3, 134.
21. Ibid., 110–5, 121–4, 129, 133.
22. Ibid., 116, 137–9.
23. Richard W. Cottam, *Nationalism in Iran* (Pittsburgh, PA, 1964), 14–5, 40–1.

24. Ibid., 58–9, 138–9.
25. *DBFP*, I, IV, 1919, No. 710, "Memorandum by Earl Curzon on the Persian Agreement," F.O., August 9, 1919, 1119–22.
26. Cmd. *(Command Papers)* 300, "Agreement between His Britannic Majesty's Government and the Persian Government" (London, 1919). Not all items of this Agreement were published.
27. Cited in Richard H. Ullman, *Anglo-Soviet Relations, 1917–1921. The Anglo-Soviet Accord*, Vol. III (Princeton, NJ, 1972), 326–7.
28. Cited ibid., pp. 327–328. Professor Ullman was the first scholar to discover the Ironside's papers.
29. *DBFP*, I, XIII, No. 181, "Note on the Military Situation," W.O., November 22, 1920, 183–9. See particularly p. 189.
30. *DBFP*, XIII, No. 171, Stokes to Curzon, November 6, 1920, Personal.
31. Cited in Ullman, *Anglo-Soviet Relations, 1917–1921*, p. 328. On Montagu see S.D. Waley, *Edwin Montagu* (London, 1964); and on his attitude to Zionism see Isaiah Friedman, *The Question of Palestine*, 22–5, 136–7, 193, 254, 257–63, 266–9, 307.
32. Ullman, *Anglo-Soviet Relations, 1917–1921*, 350.
33. Cottam, *Nationalism in Iran*, 181.
34. Harish Kapur, *Soviet Russia and Asia, 1917–1927* (Geneva, 1966), 154–7, 162–3.
35. *DBFP*, I, IV, eds. Woodward and Butler, No. 788, Cox (Teheran) to Curzon, September 22, 1919, 1174–5.
36. Ibid., No. 852, Cox to Curzon, November 21, 1919, 1241–4.
37. Ibid., I, XIII, eds. Butler and Bury (1963), No. 492, Norman to Curzon, June 26, 1920, *Most Urgent*, 546–9.
38. Ibid., No. 503, Norman to Curzon, July 7, 1920, *Urgent*, 559–60.
39. For the full texts of the treaties see Leonard Shapiro, *Soviet Treaty Series. A Collection of Bilateral Treaties, Agreements and Conventions, etc. Concluded between the Soviet Union and Foreign Powers*, Vol. I, 1917–1928 (Washington, DC, 1950), 92–5, 100–2.
40. Kapur, *Soviet Russia and Asia, 1917–1927*, 47–8; for an analysis see 182–6; A. J. Toynbee, *Survey of International Affairs, 1928* (London, 1929), 10–1.
41. Cited in Kapur, *Soviet Russia and Asia, 1917–1927*, 52.
42. Cited in Spector, *The Soviet Union and the Muslin World, 1917–1958*, 84–5.
43. Ibid., 93.
44. Ibid., 95–6.
45. *DBFP*, I, XIII, No. 434, Cox (Teheran) to Curzon, May 18, 1920, 488–9.
46. Ibid., No. 422, Cox to Curzon, May 9, 1920, 478.
47. Kapur, *Soviet Russia and Asia, 1917–1927*, 169.
48. Ibid.
49. *DBFP*, I, XIII, No. 433, Curzon to Cox, May 18, 1920, very urgent.
50. Ibid., No. 444, Earl of Derby (Paris) to Curzon, May 25, 1920, 496–8, where quotations from the French Press are reproduced.
51. Ibid., Chelmsford to Montagu, No. 662, January 22, 1921, 704–6.
52. Ibid., minute no. 7, 706.
53. Ibid., no. 624, note 3, Norman to Curzon, December 31, 1920, 675–6.
54. Ibid., no. 683, Norman to Curzon, February 25, 1921, very urgent, 731.

55. Ibid., No. 686, Norman to Curzon, February 28, 1921.
56. For the clauses of this treaty see ibid., No. 621, Norman to Curzon, December 27, 1920, 672–3, where the draft treaty is fully reproduced.
57. Ullman, *Anglo-Soviet Relations, 1917–1921*, 384.
58. *DBFP*, I, XIII, No. 29, note 1, Norman to Curzon, March 3, 1921 (not printed), 729.
59. Ullman, *Anglo-Soviet Relations, 1917–1921*, 387.
60. *DBFP*, I, XIII, No. 681, Norman to Curzon, February 21, 1921, 729–30.
61. Ullman, *Anglo-Soviet Relations, 1917–1921*, 388.
62. Ibid., 394.
63. Ibid.
64. Skillfully analyzed by Adamec, *Afghanistan, 1919–1923. A Diplomatic History*, 157–68.
65. Ibid., 162–4.
66. Ibid., 164–7.

6

Mesopotamia:
A Futile Adventure

On March 10, 1915, when the British cabinet discussed the future of Turkey-in-Asia (assuming that the Allies would emerge victorious), Lord Kitchener, the minister of war, advocated the occupation of Mesopotamia. Strategic advantages apart, he pointed to the potential agricultural and mineral resources of Mesopotamia, notably oil, and, if irrigated, the country could become again "one of the most fertile areas of the world."[1]

Kitchener was ill-informed. He had never visited Mesopotamia and was woefully ignorant of the conditions. With the exception of oil (the abundance of which was ascertained later), Mesopotamia—now Iraq—was deficient in natural wealth. Minerals and raw materials capable of contributing to industry and export were scanty. The population ekes out its livelihood from sheep and cattle herding, albeit by primitive methods. The agriculture is greatly disadvantaged by the scanty and uncertain rainfall, its frequent pests, and its damaging winds and dust. With deficient rainfall, agriculture depends on the two rivers—Tigris and Euphrates—which are both a blessing and the cause of disasters. If not harnessed by a complicated system of flood dikes and diversion of excess water to neighboring regions, the country would be under constant threat of enormous floods. These occur mostly when the spring grains are maturing. The construction of bridges, dikes, canals, and flood escapes is costly and required constant vigilance and skill. It is an illusion to assume that Mesopotamia was an ecologically favored region for agriculture.[2]

During the ancient period, Mesopotamia was one of the cradles of civilization, a veritable granary; it was a locum of the Acadian, Babylonian, and Assyrian empires. It flourished during the Islamic period, notably under rulers like Mansur and the legendary Harun al-Rashid, the builder of Baghdad, but during the days of the Abbasid Dynasty, a gradual disintegration of the empire took place followed by political feebleness and decadence. Four separate governments—Mongol, Turkoman, Ottoman, and Persian—were to exercise authority in its lifeless impoverished provinces. It was, however, the Mongol raiders, led by Hulagu, who caused the final destruction of the irrigation system (1257 CE). The second Mongol invasion, led by Timur the Lame, noted for his barbarity, crushed whatever was left of Mesopotamia's prosperity. The population was halved; living standards in town and country sank low, and trade was meager; wide areas turned into desert or camel pasture. During the Ottoman period, the government did little to improve the situation. The population remained backward, suffering from endemic diseases and neglect, accepting with helpless fatalism poverty and deprivation.

The damage inflicted on the country was cumulative, causing a complete disintegration of the rivers and creation of immense marshes. Sir William Willcocks, the eminent irrigation engineer and an adviser to the Turkish Ministry of Public Works, in his 1905 report, pointed out that the total estimated cost of the project for irrigation and agricultural work was twenty-six million pounds (equal to approximately thirty million pounds during the postwar period), giving a return of 25 percent on the cost of the whole undertaking. The cultivation of cotton by the British military administration in 1919 proved a failure. Sir George Buchanan, an eminent expert in irrigation and a leading engineer on ports, concluded despondently, that "The greater part of Mesopotamia . . . will remain the dreary wilderness that it was when the British first marched through the country." Moreover, unlike Egypt or India, in Mesopotamia, there was a population of only ten to a square mile, consisting of untamed nomadic tribes who bitterly resented the intrusion of foreigners. It was therefore "useless," Buchanan maintained, "to spend millions of pounds in irrigation schemes if there are no people to farm the land when irrigated."[3]

A.B. Buckley, in his book, *Mesopotamia as a Country for Future Development* (1919), pointed out that Mesopotamia was not a profitable venture. If £31,000,000 was spent on irrigation and three million acres were brought under cultivation, the gross revenue of Mesopotamia in fifty years' time would reach much below £10,000,000. Moreover, to achieve this objective "almost insuperable labour difficulties must first be overcome."[4]

Prime Minister Asquith was not better informed on conditions in Mesopotamia than Kitchener. He was, however, more realistic, as well as superior in common sense. On April 22, 1915, writing to Admiral Fisher, he referred to Kitchener rather dismissively thus:

> He is a man of great imagination. . . . He thinks a new country in Asia can be made as quickly as a new army in England. . . . It has taken many years to make the Punjab, [but] it is yet not self-supporting. How long will it be before Mesopotamia can give to the subjects of King George's great grandson some part of the expenditure which we have to-day will have to bear on . . . The vast army to defend it and the railway from there to Basra. [*sic*]

He added the following:

> New territories require the expenditure of more money, and even more important the expenditure of more men. We shall be short of both at the end of this War . . . Where are these to come from? . . . And if we try . . . we shall arrest progress at home . . . and we shall saddle the British taxpayer with huge liabilities.[5]

And yet, Kitchener's idea did not die, the recommendation of the de Bunsen Committee notwithstanding. The committee, it will be recalled, objected to the dismemberment of the Ottoman Empire in the aftermath of the war and opined that British interests would be better served if the Ottoman Empire remained intact, though on a federal basis. The committee's conclusion, as well as that of the Asquith-Grey school of thought, bore testimony to the nonannexationist character of British policy. "Our Empire," the committee stated, "is wide enough already and our task is to consolidate the possessions we already have."[6]

Nonetheless, for some British officers in the East, the lure of Baghdad was irresistible. Thus Lord Hardinge, the viceroy of India, writing to Austin Chamberlain, the secretary of the state for India, as early as September 1915, pointed out that the British capture of Baghdad would have a resounding effect in the East.[7] On October 6, in a private letter to Chamberlain, Lord Hardinge pressed this point again:

> From a political point of view, capture of Baghdad would create an immense impression in the Middle East, especially in Persia, Afghanistan . . . and would counteract [the] unfortunate impression created by want of success in [the] Dardanelles. It would isolate German parties in Persia. . . . While impression throughout Arabia would be striking. In India effect would be undoubtedly good.[8]

Sir Percy Cox, the chief political officer of the Indian army, seconded the viceroy. On November 23, 1914, he cabled to him, suggesting the takeover of Baghdad.[9]

He wrote as follows:

> I find it difficult to see how we can avoid taking Baghdad. We can hardly allow Turkey to retain possession and make difficulties for us at Basra; nor can we allow any other Power to take it, but once in occupation, we must remain, for we could not possibly allow the Turks to return after accepting from Arabs co-operation afforded on the understanding that the Turkish régime has disappeared for good.

This cable followed earlier attempts to persuade commanders in chief in Mesopotamia, as well as authorities in Simla (India) and Whitehall "to face the inevitable implications of a forward policy in terms of men and material."[10]

Wilson, who later deputized for Cox, testified that Cox (later Sir Cox), brought to his task as chief political officer, "a wealth of experience and exceptional qualities of mind." He had, behind him, twenty years of service in the Somaliland coast in Muscat and in Bushire and engaged the confidence of the India Office and London, as well of the viceroy. He was methodical and extremely industrious. "By temperament, he was ideally suited to face the problems that presented themselves daily." Although he read and spoke Arabic fluently, he "knew little or nothing at firsthand of Turkish Arabia."[11] This was his Achilles heel. It handicapped him in assessing the real situation in Mesopotamia, as well as the chances for the success of a military campaign in a hostile territory.

First, as the political officer, it fell upon him to examine whether the army of India was indeed fit to capture Baghdad at the time that it was almost a given that it was not capable for such an undertaking. It was prepared only for a campaign on the North-West Frontier against Afghanistan and the tribes, and maintaining internal security in India, but not for the kind of expedition required in Mesopotamia. The army was ill-equipped and not sufficiently trained. Medical services were totally inadequate and operational planning was nonexistent. Good intelligence is a must, but Cox made little attempt to organize an intelligence network, which could have supplied vital information before embarking on any military operations.

Cox seemed unaware of lack of transportation, which so seriously handicapped the Mesopotamian expedition. There was no railway system in the country, no adequate roads, and the rivers provided the only means of transportation. These, however, at times proved treacherous. The difficulty was aggravated by a shortage of boats, which at best were always exposed to sniping by the native Arab tribes. Nor did Cox consider the vagaries of the climate: the unbearable heat during the summer and unexpected torrential rains in the winter. Moreover, Mesopotamia was known as a hotbed of ravaging diseases: plague, small pox, cholera, malaria, dysentery, and typhus—always menacing in a swamp-ridden and unsanitary country. Neither Cox nor the viceroy grasped the immensity of the problems that the expedition force would have to encounter. One is forced to conclude that there was much dilettantism and wishful thinking in their suggestion to capture Baghdad.[12]

The greatest error in their thinking, however, was the expectation, bordered almost on certainty, that one could wean the Arabs away from Turkey and harness them in a war of liberation from the "Turkish yoke." Just as in the case of Syria and Palestine, this expectation proved an illusion. The Arabs of Mesopotamia, as elsewhere, would not raise their hand against the sultan-khalif and substitute domination by an infidel for a Muslim Empire. Turkish propaganda generated a dislike of the British. The latter on their part were unable to see that, far from being regarded by the native population as liberators, they were seen as unwanted intruders. Lord Hardinge erred in thinking that occupation of Baghdad by the British would create "an immense impression on the Middle East," especially throughout Arabia.[13] Quite the contrary. As shown in previous chapters, the Muslims, by and large, furiously resented the destruction of the Ottoman Empire and came to regard Britain as the chief culprit. It did not take Hardinge long to realize how mistaken he was. Perturbed by Cairo's policy, on November 28, 1915, he wrote to General Maxwell as follows:

> I fail to see why we should make any sacrifice to the Arabs . . . in view of the fact that they have been fighting against us the whole time and have no claim whatsoever upon us. I cannot tell you how strongly I feel upon this point.[14]

London urged restraint and favored a limited strategic objective viz., occupation of Basra and its environs. The objectives were defined as follows: (1) to check Turkish intrigues, (2) to encourage the Arabs to rally round the British and confirm sheiks of Muhammerah and Koweit in their allegiance, and (3) protect the oil installations at

Abadan. On October 5, 1914, the state secretary for India stated that "[t]he intention is to occupy Abadan . . . to protect the oil tanks and pipe-line . . . and show Arabs that our intention is to support them against the Turks."[15]

The expedition under General Delamain arrived from Bombay at Bahrain on October 23 and was ordered to make every effort to calm the Arab's apprehensions. On November 5, war with Turkey was declared. Basra was occupied without much difficulty after a number of skirmishes. Basra was the key to Mesopotamia, and this stage of the expedition was crowned with success.[16]

Soon after the occupation of Basra, Sir Percy Cox, the political agent, suggested that it should be announced that the occupation "would be permanent." This idea, however, was turned down by the British government on the ground that such a move would be "utterly contrary" to the agreement with the Allies, which stipulated that disposition of occupied territories should be left until the future peace conference. Lord Crewe, then secretary of state for India, agreed, though reluctantly, on advancing toward Qurna but objected to any further advance. Consequently, Qurna was captured successfully on December 9; the vali and twelve hundred soldiers were taken prisoners.

The occupation of Qurna coincided with Sir John Nixon assuming command of the Mesopotamian expedition. It signaled a landmark in the history of the operations. Henceforth, the initiative no longer emanated from London but from Nixon himself who obeyed solely the instructions of the Indian government, i.e., the viceroy. Although London urged defense and consolidation of the positions already gained, in Mesopotamia, the "desire to move forward toward Baghdad became more apparent." Concurrently, the problem of river transport became of crucial importance.[17]

On April 22, Maj. Gen. Charles Townshend arrived and took command of the Sixth Division; the total force at Nixon's disposal amounted to two divisions and one British cavalry regiment. Nixon's request to augment it by an additional cavalry regiment was rejected. On April 24, the secretary of state for India wired to the viceroy that the approach of the hot season rendered it undesirable to dispatch any more troops, especially British; the British government would not sanction any further advance. "During the summer we must confine ourselves to the defense of oil interests in Arabistan and on the Basra Vilayet. . . . Our present position is strategically a sound one, and we cannot at present afford to take risks by extending it unduly. In Mesopotamia, a safe game must be played."[18]

On May 27, Lord Crewe left the India Office and was succeeded by Austin Chamberlain who endorsed his predecessors' policy of caution. This was particularly true of Prime Minister Asquith, as well as of Sir Edward Grey, the foreign minister. Both of them were convinced antiannexationists. Asquith's note in his diary, dated March 25, 1915, is very revealing. He wrote thus:

> Grey and I . . . both think that in the real interest of our own future the best thing would be if at the end of the War we could say that we hand taken and gained nothing . . . Taking Mesopotamia, for instance, means spending millions in irrigation spending development with no immediate or early return, keeping up quite a large army in an unfamiliar country, tackling every kind of tangled administrative question worse than any we have ever had in India, with hornets nest of Arab tribes, and . . . a perpetual menace on our right flank in Kurdistan.[19]

Mesopotamia, however, at that time was not under the Foreign or the India Office jurisdiction but was within the sphere of influence of the capital of the Simla government of India. There, the viceroy, the Indian general staff, and particularly General Nixon, nourished different ambitions. Nixon's eyes were set on Baghdad.

Nixon's arrival coincided with the Turkish onslaught aiming at the recapturing of Basra. The Turkish army was composed of twelve thousand regulars and ten thousand Arab tribesmen. The battle of Shu'aiba was severe and lasted three days (April 12, 13, and 14). It ended in the complete defeat of the Turks. The British and Indian casualties amounted to 1,257 and of the Turks, double that number. The rivers were, at that time of the year, in full flood and the surrounding countryside was under water. In addition, the hot Mesopotamian weather was in full blast. Undeterred, Nixon continued to advance toward Amara, paving the way for General Townshend along the Tigris. To ensure control of the Basra province, he considered it essential that Amara be held in British hands. Concurrently, with the advance along the Euphrates, it became imperative to also occupy Nasiriyah to foil any renewed Turkish attempt to retake Basra. Nasiriyah was captured by General Gorringe on July 25; Amara was taken by General Townshend by an amphibious operation, which became known as "Townshend Regatta."[20]

General Nixon, reporting the brilliant success of operations, observed as follows:

> Seldom, if ever, have our troops been called upon to campaign in more trying heat than they have experienced this summer in the marshy plains of Mesopotamia. Many indeed succumbed to the effects of the sun when trenches had to be manned without a vestige of shade, and others were worn out by illness and restless nights . . . or disturbed by the attacks and fire of the enemy.[21]

Yet, in spite of what seemed to be insuperable difficulties, Nixon instructed Townshend to aim at a complete control of the lower portion of Mesopotamia, comprising the Basra Vilayet and to endeavor to secure the safety of the oil fields, pipeline, and refineries of the Anglo-Persian Oil Company. He added, however, that, after acquainting himself with the situation, he decided to submit "a plan for a subsequent advance on Baghdad."[22]

Whilst the overall objective was legitimate and strategically justifiable, the idea of an advance toward Baghdad had not been authorized by the British government. Lord Crewe specifically warned that "[b]oth civil and military policy should . . . be decided by the Cabinet only."[23] However, Nixon, supported by the viceroy as well as by Cox, was inclined to chart his own policy, disregarding London's instructions. His drive toward Baghdad, in the given circumstances, proved a major miscalculation and a recipe for disaster. He disregarded the fact that the forces at his disposal were woefully inadequate to meet such an ambitious undertaking, that the lines of communications would be trebled, that the means of transportation were completely inadequate, that the climate was inhospitable, and, above all, the Turkish army was still a force to be reckoned with. Surprisingly, London remained silent and did practically nothing to dampen Nixon's enthusiasm; the only explanation is that Whitehall, engaged in a titanic struggle in other theaters of war, could not pay sufficient attention to a front that was considered relatively "a sideshow" of sorts. Moreover, reports about Nixon's initial victories might have blinded British ministers to possible pitfalls.

The most vital question was that of river transportation. The waters were falling rapidly and would not rise again until the following February. Moreover, there was a desperate shortage of light-draught crafts for navigation beyond Qurna. Major General Kemball, Sir John Nixon's chief of staff, in a memorandum dated July 8, 1915, warned that, unless steps were taken in good time to meet the necessary requirements, the expeditionary army would meet "grave risks of a breakdown at possibly a serious moment; even at present, we cannot make the most effective use of the troops available owing to want of ships."[24]

Another serious drawback was the lack of adequate provision for the sick and wounded, which had become painfully apparent after the battles of Nasiriyah. There was no hospital ship on the rivers, medical staff and equipment were insufficient, and the hospitals at Basra were overcrowded. All these and a host of other problems should have made a responsible commander pause. However, as Buchanan poignantly put it, "General Nixon's temperament would not allow him to remain still, whatever the consequences." Regardless of the army's unpreparedness, he ordered an advance on Kut-al-Amara, hoping that its occupation would consolidate the military position. As events showed, however, all his calculations proved wrong.[25]

On August 23, Nixon ordered General Townshed to disperse the enemy and occupy Kut. His force consisted of 3,000 British and 8,000 Indian troops with 32 guns. Opposed to him astride the Tigris were some 6,000 Turkish soldiers and 38 guns under General Nur ud-Din Bey. In a brilliant operation, Townshed captured 1,290 Turks, killed and wounded 1,700; his own losses were 1,230 killed and wounded. Nonetheless, it was not as complete and successful a victory as previous ones; in a way, it constituted a turning point in the whole campaign. In London, the India Office doubted the wisdom of an advance toward Baghdad. Lord Kitchener, the state secretary for war too was opposed to the idea, pointing to the disadvantage of the long and imperfect line of communication.[26]

Nixon, however, held just the opposite view. He advised the government of India that in his estimate, his forces were strong enough to open the road to Baghdad, and that the capture of Baghdad was feasible, provided he had received sufficient reinforcements. He believed that he could overcome the transport difficulty. Carried away by his optimism, he even anticipated the possibility of evacuating the wounded to Baghdad. Consequently, London became infected by Nixon's optimism and, on October 23, consented to his request to march to Baghdad and that two divisions would be sent to him. However, as Buchanan prudently remarked, "No consideration seems to have been given to the almost insuperable difficulties to be encountered in conveying two divisions with equipment, stores, guns, and land transport, the five hundred miles between Basra and Baghdad. There was a considerable shortage of land transport and, although there were two thousand transport mules and many carts waiting at Basra, there was no river transport to convey them to the front."[27]

In the meantime, the Turks did not stay idle. They established themselves in a strong position at Ctesiphon with a double line of defense. Moreover, they brought in large reinforcements of which General Townshend was unaware. The fighting was severe and lasted the whole day. Encountering a superior force, Townshend had to abandon the idea of advancing on Baghdad. He was forced to fight a rearguard action all the way. With his depleted division, he retreated under heavy fire to Kut-al-Amara.[28]

A few days before the battle of Ctesiphon, the war office wired that thirty thousand troops had left Bitlis and that Von der Goltz was on his way to engage the invading army. Nixon, however, refused to credit this news. For his impetuosity and recklessness, he paid a heavy price. The troops were completely exhausted by the forty-four-mile march carried out in thirty-six hours, without sufficient food or water. Even sleep was not possible, for the cold was intense, and the Arabs were harrying the columns, pillaging and killing stragglers. For the wounded, in particular, the ordeal was supremely agonizing. Their cries and groans struck horror into their surviving comrades. Most of them had been without water, and all were chilled to the bone with the cold night breeze. It took two days to remove the casualties to the waiting steamers, on which they were "crowded, unmurmuring, like cattle." The weather was atrocious: a violent gale blew without intermission from dawn to dusk, bringing with it clouds of dust, which made adequate observation impossible. Realizing Townshend's plight, Nur-ud-Din, the Turkish commander, attacked, shelling incessantly and disorganizing the transport. Yet in spite of extraordinary difficulties, Townshend was at his best displaying courage and self-discipline.[29]

As in battle, so also during the siege of Kut-al-Amara, Townshend showed resourcefulness and fortitude. Circumstances, however, were against him. In January 1916, a relief force under General Fenton Aylmer, totaling nine thousand men, made a desperate attempt to break through and failed, suffering seven thousand casualties; three days later, heavy rain made movement in any direction impossible. The most critical problem was shortage of food and ammunition. *The Campaign in Mesopotamia, 1914–1918* testified to the "vast amount of suffering from hunger amongst the troops . . . [whose] behaviour in meeting these unfortunate conditions [was] heroic." Owing to heavy shelling by the Turks, supplies by the river had to be discounted. An attempt was made to drop food into Kut by air, but the British had neither the airplanes nor the skilled pilots necessary for success on a scale adequate for Townshend's needs. There were nineteen thousand people in town: three thousand British, eleven thousand Indians, and five thousand native Arabs. Yet in spite of dire shortage of food, Townshend decided not to expel the Arab inhabitants;[30] it would have condemned them to starvation and certain death. It was an act of supreme humanity.

The food situation grew desperate and by April 23, Townshend saw no other option but surrender on honorable terms. Gen. Percy Lake, who relieved General Nixon, concurred. Khalil Pasha, the Turkish commander, though polite, demanded unconditional surrender, adding that "General Townshend *and his soldiers* would be treated with all the honour due to them for their heroic defence." On April 29, after destroying his guns, much to the indignation of Khalil Pasha, Townshend surrendered; his force was made up of 13,309 men, British and Indians. During the siege, 1,025 had been killed or had died of wounds, 721 had died of disease, and 2,500 had been wounded. About 12,000 men in all went into captivity, of whom 4,000 died. Khalil, however, reneged on his promise to Townshend.

> The occupation of Kut by the Turks was accompanied by scenes of indiscipline, violence and savage brutality. Officers of the highest rank and men, sick and wounded, were pillaged by Turkish soldiers and Arabs under the eyes of their officers, their boots and blankets stolen, and their food seized, and resistance being met by merciless bludgeonings.[31]

The Hague Convention of 1909 (article 7) prescribes that captives of war should be treated humanely, i.e., in the same way as the soldiers who captured them. Moreover, Townshend warned Khalil Pasha that the men of his garrison were too emaciated to walk: he promised in a written reply that every care should be taken of them and that they should be transported by steamer to Baghdad and thence by carts. This promise too was not kept.

Colonel Wilson, in his book draws from *Campaign in Mesopotamia*, as well as from eyewitnesses, who were fortunate to survive the harrowing ordeal. The description is hair-raising: there was hardly any room left on the steamer and most were forced to march with their possessions on their backs. The march itself was "a nightmare. The Arab soldiers freely used sticks and whips to flog the stragglers on . . . many died by the roadside . . . some have been thrashed to death, some killed, and some robbed of their kit and left to be tortured by the Arabs." Men were dying of cholera and dysentery and often fell out of sheer weakness. Those who survived this ordeal—which involved a march of over one hundred miles in eight and a half days at the hottest time of the year—were marched through the crowded streets of Baghdad for some hours. They were denied food and water and were treated abominably. The treatment, Wilson declared,

> [c]onstitutes a record of callous brutality without parallel in civilized warfare . . . of the 2,592 British rank and file led into captivity from Kut, more than 1,700, or nearly 70 per cent, died in captivity. Of Indian rank and file about 2,500 died. . . . Turkish negligence to provide food and clothing was directly responsible for many of the deaths. In other cases, death was due to the brutality of the Arab inhabitants, who pillaged our men and habitually ill-treated them without any serious attempt by the Turks either individually or collectively to restrain them.[32]

The news about the fall of Kut-al-Amara reverberated through the East and caused considerable damage to British prestige. In England, however, the public was unaware of the full scope of the disaster at Kut-al-Amara. This was the result of excessively rigorous censorship. It was used not so much to conceal facts from the enemy as to give to the British people information that was usually tendentious or false. So long as the expeditionary army was crowned with success, censorship was lax, but after the disastrous outcome of the fighting at Ctesiphon, it became exceedingly strict clearly in order to prevent the public, both in India and the United Kingdom, of becoming aware of the appalling suffering that the troops were enduring.[33]

Censors were unprofessional officers with little or no experience. The faults of this department were pointed out by Edmund Candler, who reached Basra as the "official eye witness" on December 31, 1915. He remarked humorously that "obscurity became a tradition" and that censorship existed more as "a nursery of convenient assumptions," rather than a screen to hide secrets from the Turks.

> The most universally execrated institution in Mesopotamia was the censorship. . . . It was impossible to communicate with outside world . . . this fussy, meddling supervision, this constant fear of anything discreditable leaking out, did not increase one's confidence in the Higher Command.[34]

Candler was furious. He saw men at Amara unfed, untended, some in a dying state, their field dressings unchanged, filth too revolting to describe. He cabled to India and to England appealing for medical assistance. To his chagrin, however, the telegram was suppressed by the censor at Basra. The government in India, as well as the General Staff in Mesopotamia retained an ostrich mentality. Nevertheless, gruesome news percolated gradually to the public in England and provoked a storm of indignation and resentment. "We want to fix responsibility upon some one", protested MP. Gerald Lambert in the parliament.[35]

This was one of the tasks that devolved on a special commission appointed by an Act of Parliament in August 1916[36] under the chairmanship of Lord George F. Hamilton. Other members were the Earl of Donoughmore, Lord Hugh Cecil, MP; Sir Archibald Williamson, MP; John Hodge; Commander Josiah C. Wedgwood, MP; Admiral Sir Cyprian George Bridge; and Sir Neville G. Lyttelton. Their purpose was to enquire into the origin, inception, and conduct of operations of the war in Mesopotamia. They interviewed a large number of officers of all ranks and other witnesses in England, India, and Mesopotamia and examined the physical and climate peculiarities in the theatre of operations.

The commission was quick to observe that the Indian army, led by British officers, was totally unprepared for their assignment. It was grossly underequipped for modern warfare, not at all fit to confront the Turkish army, which had been equipped by superior German mechanical equipment. Moreover, no consideration was made of the treacherous climate and the alternation of sweltering heat and bitter cold, which requires a continuous supply of such articles as warm clothing, on the one hand, and sun helmets, mosquito nets, and other tropical prophylactics, which were indispensable, if the health and moral of the troops were to be maintained at a reasonably high standard.

Every general, who appeared as a witness, maintained that the Mesopotamian expedition was badly equipped. Heavy artillery so essential to support an attack across an open territory, as well as to crack fortified trenches, was "not only deficient in numbers but out of date in quality." Moreover, one of the most glaring defects was the want of airplanes, which seriously hindered the troops in their performance during the crucial battle at Ctesiphon. The main difficulties that the expedition encountered were connected with transport. Efficiency of the forces was absolutely dependent on supply of river craft, but before the advance from Qurna to Amara, neither the Indian authorities nor the military made inquiries as to the sufficiency of the transport. General Nixon, in particular, took the matter rather lightly, grossly underestimating the requirements. He demonstrated an insufficient grasp of the transport situation and embarked, in 1915, on a major operation with totally inadequate transport facilities and equipment. His responsibility, the commission concluded, was "a grave one."

They went on as follows:

> Looking at the facts which from the first must have been apparent to any administrator, military or civilian, who gave a few minutes' consideration to the map and to the conditions in Mesopotamia, the want of foresight and provision for the most fundamental needs of the expedition reflects discredit upon the organising aptitude of all the authorities concerned. (p. 113)

"The evidence shows convincingly," the commissioners observed that "shortage of river transport was the chief cause of the failure to relieve Kut." (p. 43) The history of the attempt to relieve Kut makes melancholy reading. The heavy flooding made all movements most difficult, and the troops, at times, could not even use their rifles, which were clogged with mud. As a result, the fighting efficiency of the force was seriously affected and all hope of relieving Kut had to be abandoned. General Lake summarized three main causes of failure: premature attacks, inadequate transport, and exceptionally unfavorable weather.

The members of the commission censured the government of India severely as follows:

> It was in a position to know the facts . . . [but] failed lamentably in anticipation of needs and ready helpfulness. We consider that responsibility for the shortage of river transportation rests mainly with the Government of India, in its various Departments. For their failure in this matter, which was the foundation of all the troubles in Mesopotamia, no censure could, in the circumstances, be too grave. (p. 49)

This was a very harsh verdict. "With Gen. Sir John Nixon in particular rests the responsibility for recommending the advance in 1915 with insufficient transport and equipment. . . . there was no imperative need to advance without preparation. For what ensued . . . General Sir John Nixon must be held to blame." (p. 61)

The transport situation could have been greatly alleviated had a railway from Basra to Nasiriyah been built as had been strongly recommended by General Bartlett in February 1915. The proposal was dealt with seriously by the government of India and finally vetoed on grounds that it could not justify the expenditure involved. In April 1916, however, under the pressure of the war office, the Indian government finally awoke to the necessity of building a railway. Ironically, the cost of all the railways in Mesopotamia proved to be less than the construction of river crafts. A railway system could have altered the course of the war in Mesopotamia and saved the lives of many wounded in the battle. Absence of speedy transport facilities delayed evacuation and increased the suffering of the wounded. The medical equipment was below the standard and the medical personnel were barely sufficient.

The commission also pointed to the lack of coordination between the India Office in London and the Indian government and to the absence of any professional intelligence service. The latter was within the purview of Sir Percy Cox, who surprisingly escaped criticism.

On matter of strategy, the commission had this to say:

> The advance to Baghdad under the conditions existing in October 1915, was an offensive movement based upon political and military miscalculations and attempted with tired and insufficient forces, and inadequate preparations. It resulted in a surrender of more than a division of our finest fighting troops and the casualties incurred in the ineffective attempts to relieve Kut amounted to some 23,000 men. (p. 111)

There was a string of errors of judgment, which caused the failure of the Mesopotamian campaign:

> The weightiest share of responsibility lies with Sir John Nixon, whose confident optimism was the main cause of the decision to advance. The other persons responsible were: in India, the Viceroy (Lord Hardinge), and the Commander-in-Chief (Sir Beauchamp Duff); in England, the Military Secretary of the India Office (Sir Edmund Barrow) and the Secretary of State for India (Mr. Austin Chamberlain).

Sir George Buchanan, former chairman and chief engineer of the Rangoon Port Trust (later general), recalled that there were no maps or other reliable data on which to formulate a plan of campaign.

Nonetheless, the lure of Baghdad was irresistible even at the early stage of the war. General Nixon's temperament, however, would not allow him to remain still, whatever the consequences.[37]

General Townshend recorded in his memoirs as follows:

> It was evident that Sir John Nixon intended me to make a dash for Baghdad with my present inadequate force, and it seemed to me that it was useless to try and argue with him any longer.[38]

And with a glimmer of irony, Buchanan remarked thus:

> I marvelled at the audacity of the authorities response for advancing so far as Kut-al-Amara, whilst to proceed further, or to ever dream of reaching Baghdad seemed to invite the awful disaster that followed.[39]

Gen. Edmund Candler, the official "eye witness" in Mesopotamia, was even more scathing in his criticism. He pointed to a struggle in which "blunder piled upon blunder, making it evident to the troops that sacrifice was in vain." Politically, he insisted, Kut was "a national disaster" and the chief blame was that of General Nixon. The tragedy of Mesopotamia hinged upon the decision to advance from Kut-al-Amara and beyond.

> If we were out for the big thing and were going to supplant the Turks in the city of the Caliphs and impress the East, we should have started with an army of at least 40,000 men and built a railway behind them. . . . Baghdad, without a railway, was an impossible ideal.[40]

In consequence, Mesopotamia became "a grave of reputations."[41] The notable exception was General Townshend. He had all the resourcefulness and personal magnetism that is so essential in the commander of a beleaguered garrison. He was, in Candler's words, "the chief fountain of optimism. He was always on his rounds, visiting the sick, chatting with the men, and inspiring confidence and cheerfulness everywhere. He was a born commander in a siege." The Arabs believed Townshend "invincible", whereas the Turks admitted that nothing short of starvation had defeated his garrison. At all events, Townshend's personality deeply impressed the Turks. Khalil Bey, the Turkish commander, spoke of him with most profound admiration and permitted him to retain his sword. Townshend's arrival in the Bosporus was "almost triumphal; he became the lion of the place." Khalil was evidently anxious that Townshend receive "every comfort and attention after the privations he had endured so gallantly."[42]

It will be recalled that toward the end of September 1914, when it became evident that Turkey would become a hostile belligerent, Sir Edmund Barrow, the military secretary of the India Office, London, strongly advocated a policy to encourage the Arabs to rally to the British. Soon after, General Delamain issued instructions to reassure the local Arabs of British support against Turkey.[43]

On December 9, a new proclamation was issued explaining the desire of the British government to be on friendly terms with the Arabs, and stating that the wish of the British government was "to free the Arabs from the oppression of the Turk and bring them advancement and increase of prosperity and trade." Unfortunately, Buchanan commented, "Many of the Arabs considered these proclamations as a sign of weakness, and so far from responding to our advances they showed intense hostility throughout the campaign."[44]

Like the British in Cairo, so also those in Basra and Delhi labored under the assumption that the Arabs desired nothing better than liberation from the assumed Turkish oppression and that, once freed, the Arabs would be beholden to the British for their liberation, as well as for the economic benefit bestowed upon them. This basic assumption, however, proved false. Unlike those in Palestine and Syria, who remained generally quiescent, those in Mesopotamia were demonstratively hostile.

A minor incident, albeit a trivial one, indicated clearly where the sympathies of the local population lay. The fighting at Shu'aba ended in the complete defeat of the Turks, but the people of Basra had confidently anticipated a British defeat. They even went so far as to prepare a celebration and an address to welcome Sulaiman Al-Askari, the Turkish commander.[45] Still worse, on May 7, during the onslaught on Amara, the expeditionary force encountered an "intense hostile Arab tribe"; their continuous snipping was quite disturbing. The Bani Lam tribe in particular was "the most hostile . . . and as savage and cruel as treacherous." General Brookings condemned their treachery and the way they killed and mutilated any of the British or Indian soldiers. The town of Hai and the district were notorious, being the headquarters of tribes who had consistently massacred the wounded and plundered the dead; "so it was not to be wondered that when the cavalry division retired they were set upon by the tribes in force."[46]

The civil administration in the occupied territories, from its inception, registered "bitter experience of Arab hostility, Arab thefts, and Arab rapacity." It did not take long for Arnold Wilson to reach the conclusion that "a policy of whole-hearted cooperation between British and Arab elements in Mesopotamia was . . . impossible. The reason was crystal clear. The Arabs of Mesopotamia . . . had always regarded themselves as part of the Turkish Empire and had never desired anything more than some form of autonomy under the Sultan." The Arab leaders remained loyal to the Turks. This sentiment was dominant among the tribes and a call to *jihad,* backed by a strong Turkish force, "met with some measure of success." Even among those tribes who were formerly at loggerheads with the Turkish government, like Bani Tar, the call of *jihad* fell on "favorable soil" and they rose in support of the Turks. On March 2, 1916, General Robinson encountered a newly arrived Turkish force aided by "greatly superior number of Arabs." During the retreat to Kut, the main assailants were the Arabs, who "harried the columns, pillaging and killing stragglers in the darkness and harrying the field ambulances when they got a chance." No wonder that

> the Army staff and regimental officers alike, could scarcely be blamed for regarding Arabs collectively, as incorrigible thieves, and murderers, faithless and mercenary. Again and again they found the wounded slaughtered, the dead dug up for the sake of their clothes and left to the jackals; the word treachery was always on their lips, and not without reason.[47]

Surgeon-General MacNeece, in a letter to Sir Percy Lake, the chief of the General Staff (November 4, 1916), described the terrible conditions in which the sick and wounded were transported down the river from Ctesiphon and complained bitterly that the steamers and barges were stopped by Arabs and had to go back three times.[48] The Mesopotamia Commission, describing the unfavorable conditions under which the troops had to operate, emphasized that were surrounded by "a hostile and marauding population."[49]

Lawrence thought that until the end of the war, the British in Mesopotamia remained substantially "an alien force invading enemy territory, with local people passively neutral or silently against them."[50]

This was an understatement. Much harsher was Kandler's judgment.

> These Tigris Arabs [he wrote] are a lower type than the Bedouin. They have no virtue. No germ of decency has begun to sprout in them.

> They are frankly plunderers, and murder is merely the preliminary to pillage. They kill their prey before they strip it. A battlefield is haunted by them for days. They leave the dead stark. . . . The Arab is out for loot, and follows no cause.[51]

The village of Khafajiyeh was a stronghold of the Beni Taruf Arabs, a truculent tribe, who had been operating with the Turks and who had mutilated the British and the Indians, wounded and dead. Even the Arab regular in the Turkish army "is the same unregenerate Arab under the leash. One could witness how the bodies were brought over and had been stripped. Corpses were carried over their shoulders like sacks of coal or bushes of hat. They dumped them on the ground . . . [and thereafter] shot through the head or the heart." Having witnessed such brutality, Candler was frank to admit, "We have no love for the Tigris Arabs, who have none of the decencies which are supposed to leaven the iniquity of primitive man." Per force, Candler juxtaposed the Arab to the Turk. "The Turkish officers," he observed, "looked warm and comfortable, and . . . they were most damnable polite. They have good manners."[52]

The Bakhtiaris, on the border of Persia, "are [a] fluctuating political element but their sympathies were undoubtedly German." When Salr-i-Masud, their chief, was asked why he had supported the Kaiser, he explained that before the World War he had visited a number of capitals in Europe and returned with the impression that the Germans were "the most warlike nation. In Berlin," he said, "every other man you met was a soldier, whereas in London you hardly ever saw a uniform in the streets." His conclusion was that ". . . a people to whom the soldiers are an object of curiosity cannot be a military force." Moreover, Candler observed, among the tribesmen there existed a prevalent notion that the Germans were "the true champions of Islam"[53]—and this made all the difference.

Lt. Col. (later Sir) Arnold Wilson too was bitter against the Arabs. During the early part of 1916, he wrote, Arab propensities for brutal murder and theft had "a disproportionate influence on the campaign." Long lines of communications were seriously menaced by hostile hordes. Shortage of transport, lack of mobile cavalry, and, above all, lack of good cavalry leadership handicapped the expeditionary force in brushing "aside these ghostly evils." Even punitive actions have had no more than a transient effect. "The tribal Arabs lacked neither leaders nor fresh recruits. . . . The motive of pillage was all-sufficient."

During the retreat to Kut on the first and second of December 1916, the Turks had been outdistanced; the only assailants were the Arabs, who harried the columns, pillaging and killing stragglers in the darkness and harrying the field ambulances when they got the chance. Later on, when the offensive was renewed under General Maude, Arab menace was responsible for immobilizing a whole brigade. They raided and looted at night, and stole horses, arms, and ammunition generally untouched.[54]

Very little, if anything, was reported about Arab antagonism. So just like in other matters, also with regard to this issue, London was uninformed. Greatly dissatisfied, Gen. Sir William Robertson, the chief of the Imperial General Staff, recommended on February 3 that the control of operations in Mesopotamia should in future be vested in the war office, in exactly the same manner as in other theatres of war. It was endorsed by the war committee and by the government of India. The decision marked an epoch in the history of the campaign in Mesopotamia and was welcomed with relief by all concerned. Henceforth, the expedition could draw on the resources of the British Empire. Lt. Gen Sir Stanley Maude, who replaced General Lake, won the affection of all ranks, British and Indian, and the spirit which animated him permeated the staff and brought new determination to the rank and file to proceed vigorously in the campaign. The force was augmented by new units from Egypt and France among whom a remarkable esprit de corps and camaraderie developed between soldiers in the British and Indian ranks. The morale of the troops was high and by the autumn of 1916 the army in Mesopotamia was ready for resumption of the offensive. General Robertson instructed that the mission of the Mesopotamia force was to protect the oil fields and pipelines and, if possible, to establish British influence in the Baghdad Vilayet, but "at present no fresh advance to Baghdad can be contemplated."[55]

Events, however, took a more favorable turn than had been expected. The rain did not fall and the attacking force was not hampered, as in every battle of 1916, by mud. Moreover, unlike Maude's force, the Turkish army was badly equipped and ill-fed. Reinforcements from Persia and elsewhere failed to arrive and, according to estimate, Maude's force was four times that of the Turks in numbers. On February 24, as a result of General Maude's operation, the Turks were retreating toward Baghdad. Maude's natural instinct as a soldier was to make the most of this victory and to pursue his opponents even to Baghdad.

He called London and asked for new instructions. General Robertson responded on March 3 thus:

> Telegrams received from you show that the defeat of the Turks is more complete than I had reason to suppose. In consequence the feasibility of occupying Baghdad at once is probably greater than I had supposed. I hope therefore that you understand that my telegram of February 28th left matters to your own judgement.[56]

Khalil Pasha, the Turkish commander was in desperate straits. He had failed to hold back Maude's advancing force. He retired at night, and on March 11, a portion of Maude's army entered Baghdad. The advance within two months, a distance of two hundred miles, to organize and direct three separate forces operating in different directions was a masterly achievement.

The battle casualties amounted to eighteen thousand, out of a total fighting force of about forty-five thousand, or 40 percent. It was a high price to pay for the victory, however brilliant.[57]

Before leaving, the Turks had been requisitioning private merchandise and destroyed much material of military use. The Arabs too had not been idle; they were busily engaged in pillage. This, Maude would not tolerate and speedily restored order; in his own words, "The city was rather in a turmoil. Kurds and Arabs began looting everywhere, and although we got into the city by about 6:00 a.m., there was time for them to do a considerable amount of damage. Still we soon reduced them to order."[58]

A few days later, Sir Mark Sykes sent General Maude a text of a proclamation to the people of the Baghdad Vilayet. It read inter alia thus:

> Since the days of Hulagu your city and your lands have been subject to the tyranny of strangers, your palaces fallen into ruins, your gardens have sunk in desolation. . . . Your sons have been carried off to wars not of your seeking, your wealth has been stripped from you by unjust men and squandered in distant places.

The proclamation dwelt on "a close bond of interest for two hundred years" between the merchants of Baghdad and Great Britain who traded together in mutual profit and friendship.

> It is the hope of the British Government that the aspirations of your philosophers and writers shall be realised, and that once again the

149

people of Baghdad shall flourish, enjoying their wealth and substance with their sacred lands and their racial ideals.

Finally, the people of Baghdad were invited to participate in the management of their own civil affairs in collaboration with the political representatives of Great Britain.[59]

The proclamation was published on March 19 in English and Arabic and was simultaneously broadcast in all neutral and eastern countries, emphasizing the historic character of the event. In Baghdad, however, and, to an even greater extent in Mesopotamia, the proclamation "fell flat": it was critically studied, and the conclusion that had been almost unanimously reached that it was "politics," and that it had been drafted in London by "a romantically-minded traveler." In some quarters it was openly derided. Nowhere did it generate enthusiasm. In short, the proclamation "failed altogether to convince. The general belief was that the Central Powers would win the war, or that at worst, it would be a drawn game."[60]

Obviously Sykes was misinformed. Had he been made aware of the true attitude of the Arab inhabitants toward British occupation, the document which he authored would have been cast in more realistic terms.

Well meant as the Sykes Proclamation was, it was based on false premises. It was unrealistic to expect that such a heterogeneous population, torn by sectarian and religious divisions, would be able to unite and develop a system of self-government in collaboration with an occupying power. The Turks, as Miss Gertrude Bell, in her classic *Review*, had pointed out, deliberately deepened the cleavage within the inhabitants of Mesopotamia. To maintain their shaky authority, they were playing upon the hereditary enmities of the great tribal groups and upon the personal rivalry that existed between individual members of the ruling houses. The tribes, in any case, for generations, had resented any governmental authority. The vilayet of Baghdad had for years presented "a comprehensive picture of lawlessness."[61] The dominant factor, however, was, as Wilson astutely pointed out, "Most of the leading men within the walls of Baghdad had pro-Turkish leanings." On the Euphrates, west of Baghdad, the turbulent Zoba' openly mocked General Maude's proclamation, as did the Dulaim, under the stout-hearted chief Ali Sulaiman. A large portion of the tribes remained on the side of the Turks, till well into the following year.[62]

Lord Curzon was in a triumphant mood when declaring to the House of Lords in November 1917 that "[b]y a single stroke, or series of strokes, General Maude may be said to have altered the history of the world." He added thus:

> It is surely inconceivable that the inhabitants of those fair regions can ever be thrust back into the servitude from which he and his forces succeeded in emancipating them.[63]

This was wishful thinking. Curzon, like other British officials, was indulging in the belief that the Arabs would cooperate with the British in the struggle for their liberation from Turkish misrule. All the documentary evidence adduced in this and the following chapter shows the contrary.

General Robertson was equally under a misapprehension when instructing Maude that the moment was opportune "to exploit our Arab policy and to foster a general movement to embarrass the Turks. The Arab movement," he continued, "has been of distinct military advantage in the past and it is unsound not to continue to encourage it."[64] Maude, in consultation with Sir Percy Cox, tried indeed to enlist the Arab tribes under the British banner, but the experiment failed abysmally. According to the *Official History* of the campaign in Mesopotamia, "They were quite unreliable, and though they might fight for us one day, they were likely to take up arms against us the next. They had, moreover, little or no fighting value."[65]

Notes

1. Friedman, *The Question of Palestine*, 16.
2. Stephen H. Longrigg and Frank Stoaks, *Iraq* (London, 1958), 29–33.
3. Sir George Buchanan, *The Tragedy of Mesopotamia* (London, 1938), 244–52.
4. Cited in *The Times*, London, August 16, 1920.
5. Friedman, *The Question of Palestine*, 18–9.
6. Ibid., 19–21.
7. Brigadier General F.J. Moberley, *History of the Great War Based on Official Documents. The Campaign in Mesopotamia, 1914–1915*, 4 vols. (HMSO 1923–1927), Vol. II, 3–4.
8. Ibid., Vol. I, 15–6.
9. Ibid., Vol. I, 134. There is a biography by Philip Graves, *The Life of Sir Percy Cox* (London, 1941).
10. Lt. Col. Sir Arnold T. Wilson, *Loyalties. Mesopotamia 1914–1917* (Oxford, 1930), 55–66.
11. Ibid., 65.

12. *Mesopotamia Commission Report* (London, 1917), 81.
13. Above, p. 113.
14. Friedman, *Palestine: A Twice Promised Land?*, 28–9.
15. *Mesopotamia Commission Report*, 12, 19.
16. Ibid., 12.
17. Ibid., 15–6.
18. Ibid., 18.
19. Herbert Asquith, Earl of Oxford, *Memories and Reflections, 1852–1927* (London, 1928), Vol. II, 60.
20. Buchanan, *The Tragedy of Mesopotamia*, 15–9; *Mesopotamia Commission Report*, 18; Wilson, *Loyalties*, 46–9, 50–1, 60–1.
21. Buchanan, *The Tragedy of Mesopotamia*, 19; also Wilson, *Loyalties*, 57.
22. Wilson, *Loyalties*, 38.
23. Ibid., 51.
24. Buchanan, *The Tragedy of Mesopotamia*, 20–1; *Mesopotamia Commission Report*, 19.
25. Buchanan, *The Tragedy of Mesopotamia*, 21–2; *Mesopotamia Commission Report*, 19.
26. Wilson, *Loyalties*, 81–3.
27. Buchanan, *The Tragedy of Mesopotamia*, 27–8.
28. Ibid., 28–9.
29. Wilson, *Loyalties*, 85–9.
30. Ibid., 95–6, 109–12. On the fall of Kut, see also Edmund Candler, *The Long Road to Baghdad* (London, 1919), Vol. I, 211–29, and Townshend, *My Campaign in Mesopotamia*, 116–358.
31. Wilson, *Loyalties*, 97–100.
32. Wilson, *Loyalties*, 129–41; also Candler, *The Long Road to Baghdad*, 229–30.
33. Wilson, *Loyalties*, 165–6.
34. Candler, *The Long Road to Baghdad*, 65–6.
35. *House of Commons*, Debates, March 14, 1916.
36. See note 12. What follows is based on this report. It contains 119 pages.
37. Buchanan, *The Tragedy of Mesopotamia*, 8–9, 26–7.
38. General Sir Charles Townshend, V.F., *My Campaign in Mesopotamia* (London, 1920), 197.
39. Buchanan, *The Tragedy of Mesopotamia*, 62. On January 18, 1916 Nixon retired, a sick man at heart, as in body (Ibid., 69).
40. Candler, *The Long Road to Baghdad*, viii, 4–7, 128.
41. Ibid., 162, 212.
42. Ibid., 212–5, 219. On Townshend's treatment by the Turkish government see Chapter 13, 15–8, 22).
43. *Mesopotamia Commission Report*, 12, 13.
44. Buchanan, *The Tragedy of Mesopotamia*, 9–10.
45. Ibid., 11.
46. Ibid., 14, 77–8, 81–2, 106, 152.
47. Wilson, *Loyalties*, 10–2, 16–7, 19, 23, 28–9, 52, 54, 89.
48. Cited in *Mesopotamia Commission Report*, 85.
49. Ibid., 115.
50. Lawrence, *Seven Pillars of Wisdom*, 59–60.

51. Candler, *The Long Road to Baghdad*, 106–7.
52. Ibid., 104–6, 167, 243.
53. Ibid., 248, 251.
54. Wilson, *Loyalties*, 89, 206–7, 214.
55. Ibid., 114, 206–8.
56. Ibid., 217, 225; Buchanan, *The Tragedy of Mesopotamia*, 148, 158–9.
57. Buchanan, *The Tragedy of Mesopotamia*, 165–9; Wilson, *Loyalties*, 226–35.
58. C. E. Calwell, *Life of Sir Stanley Maude* (London, 1920), 275.
59. Reproduced in full in Wilson, *Loyalties*, 237–8; Buchanan, *The Tragedy of Mesopotamia*, 169–72.
60. Wilson, *Loyalties*, 239, 260.
61. Cmd. 1061, *Review of Civil Administration of Mesopotamia* by Miss G. L. Bell, C. B. E. (London, 1920), 20.
62. Wilson, *Loyalties*, 255–8.
63. Ibid., 228.
64. Wilson, *Loyalties*, 260.
65. F. J. Moberley, Brig-General, *Official History of the War. Mesopotamian Campaign*, cited in Wilson, *Loyalties*, 261.

7

Rejection of British Presence in Mesopotamia

The conquest of Baghdad on March 11, 1917, was a remarkable achievement. Full credit for it should go to Gen. Sir Stanley Maude,[1] who had an extraordinary gift for organization and had built the army into an effective fighting machine. His self-confidence was infectious due to his personal magnetism and the admiration of his troops. He was "a gallant gentleman and a soldier in the best sense of the word. He was the heart and the brain of the machine. . . . He was a Commander whose character and genius had changed the whole aspect of the campaign." His untimely death on November 18, 1917, from illness, was a great loss to the Expeditionary Force.[2]

Maude, as well as his successor Lt. Gen. Sir William Marshall, proved to be good administrators. In the course of the years, the British accomplished more than what the Turkish officials had done in a century. Baghdad was changed unrecognizably. The main thoroughfare was macadamized and lighted. A police force was organized. The water supply was extended. Electric lighting was introduced into offices and billets. Mosques were repaired and schools opened; the markets became controlled, while prices moderated; two new bridges crossed the Tigris. These were only some of the visible changes that took place.[3]

In Parliament, words of praise were heaped lavishly. In his address to the House of Commons on July 23, 1918, Lord Robert Cecil, the undersecretary for foreign affairs, pointed to the "very satisfactory progress [that was] being made in redeeming the country from the state of ruin into which it had fallen under the Turk. . . . The opinion is frequently expressed that the British people mean well by the Arab race." Similarly, Lord Curzon, the acting secretary of state for foreign affairs, speaking in the House of Lords on February 20, 1919, paid tribute to the work accomplished by the British in Mesopotamia. "The population is free and happy. Justice is administered, life and property are secure. There are no shadows in this picture."[4]

This description was overly optimistic. While it is true that the Arab population in Mesopotamia benefited from the British presence, Edmund Candler astutely remarked thus:

> It must not be supposed that [the Arab] welcomed us with open arms. The Asiatic as a rule dislikes an alien tutelage, no matter what gifts it may bring; and the reality as well as the name of independence is becoming more important to his peace of soul. To the Christian population in Mesopotamia the British occupation was undoubtedly a godsend, but we must discount a great deal of the smug nonsense that has been written about the Arab eagerly waiting for the British to deliver him from the yoke of the Turk. He cares for neither of us; both are intruders. It is true that the Turk as a member of the dominant race was an unpleasant person to deal with, but the Arab often got even with him. We on the other hand are admittedly efficient and men of good faith. But the Arab does not appreciate these gifts so much as he would if he were a European; in all the simple contracts of life the Asiatic will feel more at home with the Asiatic.[5]

The depth of the antagonism toward non-Muslims transpires from a letter from Ibn Saud, the sheikh of Najd, to Lt. Gen. Aylmer Haldane, commander of the expeditionary force in Mesopotamia in 1920. Ibn Saud wrote among other things, "Never forget that the feelings which animate them are expressed in saying, 'He who even dips his pen in an inkstand on behalf of a Christian, that man becomes a Kafir.'" He warned that the tribes in Mesopotamia are unruly and antithesis to law-abiding citizens. It is "an uncontrovertible fact that it will be impossible to manage the people of that country except by strong measures and military force."[6]

Subsequently, from his personal experience, General Haldane concluded that "[t]he Arabs of Iraq respect nothing but force, and to force only will they bend." However, when beaten, they would accept the situation, "bow to superior force, and bury the hatchet till a good a chance comes of paying off the score." Once subdued, the Arabs may display their "princely hospitality," but in essence, they "are distinguished by the treachery."[7] Elsewhere, Haldane wrote that the vast majority of the tribes of the interior of the country, including the Marsh Arabs or dwellers in the swamps of the Tigris and Euphrates, are "generally regarded as quite untrustworthy."[8] This did not bode well for the British to build a durable administration. In *sum* it could be said, military achievements notwithstanding (Mosul was captured on November 7, 1918), politically the British conquest of Mesopotamia was merely a Pyrrhic victory.

In December 1918, Miss Gertrude Bell wrote gleefully to her father that "[i]n Mesopotamia they want us and no one else."[9] This assessment, however, bordered on wishful thinking.

Sir Perry Cox, the civil commissioner, was more circumspect in his evaluation. In his memorandum, dated April 22, 1918, he wrote, "As regards the elements who do count, e.g., the Jews and other denominational communities [particularly the Christians] in the large towns, they could without doubt be squared in some form to give expression to the sentiments that we desire." Hence, the elements that should be encouraged are: first, the Jewish community in Baghdad; in this connection, he recommended that Dr. Chaim Weizmann, then in Palestine, be induced to pay a visit to Baghdad to fortify the pro-British leanings of the Jewish community. The other element worthy of encouragement was the Arab notables, merchants, and wealthy landlords. On the other hand, the rural population of Iraq "as a whole is quite inarticulate and can hardly be consulted." The intelligent inhabitants are reticent; they are apprehensive that at the Peace Conference, Mesopotamia would be restored to the Turks, who would take punitive measures against any pro-British sympathizer.[10]

That Cox did single out the Jews as the most reliable element on whom the British could count is not surprising. They were the wealthiest element in Baghdad and constituted more than a third of the population. By inclination and in order to insure their security, they were loyal to the suzerain of the country and now looked upon the British as trustworthy protectors. With regard to Arab intelligentsia, however, Cox was in error. Arnold Wilson, his deputy, predicted with remarkable prescience that "[t]he Arab public at large would after a few years actively favor the return of the Turks."[11] This tallies with David Hogart's prognostication made a year earlier. Visiting Syria in 1918, after the armistice, he concluded despondently that, contrary to the view presented in the European press, the Syrian Arabs did not consider at all their "liberation" from the Turks as a "boon"; they regarded it merely as a means to achieve their independence. If they failed to achieve it, "they would rather have the Turk back and will scheme to get him."[12] This was equally true of the Arabs in Mesopotamia, who shared the aspirations of their Syrian compatriots. In April 1920, Nuri Said frankly admitted that soon after the armistice, Turkish propaganda, taking advantage of the "vexed conditions arising from the unpopular military administration, succeeded by accusations against the British in . . . alienating [Arab] sympathies and ranging them once more on their side. In some places it attained such dimensions as to give the impression that there was a strong responsible party in the Arab countries of reinstating the Turk."[13]

It is not surprising, therefore, that in this climate of opinion the Anglo-French Declaration of November 8, 1918, struck no chord among the Arab population in Syria and Mesopotamia; in fact, it had the opposite effect to what was intended.

As mentioned, the idea of the declaration was conceived in the fertile mind of Sir Mark Sykes. His purpose was to clear the Allied Powers of the annexationist taint, which had taken hold of the Arab populations following the revelation, albeit in a distorted form, by the Bolsheviks of the Sykes-Picot Agreement. The purpose of the Anglo-French Declaration of November 8, 1918, was to liberalize the Sykes-Picot Agreement and make the French acceptable to the Arabs. For this kind of policy, Sykes found Picot a willing partner. The chief concern of the French was to proceed in tandem with the British in order to secure for France a status of parity in the occupied territories. The declaration was also intended to win the goodwill of President Wilson, who was known to be a Turcophile and a strong opponent of the secret agreements with regard to the Asiatic Turkish provinces in particular.[14]

Both Britain and France intended to act as tutors and educate the Arabs in the art of self-government while simultaneously safeguarding their legitimate strategic interests. The Arabs, however, took it to mean, jointly with other declarations made during the war, a pledge of independence. They read into the Anglo-French Declaration what they wanted to read. The word "independence" is not to be found in it; nor does *Istiqlal*, its Arabic equivalent, appear in the Arabic text. The authors of the declaration studiously avoided using this term. At no time did the Allied Powers commit themselves to granting the Arabs unconditional independence.[15] As shown in our previous study, in their Turkey-in-Asia Agreement of May 1916 (commonly known as the Sykes-Picot Agreement), it was stated that Britain, France, and Russia, and later also Italy, were "prepared to uphold and protect an independent Arab State or Confederation of Arab states . . . provided that the cooperation of the Arabs is secured." From all the contemporary statements it is evident that the Inter-Allied Agreement of May 1916 and all that it entailed was contingent upon the Arabs doing their part in the struggle for their own liberation. Failing that, as Sir Arthur Nicolson, the then Permanent undersecretary for foreign affairs, made crystal clear, "all the proposals fall to the ground."[16] As we know, during the war, the Arabs did not rebel either in Syria or in Mesopotamia. Quite to the contrary, they fought shoulder to shoulder with the Turkish soldiers against the British. And yet, it was this false belief that the British had reneged on this promise of "Arab independence" given successively during the McMahon-Hussein Correspondence, in the declaration to the Seven Syrian notables in Cairo, and in the Anglo-French Declaration that fuelled Arab resentment and made them eventually turn their arms against Britain as well as against France. But the overriding reason for the deep antagonism was the objection to the presence, more precisely, to the rule, however benign, by the infidel powers over the Muslim. This, in essence, was the driving force of the nascent Arab nationalism.

Soon after the armistice, Arab Nationalists joined the Pan-Islamic Movement that was directed against Britain and the entente as a whole. This movement originated in Turkey and bore a distinct revanchist character. The avowed objective of a newly founded association, called *Mouvahidin*, was to liberate the occupied territories from the Christian powers and restore Muslim sovereignty. Shaykh al-Islam, a leading cleric in Turkey, founded a network of communities throughout the Arab provinces of the Ottoman Empire and propagated similar ideas demanding national autonomy for Syria and Mesopotamia under Ottoman suzerainty. The clerics of Karbala, a holy city in Mesopotamia, went even further. They issued a secret *fatwa* declaring that anyone who desired anything but a Mohammedan government was an unbeliever.[17]

In Mesopotamia, the effect of the Anglo-French Declaration was disastrous. J. de V. Loder, close observer of the events in the Near and Middle East, affirmed that the declaration gave an unprecedented impetus to Arab nationalism and played into the hands of agitators who wished to get rid of foreign control. "In countries with little sense of political and social unity [such] as the Arab provinces in Turkey . . . , self-determination carried to its logical conclusion is little more than a synonym for lawlessness."[18] This was particularly true of Mesopotamia, which was driven by religious and ethnic divisions. It is worth observing that until the armistice, de V. Loder served in the Political Department of the Egyptian Expeditionary Force and subsequently worked for about two years in the Eastern Department of the Foreign

Office. He was, therefore, well qualified to assess Middle Eastern complexities.

Gertrude Bell, the Oriental Secretary to the Civil Commission in Mesopotamia, was also disturbed. Before the armistice, she wrote officially in her *Review*, the people of Mesopotamia "had accepted the fact of British occupation and were resigned to the prospect of British administration. They were satisfied with the progress in their standard of living" and "[t]hroughout the country there was a conviction that the British meant well for the Arabs coupled with an appreciation of material prosperity which had followed in the train of our armies." The Anglo-French Declaration, taken together with President Wilson's Fourteen Points, declared to the US Senate on January 8, 1918, put the population in a quandary. It provoked uncertainty and had a destabilizing affect. The former officials employed by the Turkish Government returned to the country and "formed a nucleus of discontent and hostility".[19]

Miss Bell described the events in great detail. In her memorandum, entitled, "Self-Determination in Mesopotamia" (February 1919), she concluded thus:

> Given the short period of time, it would have been difficult to arouse more sound and fury, not to speak of heartburning and intrigue, that have been created in Baghdad by the declaration. . . . There can be no question that sooner or later a Nationalist Party with inflated ambitions must have sprung to life; as a result of recent processes it has come sooner to birth.[20]

Sir George Buchanan was greatly dismayed. He pointed out that in the wake of the declaration, "the country, and especially Baghdad and Mosul, soon became hotbeds of political intrigue, with the extremists and Mesopotamian officers in Syria clamouring for complete and immediate independence."[21]

Sir Arnold Wilson thought that a declaration of this nature was superfluous; its promulgation was "a disastrous error." He warned the secretary of state for India that it would involve the British Government in considerable difficulties and that setting up an indigenous government "will be the negation of orderly progress"; it would involve the local British administration in "diplomatic insincerities." Moreover, he pointed out, the "tribal element is a constant potential source of dissention and [an element of] grave public insecurity." Nor one should ignore the mutual contempt and jealousy that existed between townsmen and tribesmen that militated against the idea of independence. Wilson recommended that Mesopotamia be declared a British Protectorate, under which "all races and classes will be given forth with the maximum possible degree of liberty and self-rule that is compatible with the good and safe Government." Self-determination, he emphasized, should be "a continuous process; and not a precipitate choice between uncertain courses half understood."[22]

Edwin Montagu, the state secretary for India, responded (November 30) that the purpose of the British Government was to assist in the establishment of the native government in the liberated area.[23] Montagu was liberal-minded and did not see eye to eye with Wilson's idea. Wilson found more comfort in the press, *The Times* in particular, as well as in the French journals, in parliamentary debates. The general impression indicated that the French in Syria and the British in Iraq intended to create effective protectorates and that the Anglo-French Declaration "was not intended to be taken seriously."[24] However, the Arab Nationalists in Mesopotamia took it very seriously. The clash between them and Allied Powers, both in Syria and Mesopotamia, was inevitable.

In April 1919 Wilson went to London. He had a comprehensive discussion with Balfour, Lloyd George, and Lord Curzon on the situation in Mesopotamia. He was granted an audience with King George and appeared before the Eastern Committee, where he unfolded his proposal. First, he ruled out the option of an Arab Emir and advocated the appointment of a British High Commissioner instead. The person most qualified was Sir Percy Cox, then in Persia. Under the high commissioner, there should be four governors over the vilayet of Basra, the vilayet of Baghdad, the Euphrates districts, including the towns of Najaf and Karbala, and the vilayet of Mosul. Dair al-Zor should be included in Mesopotamia. The country should be united into one unity and run by the British officials. Arab officials selected on merit and character should assist in administration of the provinces. In conclusion, Wilson admitted, however, that the problem confronting Britain in the Oriental world

> is in a large measure insoluble. Political discontent, always with us, will increase, the Arab Nationalists will return to Baghdad and will grudge if they be not satisfied. These difficulties are inherent in the otherwise favourable position which our army has won for us in the East.[25]

Wilson was fully aware of the prevailing mood and that it would hardly be possible for the British to stem the tide of nationalism. In April 1919, he drafted a note on the treatment of Turkey that coincided entirely with the views held by Winston Churchill, the minister of war. Wilson wrote as follows:

> Muslims all over the world, including Mesopotamia . . . will join with the Turks and Kurds in actively resenting the dismemberment of . . . the Turkish Empire and its partition by a Christian Peace Conference on selfish lines.

He went on,

> We cannot do now what we might have done three months ago. In the East as in the West there is a new spirit in men's minds. The Turkish Empire cannot be destroyed: it is the embodiment of the Muslim ideal of temporal rule on earth of Muslim rulers. . . . The only solution I can now see is the recognition of the Turkish Empire from Constantinople to the Caucasus. . . . This will commit us to support Turkey—and to this extent will be satisfactory to our Muslim clients.[26]

Like Churchill, Wilson was also speaking in the wilderness.

A few days later, on March 25, a debate of great importance took place in the House of Commons. It was initiated by Herbert Asquith, the former prime minister. Supported by Sir Charles Townshend, Asquith urged that the British Government confine its obligations to the zone of Basra. Lloyd George, however, totally dissented from this advice. To abandon Mosul—a country that contains some of the richest natural resources of any country in the world, immensely rich in oil deposits—would be impolitic. Should Britain withdraw from Mesopotamia, some other country would fill the void.

> After enormous expenditure which we have incurred in freeing this country from the withering despotism of the Turk, to hand it back to anarchy and confusion, and to take no responsibility for its development would be an act of folly and quite indefensible. . . . We should be responsible as the mandatory . . . for advising, for assisting, but that Government must be Arab. . . . We will respect the solemn undertaking which we gave to the Allies in November 1918 . . . [The Arabs] absolutely agree that they do not want Turkish rule again.[27]

Lloyd George was under a misapprehension in thinking that the Arabs did not wish to see the Turks ruling over them again. He also underestimated the enormous expenditure required to administer and develop a country like Mesopotamia at the time when Britain in the postwar period was in severe financial straits. Nor were any steps taken to put into effect for the policy that the prime minister had been advocating in Parliament.

Unlike the members of Parliament, Wilson was aware of the inherent difficulties. Although the great majority of the population had accepted the occupation, there were various sectors that were not content. These included some of the most important religious authorities; a small but active section of political agitators, mostly centered in Baghdad; all the pro-Turk elements; and a small Syrian party. "It would be difficult, therefore, for people of moderate views to resist the pressure which extremists would exert upon them, pointing out that in accepting tutelage by a Christian Power, they are betraying their faith and their race. The extremists have on their side all the strength of an appeal to emotion and to religious prejudice."[28]

Wilson was better informed than the politicians at Whitehall and his assessment of the mood among the people of Mesopotamia was more realistic. In December 1918 his friend, the Reverend J. Van Ess, of the American Presbyterian Mission at Basra, told him that mainstream public opinion had turned against the British; "some favoured the return of the Turk."[29] Several months later (November 15, 1919), Wilson confirmed that "the prestige of the Turkish Government was still strong" and that "[t]he Arab public at large would after a few years actively favour the return of the Turks [who] still retained the respect of devout Muslims."[30] This was the case in Mosul, where the majority of the population was Kurds and Turks, not Arabs. The geographical proximity to Anatolia made them naturally turn toward Turkey rather than to Baghdad. Ismet Pasha, Atatürk's aide, made this point when arguing vis-à-vis the British that

> [t]he inhabitants of the vilayet of Mosul demand that they may be restored to Turkey, for they know that in that event they will cease to be a colonized people and become citizens of an independent state.[31]

Both the Christian and the Jewish communities in Mosul, Baghdad, and Basra before the war were loyal Ottoman subjects but, soon after the armistice, submitted numerous petitions asking for British protection; they viewed with "alarm" the prospect of the creation of an autonomous Arab Government. The archbishop of the Syrian Catholics, supported by prominent members of his congregation, priests, and notables, submitted a petition declaring their submission to the British Government and requesting that "no Arab Government should rule over us." The Armenians and some of the Kurds did the same.[32]

The Ottoman Government treated its Jewish and Christian subjects (the Armenians excepted) benevolently and granted them special constitutional privileges. These, they feared, would be forfeited under an Arab administration and a retrogressive regime would take over. In addition, Arab nationalism was tinged with strong Islamic undertones, in which case the Sháriya law would be discriminatory and reduce non-Muslims to the status of second-class citizens. This would be an irreparable blow to Jews and Christians who, both socially and culturally, were superior to their Muslim counterparts. On the other hand, under British administration, they would feel more secure and their prospects for commercial prosperity much brighter.

Wilson affirmed that the non-Muslims were less than sympathetic toward the Nationalists, an opinion that was confirmed later by the political officer in Mosul.[33]

Rumors that installation of an Arab Government was imminent produced a state of panic among religious minorities.[34] These rumors emanated from Damascus, the seat of Iraqi Sharifian officers, who aspired to achieve the "complete independence" of Mesopotamia without foreign interference. British Intelligence became aware of their activities, commenting that they were "sowing the seed of future trouble by exciting a number of unattainable ambitions."[35]

During the following month, the British intercepted some "agitating" letters from Sharifian agents to certain Nationalists in Mesopotamia.[36] Intoxicated by the capture of Damascus, the Iraqi, like other officers in the Sharifian army, seized power and were, in Miss Bell's words, "in a fierce pursuit of an exaggerated political ideal for the attainment of which . . . they were prepared to set the Syrian province in a blaze." Their unabated ambitions defied realism and stood in inverse ratio to their ability to govern. Their leader and chief of staff of the new Arab army was Yasin al-Hashimi. He impressed Miss Bell as "the most forcible personality" she had ever met and became one of the most extreme exponents of Arab independence. On the eve of the arrival of the King-Crane Commission of Inquiry, he circulated a letter to the tribal chiefs of Mesopotamia, asking them to demand "complete independence as one nation, with the assistance [as opposed to a

Protectorate] of a single Power." The political officer in Baghdad sounded an ominous note thus:

> The Arab movement is becoming steadily more anti-foreign and more anti-British. It shows, however, no sign of being constructive, nor does it promise to develop on peaceful lines.[37]

General Haldane affirmed that from April/May 1919, propaganda directed from Syria was poisoning the minds of the inhabitants of Iraq, especially those in the Lower Euphrates tribes.[38] "The Mesopotamians in Faisal's Army," wrote Miss Bell in her *Review of the Civil Administration of Mesopotamia*, "were at the root of the national agitation." Nationalism apart, they also had a vested interest in freeing Mesopotamia from British control. The Syrians claimed the important posts for themselves and the Iraqis, as "foreigners" felt themselves to be marginalized. With their prospects in Syria diminishing, "A Mesopotamia, free from British control seemed alone to offer them hope of office."[39]

Returning from London, Wilson made a stopover in Damascus where he met an Iraqi delegation composed of Yasin al-Hashimi, Nuri al-Said, and Naji al-Suwaidi who raised the issue of the political future of Mesopotamia. What he did hear from them did not surprise him, since as early as February 1919, he had complained about "Sharifian" interference in Iraqi affairs.[40] Gertrude Bell was present and made some critical observations. According to Bell, Wilson dismissed their demands for independence "brutally," telling them that it was "all moonshine"; they should satisfy themselves with running municipal councils instead. This infuriated the delegates and from that day onwards

> Yasin, being the violent, active creature that he was, urged on the Mesopotamian League, of which he was the leading spirit, to intensify anti-British propaganda. . . . And it was because he [Wilson] outraged nationalist feeling, underestimated the strength of it and wholly misunderstood it that A. T. Wilson stands convicted of one of the greatest errors of policy we have committed in Asia.[41]

This was an unprecedented affront against her superior. Unmoved, Wilson enclosed Bell's note and commented in a dispatch to the Foreign Office. His experience led him to the conviction that the assumption that an Arab state in Mesopotamia within a foreseeable future was feasible was erroneous. "I am aware," he added, "that in holding this view I differ from authorities and observers at home and abroad."[42]

In May, Faisal asked Lawrence to facilitate the repatriation of the Iraqi officers in Syria to Mesopotamia. Lawrence recommended this move and wrote to Foreign Office, "They are officers who served us very well and are mostly pro-British. . . . I need hardly say that they all expect and want a British mandate in Mesopotamia."[43]

This was a blatant distortion of truth. The India Office strongly protested Lawrence's unwarranted interference, pointing out that on their return to Mesopotamia, Iraqi officers would pursue their propaganda campaign zealously. Moreover, the India Office asked that the British authorities in Cairo be instructed that no person in the Sharifian service of Iraqi origin should be permitted to proceed to Mesopotamia without prior concurrence of the Civil Commission in Baghdad.[44] Curzon eventually agreed with the request of the India Office.[45] Wilson was unequivocal in his observation:

> Individuals like Jafaar Pasha, Maulud, Nouri Said and others have written to their friends and relatives in Baghdad . . . they are coming to Baghdad before long to prosecute a political campaign in favour of an Arab Government . . . they have already sent a number of representatives who are conducting active secret propaganda on these lines, but with strong anti-foreign bias . . . recommend . . . to inform them and others of the same colour that they cannot be permitted at present to return to this country.[46]

Wilson favored a British-administered Mesopotamia assisted by native Arab officials of merit and experience. Sir Arthur Hirtzel, head of the Political Department of the India Office, was of the same opinion.[47] However, by July, he changed his views drastically. He told Wilson as follows:

> As regards Arab nationalism I think you will soon find yourself in pretty deep waters and, to be frank, I do not think you are going the right way to work with it . . . you appear to be trying impossibly to turn the tide instead of guiding it. . . . You are going to have an Arab state whether you like it or not, whether Mesopotamia wants it or not. . . . There is no getting out of it, and it is much wiser to face the fact. . . . Otherwise we shall have another Egypt on our hands. All these things are going to be contrary to our most cherished hopes, and nothing that you or I can say or do will alter them . . . the idea of Mesopotamia as the model of an efficiently administered British dependency or protectorate is dead. . . . We must adapt ourselves

to the new order of ideas and find a different way of getting what we want.[48]

Wilson was not convinced and some time later responded thus:

[T]he creation of an Arab Government on the lines advocated by Yasin . . . and Naji . . . [is] inconsistent with . . . effective control of any sort. For some years to come the appointment of Arab . . . officials except of an advisory capacity would involve the rapid decay of authority, law and order . . ."[49]

The position, however, was even more serious than the British had imagined. On June 16, 1919, Emir Feisal concluded a formal agreement with Mustafa Kemal according to which Arabia would be attached to Turkey on a federal basis. Arabia would be comprised of Syria, Palestine, Mesopotamia, and the Hedjaz; military alliance would be concluded, and a holy war (*jihad*) would be declared against the foreign powers.[50]

The results were not long in coming. In the same month, Sir William Tyrrell, assistant undersecretary of State, cautioned Sir Reginald Wingate about the rise of anti-British and antiforeign feelings among the Muslim population of Syria and Mesopotamia.[51] Curzon complained about the effect of Feisal's propaganda in Mesopotamia; it was causing "considerable apprehension" both in London and in Baghdad. He asked Clayton to instruct all responsible British officers "to discourage the movement by all means in their power."[52] Feisal urged the sheikhs of the Tai and Shammar tribes not to accept the rule of the British, who were Christians; they should help the Sharifian Government, which aimed at Arab independence, instead.[53] G.K. Kidston, at the Foreign Office, observed correctly that Feisal was advocating independence and was spreading propaganda in this sense in Mesopotamia.[54] Captain C.D. Brunton of the General Intelligence Staff disputed the belief that Feisal was a friend of the British. The aim of the Arab national movement, he asserted, was to free Syria, Palestine, and Mesopotamia from foreign control and "the establishment of Arab states under nominal Turkish suzerainty." Brunton's assessment was shared by Major Camp, as well as by Captains Peak and Kirbride.[55]

The majority of Sharifian officers were members of the *al-Ahd* society. During the Ottoman period, the *al-Ahd* was a miniscule and marginal political body. During British occupation, it grew in membership and in motivation. Cells were established in Baghdad, Mosul, and elsewhere. British Intelligence was able to uncover the names of the prominent members. The list, quoted below, gives us a general idea of the social composition:

Dr. Daud Chalubi, a medical doctor, presumably the head of the *al-Ahd* committee in Mosul.

Amin al-Umari, first employed by the British army, he later resigned and became a liaison officer between the Sharifians and the Kemalists.

Aziz Arab, a young merchant, accused of sedition and arrested by the British administration.

Aziz Ismail al-Umari, young teacher, propagandist and suspected of spying on Britain agents.

Mulla Muhammad Arab, the Imam of the Nabi Jarjis Mosque. Believed to be extremely fanatical and extremely anti-British.

Mustapha b. Haji Hussein Agha, a lawyer and a head of a local society in Mosul.

Mustapha Ahmed al-Umari, a law student at Baghdad, extreme Nationalist, and the Baghdad correspondent of *al-Ahd*.

Said b. Haji Thabit, merchant, escaped from arrest.[56]

Even from this selected sample, it is possible to see that *al-Ahd* had made substantial inroads into the middle-class section of the population. The political officer in Mosul ascertained that Sharifian propaganda found "considerable adherence" also among the city magnates and landowners, as well as intellectuals who "did not, as a rule, feel the hardships of Turkish administration." Hence, "Leaning toward Turkey," he predicted, "is to be expected."[57] In October 1919 Major J. N. Clayton, the political officer in Damascus, predicted that the leaders of the Baghdad party, as well as other extreme Nationalists, might be tempted to declare a *Jihad* against the foreign Powers, which "will inevitably lead to rapprochement with the Turks and with Mustafa Kemal."[58]

Clayton was unaware that the rapprochement had, in fact, taken place and was formally enshrined in the treaty between Emir Feisal and Mustafa Kemal. The idea of rapprochement had originated with Yasin al-Hashimi and was seconded by Ja'afar al-Askari.[59] Yasin was the undisputed leader of *al-Ahd*. Gertrude Bell, in her memorandum, "Syria in 1919", quoted previously, asserted that Yasin was its "moving spirit." His followers were working for "Arab independence without foreign control." Some of his moderate adherents were not in full accord with his policy, but Bell was doubtful whether they would carry much weight. The extremists, on the other hand, were convinced that "[u]nder a British mandate no attempt will be made to set up responsible government." Bell added that "[g]rave discontent exists among all classes in the Iraq."

The British Intelligence described Yasin as being "capable, a good soldier, intelligent, ambitious, fanatical supporter of complete independence, and potentially dangerous."[60] Gravely concerned, Wilson reported to the India Office that Yasin, as well as Naji Suwaidi, were actively working for the establishment of an Arab government on "pro-Turkish lines."[61] Earlier, the headquarters in Cairo suggested to the War Office that it was "desirable, for political reasons, to get Yasin Pasha . . . out of Syria."[62] Overconfident, Yasin overplayed his hand and, as a result of his contacts with the Kemalists and his subversive anti-British activities in Mesopotamia, was arrested by General Allenby on November 22, 1919, and exiled to Palestine. Here he was kept under house arrest and could not return to Syria until May 1920.[63]

It was also Yasin al-Hashimi who conceived the idea of capturing Dair al-Zor. The political officer at Dair had no doubt that Yasin and his followers "not only counteracted but also encouraged it."[64] On January 14, 1922, Feisal, then king of Iraq, confirmed it during an interview with Miss Bell.[65]

During the Ottoman period, the town Dair al-Zor was the headquarters of a Sanjak lying between the vilayets of Aleppo and Baghdad and was administered directly from Constantinople. It was situated on the Euphrates River some four hundred miles from Baghdad. On the date of the armistice, the frontier between Syria and Mesopotamia had not been defined. This was the cause of friction between the Sharifian Iraqi officers in Damascus and British administrative officers of Mesopotamia.

Toward the end of November 1918, the inhabitants of Dair al-Zor requested the British to dispatch a unit to preserve law and order. Wilson was not enthusiastic, while General Marshall declined to extend his sphere of military protection. However, as it was dangerous to leave a "no man's land" between Mesopotamia and Syria so close to Turkey, with London's approval, an officer was sent, assisted by a couple of armored cars and a handful of Arab levies. The Arab Government in Damascus protested, claiming that the region was part of Syria. The British, however, regarded the move as a temporary measure pending the decision of the Peace Conference.[66]

On his arrival in Dair, the British officer, Captain Chamier, found that the governor of Aleppo, Ja'afar al-Askari, had already appointed an Arab governor who was administrating the town. His name was Ramadan al-Shallash, head of the local tribe, who had a reputation of being an "irresponsible firebrand." His mission was to raise his own tribe and capture Dair al-Zor, while the Sharifian government, "disclaiming all responsibility, but hoping to profit by his action, would be ready to express regret that they possessed no power to control him." The scheme was carried out smoothly, and Dair al-Zor was captured on December 13, 1919.[67] It was not a glorious victory.

Soon after the takeover, the tribesmen raided the hospital, the church, and private homes. The inhabitants were in a state of panic. An armored car was damaged, and Captain Chamier was requested to leave, while other British personnel were held as hostages "for the safety of the town." Ramadan launched a vicious anti-British propaganda campaign. Feisal, at the time attending the Peace Conference in Paris, sent a cable to Zeid, his brother, who was deputizing for him at Damascus, repudiating Ramadan's actions and ordering him to withdraw from Dair. On December 21, two emissaries of Ja'afar Pasha, then military governor of Aleppo, arrived in Dair with instructions to release British prisoners and to offer reassurance that the Christian population on the town would not be harmed. In mid-, Ramadan left for Aleppo and was replaced by Mawlud Mukhlis.[68]

Like his predecessor, Mawlud Mukhlis was a Mesopotamian (he hailed from Mosul); he had previously been in command of a division and was a prominent member of the *Ahd al-Iraq*. Ostensibly, his appointment was meant to mollify the British, but in fact, he was no less of an extremist. He was actively engaged in hostile anti-British propaganda, which was of a "fanatical character." His letters inciting to *jihad* addressed to the sheikhs of the tribes reached as far as Karbala and Najaf. Moreover, he demanded that the British cede territory far beyond Dair, which should be placed under the jurisdiction of the Damascus Government.[69] Wilson described the events vividly as follows:

> Seizure of Dair-ez-Zor was the first step in [the] campaign of penetration from Syria to Mesopotamia. Occupation of Albu Kamal . . . is the second step . . . for last week our troops have daily been in action against well-organized raids. Occupation of Ana is the third step, and if made effectively by Arab Government, would imperil our position at Mosul. There are indications that in near future we may be faced with a recrudescence of fanatical Arab activity.[70]

Wilson complained that Mawlud, "far from adopting a different attitude [than Ramadan], is also actively inciting tribes throughout Mesopotamia to active revolt and rebellion. His letters have reached as far as Amara."[71] Mawlud warned Wilson that, unless the British retreated, his tribes would be unrestrained. On February 11, General Haldane informed the War Office that Mawlud was "still threatening."[72]

In his drive, Mawlud was assisted, if not inspired, by the Iraqi officers in the Sharifian Government and has at his disposal considerable sums of money in order to win over the local sheiks. Wilson learned that, contrary to Ja'afar's promise, Ramadan Shalash had never been arrested. Quite the contrary, he returned, "styling himself as leader of Arab party with the connivance, if not with the active assistance of Mawlud Pasha at Dair-ez-Zor, who is Feisal's own nominee."[73] Several weeks later, Wilson added as follows:

> There is a continual flow of money and propaganda employing the name of Abdullah, as well as that of Feisal and the Syrian State, from Dair-ez-Zor into this country, and it is not too difficult to see where this can come from . . . if not from Damascus Government or officers of that Government.[74]

Wilson was confident that, should the funds flowing from Syria be stopped, external hostile propaganda would be much emasculated.[75]

Feisal, on his return to Damascus, kept apologizing, while his foreign minister assured the British authorities in Cairo that the Syrian Government "has no connection" with the affairs at Dair al-Zor, and he emphasized that Emir Feisal is taking pains to quiet the Arabs at all occasions.[76]

Neither the War Office nor Young at the Foreign Office could give credence to the claim that Feisal was implicated in the assault at Dair.[77] Wilson, however, was quick to point out that

> the sending of a succession of extremists to Dair al-Zor in an official capacity from Ahd el-Iraq is in itself sufficient proof of their lack of desire to help.[78]

Wilson insisted that Feisal be asked to remove the Mesopotamian Nationalists, his de facto representatives at Dair, since in his opinion, "a virtual state of war" existed between the Sharifian forces and those of the British Government in Mesopotamia.

Although it sounded alarmist, Wilson's assessment was essentially correct. For this kind of war, however, the British were ill-equipped.

The military forces were in a state of demobilization. Dair was too far from Baghdad to wage a successful counteroperation to subdue a budding insurgency. Moreover, a raison d'être for launching such an operation was wanting since at the Peace Conference, at that time, it had been decided that Dair al-Zor be included in the Syrian State.

Nonetheless, both Wilson and Haldane thought that submission to force was a bad policy. However, their request to use the air force, the only weapon available, was flatly rejected.

> The India and Foreign Office deprecate the bombing of Dair-ez-Zor and Jazáiri-Ibn-Omar on political grounds. The Air Ministry has also been consulted and is of the opinion that for technical reasons it is out of the question to bomb Dair-ez-Zor effectively.[79]

The War Office did not clarify the nature of "political grounds" that precluded the option of bombing Dair. We can only surmise. Feisal had been officially recognized as an ally, and it was, therefore, inappropriate to resort to force in a region that had been designated for his jurisdiction. If this was the reasoning, it was based on mistaken premises. First, as shown in our study, Feisal was not a reliable ally and hardly deserved to be treated so leniently. Second, submission to violence dented British prestige and established a dangerous precedent.

Inaction inadvertently invites repeated violence. What mattered was how the episode was seen by the Arabs. General Haldane pointed out that if it was possible to "expel the British at their pleasure, how much more easily could the more warlike inhabitants of the Lower Euphrates achieve the same results." A few months later, the loss of some vessels on that river, coupled by the defeat of a detachment of British soldiers elsewhere, served as grit to Arab propaganda among credulous tribesmen that the British fleet and army had been routed. It had a "disastrous" effect on those Arabs who remained friendly toward the British. Fahad Bey ibn Madhal, the chief of the Amarat section of the Anizah tribe, prophetically remarked in February 1920 thus:

> If you do not reoccupy Dair-ez-Zor, you will have a rebellion on the Lower Euphrates within six months.

Haldane commented that, after the reoccupation, Dair could have been handed back to Feisal, but the main thing was "to show our power . . . and our determination not to accept with misplaced Christian weakness the insult offered to us."[80]

Unlike Curzon, Montagu, the state secretary for India, was soft on Mesopotamia. To mollify the Nationalists, he proposed to introduce some constitutional changes—creation of the institution of the President of Council and a Council of State, to be followed by the constitution of a Legislative Assembly.[81] Wilson, who had been briefed about the proposal earlier, responded unequivocally as follows:

> An announcement of the Constitution that we propose for [Mesopotamia] is unlikely to have any appreciable effect on this agitation; population led by extremists whose cry is complete independence, exclusive of any sort of foreign influence . . . [have the upper hand.] Further concession in constitutional direction will not affect this issue.[82]

Wilson was in full accord with Winston Churchill's opinion expressed in his speech in Parliament on February 23, 1919. Churchill declared thus:

> Mesopotamia is disturbed by the excitements of the Arabs due to the situation in Syria and by the increasing movement and power of the Turkish Nationalist forces in Asia Minor, and by Bolshevik advances in the North.
>
> No further relief can be looked for till a real peace can be made with Turkey. We have lost ground steadily throughout the year . . . because our resources are not equal to the discharge.[83]

Churchill's views had no appreciable effect on formulation of policy. The decision was in the hands of Lloyd George, the prime minister. He was anti-Turkish and favored a British mandate over Mesopotamia, i.e., Britain should not govern it as a colony; "the government should be Arab" but advised and assisted by British officials until the country became fit for independence.[84] Whether this formula satisfied Iraqi Nationalists is another matter.

Feisal's objective was to achieve independence by peaceful means. In a cable to his father, dated February 24, 1920 (intercepted by British intelligence), he wrote, "Unity and independence are the objects of all of us." But since the Anglo-French Declaration made no reference to the "covenant" made by McMahon with yourself, we must oppose these Allies if we wish to obtain our objective "soon." It would oblige the Arab nation to rely on her own financial resources, as well as in procurement of armaments. This task, Feisal admitted, "at present is very difficult. My political plan is the same as Yours, but peaceful."[85]

Needless to say the so-called covenant did not exist. It was a product of Hussein's imagination in a letter to Sir Reginald Wingate on August 28, 1918[86] that remained unanswered. The Arabs were not slow to take advantage of Wingate's negligence to blame the Allies, Britain in particular, of reneging on the promises to the Arabs to grant them independence. The claim that the British offered independence to the Arabs was false. And yet, it was universally believed by the Arabs and colored their attitude toward the British.

Feisal treaded carefully. Aware that his well-being and, indeed, his political future depended on Britain's goodwill, he proffered friendship toward the British and condemned Ramadan and Mawlud's activities at Dair al-Zor. On the other hand, he took care to provide them with sufficient funds to ensure their success in their campaign against the British. Parenthetically, it is worth mentioning that the money at Feisal's disposal came from British treasury. Skillfully and discretely he was playing a double game. However, his propaganda for "complete independence" in Mesopotamia could not be concealed and caused Curzon to express his displeasure.[87]

Unlike Feisal, the Iraqi Nationalists, most of them members of the *al-Ahd* society, were impatient and militant. They made no secret of their ultimate goal: for them independence meant emancipation from foreign interference. The decision taken by the Allied Powers at the San Remo Conference on April 24, 1920, infuriated them. The Allies decided that both Syria and Mesopotamia should become independent states, subject to a mandate only until they were able to stand alone. The Arabs, however, did not understand the meaning of the mandate and its underlying purpose. The Nationalists, in particular, equated it with annexation. In this, they were mistaken. Lloyd George, in a debate in Parliament on March 25, unequivocally clarified thus:

> It is not proposed that we should govern this country as if it were an essential part of the British Empire, making its laws. That is not our point of view. Our point of view is that they should govern themselves and that we should be responsible as the mandatory for advising, for counselling, for assisting, but the government must be Arab . . . We will respect the solemn undertaking which we gave to the Allies in November 1918.[88]

This was in line with the principle of trusteeship which had been endorsed by President Wilson in January 1919. Moreover, on May 5, Colonel Wilson received instructions to publish an announcement that it was the "firm intention" of the British Government "to promote the creation of the form of civil administration based upon representative indigenous institutions which would prepare the way for creation of an independent Arab State of Iraq."[89] Earlier, in April 1919, Wilson had appointed a committee headed by Sir Edgar Bonham-Carter, a former legal secretary in the Sudan government, to prepare proposals for a constitution for Iraq in accordance with the covenant of the League of Nations. The committee recommended establishing a Council of State, to act as the principal executive authority of the state, that the president should be an Arab, and a legislative body should be either elected, or preferably appointed, by local Arab bodies.[90] This was a blueprint for an embryo state. The document was published both in English and in Arabic. The impact of all the announcements was practically nil. The heart of the Nationalists was with Turkey, not with England.

In mid-March a formal treaty was concluded between Kemal Atatürk and the Sharifian Government. Kemal obligated himself, among other things, to supply arms and instructors to train the Syrian army. The Alliance bore both a military and a religious character, and its aim was to liberate all the Muslim countries from the control of Christian powers and undermine Christian supremacy.[91] Iraqi officers in the Sharifian army were privy to the move; it was Yasin al-Hashimi who, soon after the armistice, conceived and pioneered the rapprochement with Turkey. Indicative of much was the fact that a large number of Mesopotamians joined Mustafa Kemal's army and were susceptible to the Bolshevik anti-British propaganda. Miss Bell was bitter toward Iraqi officers in the Sharifian army for their subversive activities in Mesopotamia. They attributed the creation of the Syrian State to "the victory of Arab arms" and argued that only by resorting to force could similar liberties in Mesopotamia be won.[92] In September 1920, General Gouraud recalled that, before Feisal's eviction from Damascus, Feisal had proposed, if supplied with French arms and money, "to drive the English out of Palestine and Mosul." Moreover, Iraqi officers in his army were fighting the British in Mesopotamia with Feisal's knowledge, if not blessing.[93]

Churchill, like other Britons, was not fully aware of Feisal's duplicity but, as early as February 1920, in a cabinet memorandum, warned his colleagues that the campaign in Mesopotamia was a thankless task.[94]

Lloyd George was not as far-sighted as Churchill. He misread the situation, claiming in his speech in Parliament on March 25 (quoted above) that "almost without exceptions [the people of Mesopotamia] are anxious that the British Government should stay. . . . To hand it over to anyone else would be contrary to the wishes of the Arab population there. They absolutely agree that they do not want Turkish rule again."

It is true that there were some sizeable sections of the population that would have been quite content to live under the British mandate. However, they found it difficult to resist the appeal to religious and national feelings made by the extremists, nor could they rebut the argument that "in accepting the tutelage of Christian Power they were betraying their faith and their race."[95] The factor determining the attitude of the nationally conscious Muslim population toward the British was religion.

The statement made by Sulaiman Faidi during an interview with Ms. Bell in June 1920 is illuminating. Faidi frankly admitted thus:

> The Agitation is taking dangerous proportions. I very much fear open disturbance, not perhaps in Baghdad but in the provinces, for all the tribes are affected . . . I look upon the combination of religion and politics as especially dangerous for it is almost impossible . . . to stand up against it. Though I dislike the Mauluds intensely, I find myself obliged to go to them . . . the boasted reconciliation of Sunnis and Shi'is is most distasteful to me and I should regard Shi'ih domination as an unthinkable disaster.

Wilson forwarded a copy of Bell's memorandum to the India Office, commenting, "This may be regarded as a fair exposition of the present moderate view."[96]

In contrast to Faidi, the activists of both Sunni and Shi'ih regarded their mutual reconciliation as a triumph. It was an event unprecedented in Iraqi history. In spite of centuries-old animosity, they had now found a common cause. They buried the hatchet in order to facilitate their struggle against the foreign power. The first sign of a rapprochement appeared in the summer of 1919, when, on two occasions, the Sunnis attended the religious meetings that were held in memory of the deceased Shi'ih mujtahid, Sayid Muhammad Kadhim Yazdi. It was, however, not until May 1920 that the political significance of the reconciliation became apparent. Members of both sects were attending services in Sunni and Shi'ih mosques in turn, during which political speeches and recitations of patriotic poetry were intertwined with religious ceremonies.[97]

Such a thing, the police intelligence commented, "has never before occurred in Islam. People who objected were silenced and told that all must combine as long as the common enemy—Britain—is before them." Political matters were being discussed freely and unreservedly.

> They have gained confidence by this union . . . and criticize Government with far greater license than before. The great object of these *Mauluds* is to reach the lower classes and excite them to take an interest in political affairs. It is from this class that danger threatens.[98]

Miss Bell remarked that by this method, the Nationalists "have adopted a line difficult in itself to combat."[99] Wilson detected yet another source of danger.

> The priesthood of Karbala, Najaf, and Kadhiman were, with notable exceptions, frankly hostile to organized secular government of whatever kind. . . . They allied themselves to the nationalist movement in its most reactionary aspects, and lent the weight of their authority to arguments which would be understood by the most ignorant. They sought and found their opportunity in an appeal to religious fanaticism.[100]

Wilson, therefore, was reluctant to imprison or deport members of a group, some of whom would, he was certain, be called upon to assist him in the task of forming an indigenous government. Thus, the Nationalists' propaganda was allowed to gather momentum, unabated and undisturbed.

The Nationalists were astute enough to rally the non-Muslim sectors of the population, Jews and Christians alike, to their cause. The latter were happy, even relieved, when, instead of becoming objects of xenophobic attacks and abuse, they were receiving letters of friendship. In return, a great number of them "declared their intentions of supporting the Mohammedans in their demand." Leaflets were distributed among Jews and Christians appealing for unity and brotherhood in the struggle for Iraq's independence.[101]

In response, on June 18, 1920, the Syrian and Chaldean archbishops of Baghdad, jointly with Latin Chaldean and Armenian priests, accompanied by some notables, proceeded to Kadhimain to congratulate the Ulema, Sayyid Muhammad al-Sadr, and others on the occasion of *Id al-Fitr*—a Muslim holy day. A Jewish deputation, led by the Chief Rabbi, also waited upon the Ulema.[102] On the other hand, as British

Intelligence described, there was an "unprecedented spectacle" and "a good deal of sentimental talk" when a delegation of Muslim notables and a mixed group of Sunni and Shi'ih young educated individuals threw flowers and scented water on a Christian procession as it passed and shouted, "Long live our brothers the Christians; long live the Iraqi Union." The Christians, including some priests responded, "Long live our brothers the Muhammadans—Long live the Arabs." The Muslims entered the church and stayed there until the end of the service.[103]

In contrast, the animosity toward the British intensified. On March 14, 1920, Miss Bell wrote to her father that the Shi'ihs and, more especially, the *Mujahids*, the leaders of religious opinion, were "very hostile to us, a feeling we can't alter because it is so difficult to get at them." On April 10, she frankly admitted that Mesopotamia was "on the edge of a pretty considerable Arab Nationalist demonstration with which I'm a good deal in sympathy." She might have had some second thoughts when on June 14 she was facing reality.

> We have had a stormy week. The Nationalist propaganda increases. There are constant meetings in mosques where the mental temperature rises a great deal above 113. The extremists are out for independence without a mandate. They play for all they are worth on the passions of the mob and what with the unity of Islam and Rights of the Arab Race they make a fine figure. They have created a reign of terror; if anyone says boo in the bazaar, it shuts like an oyster.[104]

Six months earlier she analyzed quite correctly that

> [i]t was this [Nationalist] propaganda which was the sole and only cause of the stirring up of revolt here. For the primary movers were actuated by the pure spirit of nationalism. It is true they had to add to it Pan-Islamism before they could stir the mass, true again that the tribes would not have come out but for hope of loot, and the prospect of paying no taxed; none of these passions and prejudices would have been mobilized if the Nationalism had not called them to arms.[105]

By July, she concluded that the British "could not crush a universal sentiment" since even if they restored repressive measures, it would only temporarily produce silence. Hence, she concluded, if the British wished to play a role in shaping Mesopotamia's future, they must make themselves "acceptable" to the local population.[106]

The imponderable question, however, was whether the Iraqi Nationalists were willing to accept British presence however benign and beneficial that administration might be.

Undoubtedly, there was a newly found spirit of nationalism among the people of Mesopotamia, albeit in a rather primitive form. There were, however, also external forces that inflamed anti-British sentiments and stimulated the desire for independence. Wilson time and again pointed out that "the Sharifian intrigues were the mainspring and almost the sole source of our troubles."[107] Another source was the Nationalist Turkey, as well as ex-Turkish officers and officials who, after the armistice, were returning to Mesopotamia. In April 1920, the Intelligence Department reported, "There is little doubt that ex-Turkish officials are fanning the sparks of unrest and excitement and look forward to open demonstration, if not actual open revolt in the near future."[108]

After the riots, Wilson again became convinced that the "steady inflow of propaganda from Syria and . . . Turkey, supported by ample funds," played a major role in the outbreak of violence.[109] Montagu did not demure and thought that the ultraextremists desired to see "the abolition of European control" and that they commanded the sympathy of the Bolsheviks, the Indian anarchists, and the Kemalists.[110] In September, the Foreign Office advised the India Office that, in Curzon's opinion, "one of the principal dangers not only to British policy in Mesopotamia, but to British policy elsewhere, is the relation between Mustapha Kemal and the Mesopotamian extremists."[111]

Notes

1. There is a biography by Sir Major General Calwell: *Life of Sir Stanley Maude* (London, 1920).
2. Edmund Candler, *The Long Road to Baghdad* (London, New York, 1919), 2:246–51.
3. Ibid., 184–6.
4. Cited in George Buchanan, *The Tragedy of Mesopotamia* (London, 1938), 264–6.
5. Candler, *The Long Road to Baghdad*, 188.
6. Lt. Gen. Sir Aylmer L. Haldane, *The Insurrection in Mesopotamia, 1920* (London, 1922), 314.
7. Ibid., 312–3.
8. Ibid., 23.
9. *The Letters of Gertrude Bell*, ed. Lady [Florence] Bell (London, 1927), 2:484. Letter to H[ugh] B[ell], Baghdad, December 27, 1918.
10. F.O. 371/3387/856, "The Future of Mesopotamia," memorandum by Sir Percy Cox, April 22, 1918.

11. F.O. 882/24, Wilson (Baghdad) to secretary of state for India, November 15, 1919.
12. Isaiah Friedman, *Palestine: A Twice Promised Land? The British, the Arabs and Zionism 1915–1920* (New Brunswick, NJ: Transaction Publishers, 2000), 212–3.
13. F.O. 371/5226/2719, Nuri Said to Major Young (F.O.), April 5, 1920.
14. Isaiah Friedman, *British Pan-Arab Policy, 1915-1922: A Critical Appraisal* (Transaction, New Brunswick, 2010), pp. 209-234. For a full text of the Anglo-French Declaration of 8 November 1918 see ibid, pp. 214-5.
15. Ibid., 9–10.
16. Friedman, *Palestine: A Twice Promised Land?*, 56–7.
17. Isaiah Friedman, *British Pan-Arab Policy 1915-1922. A Critical Appraisal* (Transaction, NJ 2010): p. 221.
18. J. de V. Loder, *The Truth About Mesopotamia, Palestine and Syria* (London, 1923), 53.
19. Gertrude Bell, *Review of the Civil Administration of Mesopotamia*, Cmd. 1061, 1920, 126–7.
20. "Self-Determination in Mesopotamia," Memorandum by Miss G. L. Bell, February 1919; reproduced in Lt. Col. Sir Arnold T. Wilson, *Mesopotamia 1917–1920: A Clash of Loyalties* (Oxford, UK, 1931), 2:330–6.
21. Sir George Buchanan, *The Tragedy of Mesopotamia* (London, 1938), 271–2.
22. Wilson, *A Clash of Loyalties*, 2:104–9.
23. Ibid., 110, 114–5; dispatches, dated November 20, 1918 and February 16, 1919.
24. Ibid.
25. Ibid., 116–8.
26. Ibid., 239–40.
27. Ibid., 240–1.
28. Ibid., 242–3.
29. Ibid., 112n1.
30. Ibid., 314–5.
31. Cmd. 1814, *Turkey*, No. 1 (1923), 351–2, clause 2.
32. F.O. 371/4150/5394, "Self-Determination in Mesopotamia," memorandum by A.T. Wilson to secretary of state for India, February 22, 1919, No. 14, paragraphs 3, 4, 6, 7, 10, pp. 26–7.
33. F.O. 371/4147/146, Wilson to India Office, December 26, 1918; C.O. 696/21 Administration Report, Mosul, 1919, 7.
34. C.O. 696/3, Administration Report, Mosul, 1920, 25.
35. F.O. 371/4144/17618, an extract from the "Arab Bulletin," February 1919.
36. F.O. 371/4145/43823, Political Officer in Baghdad to India Office, March 14, 1919.
37. Friedman, *Palestine: A Twice Promised Land?*, 215, 255.
38. Haldane, *The Insurrection in Mesopotamia*, 32.
39. Miss G.L. Bell, *Review of the Civil Administration of Mesopotamia*, Cmd. 1061 (1920), 138.
40. F.O. 882/23, Wilson (Baghdad) to the Arab Bureau (Cairo), February 23, 1919.

41. *Private Letters and Papers of Gertrude Bell* (Newcastle upon Tyne: University of Newcastle Library, n.d.).
42. F.O. 371/5228, No. 172818, Wilson to F.O., November 5, 1919. Quoted in "A Summary of Correspondence in regard to the political situation in Mesopotamia" by Major H. Young.
43. F.O. 371/4146/142, letter dated May 22, 1919.
44. F.O. 371/4145/142, I.O. to F.O., May 26, 1919.
45. F.O. 371/4146/142, summary dated June 16, 1919.
46. F.O. 371/4145/142, Wilson to I.O., May 14, 1919; repeated to H.C. Cairo.
47. CAB 27/23, Memorandum by Sir A. Hirtzel, "Future of Mesopotamia," January 11, 1918.
48. Hirtzel to Wilson, letter dated July 11, 1919, cited in John Marlowe, *Late Victorian* (London 1947), 165.
49. F.O. 882/24, Wilson to I.O., November 15, 1919.
50. See above, pp. 50–3, and for a discussion ibid., 3–13.
51. University of Durham, Sudan Archive, S.A.D. 15/5/10, Tyrell to Wingate, July 2, 1919.
52. *DBFP*, I, IV, No. 204, Curzon to Clayton, January 24, 1919, 296–97.
53. Above pp. 76, 87.
54. F.O. 371/4181/2117, fols. 159–60, minute by Kidston, June 20, 1919.
55. Above, p. 56.
56. C.O. 696/3, Administration Report, Mosul (1920), P. 26; F.O. 371/6349/171, "Personalities in Mosul," n.d.
57. C.O. 696/2, Administration Report, Mosul, 1919, 7.
58. *DBFP*, I. IV, doc. No. 391, Report by J.N. Clayton, Damascus, October 15, 1919, encl. in Meinertzhagen to Curzon, December 2, 1919, 565–7.
59. W.O. 106/196, fols. 136–37, "Nationalists and Arabs", Constantinople, April 15, 1920; also Friedman, *Palestine: A Twice Promised Land?*, 279.
60. F.O. 882/24, "Who is Who," Damascus, 1919.
61. F.O. 882/23, Wilson to I.O., December 24, 1919.
62. F.O. 371/4235/120164, H.Q. (Cairo) to W.O., August 21, 1919.
63. *DBFP*, I, IV, Nos. 339, 413, Meinertzhagen to Curzon, October 21, 1919, January 13, 1920, pp. 495, 613–5, W.O. 106/195, fols. 55, 59.
64. F.O. 371/5128, E 2164, Report by Political Officer in Dair al-Zor, January 1920.
65. "Gertrude Bell Interview with King Feisal," January 14, 1922 in *Gertrude Bell Letters and Papers*.
66. Wilson, *Clash of Loyalties*, 2:228–9.
67. Haldane, *The Insurrection in Mesopotamia, 1920*, 32–3.
68. Wilson, *Clash of Loyalties*, 2:230–3; Cmd. 1061, Bell, *Review of the Civil Administration of Mesopotamia*, 134–6.
69. Ibid.
70. F.O. 371/5073, Wilson to I.O., May 15, 1920.
71. F.O. 371/5278, E 115, Wilson to I.O., January 30, 1920.
72. Ibid., E 114, Wilson to I.O., February 4, 1920; Ibid., E 282, Haldane to W.O., February 11, 1920.
73. F.O. 371/5129, E 2577, Wilson to I.O., May 24, 1920.
74. F.O. 371/5130, E 7219, Wilson to I.O., June 18, 1920.
75. Ibid.

76. F.O. 371/5130, E 9297, Foreign Minister, Damascus, to G.O.C. E.E.F. Cairo, July 2, 1920.
77. F.O. 371/5129, E 6729, W.O. to I.O., n.d.; Ibid., E. 6324, Young's minute (14.6.20) on Wilson's cable no. 6806.
78. F.O. 371/5130, E 7219, Wilson to I.O., June 19, 1920; F.O. 371/5129, E 6324, note dated June 8, 1920.
79. F.O. 371/5129, E 6543, W.O. to G.O.C. Mesopotamia, March 15, 1920.
80. Haldane, *The Insurrection in Mesopotamia, 1920*, 33–4.
81. F.O. 371/5226, E 5113, Hirtzel (I.O.) to F.O., May 20, 1920.
82. F.O. 371/5073, Wilson to I.O., May 15, 1920.
83. Cited in Wilson, *Clash of Loyalties*, 2:238. For Churchill's view in November 1920 see above, 98–101.
84. Ibid, 241.
85. F.O. 371/5216. E 2896, Feisal to King Hussein, telegram dated February 24, 1920 (intercepted).
86. Friedman, *Palestine: A Twice Promised Land?*, 62–3.
87. See note 52 above.
88. Wilson, *Clash of Loyalties*, 2:251.
89. Ibid., 249.
90. Ibid., 242–7.
91. Above, pp. 49–53.
92. Above, pp. 60–2.
93. Isaiah Friedman, *British Pan-Arab Policy*, pp. 285–6.
94. Above, p. 99.
95. Wilson, *A Clash of Loyalties*, 2:242–3.
96. F.O. 371/5228, E 8915, Wilson to I.O., June 14, 1920, and Bell's memorandum titled: "Conversation with Sulaiman Faidi." *Mauluds* stands for joint demonstration staged by Sunni and Shia to assert Muslim solidarity.
97. Wilson, *Clash of Loyalties*, 2:253–4.
98. F.O. 371/5076, Police Intelligence Report, No. 21, paragraph 388, dated May 22, 1920.
99. University of Newcastle Library, Gertrude Bell Private Letters, dated June 1, 1920.
100. Wilson, *Clash of Loyalties*, 2:253.
101. F.O. 371/5076, Rep. No. 22, paragraphs 418 and 428, dated May 29, 1920.
102. F.O. 371/5077, Report No. 24, paragraph 484, dated June 19, 1920.
103. F.O. 371/5076, Abstract of Intelligence, No. 23, dated June 5, 1920.
104. *The Letters of Gertrude Bell*, ed. F. Bell, 483, 486, 489.
105. *Gertrude Bell Private Letters*, January 30, 1920.
106. Ibid., "Note by Miss Gertrude Bell," July 1920.
107. Wilson, *A Clash of Loyalties*, 2:264–5.
108. F.O. 371/5074, Mesopotamian Police, Abstract of Intelligence, Rep. No. 14, dated April 3, 1920.
109. F.O. 371/5228, E 9849; F.O. 371/5229, E 10129, Wilson to I.O., August 5 and 12, 1920.
110. F.O. 371/5229, E. 10440, "Note on the Causes of Riots," August 1920.
111. F.O. 371/5229, E 10440, F.O. (signed by J.A. Tilley) to Montagu, September 11, 1920.

8

Rebellion in Mesopotamia

At the end of May, a self-appointed committee of fifteen persons asked Wilson to transmit their views to the British government. Wilson refused to accept them as "representatives of the Iraqi nation" and invited an additional forty persons, all notables of Baghdad, regardless of their political affiliations, including representatives of the Jewish and Christian communities. The meeting took place at the *Sarai* (i.e., residence of the government) on second June. Wilson assured the delegates that the civil administration proposed to establish a Council of State under an Arab president, who would hold his office provisionally until the question of the final constitution of Iraq was confirmed by the nascent legislative assembly. Responding, the delegates produced a document in which they demanded "the immediate formation of a convention for Iraq, elected in conformity with Turkish electoral law; it would be empowered to draw up proposals for a National government for Iraq as promised in the Anglo-French Declaration of November 8, 1918." The proceedings were conducted with dignity and restraint.

On June 20, Edwin Montagu, the secretary of state for India, authorized Wilson to make a statement that the mandate, under the guarantee of the League of Nations, " will contain provisions to facilitate the development of Iraq as a self-governing state until such time as it can stand by itself, when the mandate will come to an end." When the delegates met again, they declared categorically that "between the British and ourselves, there was a great gulf . . . the mandatory system was a disguised form of annexation." Wilson commented that the scheme that had been outlined was "inadequate and unacceptable. For them to accept anything short of complete independence would be disastrous."

Wilson warned the delegates that the British government might be compelled to resort to military force. They replied that it would be a small price to pay for independence. Wilson responded that a "revolution" might be counterproductive, to which they answered without cynicism that

> [b]etween nations liberty was not given, but taken; a rebellion, whether successful or not, was not only the best but the sole way to advance the cause of freedom. The nations of Europe," they concluded, "always yield to force: Great Britain has yielded in the case of Afghanistan, it is weakening in Egypt, it has yielded even in India, and will eventually give way in Ireland. The British nation is weary of wars and will make no more sacrifices; once the Mandate is granted and its terms settled, we shall lose the chance of obtaining complete independence; nothing short of this will satisfy us.

After hearing two hours of discussion, conducted with courtesy and restraint, it became clear that no compromise or understanding was possible.[1] It was a bad omen for future Anglo-Iraqi relations.

With this kind of philosophy, outbreak of violence was inevitable. In fact, at the time that negotiations with the acting civil commission were taking place, the Sharifian Iraqi officers launched an attack on Tal'Afar, a town twenty miles westward of Mosul. The attack was preceded by violent propaganda conducted by *al-Ahd* members at Mosul during May and June. On May 26, a unit of Iraqi troops led by Jamil al-Madfai arrived at Tal'Afar calling on the inhabitants to be ready for the Sharifian forces. On June 4, telegraph lines were cut and tribesmen rode into the town.

Captain Stuart was shot dead by one his native officers and no resistance was made by gendarmes; their British instructor, the clerk, and the Vickers gunner were also killed; so was Major Barrow. On June 5, a punitive column of armored cars was ambushed near Tal'Afar; none of the crews escaped.

The fall of Tal'Afar was the signal for a general uprising of all the tribes in the district. Pro-British Christian villages were raided, wires were cut, and all roads to Mosul were rendered unsafe. Jamil was aiming to march on Mosul itself, known for its pro-Turkish leanings, but was repulsed by newly arrived British troops. Wilson commented, "This murderous exploit . . . was the work of the Sharifian force, assisted by the townspeople, whose treachery was afterwards punished, however inadequately."[2]

Although Jamil and his crew failed to capture Mosul, which has been their main objective, nonetheless the fall of Dair-ez-Zor and Tal'Afar had a tremendous impact on the Arabs in Mesopotamia and were considered a prelude to the general uprising.

A few days after Wilson's meeting, widespread disorders broke out on the Middle Euphrates and the Diyala, which would be described later. Wilson commented sarcastically that had the British military dispositions been more effective, the disorders could have been suppressed.[3] Faced with a two-pronged onslaught at Tal Afar and on the Middle Euphrates, the position was becoming serious. On June 9, Wilson reminded the India Office that, as early as February, he warned that the British must use their troops available in the country:

> We cannot give effect to mandate without risk of disaster, unless we are prepared to maintain for the next two years at least as many troops in the country as we may have, and in a state considerably more efficient than they are now . . .
>
> We must regain possession of Dair-ez-Zor up to Rakka inclusive . . . we cannot maintain our position as mandatory by a policy of conciliation of extremists. . . . We must be prepared, regardless of League of Nations, to go very slowly with constitutional or democratic institutions. . . . If [H.M.G.] regard such policy as impracticable or beyond our strength (as well they may), I submit they would better to face the alternative . . . and evacuate Mesopotamia . . . [I]t is my conviction that half measures will end in disaster . . .[4]

Wilson saw clear-cut courses: either to hold Mesopotamia by force or to withdraw altogether. In response, Hubert Young, head of the Middle East Department at the Foreign Office, suggested a third course "to remain in Mesopotamia with the goodwill of the people."[5] This sounded like an ideal solution, although, in the given political climate, hardly feasible. The extremists called the tune, and the moderates were silenced. Miss Bell described it vividly, "The extremists had created a reign of terror; if anyone says boo in the bazaar, it shuts like an oyster."[6]

Curzon followed Young's advice and, in the interdepartmental meeting, declared that the British government ". . . should continue the middle course of retaining [the] position in the country with the goodwill of the people."[7]

Four months later, after the riots, Young ventured to go further. He wrote thus:

> I believe that peace cannot be permanently restored unless this society [al-Ahd] is on our side but would point out that the society, which I believe is the moving power of the patriotic movement in Mesopotamia, is fighting for an ideal and that until this ideal is

satisfied to an extent which will content its moderate members, there is no possibility of enlisting its wholehearted support.

A nation which, according to a recent report from Baghdad, has suffered at least 8,000 casualties in a few months and is still unsubdued, is not going to be convinced of our honesty of purpose by words.[8]

It seems that Young was out of touch with the reality. The *al-Ahd* society was in collusion with the Turkish Nationalists to oust the British from Mesopotamia, and there was not the slightest chance of winning them over. Major N. N. Bray, an Intelligence Officer attached to the Political Department of the India Office, similarly was in error when asserting, in his memorandum "On Causes of Unrest in Mesopotamia," that the *al-Ahd* Society was "at heart anti-Turk."[9]

So what were, in fact, the causes of the uprising?

First, there was a deep distrust of Britain caused partly by a misunderstanding of Britain's intentions but primarily by the innate suspicion against any foreign power, particularly non-Muslim.

Second, for centuries, the Mesopotamians, as Arabs in general, were linked to Turkey by bonds of religion and custom and resented any incursion by a foreign power; to be ruled by an infidel was an anathema. As Edmund Candler aptly pointed out, "The Asiatic, as a rule dislikes an alien tutelage, no matter what gifts it may bring." It was a fallacy, he maintained, that "[t]he Arab [was] eagerly waiting for the British to deliver him from the yoke of the Turk."[10] The British a priori were not wanted.

Britain's weakness during the aftermath of the war served as an open invitation to violence. The takeover of Dair-ez-Zor, Albu Kamal, al Qaim, and Tal Afar demonstrated to the people of Mesopotamia that the British could be dislodged by armed force. Trains between Baghdad and Mosul were derailed and British officers murdered with impunity. Consequently, public confidence in Britain's ability to maintain order began to wane. "Extremists began to hope that they might be successful in attaining their object, viz., complete independence and freedom from all foreign interference by direct action. Karbala and subsequently Najaf became the principal centers of agitation." Religious leaders demanded "the complete expulsion of the British from Mesopotamia and [foundation of] an Islamic Kingdom."[11]

As mentioned earlier, the Sharifian government had initiated and inspired the subversive activities in Mesopotamia, supplying the rebels with arms and ample funds. The Bolsheviks also played a role in fanning anti-British sentiments. Administrative mistakes with regard to taxation policy and support of unpopular sheiks, among other missteps, caused resentment, but the overriding reason that had inflamed the Muslims at large was the destruction of the Ottoman Empire coupled by the explosive ideas of self-determination. When the Allies, in the eyes of the local population, failed to live up to their solemn proclamations, the emotional ground for a rebellion was ripe.

Finally, at the end of his term, Wilson himself recognized the force of nationalism in the East. On September 20, 1920, during a complimentary dinner given in his honor by the Railway Directorate, he stated thus:

> Nationalism is the basis of the latest Peace Treaties. We entered the way to protect the rights of small nations [but] critics of Nationalism as a constructive policy were silenced; doubters were perforce dumb; Nationalism held the field, and every official utterance of the Allies . . . emphasized this as the basis of future policy.
> The seed of Nationalism had grown in Europe meanwhile, and the plant had borne fruit in the East. . . . In Mesopotamia the new vine was fermenting in the old bottles.[12]

Gertrude Bell was of the same opinion. In a note, dated July 20, 1920, she wrote as follows:

> The movement in this country is one aspect of a very strong nationalist sentiment . . . and has immensely gained in strength and definition from the very principles of defence of which we fought. . . . We are in presence of a sentiment the roots of which go further and deeper . . . the roots of our own action [during the World War] in the greatest trial which we as a nation have known.[13]

In Mesopotamia, as in Muslim countries in general, nationalism was intertwined with religion. In Karbala, one of the holy cities, Imam Shirazi issued a *fatwa* to the effect that "None but Moslems have any right to rule over Moslems." Shirazi had succeeded the deceased Yazdi as the grand *mujtahid* and of his political activity in the cause of independence, earned him the title, "The Spiritual Leader of the Revolt." His son, Mirza Muhammad Riza, played a crucial role as a liaison between Najaf, Baghdad, and neighboring tribes. Printing presses were set up in Najaf and Karbala; leaflets were printed inciting the tribes to prepare for a revolt. Thousands of copies were distributed all over the region; so were Arab flags.[14] Thus, as Haldane commented aptly, "The seeds of Sharifian and religious propaganda fell on fertile soil, and, ultimately ferminating [sic], produced a rich crop of armed insurrectionists."[15]

In addition, there were also some mundane reasons that caused resentment. They were the method of assessment and collection of land revenues—totally different from that used by the Turks—and forced labor. The inhabitants were requested to provide manpower for making or repairing flood banks or for other public works. In theory the British administration was right, but the Arabs regarded this as "oppression . . . a flood, even if it ruined a large cultivated area, was accepted with equanimity as being a manifestation of the hand of God." Houses requisitioned during the war to house the troops were another cause of resentment. The effendi class, who were used to the Ottoman system of government, were also dissatisfied.[16]

They feared lest Mesopotamia became a British dependency. "This at all costs they were determined to prevent." So it would not be an exaggeration to say that toward the summer there was a buildup of an army of malcontents, ready to challenge the British control.

On June 30, 1920, when the rebellion broke out, the British were at a disadvantage. The number of British troops numbered (in round figures) 7,200 British and 53,000 Indian soldiers, in all some 60,200 men. These figures included 3,000 British and 23,000 Indian troops, who were employed on noncombatant duties in various departmental services.[17] Wilson estimated that owing to demobilization during May, there were only 5,000 British and 30,000 Indian combatants in Mesopotamia.[18] Early in July 1920, General Haldane informed the War Office that the position was "serious" and requested more troops.[19]

The request was turned down. At the Foreign Office, Hubert Young had strong reservations with regard to a military solution. He suggested that Ja'afar and Nuri, who were protesting their loyalty to Britain, might be more useful to quell the unrest.[20] Moreover, at the time when disarmament was in swing, recruitment of new troops was difficult. Haldane was thus bogged down with inadequate combatant force, a third of which was "useless" in the field.[21] The British troops were "almost without exception, new to the country, and without previous experience." The lines of communication in Mesopotamia, the maintenance of which was necessary for military purposes, totaled two thousand miles. By railway, it was not possible to transport more than a quarter of the tonnage needed by the force; with the result, the army had to depend on navigation along the Tigris and Euphrates rivers.

These were vulnerable to sniping and required guarding by some ten thousand noncombatant soldiers.[22]

In contrast, the Arab tribes were swift and mobile; they could be mobilized at short notice; they were familiar with the terrain and were highly motivated. Xenophobia and religious fervor fed their aggressive instincts. In these circumstances, any commanding officer would have encountered insuperable difficulty in nipping the rebellion in its bud. In this respect Wilson's criticism of Haldane is not fully justified. Wilson himself admitted that the military position with which Haldane was confronted was "one of extreme difficulty."[23]

Lt. Gen. Sir Aylmer Haldane was fifty-eight years of age when Churchill appointed him the chief of command in Mesopotamia. General Sir George MacMunn, his predecessor, left his position before Haldane's arrival, and the latter was deprived of the advantage of personal discussion with an officer who had special experience and qualifications to tackle complicated administrative and politically delicate situations. Haldane was a novice and ignorant of the problems he had to confront. Nonetheless, judging by the final results, he acquitted himself well. His book, *The Insurrection in Mesopotamia, 1920*, is a testimony to his personal stamina, as well as to an intelligent comprehension of military situations. In it he gave his readers a detailed description of the military campaign vis-à-vis the rebellion. Repetition, therefore, is superfluous. Our purpose is to sketch its salient features and analyze its political effects.

The rebellion broke out first at Rumaytha in the Diwaniya Province. A sheik of the Zawalim tribe, a noted activist, was arrested for refusing to pay taxes. On the same day an armed band of his followers stormed the prison and set him free; hereafter, they declared rebellion and began to destroy the railway tracks and nearby bridges. The fighting soon spread to Samawa where the British garrison, taken by surprise, surrendered after having suffered a number of casualties. The tribal warriors " displayed courage, coordination and ingenious military tactics."[24]

When a force, under the command of Captain Bragg, was sent to occupy Rumaytha, it was soon noticed that the Arabs responded by constructing a trench system round the town in order to put it under a siege. Haldane saw in it an indication that "[e]x-Turkish Army officers were probably in control." Moreover, the Arabs, numbering from fifteen hundred to two thousand began converging from every side. The two British-led platoons were overwhelmed; forty-three soldiers were reported missing and fourteen were wounded. The townspeople and the tribesmen in the neighborhood became "unmistakably hostile" and opened fire from all quarters of the village, killing six men and wounding fourteen. Captain Bragg ordered the troops to withdraw to the building of the Serai. There, however, food and ammunition were running short, while medical supplies did not exist. The insurgents, estimated from three thousand to five thousand men, launched a concerted attack and the position of the beleaguered soldiers became precarious. The commander, however, resolutely took advantage of a dust storm and managed to break through to relative safety.[25]

Elsewhere the position was even more severe. General Haldane likened the state of Mesopotamia to "a sheet of parchment which rises at any point where a weight is lifted from its surface." The dispatch of troops from Hilla to Diwaniya resulted in a rising in the Hilla district, where a section of Bani Hasan tribe seized the town of Kifl on July 20. A force consisting of three companies of Manchesters, augmented by Sikh Pioneers, and a battery of field artillery was sent out. The heat was unbearable and the operation was mismanaged. They were attacked by superior forces and General Leslie, the commander, decided to retire. The retreat became a rout: some soldiers lost their way and less than half of the force reached Hilla. The retreat cost 180 killed, 60 wounded, and 160 taken prisoners. Wilson observed succinctly: "No one with the column had knowledge of either Arab warfare or the country."[26]

The Shamiya region, along with Sukhair and Kafal, was dominated by the powerful Khazail confederation, which maintained virtual independence during the Ottoman period. On July 11, 1920, several leading sheiks approached Major Norbury, the political officer, asking for the complete independence of Mesopotamia. When their request was rejected, they took over the town and set up a provisional revolutionary government with four departments. The revolt thereafter spread to Kufa, Rustamiya, Hindiya, and elsewhere.[27] By August 25, practically all the tribes north of Diyalah, north-east of Baghdad, became implicated in the rising; lawlessness and disorder spread as far as Kirkuk and thereafter to Arbil. Several British outposts on the Baghdad-Quvaintu line were attacked and temporarily cut off. Relief of beleaguered garrisons became difficult since the railways were cut off and use of armored cars, because of the intricacies of the terrain, was not always possible. By the end of August, the number of armed men among the insurgents reached 131,000, nearly half possessing modern rifles.

The sheiks claimed that they were being assisted in arms and money by the Turkish Nationalists.[28] The long hand of the Bolsheviks too reached the insurgents. In its report, "Cause of the Outbreak in Mesopotamia," October 1920, the General Staff concluded that "the malign influence of Moscow" partly contributed to the insurrection.[29] Earlier, Wilson suspected that Mirza Muhammad Rida, the son of the chief mujtahid al-Shirazi, was "working for the Bolshevik cause in Karbala."[30] This information was confirmed few months later by Sir Percy Cox, then high commissioner for Mesopotamia, in the sense that Mirza Muhammad Rida "has been advocating an understanding with the Bolsheviks."[31] Moreover, the British Intelligence ascertained that the Bolshevik government, in a letter to an underground cell called Haqq (Right), promised assistance to the rebels' cause.[32] It was also reported that Bolshevik agents were in communication with Sheikh al-Shariah al-Isfahani.[33]

Jihad was being preached with frenzied fervor by numerous emissaries from the holy cities of Najaf and Karbala. Mirza Muhammad Shirazi was offering prayers on the corpses of Arabs killed in battle, an act which "conferred on the inanimate warriors the crown of martyrdom."[34] Gertrude Bell was in a state of despair. She revealed her thoughts to her father thus:

> We are now in the middle of a full-blown Jihad, that is to say we have against us the fieriest prejudices of a people in a primeval state of civilisation. Which means that it's no longer a question of reason. It has on its side the tendency to anarchy. . . . We've practically come to the collapse of society here and there's little on which you can depend for its reconstruction. The credit of European civilisation is gone.[35]

The situation seemed to be so precarious that Wilson, in view of the inadequate defense force, suggested evacuating the whole of Mosul Vilayet.[36] It was Winston Churchill, the secretary of state for war, who saved the situation. He was not only sympathetic but helpful. Responding to Haldane's plea to send reinforcements to the beleaguered British garrisons, he wrote, "The Cabinet have decided that the rebellion must be quelled effectively, and I shall endeavour to meet all your requirements." He added that troops and air squadrons were on the way to Mesopotamia.[37]

Three days later, Haldane sent yet another telegram, explaining in some detail the gravity of the situation and the dangers with which his forces were threatened. In spite of the great strain on resources, of both the United Kingdom and India, Churchill was forthcoming, so was Field-Marshall Sir Henry Wilson, who, in February 1918, succeeded Robertson as chief of the Imperial General Staff.[38]

In the concluding chapter of his book, General Haldane admitted that from the beginning of July until well into October, "[w]e lived on the edge of a precipice where the least slip might have led to a catastrophe" but thanks to the resolution and valor of the troops, both British and Indian, it was possible to temporize and maintain the situation until the reinforcements arrived.[39]

Now better equipped, Haldane was able to launch a counteroffensive. Particularly helpful was the Royal Air Force, which bombed and devastated villages and locations of tribes indiscriminately. Haldane thought that "there could be no security for the future peace of Mesopotamia unless the punishments awarded were such as would discourage a repetition of this foolish outbreak. . . . After that stage had been attained, when all hope of further resistance had been obliterated, the time for amnesty would come, and relations of a friendly nature could be established." In this ruling, Haldane took a leaf from a sheikh in the Middle-Euphrates region. Speaking about his fellow countrymen with conviction, the sheikh said, "The Arab is a slave, and requires a hard master; give him a stick first, then the sugar." Haldane concurred, observing that the employment of any other method "would be accepted as weakness."

The punishment meted on the rebellious tribes was surrender of all the weapons of any kind. The total number of rifles, modern and other, amounted to three hundred thousand and the tribes who had participated in the uprising possessed between fifty thousand to sixty thousand rifles.[40] Thus, the general, who, by his own admission, was on the brink of catastrophe, was now residing over a total disarmament.

Cox and Bell subscribed to Haldane's method. Miss Bell wrote to her father thus:

> Sir Percy, I think, rightly decided that the tribes must be made to submit to force. In no other way was it possible to make them surrender their arms, or teach them that you mustn't lightly engage in revolution, even when your holy men tell you to do so. . . . Without the lesson and without drawing their teeth by fine of arms (impossible to obtain except by force), we should have left an impossible task to Arab Govt.[41]

It was, however, not only the superior British force that subdued the rebels. With their ammunition running low, and depleted of food and other basic necessities, they had no choice but to surrender. Expulsion of Feisal from Damascus in July 1920 had a sobering effect; the Arabs lacked the stamina and were not fortunate to have a leader with the stature of Kemal Atatürk.

Haldane earned well-deserved praise from his superiors. Wilson, too, admitted that the principal object of Haldane's operations had been achieved. He defeated the insurgents at every point, restored communications, and above all, prevented the recurrence of disorders in the foreseeable future.[42]

Although a victory was finally achieved, it was nevertheless a bitter victory. Between July 2 and October 17, 1920, the grand total of British and Indian casualties amounted to 2,269. It was estimated that Arab casualties, killed and wounded, amounted to 8,450.[43] Berton C. Busch estimated that suppression of the uprising in Mesopotamia cost the British nearly 2,000 casualties, including 450 dead and a loss of forty million pounds to the treasury.[44] During a debate in the Parliament, Winston Churchill declared that the total war in Mesopotamia since its inception cost the British 100,000 casualties and approximately 350 million pounds.[45]

The British people were outraged by the scope and ferocity of the Arab rebellion in Mesopotamia. *The Times* (August 7, 1920), in its leader, gave vent to the prevailing frustration: "How much longer are valuable lives to be sacrificed in the vain endeavour to impose upon the Arab population an . . . expensive administration which they never asked for and do not want?" A few days later *The Times* resorted to even stronger language: "We are spending sums in Mesopotamia . . . which may well reach a hundred million pounds this year" in support of what the paper described as "The foolish policy of the Government in the Middle East."

Drawing on a number of studies,[46] *The Times* (August 16, 1920) asserted emphatically that Mesopotamia ". . . will not pay in a thousand years . . . Our object should be to get away our troops as soon as we can." Three days later, *The Times* pointed out the economic difficulties confronting Britain caused partly by "the huge and wasteful squandering by the Government in distant lands." Hence, the paper concluded, "The determination of the Cabinet to incur a vast outlay in fighting Arabs, who reject us . . . seems to us almost insane." The *Daily Mail* (July 12, 1920)

was of the same opinion: "There is nothing in all our history to com-
pare with our folly in Mesopotamia." A sizeable body of members in
the Parliament voiced similar sentiments. Some members argued
that there was no palpable need that had required British presence
in Mesopotamia.[47] This point was argued most potently by Churchill,
the secretary of state for war. In a memorandum dated December 10,
1920, he emphasized that it had been for military reasons that Britain
became involved in Mesopotamia.

> The idea of maintaining troops in Mesopotamia or Persia for the
> defence of India is radically unsound, and has never been contem-
> plated by [H.M.G.]. . . . From the strategical point of view the only
> justification for the maintenance of military forces in Mesopotamia
> is . . . to keep control of the Persian Gulf and to protect the Anglo-
> Persian Oilfields, which were, and are vital to the navy.[48]

Churchill realized that, since the British were not wanted in
Mesopotamia, it would not be more prudent to cut the losses and
concentrate on vital British interests instead, such as had been originally intended at the beginning of the war in 1914, i.e., Basra and the
oil-fields in its neighborhood. Churchill, however, failed to carry the
cabinet with him.

Had the British government followed Churchill's advice, it might be
assumed that there was a good chance of achieving a healthy modus
vivendi between Basra and Britain. Unlike in the north, Basra and
environs did not participate in the rebellion, and there were strong
commercial interests between Basra and British companies which
lasted for generations.

Most telling was the farewell ceremony arranged by the local
community, as well as by the Chamber of Commerce in honor of Sir
Arnold Wilson, on the occasion of his retirement in October 1920.
In the presence of all the notables of Basra and representatives of all
parties, Wilson was presented with a special gift: a sword of honor.
The principal speakers were his personal friends Abdul Latif Pasha
Mandil and Muzahim Bey Pachali. The latter described himself as
"an extreme Nationalist and one of the founders of the general Arab
movement since 1906. . . . I very much regret," he stated in his speech,
"that the follies of some individual Arabs have served to disappoint the
British nation in its honorable undertaking." He attributed their acts
partly to "unattainable dreams and partly to selfish material interests."
He went on as follows:

The present movement is not purely an Arab movement, but it is mixed with an alien element, who have been, to my deepest regret, successful in using Arab fame, wealth and blood for their own benefit, in the hope of weakening the position of Great Britain elsewhere. . . . Do not consider that the present revolt of some nomad tribes is really a national revolt seeking for independence. Such a movement cannot be taken as representing the feeling of the whole community. . . . Those who are advocating the withdrawal of Britain from this country cannot realize that withdrawal means no less than breaking up the law, and ruin of the people, followed by anarchy throughout the country . . .

The meeting was presided over by Sir Percy Cox to whom, on October 4, Wilson handed over the keys of the office of civil commissioner of Mesopotamia and under whom he had acted for two and a half years.[49] Sir Percy took up now the post of high commissioner in accordance with the official announcement made on June 20. With Cox's appointment, military control ceased. In the final analysis it was Cox who shaped the future destiny of Mesopotamia, not Churchill. Years later, in a "tribute to Gertrude Bell," he wrote thus:

Asked for my opinion . . . I replied that . . . evacuation was unthinkable; it would mean the abandonment of the Mandate and of the seven or eight millions worth of capital assets which we had in the country; the complete violation of all the promises we had made to the Arabs during the war. As to whether the alternative policy of establishing forthwith a national Government had a reasonable chance of success, I replied that without being too confident, I thought it had, and that the risk at any rate worth taking if regarded the only alternative to evacuation.

Cox also maintained that premature evacuation would expose the local inhabitants to "their inevitable re-subjection to chaos and the hated yoke of the Turk."[50]

On certain points, Cox was in error. The promises by Sir Henry McMahon were made to the sharif (later King Hussein), not directly to Arabs of Mesopotamia. They were predicated on Arab revolt against Turkey. This did not happen. Moreover, the "hated yoke of the Turks" was a figment of imagination. It is worth recalling that it was Cox with whom the idea of capturing Baghdad had originated early in the war,[51] the consequences of which were dire.

Having no support, Churchill abandoned the idea of retaining Basra; his principal concern was the economy. In a speech in Parliament on

June 14, 1921, he declared, "I cannot say in regard to Mesopotamia that there are primary, direct, strategic British interests involved . . . our policy in Mesopotamia is to reduce our commitments and to extract ourselves from our burdens while at the same time honourably discharging our obligations and building up a strong and effective Arab government which will be a friend of Britain."[52]

British officials considered Emir Feisal to be the most suitable candidate for this task.

It was Wilson who, as early as July 1920, suggested that Feisal be invited to assume the emirate of Iraq on grounds that no local candidate would succeed in garnering sufficient support. Moreover, Wilson was confident that Feisal could "scarcely fail to realise that foreign assistance is vital to the continued existence of an Arab State."[53]

Practically at the same time Cox, then in Persia, reached a similar conclusion. Writing to Churchill, he objected to the separation of Basra from the rest of the country and, pointing to the fruitful Anglo-Hashemite cooperation, advocated Feisal's nomination as the emir of Mesopotamia. Reports that he had been receiving from Mesopotamia indicated that this was a "solution desired by a preponderant body of opinion in Iraq."[54] In February 1920, the General Staff proposed the same idea, arguing that Feisal's appointment would enhance Britain's prestige, that he was familiar with British methods of administration, that he would be acceptable to both Shi'ihs and Sunnis, that he was hostile to Bolshevism, that intrigues with Mustafa Kemal would cease, and that his rule would have a "steadying effect on the Middle East."[55]

The memorandum was based on mistaken premises. The General Staff was unaware that during the war Feisal was negotiating with Djemal Pasha with the purpose of defecting to the Ottoman camp, that in June 1919, he concluded an agreement with Mustafa Kemal aimed against the Allied powers, and that, far from having a "steadying effect" in the Middle East, he was actively promoting and condoning subversive activities.[56]

In August 1920 the British government advised Sir Percy Cox, now high commissioner, of its intention to appoint Feisal as emir of Iraq. This was predicated on two conditions:

1. That his appointment would follow "a spontaneous demand . . . from a sufficiently representative body of public opinion".
2. And that Feisal was prepared in principle to accept Great Britain as mandatory power.[57]

Having acquainted himself with the above conditions, Feisal promised to do all he could "to make his part of the [scheme] work."[58]

Feisal's candidature for the throne was assuming particular urgency because, in the meantime, the idea of nominating a Turkish candidate was gathering momentum, especially among former Ottoman servicemen and officials; their chosen man was Abd al-Rahman al-Naqib, a person of standing and of some consequence.[59] Moreover, the Sunnis of Baghdad were considering whether it would not better suit their interests to have "a Turkish prince as King. They are afraid," Miss Bell wrote to her father, "of being swamped by the Syrians, against whom a Turk might be a better bulwark than a son of the Sharif."[60] This trend, Cox warned Churchill, was dangerous.[61] Miss Bell too, in her letter of January 22, quoted above, opined, "I believe if we could put up a son of the Sharif at once, he might yet sweep the board; if we hesitate, the tide of public opinion may turn overwhelmingly to the Turks."

Curzon lost no time in suggesting that it was necessary to work for Arab independence in the hope that it would lead to "a division between Turks and Arabs and unity between Arabs and Britain."[62]

It was in these circumstances that it was decided during the Cairo Conference, March 1921, under Churchill's chairmanship, that Emir Feisal would become king of Iraq. The reduction of military expenditure was uppermost in Churchill's mind. Thus, Churchill advised the prime minister that he had "no doubt" that Feisal offered the best chance of saving our money; it would cut the "incredible waste" in Mesopotamia.[63]

Feisal's coronation took place on August 23, 1921. It was, as Bell described it, "admirably arranged" in presence of English and Arab officials, townsmen, and local deputations to the number of fifteen hundred. Feisal looked "very dignified . . . it was an agitating moment."[64]

However, high as the hopes were, so deep was the disappointment. The British were completely unaware of his shortcomings, as well as of his mental predisposition. During his talk in April with Lawrence in Cairo, Feisal revealed his predicament. The people of Iraq, he said, were not yet fitted for a responsible government; he would require British help, otherwise "there will be a disaster." He invited also military protection, thereby inadvertently agreeing to become a vassal of the British. A few days later, however, when on a steamer heading toward Iraq, he declared to the Indian caliphate official that the destruction of the Ottoman Empire was "an offence to Islam as a whole; that he wished to restore peace and concord in the Islamic world; that he had no faith in England; and that, should Turkey be attacked at any time in the future, the Arabs, as brothers in faith, would volunteer to fight even their Ally England."[65]

Feisal tried thus to rehabilitate his name, as well as of his family in the eyes of Muslims in general and Mesopotamia in particular. The stain, however, could not be removed. Feisal was blamed for deserting the Ottoman realm in the hour of its need and of collaborating with the infidel power, whereas his father had been denounced as a traitor.

As Thomas Owens, the American consul in Baghdad, observed, "Feisal has never been popular. He was forced upon the country and all Arabs are said to harbor a resentment . . . the opposition is quite open and often very bitter. The installation of Feisal in Baghdad never has been possible without the exertion of British power and prestige."[66] However, reliance on British force made him even less acceptable to his fellow Arabs.

Cox was misinformed when writing to Churchill that Feisal's nomination to the throne was "desired by a preponderant body of opinion in Iraq."[67] Cox's report misled not only Churchill but also Lloyd George. The disillusionment was therefore even greater.

First came the bad news delivered by Curzon to Churchill that Feisal had been negotiating with the Turks "behind the backs of Cox and ourselves."[68] Churchill himself was very much annoyed with Feisal. "I am getting tired of all these lengthy telegrams about Feisal and his state of mind. There is too much of it," he wrote to his staff.

> I am forced to read day after day 800-word messages on questions of his status and his relations with foreign powers. Has he not got some wives to keep him quiet? He seems to be in a state of perpetual ferment. . . . Cox ought to go into the financial aspect with him and show him that the country on to whose throne he has been hoisted is a monstrous burden on the British Exchequer, and that he himself is heavily subsidised. Let him learn to develop his country that he can pay his own way.[69]

Churchill was concerned that by the end of 1921, he would be confronted with about a three-million-pound civil deficit and that administration of Iraq constituted an "enormous burden." Feisal's primary task should be to save money and promote internal tranquility. "His talk about extending Arab control to Nisibin etc. is merely fantastic, seeing that he cannot even pay his Arab army for home defence."[70]

It would be recalled that before his accession to throne, Feisal had agreed to accept a British Mandate over Iraq. It did not take him long, however, to renege on his agreement. He succumbed to the pressure of Nationalists and political agitators who claimed that they were "quite competent to administer their country free from tutelage in any shape or form." In consequence, with Feisal's support, a violent campaign of calumny and vituperation was launched against the mandate. "The very word was anathema and in a short time," Buchanan commented bitterly, "the nation that had rescued the Iraqis from the oppression of the Turks became more hated than the Turks themselves had ever been."[71]

Feisal demanded to substitute a treaty with Britain for a mandate, but even a treaty failed to satisfy him, and he continued to make difficulties. Churchill was also outraged. "The Treaty was Feisal's plan, not ours. We consented in order to meet his views. If he obstructs the Treaty and will not sign it, it is for him to suggest a method of avoiding a deadlock," Churchill wrote to Shuckburgh.[72]

On the same day Churchill drafted a strong-worded letter to Feisal in which he wrote as follows:

> I have learned with profound regret of the course Your majesty is resolved to persevere. It can only lead to the downfall of those hopes of cooperation between the British Govt & the Sherifian family in pursuance of which we have with so much labour & expense facilitated YM's accession to the throne of Iraq. Having laboured so long to serve your interests & to create for YM [a] stable throne & prosperous country I cannot view without sorrow the return which the exertions & sacrifices of Britain have received. The prophecies of the French & of General Gouraud which I have so often repulsed are apparently to be fulfilled to the letter.[73]

He decided, however, not to send this letter because, in the meantime, he learned that Cox had already warned Feisal that he would bear full responsibility for his conduct. "Rightly or wrongly," Cox cabled to Churchill, "I regard Feisal's letter as pure bluff."[74]

On August 28, Churchill briefed eight cabinet ministers on the situation in Iraq and pointed to the difficulties that Feisal had been creating. He had allied himself with the extremists and regarded the mandatory system as "a slur on Iraq." In Cox's opinion, Churchill disclosed, Feisal was "quite unfitted for his position and was directly responsible for unrest in Iraq, and for bad administration."[75]

In despair Churchill turned to the prime minister. "The task you have given me is becoming really impossible. Our forces are reduced to very slender proportions. . . . Feisal is playing fool, if not the knave; his incompetent Arab officials are . . . failing to collect the revenue; we overpaid £200,000 on last year's account which is almost certain Iraq will not be able to pay this year." Churchill feared "a disaster" to come and suggested that the Iraqis should be warned "in the most brutal way" that, unless they "beg us to stay on our own terms in regard to efficient control . . . and cooperate in every manner. . . . We shall actually evacuate before the close of the financial year." Whether Britain should clear the country altogether, or hold on to a portion of Basra Vilayet, was an issue which would require a special study.

The victories of the Turks [Churchill predicted]

> will increase our difficulties throughout the Mohammedan world. At present we are paying eight million a year for the privilege of living on an ungrateful volcano out of which we are in no circumstances to get anything worth having.[76]

The tone of Lloyd George's reply was friendly ("My dear Colonial Secretary"). He agreed with Churchill's analysis and suggested that he present his views to the cabinet. Lloyd George went on to say that

> [t]he whole problem has arisen out of the decision to attack the Turks in Mesopotamia. Strategically, I think that decision was faulty. . . . The decision was taken when I was hardly on the fringe of the War Cabinet. Having provoked war with the Turk we had to fight him somewhere, but the swamps of the Tigris were a badly chosen battleground . . . it certainly is responsible for our difficulties now.

Lloyd George thus admitted that the campaign in Mesopotamia was a mistake. This was an important statement. He disclaimed, however, personal responsibility for it since at that time he served in a junior position as minister of munitions. When he became prime minister, however, it was impossible to relax the campaign against the Turks; it would have weakened the British position throughout the Muslim world while withdrawal from Mesopotamia after the armistice

> would have repudiated all our undertakings towards the Arabs. We were responsible for liberating them from Turkish sovereignty, and we were absolutely bound to assist them in setting up Arab governments, if we were not prepared to govern them ourselves.[77]

Lloyd George committed a double error. First, Britain was able to extricate itself from the Mesopotamian imbroglio during the spring of 1917, when the Tala'at–Djavid Government tried to opt out of the war and conclude a separate peace. Lloyd George and Sir Mark Sykes unequivocally rejected the Turkish overtures.[78] Second, after the armistice, there was a golden opportunity to obtain most favorable terms from the Izzet Pasha government for a peace settlement. That opportunity was missed.[79]

The argument that Britain was obligated to liberate Arabs from Turkish sovereignty was erroneous. The Allied powers obligated themselves merely to "recognize and uphold" the Arab independence provided the Arabs liberated themselves from the Turkish realm. This, however, was not the case.

Churchill replied the following day. It was true that the Government of India, as well as Lord Crewe, then secretary of state for India, were "the prime movers in the original expedition to Basra" but at that time "both you and I were members of the War Committee . . . and are therefore responsible" for the Mesopotamian expedition. Moreover, when victory was achieved and Turkey was prostrate,

> we were undoubtedly free to decline the Mandate for Iraq and to quit the country as rapidly as our troops could be withdrawn. We were also free to make a treaty with Turkey which would have secured peace on the general basis of the victories which we had won over the Turks. Such a peace could certainly have provided . . . for the creation of a quasi-independent Iraq under Turkish suzerainty.

Churchill thought that, despite the lamentable events taking place in Anatolia, Britain should come to terms with Turkey which would insure a stable peace; "a very great easement would result."[80] Peace with Turkey was Churchill's hallowed credo; however, it clashed with Lloyd George's policy.

For installation of Feisal as king of Iraq, Churchill alone was responsible, albeit his responsibility was merely ministerial. He acted on the advice of Cox and was urged to do so by Lawrence.

The record of Feisal's reign was grim. In Baghdad, he showed the same unreliable character that he had displayed during his rule in Damascus. He was devious, weak, and ill-fitted to govern. Even Miss Bell, his warm partisan, confessed her unhappiness with Feisal's character and, particularly, "the backing he was giving to the most ignoble extremists. . . . I had formed a beautiful and gracious snowman which

I had given allegiance," she wrote to her parents, "and I saw it melting before my eyes. . . . I could not bear to see the evaporation of the dream which had guided me day by day."[81] Bell's disillusionment was shared by Cox and Cornwallis.

Feisal's ambition in foreign policy stood in inverse ratio to his domestic weakness. His policy of sectarian discrimination nurtured deep grievances among Shi'ites that Feisal did not care to mitigate. In a memorandum that he wrote and circulated among his intimates in 1932, Feisal expressed himself rather disdainfully that "[t]he Shi'ites believed that death and taxes were their lot, while official positions went to the Sunnis, and that even the holy days of the Shi'ites were not respected."[82] Shortly before his death in September 1933, he had the dubious honor of acclaiming against his will and celebrating Bakr Sidqi's victory over the Assyrians who had been ruthlessly massacred.[83]

The Sharifian officers, who propelled the rebellion, were too few to govern the country on their own. Perforce Feisal had, therefore, to co-opt the former Ottoman officials, who had remained loyal to Turkey during the war. Between these two camps a fierce ideological controversy raged as to who had contributed more to the Arab national cause. What Fahmi al-Mudarris wrote on this matter is extremely enlightening. As a partisan of Yasin al-Hashimi, it was natural to defend his patron's record. Nonetheless, his argument reflects on all fellow Arabs who remained loyal to Turkey. Al-Mudarris wrote that, as a faithful commander, al-Hashimi had the duty "to preserve the army and his honour." Moreover

> [h]e believed that the destruction of the Turkish army would lead the Arabs to be delivered over and to submit to the Allies who would divide up their country into zones of influence, which is in fact what happened . . . had al-Hashimi abandoned the Turks, he would have included himself in the category of traitors.[84]

Mudarris challenged Feisal and his family's claim "to be the leaders of the Arabs and to have saved them from Ottoman despotism." It was fanciful to claim that the Turkish regime was despotic toward the Arabs. Quite the contrary.

> Iraq [al-Mudarris wrote] never was a Turkish colony; it was part of the Ottoman Empire which had been independent and autonomous for more than six centuries. Neither was the state Turkish, but Ottoman. This meant that it gathered under its banner different races in the same manner as the Iraqi state would today, had it

been independent. The Iraqis were not under the yoke of Turkish rule, as they are today under the yoke of the British mandate. They shared, rather, in the rule together with the Turks and other races, in all the departments of the state; there was no discrimination in rights or duties between the Turks and the Iraqis; and they shared offices, high positions, and the good and the bad equally. The Iraqi exercised rule, justice, administration and politics for succeeding centuries, not only in Iraq, but in all parts of the Ottoman Empire, which extended to Europe, Asia and Africa.[85]

This statement tallies with that made by the British-oriented Nuri al-Sai'id, then prime minister of Iraq.[86] These statements are enlightening as to the essence of the Ottoman realm. The Arabs lived quite comfortably within this framework, while the hallowed institution of the sultan-caliph served as a unifying factor for the whole Muslim world. The destruction of the Ottoman Empire, "the independent State of Khalifa," as Feisal had declared to Kaderbhoy in April 1921, was "an offence to Islam as a whole."[87] This is the origin and explanation of the rabid anti-British feelings in Iraq and throughout the Muslim world. Feisal, like his father, felt guilty for the role he had played during the war and for siding with the infidel against the sultan. He, therefore, hardly ever showed gratitude to his patrons and always complained and demanded further concessions. On the other hand, the British, by hoisting an unpopular king on the unwilling Iraqis, inevitably undermined their own prestige. A priori they were in a no-win situation, their benign intentions notwithstanding.

In the early stages of the war, it was taken for granted that at the end of the campaign Mesopotamia would become a British Protectorate. This did not happen. The mood prevailing among the Iraqi people was decisively pro-Turkish. In a lecture given by Sir Arnold Wilson on April 15, 1921, he stated that, were a plebiscite to be taken in Iraq "on the issue of Turkish versus Arab government, there would be a large majority in favour of the return of the Turk." Sir George Buchanan assumed that it was thanks to the treaty with England that Iraq had maintained its integrity. Otherwise, he thought, "Large sections of the populace would not be averse to the return of the Turk under Kemal Atatürk."[88]

The treaty, meant for twenty years, was subsequently reduced to four years; it was ratified in June 1924 after an ultimatum issued by the high commissioner. In October 1932, on the recommendation of the British government, Iraq was admitted to the League of Nations.

As Churchill stated on March 9, 1922, in the Parliament, the total British casualties in Mesopotamia amounted to hundred thousand, and the approximate cost was 350,000 million pounds.[89] In addition, in 1920–21, the financial commitments of Britain to security maintenance and development of Iraq amounted to thirty-two million pounds, which by 1925–26 was reduced to four million.[90] However, gratitude, if any, was in short supply.

Sir Henry Dobbs, high commissioner for Iraq from 1923 to 1929, gave an address to the Royal Empire Society in February 1933, entitled, "Britain's Work in Iraq and Prospects of the New State." He concluded with the following melancholy words:

> So now to raise up this Iraq we have squandered blood, treasure and high ability. We have bound debts and taxes on the necks of generations of our descendants. We have seemed by the abandonment of the Assyrians and Kurds to sacrifice our very honour. We have suffered the imputation that on the scene of their agony we living have betrayed the hopes of our dead. You ask, for all this shall we have our rewards?

I answer, that I cannot say.[91]

Lloyd George had an answer: in his letter to Churchill on September 5, he admitted that the campaign in Mesopotamia was a mistake. Churchill, for his part, had claimed all along that occupation of Mesopotamia was a "thankless task." Buchanan referred to it as a "tragedy"—

> a tragedy of heroism, suffering, wasted lives, and wasted efforts, which began in 1914, when the Indian Expeditionary Force entered the Shatt-el-Arab River and which had not ended when military control ceased in 1921.[92]

Notes

1. Wilson, *A Clash of Loyalties*, 2:255–8, 266–9.
2. F.O. 371/5129 E 6165, Wilson to I.O., June 4, 5 and 7, 1920; F.O. 371/5130, E 9897, note dated August 14, 1920; Wilson, *A Clash of Loyalties*, 2: 273–4.
3. Wilson, *A Clash of Loyalties*, 2:267.
4. F.O. 371/5227, E 6509, Wilson to I.O., June 9, 1920.
5. Ibid., minute dated June 16, 1920.
6. Above, p. 160.
7. F.O. 371/5226/48n, minutes of the military, 21, June 1920.
8. F.O. 371/5231, E 12966, minute dated October 23, 1920.
9. Ibid.

10. Edmund Candler, *The Long Road to Baghdad* (London, New York 1919), pp. 2, 246–251.
11. Wilson, *A Clash of Loyalties*, 2:310–1.
12. Ibid., 318–9.
13. University of Newcastle Library, Gertrude Bell Private Letters, note, dated July 1920.
14. Amal Vinogradov, "The 1920 Revolt in Iraq Reconsidered: The Role of Tribes in National Politics," *International Journal of Middle East Studies*, 13 (1972): 135–6.
15. Haldane, *The Insurrection in Mesopotamia, 1920*, 28.
16. Ibid., 23, 25, 27, 29.
17. Ibid., 64–5.
18. Wilson, *A Clash of Loyalties*, 2:271, 319.
19. F.O. 371/5227, E 8071, G.O.C. in Mesopotamia to W.O., July 7, 1920.
20. F.O. 371/5228, E 8483, "British Policy in Mesopotamia," memorandum by Young, pp. 1, 13.
21. Haldane, *The Insurrection in Mesopotamia, 1920*, 64.
22. Wilson, *A Clash of Loyalties*, 2:272.
23. Ibid., 271.
24. Vinogradov, "The 1920 Revolt in Iraq Reconsidered," 136.
25. Haldane, *The Insurrection in Mesopotamia, 1920*, 76–8; Wilson, *A Clash of Loyalties*, 2:277.
26. Wilson, *A Clash of Loyalties*, 2:277–80; Haldane, *The Insurrection in Mesopotamia, 1920*, 91–103.
27. Vinogradov, "The 1920 Revolt in Iraq Reconsidered," 136–7.
28. Haldane, *The Insurrection in Mesopotamia, 1920*, 124, 157, 165, 178.
29. W.O. 33/969, General Staff, W.O., October 1920.
30. F.O. 371/5078, Baghdad Report, no. 20760, July 14, 1920, encl. Report by A. P. Q., Karbala, on "Activities of Anti-Government Party."
31. F.O. 371/6349/2172, Intelligence Report, No. 3, December 15, 1920, p. 7.
32. Ibid., Intelligence Report No. 2, November 30, 1920, p. 4.
33. F.O. 371/6349/2172, Intelligence Report, No. 3, December 15, 1920, p. 7.
34. Haldane, *The Insurrection in Mesopotamia*, 214.
35. *The Letters of Gertrude Bell*, 497–8.
36. Haldane, *The Insurrection in Mesopotamia*, 235.
37. Ibid., 215.
38. Ibid., 216–30.
39. Ibid., 299.
40. Ibid., 257, 313.
41. *Letters of Gertrude Bell*, November 29, 1920.
42. Wilson, *A Clash of Loyalties*, 2:301.
43. Haldane, *The Insurrection in Mesopotamia, 1920*, 331, App. VIII where a chart of killed, wounded, missing and prisoners of war is printed.
44. Briton Cooper Busch, *Britain, India and the Arabs, 1914–1921* (University of California Press 1971), pp. 408–10.
45. Commons Debate, March 9, 1922. Buchanan corrected the figure to 500 million pounds (p. 284).
46. e.g., Mesopotamia Commission Report (London: HMSO, 1917).

47. Parliamentary Debates (1920), Vol. 127, col. 644–5, 662, 712; Vol. 130, cols. 1468, 1991; Vol. 132, col. 959–60.
48. F.O. 371/5232 E 15721, memorandum dated December 10, 1920.
49. Wilson, *A Clash of Loyalties*, 2:321.
50. *The Letters of Gertrude Bell*, 526.
51. Above, p. 132.
52. Parliamentary Debates, House of Commons, Vol. 143, col. 276.
53. F.O. 141/444/12215, Wilson to I.O., July 31, 1920.
54. F.O. 371/6351/6834, Cox to Churchill, July 9, 1920.
55. W.O. 33/988, "The Proposed Kingdom of Mesopotamia," memorandum by General Staff, W.O., February 17, 1920.
56. Above, pp. 50–3.
57. F.O. 371/5229/5140, "Instructions of H.M.G.," August 28, 1920.
58. F.O. 371/6350, E. 4509, Allenby (Cairo) to Curzon, April 15, 1921.
59. C.O. 370/13/8843, "Note on Mesopotamia: Question of a Turkish Ruler," February 15, 1921; F.O. 371/6350/116, Mesopotamian Intelligence, Rep. No. 6, January 31, 1921; F.O. 371/6351/6185, Intelligence Rep. Nos. 10–11, April 4, 1921.
60. *Letters of Gertrude Bell*, 2:585, January 22, 1921.
61. F.O. 371/6349/13, Cox to Churchill, February 13, 1921.
62. F.O. 371/5229/10440, note, dated February 14, 1921.
63. F.O. 406/46/5408, Churchill to Prime Minister, Cairo, March 14, 16, 18, 1921. Also C.O. 935/1 1921; a copy in AIR/5/829, Minutes of Cairo Conference, app. 6, Mesopotamia. Political, March 1921.
64. *Letters of Gertrude Bell*, 2:619–21, August 28, 1921.
65. Isaiah Friedman, *British Pan-Arab Policy*, pp. 310–11.
66. Ibid., p. 308.
67. Ibid., pp. 308–9.
68. Martin Gilbert, ed. *Winston Churchill 1917–1922*, Companion IV, Pt. 2 (London, 1977) 1662–3, Curzon to Churchill, November 8, 1921, Private.
69. Ibid., 1675–6; Churchill to Masterton-Smith and Shuckburgh, November 24, 1921.
70. Ibid., 1677–8; Churchill to Cox, November 28, 1921, Personal and Private.
71. Buchanan, *The Tragedy of Mesopotamia*, 278.
72. Gilbert, *Companion*, 1959–60; Churchill to Shuckburgh, Biaritz, August 17, 1922.
73. Ibid., 1960; Churchill to King Feisal, August 17, 1922.
74. Ibid., 1961–2; Cox to Churchill, August 23, 1922, telegram.
75. Ibid., 1967–9; minutes of the Conference of Ministers, August 28, 1922.
76. Ibid., 1973–4; Churchill to Lloyd George, September 1, 1922.
77. Ibid., 1977–8; Lloyd George to Churchill, September 5, 1922.
78. Above, pp. 6–8; Gilbert, *Companion*, 60.
79. Above, pp. 9–12, 23.
80. Gilbert, *Companion*, 1978–9; Churchill to Lloyd George, September 6, 1922.
81. Isaiah Friedman, *British Pan-Arab Policy*, p. 309.
82. Elie Kedourie, *The Chatham House Version and Other Middle-East Studies* (Hanover and London, 1984), 253.

83. Ibid., 247.
84. Cited ibid., 277–8.
85. Elie Kedourie, The Chatham House and other Middle-Eastern Studies (Brandeis University Press 1984), pp. 277–8.
86. Isaiah Friedman, *British Pan-Arab Policy 1915–1922: A Critical Appraisal* (New Brunswick, NJ: Transaction Publishers, 2010), 19.
87. Buchanan, *The Tragedy of Mesopotamia*, 283. On the Treaty with Britain see Michael Eppel, *Iraq from Monarchy to Tyranny* (University of Florida Press, 2004), 18–21. It is an excellent study on the modern State of Iraq. It follows the admirable work by Philip W. Ireland, *Iraq: A Study in Political Development* (London, 1937).
88. Cited in George Buchanan, *The Tragedy of Mesopotamia* (London 1938), p. 262. Buchanan estimated the cost to be 500 million pounds, or £160 per capita of the population. (Buchanan, *The Tragedy of Mesopotamia*, 284).
89. Buchanan, *The Tragedy of Mesopotamia*, 279.
90. Cited ibid., 285.
91. Ibid.
92. Cited ibid., 285.

9

Great Britain and the Greco-Turkish Conflict, 1918–1920

Traditional British policy from Palmerston through Disraeli, practically until 1915–16, was the preservation of the Ottoman Empire. The vast lands of the empire served as bulwark against encroachment by other rival powers. Turkey-in-Asia served as a cordon sanitaire needed for the defense of the Suez Canal, the "jugular vein" of the British Empire.

By protecting the Ottoman Empire, Britain earned the gratitude of Muslims all over the world for whom the Ottoman Empire was synonymous with Islam itself. Its territory symbolized the power of the sultan-caliph and therefore assumed a religious significance. It was out of consideration for "the intense feeling of loyalty of the Muslim world toward Turkey, their political and religious centre"— among other reasons—that Sir Edward Grey, the minister of foreign affairs, objected to the idea of partitioning the Ottoman Empire in the aftermath of the war. The de Bunsen Committee was very clear on this matter: partitioning of the Ottoman Empire would deeply offend the Muslims and entail extensive military liabilities. "Our Empire is wide enough already, and our task is to consolidate the possessions we already have." The committee recommended the maintenance of an independent Ottoman Empire, but with a decentralized system of administration. Palestine was a unique case. It must be recognized as a country, whose destiny must be the subject of special negotiations, in which both belligerents and neutralists are alike interested.[1]

William Yale, the American Intelligence Officer, in February 1918, warned that dismemberment of the Ottoman Empire in the aftermath of the war would engender a general national Turkish revival;

moreover, Turkey would incite the Arab-Muslim population in the occupied territories undermining British and French rule.[2]

Sir Theodore Morison, a keen observer and a pundit, testified that throughout Islam there was a furious agitation against the dismemberment of the Ottoman Empire. He warned England not to destroy the Turkish Empire; it would be "a disastrous blunder." Hugh E. C. Whittal, the chief British intelligence agent in Switzerland, pointed out that "the Eastern enemies of Great Britain have united with the avowed object of overthrowing British rule in the East."

Leone Caetani, a leading Italian authority on Islam, was alarmed: "the entire oriental world, from China to the Mediterranean," he stated in the spring of 1919, "is in ferment. Everywhere the hidden fire of anti-European hatred is burning." The discontent was particularly evident among the Muslims in India. Delegation after delegation pleaded with the British Government to prevent the "calamity" of dismemberment of the Ottoman Empire. Eventually, Mahatma Gandhi, himself a Hindu, in an act of solidarity, joined the Muslims in their campaign to prevent a total dismemberment of the Ottoman Empire and any infringement on the sovereignty of the sultan-caliph.[3]

However, to no avail. All warnings went unheeded and pleadings were brushed aside. Turkey *delenda est* was the motto. The consequences were inevitable. Britain, formerly a friend, came to be regarded almost overnight as an enemy of Islam.

Before World War I, Turkey, on her part, reciprocated and valued British friendship. If she did join the Central Powers in the war, it was not because of an inherent antagonism against the British but because of fear of Russia's designs. Russia was bent on acquiring the straits and Constantinople. Britain was an ally of Russia and could no longer guarantee the integrity of the Ottoman Empire. But Germany could. This was done formally on September 28, 1915; the Turco-German Treaty was ratified thereafter twice.

The February–March 1917 Revolution in Russia changed the strategic position radically. Prince Lvov, the head of the provisional government, and Alexander Kerenski, his successor, renounced all territorial claims and propounded the principle of self-determination of peoples. Turkey could now sigh with relief as the Russian danger receded completely.

The Russian Revolution coincided with Tala'at's Bey accession to power as grand vizier. Jointly with Djavid Bey, the finance minister, he tried to take advantage of the new situation to liberate Turkey from

German embrace and, if possible, to defect to the Allied camp. Tala'at and Djavid planned to reform the empire and to decentralize the system of government. A number of feelers were put on this account, and President Wilson, in particular, was keen to detach Turkey from the Central Powers. Initially, Balfour, Lord Hardinge, and General Robertson, the chief of the Imperial General Staff, supported the idea, while Lord Milne thought that it would be "madness" to miss such an opportunity. The only dissenting voice was that of Sir Mark Sykes. He thoroughly distrusted the Turks. Enjoying Prime Minister Lloyd George's support, he delivered a scathing attack against proponents of a separate peace with Turkey; Turkey's secession from the Central Powers' was thus nipped in the bud.[4]

On October 14, 1918, a new cabinet was formed in Turkey with Izzet Pasha as prime minister (grand vizier) and minister of war, Djavid Bey, minister of finance, and Hussein Rauf Bey as minister of marine. Turkey had suffered enormous losses in the war, and her economy was completely devastated. She needed peace desperately and hoped that the terms that Allies offered would be lenient. President Woodrow Wilson, in his celebrated Fourteen Points enunciated that "the Turkish portion of the Ottoman Empire would be assured of their sovereignty" (Point 12), whereas Prime Minister Lloyd George declared on January 5, 1918 that Turkey would not de deprived of its capital, nor its territories in Anatolia and Thrace, which "are predominantly Turkish." However, the Turks were bitterly disappointed. The British cabinet offered Turkey an armistice, not a separate peace. The terms were extremely severe. Turkey was no longer an independent country. She was treated not as a vanquished adversary but as a hostile power.[5]

However humiliating the terms, the Turkish Government had no choice but to accept them. Their chief concern was to revive the friendship with Britain. There was one point on which they remained adamant: viz., that no Greek warship would land in Istanbul or Izmir and that Istanbul would not be occupied by the Allies. Admiral Calthrope passed on the message to London, and the British Cabinet, in its meeting on October 31, confirmed the Turkish request.

Nonetheless, at the Peace Conference in Paris the Turks were humiliated; their pleadings fell on stony ground. Insensitive, the Allied Powers were bent on revenge rather than on reconciliation with their former adversaries. The biggest blow, however, was the occupation of Smyrna by the Greek army. It was abetted and assisted by the Allied, particularly British fleet. This was a blatant violation of an agreement with the British authorities. It touched the raw nerve of every Turk and rekindled Turkish nationalism. The event had far-reaching consequences in the history of modern Turkey. It made the Turks more determined than ever to get rid of foreign invaders and assert their independence.

Strangely, during and even after the occupation, the Turks remained relatively quiescent. Only when the invading Greek army embarked on unexpected cruelties, burning of villages, massacres, rape of women, and murder of children did resistance became apparent. Hatred of the Greeks became so intense that the British high commission saw no hope of peace between two races except by the withdrawal of Greek troops from Asia Minor—a return to status quo ante—although this was not possible.[6]

Adm. Sir Francis de Robeck, who succeeded Calthorpe as high commissioner, admitted that occupation of Smyrna had damaged the British reputation "very considerably." Heretofore well disposed to the British, the Turks felt betrayed and not treated in accordance with the principles that the Allies had proclaimed. Turkish patriotism, he asserted on November 18, 1919, had been stimulated by the Greek occupation of Smyrna, more than by any other event during the war.[7] Three months later, Robeck predicted that the Turkish Nationalist antagonism against the Allies "would have most disastrous repercussion on Eastern situation, which it would . . . be most desirable to avert."[8] Robeck's warning went unheeded.

It fell upon Mustafa Kemal, later known as Atatürk (Father of the Turks), to lead the war of liberation. He was endowed with all the qualities necessary to fulfill a historic role. He was also a gifted orator and a superb organizer. His physical strength and unparalleled courage stood him in good stead when overcoming numerous challenges. Of steely determination, he radiated confidence, which infected his followers. A flexible tactician, he never lost sight of his ultimate objective. He was single-minded, shrewd, unscrupulous, and at times could be cruel toward both friend and foe but also generous if it suited the occasion. Above all, he was a dedicated patriot. He managed to repulse the Australian forces and save the straits and Constantinople for the Turks—an act that earned him the title of national hero.[9]

He was shocked by the terms of the armistice which, in his opinion, violated the Allies' self-proclaimed principles. He resolved to fight for Turkish independence: only Turkish bayonets could ensure Turkey's existence—was his motto.

Kemal's fist task was to rally the army general and district governors in eastern Anatolia to his cause, to abandon the disarmament, and to build a national army—in defiance of the occupying powers, England in particular. The second undertaking was to enlighten the farmers about the situation and to stir up national sentiment. The third objective was to outline a national program and build a rival government to that in Constantinople. This was done at Amasia on June 19, 1919. It was there that Kemal triumphantly proclaimed, "Henceforth Stamboul does not govern Anatolia, but Anatolia, Stamboul." It was also at Amasia that Kemal emerged as the undisputed leader of the movement.

Amasia was followed by a more meaningful development at Erzerum in Eastern Anatolia where the first Turkish National Congress met on July 23, 1919. Its manifesto proclaimed that the object of the movement was "to establish the will of the nation as sovereign power."

This principle sowed the seeds of a future Turkish republic. The delegates at the congress also declared that the entire country, which constituted "an individual whole," should be free of foreign occupation or any interference in its internal affairs. The congress reconciled itself to the loss of the Asiatic provinces of the empire and resolved that a new and homogenous Turkish state should be built. This was a momentous decision that signaled a finis to Ottomanism. The Erzerum Manifesto was the Magna Carta of the new Turkey and served as a blueprint for the subsequent congress that met at Sivas on September 4, 1919 for a week-long session.

The phenomenal growth of the Kemalist movement did not escape Admiral Robeck's attention. He pointed out that the Allies were confronted with a "new situation" and that "it would be more difficult today than it would have been eight months ago to impose on Turkey a distasteful peace treaty without fresh resort to force." The national leaders, he went on, have become more reassured and aggressive; aware of Britain's predicament, they were convinced that they would be able to expose Britain's weakness and thus the British lion would eventually cower "on the first display of Mustapha Kemal's teeth."[10]

And yet, contrary to the views held in London, Mustafa Kemal did not nourish anti-British sentiments. Quite the reverse. He aimed at a rapprochement with England, provided Turkish sovereignty and integrity were respected. This was the message delivered by Kemal Bey, a former ACDX to the grand vizier, to Lt. Col. Ian Smith, the military attaché to the high commissioner. The Nationalist's confidence in

England had been badly shaken by the events in Smyrna. Nonetheless, as realists, they appreciated that it would be fatal for them to drift into hostilities against England. Kemal Bey urged the British Government to come to terms with the Turkish national movement. It lay in Britain's own interest, he argued, to deal with a well-disposed Turkish nation, rather than a hostile one.[11]

The plea fell on stony ground. Lord Curzon, the foreign minister, remained unmoved. The British regarded Kemal as an outcast and a rebel. Subsequently, Britain became involved in a plot that had been concocted by the Ferid government to crush the Nationalists. The plot was foiled, and Mustafa Kemal was quick to realize that Britain was his chief adversary. Ruling out direct confrontation as imprudent, Kemal resorted to the indirect strategy of fomenting the Muslim world. When he joined forces with the Bolsheviks, he was able to cause considerable damage to the British standing in the East.[12]

Britain's negative opinion about the Nationalists was reinforced by Venizelos, the Greek prime minister. In an interview with Philip Kerr, Lloyd George's private secretary, he contended that the notion that Mustafa Kemal commanded a formidable force was "pure bluff." He was confident that, if the Greek force advanced beyond Smyrna, the Turkish troops "would be swept aside."[13]

> Robeck thoroughly disagreed with Venizelos and was shocked when learning that the Supreme Council of the Allied Powers supported Venizelos. Was it prudent, he asked, to call upon Allied officers and men "to sacrifice themselves in order to join Greeks in killing Turks."?
>
> The policy adopted by the Allies would perpetuate bloodshed indefinitely in the Near East and for what? To maintain M. Venizelos in power in Greece . . . is the game worth the candle . . . is it wise to run the almost certain risk of plunging Asia in blood in order to reward Greece according to the desires of M. Venizelos which are very different from the desires of Greece?

Robeck thought that the rulers, who were responsible for having brought Turkey to the war, should receive "drastic punishment." Generally speaking, Turkey should be demoted from the position of a great power. He was equally emphatic, however, in demanding that the terms imposed on Turkey should be compatible with the principles enunciated by the Allies during the war and that the terms "should pave the way for a lasting peace in the Near East."[14] Robeck questioned the very *raison d'être* of the Allies'—having in mind British—policy.

On March 15, the General Staff produced a comprehensive and a penetrating analysis of the military balance. The political power, the General Staff asserted, had passed to the Nationalists, and they soon would be able to function independently of the government in Constantinople. The mass of the population is absolutely war-weary, but the nation would be prepared to fight bitterly to avoid parts of its territory being handed over to a foreign power, especially Greece or Armenia. In this case, the Turkish regular forces would "almost certainly place themselves at the disposal of the Nationalists." Their forces are well officered and capable of a high degree of mobility. "The Turk is an excellent fighter individually, especially on the defensive."

The General Staff estimated that the Turks could raise about sixty thousand armed men, practically equal to the Greek army. However, both tactically and strategically, the position of the Greek is not good. An attempt to occupy the Anatolian Railway between Konia and Eskishehir "holds no definite promise of decisive result." It would entail the maintenance of a large Greek force for an indefinite period, which Greece is unlikely to afford. Moreover, one should take into account a combined action in Asia among the Turks, the Arabs, and the Bolsheviks. The Arabs generally sympathize with the Turks; the Damascus Government is in touch with the Nationalists and is associated with Pan-Islam.

The General Staff concluded that the difficulties that the British would encounter with the Muslim population of the British Empire would be proportionate "to the severity of the terms of the treaty with Turkey." Nor did the conditions of the treaty contain any promise of bringing peace to a country that needed it so sorely, while to the British, from a military point of view, it would "bring nothing but added anxiety and responsibility."[15]

Curzon, however, disregarded the opinion of the General Staff as he failed to take any notice of Admiral Webb's stern warning.[16] Nor did he take advice of Admiral Robeck, Webb's successor. It was, however, Prime Minister Lloyd George that was chiefly responsible for the anti-Turkish policy.[17] The rise of the Kemalist movement concerned him. The nascent Turkish national army was becoming aggressive and its sorties were endangering the British position in Constantinople. Moreover, Turkish intelligentsia and members of Parliament sympathized with the Nationalists; so did the press. Photos of Kemal and of those of his friends were demonstratively displayed in public places. Likewise, Gen. Sir George Milne, the commander of the British army in the Near East, was perturbed. He recommended that all British forces be concentrated in Constantinople and the straits. In contrast, Robeck, suspecting what was afoot, thought that it was "imperative, more than ever," to conclude peace with the Nationalists.[18] He was overruled, however, by the Supreme Council, which unanimously decided that strong measures should be taken to stem the rising tide of Turkish nationalism. On the night of March 15, General Milne's troops occupied Constantinople, arrested leading members of Parliament, and, next morning, deported them to Malta.

This was yet another serious blunder. The occupation of Constantinople infuriated the Turks still further and humiliated every Muslim. In response, Kemal decided to forge an alliance with the Bolsheviks and called for an election of a National Assembly, which met for the first time in Ankara on April 23, 1920.[19]

Ankara, or Angora, as its original name was, derives from the Greek Ancira meaning anchor. After becoming the capital of the modern Turkish state, it was regarded symbolically as the Turkish national anchorage. When Kemal chose Angora as his headquarters, it was still a primitive town devoid of suitable facilities. The advantages however were too apparent. About two hundred miles of mountainous terrain separated Angora from Constantinople, while the town itself was built some three thousand feet above sea level, giving it the appearance of veritable fortress. It had good rail connections to Anatolia and elsewhere.

Enjoying relative safety, Kemal lodged a stern protest against the occupation of Constantinople by the Allied Powers. It was "an arbitrary act contrary to the terms of the armistice," he wrote to Curzon. Members of Parliament and senators were ill-treated by British soldiers and, in violation of their human rights, deported. The sultan-caliph became a de facto prisoner, and therefore, his decrees, legally, were invalid. The National Assembly, which convened at Angora on April 23, resolved to struggle for Turkey's independence, to defend the "sacred rights" of the nation and expected to obtain an "equitable and honorable peace terms." The civil rights of the Christian Ottoman population, as well as other foreign elements, would be safeguarded, provided they do not endanger the security of the Turkish state.[20]

Curzon did not reply. Nor was Kemal's letter acknowledged by the Foreign Office. Robeck admitted that occupation of Constantinople was "a severe blow for the Nationalist movement." He regretted, however, that the Allies did not offer any policy that could form a basis for collaboration with the moderates to produce "tolerable peace terms."[21]

The Allies, however, did just the opposite. After a series of meetings in London in March 1920 and San Remo on April 18, the provisions of the treaty were finally ratified in Sèvres, a Parisian suburb, on May 11. The treaty was very harsh. The Asiatic provinces of the Ottoman Empire were detached and placed under British and French mandates. In the east, Armenian and Kurdish states were to be created, whereas the whole southern half of Anatolia was to be ceded to Italy and France. The straits area was to be demilitarized, controlled, and administered by the Allied Powers. Constantinople, though nominally Turkish, was placed under strict Allied control. It was completely isolated since the Greeks were assured sovereignty over Gallipoli, and Western Asia Smyrna area, though under Turkish nominal sovereignty, was placed under Greek administration. It was a humiliating document. Not only the Ottoman Empire, but Turkey proper also was partitioned and mutilated. Turkey became a shadow state living at the mercy of the victors. The terms were far more severe than those imposed on Germany.[22] For the Turks, it became a day of mourning.

The General Staff was aghast. Like Marshal Foch, the chairman of the Inter-Allied Military Committee at Versailles, the British General Staff was of the opinion that the force required to implement the Sèvres Treaty was beyond the Allied capabilities. British military resources were strained "to a dangerous extent," and there were no reinforcements available. The treaty would increase Greek ambitions, without improving the general situation, while the position of Christian minorities "would be aggravated beyond hope of relief." To maintain peace in the Near East, the argument of the military went on: Greek ambitions should be curbed, the Turks should retain their administrative position and access to Adrianople, while Smyrna should remain under the Turkish flag. By the present policy, Britain is risking a severe blow to her prestige without any corresponding return.[23]

The Sèvres Treaty was not implementable. The policy was bankrupt even before it was borne. It was an arbitrary act of dubious moral and legal validity.

It was Winston Churchill, then state secretary for war, who, more than any other British statesman, appreciated the situation correctly. He gave the General Staff his wholehearted support with force and eloquence that matched the sharpness of his mind. He was convinced that Britain must make peace with Kemal Atatürk and saw no merit in supporting Greek territorial ambitions. On August 12, 1919, he wrote to Balfour, then at the Peace Conference in Paris, that British forces were limited and insufficient to overawe Turkey. On August 23 he wrote to Balfour again stating unequivocally that, with regard to Turkey, Britain "must either quit or stay. If we stay, we must stay in sufficient strength to be safe." To keep an effective army at Constantinople would cost at least £50,000 a day. On September 22 Churchill wrote to Lloyd George reiterating his plea for an early peace with Turkey.[24]

Lloyd George's sympathy toward Greek ambitions did no diminish. He regarded the Turk as "ruffians of Europe . . . who had put themselves irredeemably beyond the pale of civilized society." Constantinople was a hotbed of intrigue and corruption; it was "not Turk, and the majority of the population was not Turkish,"[25] He justified the occupation of Constantinople just as he had no regrets over the Greek landing at Smyrna.

Churchill's views were diametrically opposed. During a cabinet meeting on January 6, 1920, Churchill pointed to the overwhelming evidence supplied by the secretary of state for India to the effect that "expulsion of the Turks" from Constantinople would cause an extraordinary resentment throughout the Muslim World, especially in India. It would also impose a severe strain on Indian troops serving in the British army. Churchill's fundamental belief was that Turkish nationalism was a force, which should be won over, not provoked. On March 24, he entreated Lloyd George to come to terms with it; "The Turkish Treaty means indefinite anarchy." Lloyd George did not reply.[26]

Early in June, when the Kemalist forces went to an offensive and were advancing toward Ismid on the edge of the straits, Churchill wrote to Lloyd George again (June 7). He warned him of the imminent danger if the British persist in occupation of Constantinople and that there were no sufficient troops to defend the city and "we have no reserve anywhere." Lloyd George was not impressed. He was convinced that the Greeks were "the coming power in the Mediterranean, both on land and sea," whom he wished to befriend. On June 16, General Milne cabled to the War Office, stating that he had insufficient forces to hold Constantinople and Ismid and asked for orders what he was to do. On the following day, seven senior ministers, concerned with Eastern affairs, met with Lloyd George, and thereafter, the cabinet concluded that "to retire from Constantinople before a bandit like Mustapha Kemal would deal a shattering blow to [British] prestige in the East."[27]

It was the appearance of Venizelos at the meeting of the ministers and his offer to send troops to help General Milne to defend Constantinople and the Ismid peninsula that convinced the majority of the ministers that prime minister's policy was a sound one. Venizelos' offer and his persuasive arguments were decisive. On June 26, Lord Riddell recorded Lloyd George's remark in his diary as follows:

> The Turks brought about our defeat in the war. It was a near thing. You cannot trust them and they are a decadent race. The Greeks, on the other hand, are our friends and they are a rising people. We want to be on good terms with the Greeks and Italians.
>
> We must secure Constantinople and the Dardanelles. You cannot do that effectively without crushing the Turkish power. Of course the military are against the Greeks. They always have been. They favour the Turks. The military are confirmed Tories. It is the Tory policy to support the Turks. They hate the Greeks. This is why Henry Wilson, who is a Tory of most crusted kind, is so much opposed to what we have done.[28]

Venizelos took advantage of the favorable atmosphere. On July 8, the Greek commander in chief informed General Milne that he had received orders from the Prime Minister Venizelos to occupy Eastern Thrace and transfer troops from Asia Minor for this purpose. Robeck had serious reservations and considered the proposal "most rash and ill advised." To Robeck's surprise, the Greeks managed to repulse the Nationalists forces, albeit only in relatively small part of Asia Minor.[29]

The Greeks, however, nourished wider territorial designs. General Paraskevopoulos, the Greek supreme commander, proposed a new offensive in Asia Minor against Mustafa Kemal. His plan was to advance up to the Anatolian railway, to occupy the strategic location in Eskishehr and to send a column up to Angora. For this purpose, he began to transfer troops from Thrace to Asia Minor.

The French, who had hitherto been against giving a mandate to Greek army in Asia Minor, changed their mind and strongly favored the Greek advance. Marshal Foch gave his imprimatur to General Paraskevopoulos.

Both General Milne and Admiral Robeck were strongly averse to any Greek advance. Militarily they feared lest the Greek army might be seriously compromised, while politically such a move was bound to cause a general revival of Turkish Nationalist movement and awaken among the Turkish masses the urge to defend their country. It "would alienate all moderate elements . . . and would much discredit British prestige in Muslim world, and would be used against us by our enemies as a sign that we intended to make no peace with Islam."[30]

Prudent as this advice was, Milne and Robeck were overruled by Curzon. "It should be borne in mind," Curzon replied to Robeck, "that Mustapha Kemal is the enemy of Turkish Government no less than of the Allies, and his defeat or disappearance . . . would be most effective guarantee for ratification of Treaty and setting up of new conditions created thereby."[31]

Ferid, the grand vizier, had been demanding for a long time that the British undertake measures to suppress the so-called national movement. The imperial decree condemned it in outspoken terms as "rebellion . . . detrimental to the interests of the country."[32] And yet, however inimical to the Kemalists, the government in Constantinople was reluctant to assume the responsibility of signing the treaty, which entailed ceding of Smyrna and the whole of Thrace to Greece. Curzon hoped that the Turkish Government "should swallow their medicine as quickly as possible," but this, to his dismay, never happened. The tone of the press in Constantinople was one of "extreme depression"; so was the mood of the grand vizier.[33]

On the other hand, report from Athens was good news for Curzon. There, the atmosphere was euphoric. The success of Greek arms in Eastern Thrace, the speedy fall of Adrianople and the capture of Tayar were welcomed with great joy. Flags bedecked the houses everywhere. A Te Deum, at the Cathedral, was played in the evening, and the town was illuminated at night. The press, without exception, overflowed with panegyrics on "the wonderful valor and efficiency of the Greek troops." As a by-product, Lord Granville, the British minister to Greece, recorded thus:

> British prestige and popularity stand very high indeed: it is universally believed that it is due to His Majesty's Government alone that the Greeks have been allowed to go ahead in Asia Minor and Thrace, and the Prime Minister's eulogistic speech on Greece in the House of Commons has given universal and unbounded pleasure . . .

As a sign of British popularity, Lord Granville mentioned that, when he came out of the Cathedral after the Te Deum, he was met by the crowds with a great elation, which continued in the streets as he drove away; no similar cheering was given to any other Allied minister.[34]

However, appearances were deceptive. The British—with the exception of a few individuals, like Churchill, Meinertzhagen, Robeck, as well as the General Staff, and definitely the Greeks—underestimated the vitality of the Turkish nationalism and the tenacity of the Turkish soldier. The Greeks aspired to found a Hellenic Empire on the ruins of its neighbor, whereas the Kemalists fought for the independence of their country.

In a parenthesis, it should be pointed out, that Kemal was not an enemy of the Allies, as Curzon imagined. As we shall see later, he found common ground with the Italians, as well as with the French, and made numerous attempts at rapprochement with the British. It was the latter's and support of the Greek that provoked his hostility.

Three events, discussed in our study already, were of far-reaching significance; they eventually tipped the scales in the Kemalists' favor.

First, Kemal forged an alliance with the Bolsheviks (March 16, 1920), which subsequently developed into a formal Turkish-Soviet Treaty (March 16, 1920). It was designed to undo the Sèvres agreement. In addition to political and moral support, the Soviets supplied the Turkish Nationalists with arms, ammunition, and money—generously.[35]

The second event was the defeat of General Denikin's White Army by the Soviet forces and the third, Kemal's capture of Cilicia from the French. General Dufieux's defense force of thirteen thousand, like the population of "Little Armenia" itself, consisted for the most part of refugees. It was pitiably weak. The attack of the Turks was devastatingly effective. In less that thirty-six hours half of General Dufieux's force was wiped out, Marash was captured, and its population of twenty thousand was slaughtered almost to the last soul.[36] A territorial link between the Soviets and Angora was thus created.

While the Kemalists were gaining strength, the government in Constantinople was proportionally losing its grip. Turkish troops in the Ismid area, who were loyal to the government, declared their inability to maintain their position and their intention of withdrawing. This dangerously exposed the British, and General Milne estimated that, at least, a division would be required in Ismid peninsula to fend off any attack by the Nationalist forces.[37] The position was aggravated still further when the Turkish troops defected to the Nationalists. The acute financial crisis made the position of Damad Ferid and of the central government "untenable."[38]

The sultan impressed Admiral Robeck as a man of "no great force of character or personality." During his audience (August 21), which lasted about forty minutes, the sultan bemoaned the black days that

Turkey had passed in the course of the last ten years and blamed the "clique [which] consisted of men who were no Turks at all for the disaster. They had trodden underfoot . . . the tradition of friendship with Great Britain." The ambition of "the Turks, who were the great majority in the country, is to revive to abide by it."

The sultan insisted that Turkey's wounds were deeper than those of any other country and warned that a signing to the Sèvres Treaty would be tantamount to Turkey's "death sentence."[39] The position of the government in Constantinople was practically identical. On June 10, the Grand Vizier Ferid made an urgent appeal for revision of the peace terms, i.e., to leave all the territories where the Turkish language predominated to Turkey. This conformed to the statements made by Prime Minister Lloyd George and Arthur Balfour, the foreign minister. The Turks expected a "peace of justice, not of punishment." He added that it was an illusion to assume that Greek predominance would bring a durable peace. "Greece could never hold on to great possessions." Moreover, in Europe, Greece was "under perpetual threat from Slavdom."[40]

On July 16, having returned from the Peace Conference in Paris, Ferid bitterly complained to Admiral Robeck that Turkey had been presented with a treaty of "utmost severity," signing of which would spell a "total ruin" for Turkey. The extremists regarded it as a "death sentence" and clamored that Turks "should not put a rope round their necks . . . they fixed their hopes on support of Islamic world and Bolsheviks." The government, Ferid insisted, would not put its signature until Kemal had first been repressed.[41]

Beset by severe financial difficulties and confronted by political opponents, Ferid began to show signs of breaking down, and on August, he collapsed, albeit temporarily. His position became untenable. The French High Commissioner was of the opinion that the Allies should compel Ferid to resign and bring about a reconciliation between the Central Government and Angora. Ferid's personality, he pointed out, was one of the greatest obstacles to such a move.[42]

All the same, the Turkish Government was disinclined to ratify the Sèvres Treaty. Its foreign minister told Sir Horace Rumbold, the new high commissioner, that ratification would result in "irretrievable disaster and . . . would produce a deplorable effect." He pleaded, therefore, for still further delay.[43] The treaty was never ratified. The benefit that the British devised from their support of the Constantinople Government was practically nil.

In August 1920, Kemal Pasha put out feelers to the British Government about possibility of peace. This was done through the good services of Francois Stern, a young Rumanian, who had once been employed by the British Intelligence in South Russia and Rumania. He later moved to Switzerland and was in close touch with Turkish Nationalist circles. Approached by Subhi Bey, an emissary of Mustafa Kemal, he was authorized by the latter to make the following proposal:

1. Mustafa Kemal renounced all claim to Thrace.
2. Turkey should be given an assured outlet at Smyrna.
3. Greek troops should be removed from Turkey and Great Britain should cease to support the Greek.
4. The Straits should be controlled, if at all, by Great Britain.
5. Damad Ferid should resign.
6. Mustafa Kemal would welcome British technical advisers.
7. Mustafa Kemal would disband his forces and surrender his arms. He would discontinue anti-British propaganda in Egypt, India, Mesopotamia, and elsewhere.

Mr. Stern endeavored to enlist the support of the War Office and that of the prime minister but was received only by a subordinate official at the Foreign Office. In each case, he was told that while peace with Kemal was "desirable, the precondition was his acceptance of the Sèvres Treaty.[44] The Stern mission had led to nothing.

The treaty was the cornerstone of British policy, and the idea of abandoning the Greeks was not on the cards. This was particularly so since Venizelos made a passionate plea to Lloyd George that "the only remedy [to the impasse] would be a new campaign with the object of destroying definitely the Nationalist forces around Angora and the Pontus." The newly created Greek state in Pontus, in collaboration with Armenia and Georgia, would form "a solid barrier against Islamism and eventually against Russian imperialism." He assured the prime minister that the forces at Greece's disposal were "sufficient to ensure the complete success of this expedition." Greece, however, needed financial assistance to that effect.[45] Lloyd George was impressed and forwarded a copy of it to Sir Eyre Crowe at the Foreign Office.

While Britain remained steadfastly pro-Greek, regarding the Nationalists as enemies, France and Italy began to veer in the opposite direction. Early in June, Admiral de Bon, commander in chief of the French Mediterranean Fleet, as well as the French High Commissioner, confirmed that General Gouraud had arranged an armistice with Mustafa Kemal, pointing out that the French did not intend to retain Cilicia and that he did not wish for "further bloody fighting for a country in which the French no longer interested themselves."[46]

A few days later, the secretary general of the French Ministry for foreign affairs told Sir G. Grahame, the British ambassador, that it was "practically certain that the French Chamber would not ratify the treaty as it stands."[47] Nationalist agents were operating in Paris, making every effort to persuade Allied public opinion that Mustafa Kemal and his associates were the sole representatives of Turkey. Reshid Pasha was on most intimate terms with the French and consequently was reported to have succeeded in reorienting the French policy aiming at establishing understanding with Mustafa Kemal. Admiral Robeck deduced that a compromise with the Nationalists was in accordance with French interests.[48]

Lloyd George's remark on the Treaty of Sèvres in the House of Commons on December 22 was greeted by the French Press with a chorus of resentment and disappointment. The leading article in *Le Temps* was severely hostile and couched in unusual aggressive language against Great Britain. On the strength of the treaty, England apportioned to Greece Smyrna, Gallipoli, and Adrianople, thereby prejudicing both French and Italian interests. Britain, *Le Temps* maintained, is attempting to achieve the mastery of the Eastern Mediterranean and of the straits, as well as the establishment of a Zionist State in Palestine; she is encouraging Emir Feisal in Syria, using the Greeks against the Turks at Angora; she had occupied Mesopotamia and aspires to dominate Persia, both politically and militarily. Having indicted the British policy so heavily, the paper exhorted the French Government "to enter into an immediate and independent agreement with the Angora Government so as to bring about the evacuation of Cilicia and the French zone of occupation in Northern Syria and to reinforce the French troops in the neighborhood of the straits.

The article was replete with exaggerations and inaccuracies but it reflected the kind of mood that pervaded among the Frenchmen. Other journals, like *Pertinax*, *Echo de Paris*, and *Action Française*, followed suit. The *Figaro* endorsed the views of *Le Temps*, while the *Journal* published an article entitled, "England desires the hegemony of the East." Lord Hardinge, the British ambassador, who reported the above, pointed out that the underlying reason for these attacks was the disappointment with Lloyd George's refusal to revise the Treaty of Sèvres. The French regarded the Greeks as unwelcome competitors, whom Britain used as an instrument to establish her hegemony in the Eastern Mediterranean. Constantine, the new king of Greece was thoroughly hated. France regarded the maintenance of the Sèvres Treaty too burdensome and costly. Consequently, she began to reorient her policy toward the rising force of Turkish nationalism.[49]

Besides, France nourished a long-standing grievance against Britain. Before the war, France enjoyed a locus standi in the East. Her interests there dated back to the Crusader period. The Sublime Porte had granted France exceptional privileges, known as capitulations. France was recognized as protector of the Christians, throughout the Ottoman Empire. Her huge investments in Syria and Palestine accorded her a predominant position in this region. This was recognized officially in the Anglo-French Agreement of 1904. On the eve of World War I, France formalized her position still further, initiating an agreement with Germany (February 15, 1914) and two months later with Turkey. By this agreement France gained a free hand in Central and Southern Syria, including Palestine. In 1915 Georges Picot, like his contemporaries, insisted that Syria was a purely French possession, and, by Syria, he meant the region bounded by the Taurus ridges in the north and the Egyptian border in the south.[50]

In 1915, subjected to considerable British pressure, and against their better judgment, the French consented to support the Arab revolt and made substantial territorial concessions in the Sykes-Picot Agreement, 1915/6.[51] The French were in no position to provide troops on a par with the British. They expected, nonetheless, to be accorded a status of parity. They had a rude awakening when the Zionists opted for a sole British mandate in Palestine, whilst in Syria, to their chagrin, British officials were intriguing to eliminate the French position altogether. The installation of Emir Feisal in Damascus acted as a red flag.

The exclusion from the armistice negotiations with the Turkish delegation at Mudros was an additional insult. The prevailing feeling in France was that the British were trying to steal a march in order to establish their hegemony in the East. This chain of events was far removed from Sir Mark Sykes's ideal of a genuine entente cordiale.

The Italians too embarked on an independent course, though differently. Count Carlo Sforza, who was appointed high commissioner in Constantinople, was a pragmatic statesman imbued with liberal ideas who nourished a sneaking sympathy toward Turkish national aspirations. The Italians made no secret of their opposition to the Sèvres Treaty by regarding it unpractical and immoral. They felt

particular grudge against Britain being double-crossed and for allowing the Greeks to occupy Smyrna. They felt discriminated against by
the Allies and that Greece, their erstwhile competitor, was emerging
as chief beneficiary.

Moreover, in Italy's assessment, the balance of power was visibly
tilting in favor of the Kemalists, and therefore, it made sense to conclude a deal with them on a variety of economic concessions, rather
than toeing the British line. This policy dominated when Count Sforza
became foreign minister in 1920. At the same time he endeavored to
avoid a confrontation with the British.[52]

In June 1920, Robeck advised Curzon that frequent visits of Italian
officers and other persons to Nationalist leaders in Anatolia were "so
openly directed against common interests of the Allies, that, from
purely military point of view, presence of Italian troops in Ismid area
might constitute a grave danger to [Allied] forces by transmission to
enemy of military information as to forces and dispositions."[53]

During a number of meetings with Count Sforza at the Inter-Allied
Conference at Spa (July 5–16, 1920), Curzon aired his displeasure
concerning the independent, and, in some cases "scarcely loyal" attitude pursued by Italian officials, military officers, and agents in almost
every part of the Near and Middle East. Curzon presented a resume
of Italian intrigues with the Turkish Nationalists against Allied policy
and interests. The Italians reportedly assured the Turks that they were
behind them in resisting the Peace Treaty. Their actions were "so notorious that it was a matter of common belief that the alliance no longer
existed." This kind of conduct, Curzon maintained, was inexcusable.

Sforza divulged frankly that his government entertained "very serious doubts" about the Thracian and Smyrna policy of the Allies but
acknowledged the justification of Curzon's complaints. He pointed out,
however, that in the judgment of the Italian agents in the East, "the
Nationalist forces in Turkey would be in the ascendant in the future,
it was politic therefore, with a due regard to Italian interests, to be on
good terms with that section of the Turkish community." Moreover,
the Greeks were behaving in a provocative manner, and consequently,
Italian agents were responding in kind. In conclusion, Sforza assured
his British opposite number of his government's unwavering loyalty
to the Allies.[54]

In spite of this reassurance, the situation did not change appre-
ciably. On November 6, Ambassador Buchanan regretfully reported
that the Italian agents in Caucasus and Asia Minor refrained from

giving the British the "loyal support . . . and that their sympathies seemed to be rather with our enemies, and more especially the Turkish Nationalists."[55] A fortnight later, Rumbold confirmed that, although the Italian representatives have been ostensibly scrupulously correct in their attitude throughout, "[t]he whole Italian atmosphere has been pro-Kemalist, and there is no doubt that Italian agents have had dealings with Nationalists." In Rome, Kemalists envoys enjoy a privileged position.[56]

The conclusion that the General Staff reached approximated to that of the French and of the Italians. The defeat of General Wrangel of the White Russian army, the capitulation of Armenia, and the imminent threat to Georgia by the Bolsheviks altered the strategic position in the Near East dramatically. So much so, that it "may be beyond [the British] power to cope without a change of policy." The French and British troops in the neighborhood of Constantinople amount to fifteen battalions, plus one cavalry regiment. This force was about to be decreased by the departure of three battalions. There remained the Greek army in Asia Minor, which amounted to eight divisions (110,000 soldiers), holding a line from the Black Sea, north of Ismid, to the southern end of the Smyrna enclave. However, in the opinion of the General Staff, it would be "unsafe to rely upon the Greek army to cover the Allied position in Turkey." With the likelihood of British forces reduced, the general staff favored readjustment of Allied policy. They believed that

> a drastic revision of the territorial terms of the Turkish Treaty in respect of Smyrna, the province of Kars, and possibly of Thrace, would induce the Turkish Nationalists to break with the Russian Soviet Government . . . [Moreover,] gracious concessions to the Turks [would] wean them from their alliance with the Russian Bolsheviks, by this means recreating Turkey as a buffer state between the Entente Powers and Russia, and removing some of the principal underlying causes of unrest throughout British dominions in Egypt, Mesopotamia and India.[57]

Earlier, Colonel Stokes, the British commissioner in Trans-Caucasia, advocated the renewal of the traditional friendship with Turkey. Inevitably it would involve the abandonment of support of Greece in her expansionist policy in Turkey. On the other hand, "it will bring to our side whole of Islam . . . From Bokhara to Kabul . . . we can have Islam on our side." This is "vital to [insure] the continuance of our Eastern Empire."[58]

Sir Horace Rumbold, soon after his appointment as high commissioner in Constantinople in mid-November 1920, concluded that the "present situation must inevitably lead to considerable modification of Turkish Treaty." And, unless the Allies were willing to undertake difficult military operations in the interior of the country, they should go a long way to meet the Nationalists. The position of the Nationalists had become so strong that the need for entirely new policy had become urgent. An accommodation with the Nationalists would bring, in his estimate, the following benefits:

1. It would accelerate the pacification of Asia Minor.
2. It would enable the Allies to emerge from a difficult situation with minimum of damage to their credit in the eyes of Eastern peoples, Turkish Nationalists in particular.
3. It would secure the well-being of non-Muslim minorities.
4. If properly manipulated, and, should Britain reappear as "protector of Islam," she may drive a wedge between the Kemalists and the Bolsheviks.

The latter object, Rumbold emphasized, was "very important."[59]

Rumbold was a professional diplomat, of an agile mind.

He had served in Cairo, Madrid, Munich, Tokyo, Berlin, London, Berne, and Warsaw. Son of a former ambassador, he was fifty-one years old when he reached Constantinople. He stayed there until 1922. In 1936, he was appointed a member of the Palestine Royal Commission, the Peel Commission. From the start, he did not believe that Britain was able to keep the Turkish Nationalists at bay. He felt that by force of events Britain should be "compelled" to recognize the Angora Government. On January 20, 1921, he cabled to Curzon:

> It is useless to regard Mustapha Kemal any longer as a brigand chief. Angora Government has tight grip on the whole of Asia Minor not in effective foreign occupation . . . It exercises all functions of Government with average efficiency . . . Bulk of population, sheep-like as always, recognized its authority without demur and majority [of] Moslem element[s] support it strongly as standing for the best interests of Turkey . . . native Christians do no fare badly at present.

The leaders of the Nationalist movement, Rumbold went on, were elated and self-confident. They were said to be "intensely hostile to Allies, with the exception of Italy. . . . They are especially hostile to Great Britain." Yet some of them "would even like to revert to traditional friendship with Great Britain if only Great Britain would transfer her affections from Greece to Turkey."[60]

Viceroy Chelmsford was greatly disturbed. On November 23, he wrote to the secretary of state of India, urging the desirability, "even at eleventh hour," of modifying the terms of the Turkish Peace Treaty in order to conciliate Muslim opinion. Its progressive embitterment made British position "much less secure than before the war."

> Before the war, British were . . . regarded by bulk of Moslem opinion as friends of Islam, while Russians were considered its enemies; but since announcement of terms Britain has, in eyes of Asia, become arch enemy of Islam. . . . In India itself, feeling against Turkish peace terms has steadily intensified under pressure of religious leaders and great personal influence of "Ghandi." [sic][61]

It will be recalled that since 1919 a revision of the treaty and reorientation of policy had been advocated by Winston Churchill, as well as by Colonel Meinertzhagen. In the following chapter, we shall see whether these voices of reason found an ear at Whitehall.

Notes

1. Isaiah Friedman, *The Question of Palestine, 1914–1918. British–Jewish–Arab Relations*, 2nd edition (New Brunswick, NJ: Transaction Publishers, 1992), 18, 20–1, where an analysis is provided.
2. Above, p. 1.
3. Above, pp. 17–23.
4. Above, pp. 6–8.
5. Above, pp. 9–12, 23.
6. Above, pp. 33–44.
7. Above, pp. 35–6.
8. *Documents on British Foreign Policy, 1919–1939*, eds. Rohan Butler and J. P. R. Bury, I series, vol. XIII (London, H.M.S.O., 1963); Robeck to Curzon, Constantinople, February 12, 1920, Urgent, p. 1 (Hereafter *DBFP*).
9. On Mustafa Kemal see also above, pp. 35–43.
10. Above, pp. 38–40.
11. Above, pp. 41–2.
12. Above, pp. 212–3.
13. *DBFP*, I, Vol. XIII, No. 18, Kerr to Campbell, London, March 9, 1920, 20–1.
14. Ibid., Robeck to Curzon, March 9, 1920 (My dear Lord Curzon), 17–9.
15. Ibid., "General Staff Memorandum on the situation in Turkey," Secret, W.O., March 15, 1920, No. 23, 26–38.
16. Above, pp. 90–2.
17. Above, pp. 23–34.
18. *DBFP*, I, XIII, No. 681, Robeck to Curzon, February 6, 1920, 1085–7.
19. Above, pp. 94–8.
20. *DBFP*, I, XIII, No. 58, Kemal to Curzon, Angora, April 30, 1920 (French), 67–8.
21. Ibid., No. 32, Robeck to Curzon, March 25, 1920, 47–9.

22. For the text of the Treaty see: *British and Foreign State Papers*, vol. 113 (London, 1920), 652–776; J. C. Hurewitz, *Diplomacy in the Near and Middle East: A Documentary Record*, Vol. II (Princeton, 1956), 81–7.

23. *DBFP*, I, XIII, No. 40, "General Staff Memorandum on the Turkish Peace Treaty." W.O., April 1, 1920, pp. 54–7. A copy of this memo was sent to the F.O. on April 15.

24. Martin Gilbert, *Winston S. Churchill 1916–1922, Vol. IV. The Stricken World* (Boston, 1975), 473–6.

25. Above, pp. 23–4.

26. Gilbert, *The Stricken World*, 477, 480.

27. Ibid., 486–7.

28. Ibid., 487–8. The quotation is taken from Lord Riddell's *Intimate Diary of the Peace Conference and After: 1918–1923* (New York, 1934), 208.

29. *DBFP*, I, XIII, No. 97, Robeck to Curzon, July 8, 1920, 97–8.

30. Ibid., No. 102, Robeck to Curzon, July 28, 1920, 106–7.

31. Ibid., No. 106, Curzon to Robeck, July 30, 1920, 110.

32. Ibid., Nos. 45, 48, Robeck to Curzon, April 5, 11, 1920, 59, 61.

33. Ibid., Nos. 59, 60, Curzon to Webb, May 5, Web to Curzon, May 11, 1920, Robeck to Curzon, May 17, 1920, 68–9, 73.

34. Ibid., No. 108, Granville to Curzon, July 30, 1920, pp. 112–13. The Speech of Lloyd George took place on July 21 (Commons, Deb. 5s, cols. 477–80).

35. Above, pp. 95–7.

36. Howard M. Sachar, *The Emergence of the Middle East: 1914–1924* (New York, 1969), 321. Also see *DBFP*, I, XIII, No. 174, Robeck to Curzon, November 10, 1920, 174–5.

37. *DBFP*, I. XIII, No. 79, Robeck to Curzon, June 10, 1920, Very urgent, 3–84.

38. Ibid., No. 123, Robeck to Curzon, August 23, 1920, 125–8.

39. Ibid., Nos. 135, 136, Robeck to Curzon, September 10, 1920, 138–9.

40. Ibid., No. 78, Robeck to Curzon, June 10, 1920, *Urgent*, 81–3. For Balfour's memorandum and statements by Lloyd George see: *Papers Relating to the Foreign Relations of the United States. The Paris Peace Conference, 1919*, V:669–72, 756–7; also *Documents of British Foreign Policy*, Vol. IV, Appendix II, No. 278.

41. *DBFP*, I, XIII, No. 99, Robeck to Curzon, July 7, 1920, 101–3.

42. Ibid., Nos. 121 and 136, Robeck to Curzon, August 12, September 10, 1920, *Confidential*, 123, 139–40.

43. Ibid., Nos. 196, 198, Rumbold to Curzon, December 16, 21, 1920, 203–4, 206–7. There is an admirable biography by Martin Gilbert: *Sir Horace Rumbold. Portrait of a Diplomat 1869–1941* (London, 1973).

44. *DBFP*, I, IV, No. 132, Curzon to Buchanan (Rome) and Robeck, September 3, 1920, 135–7.

45. Ibid., No. 152, Venizelos to Lloyd George, Athens, telegram October 5, 1920, *Secret*, 157–8.

46. Ibid., No. 76, Robeck to Curzon, June 4, 1920, 81.

47. Ibid., No. 82, Graham to Curzon, Paris, June 15, 1920, 86.

48. Ibid., Nos. 91 and 94, Robeck to Curzon, June 23, 26, 1920, 91–3, 95.

49. Ibid., No. 200, Hardinge to Curzon, Paris, December 24, 208–9. For Lloyd George's speech see: *Commons*, vol. 136, Deb. 5s., Cols. 1893–901.

50. Isaiah Friedman, *Palestine: A Twice Promised Land? The British, the Arabs and Zionism 1915–1920* (New Brunswick, NJ, and London: Transaction Publishers, 2000), 13–6.

51. Isaiah Friedman, *The Question of Palestine, 1914–1918, British–Jewish–Arab Relations.* 2nd edition (New Brunswick, NJ: Transaction Publishers, 1992), 102–7.

52. Salahi Ramsdan Sonyel, *Turkish Diplomacy, 1918–1923: Mustapha Kemal and the Turkish National Movement* (London and Beverly Hills, 1975), 83, 87.

53. *DBFP*, I, XIII, No. 88, Robeck to Curzon, June 23, 1920, 89–90.

54. Ibid., No. 98, Curzon to Buchanan (Rome), Spa, July 10, 1920, 98–101.

55. Ibid., No. 170, Buchanan to Curzon, November 6, 1920, 160.

56. Ibid., No. 180, Rumbold (Constantinople) to Curzon, November 23, 1920, 182.

57. Ibid., 181, "Note on the Military Situation" by the General Staff, W.O., November 22, 1920, 183–9. The author of this memorandum was General Radcliffe, the Director of Military Operations.

58. Ibid., No. 171, Stokes (Tiflis), to Curzon, November 6, 1920, 170.

59. Ibid., No. 186, Rumbold to Curzon, November 27, 1920, 193–4.

60. Martin Gilbert, *Sir Horace Rumbold. Portrait of a Diplomat, 1869–1941* (London, 1973), 228–9.

61. *DBFP*, I, XIII, No. 186, note 1, Viceroy to Secretary of State for India, November 23, 1920, 194.

10

Great Britain and the Greco-Turkish Conflict, 1920–1922, Heading toward War

As has been pointed out already in our study, Lloyd George's concept of the Greco-Turkish conflict differed sharply with that of Churchill, Meinertzhagen, and the General Staff, as well as a number of British diplomats. Churchill, who had persistently crossed swords with Lloyd George, described Lloyd George's outlook faithfully thus:

> The Greek [Lloyd George asserted] are the people of the culture in the Eastern Mediterranean. They are prolific and full of energy. They represent Christian civilization against Turkish barbarism. Their fighting power is grotesquely underrated by our generals. A greater Greece will be an invaluable advantage to our British Empire.... They are good sailors; they will develop a naval power; they will possess all the most important islands in the Eastern Mediterranean. These islands are the potential submarine bases of the future; they lie on the flank of our communications through the Suez Canal with India, the Far East and Australia.[1]

In December 22, 1920, Lloyd George declared that the friendship of the Greek people in Asia Minor was "vital to Great Britain, more vital than to any other country in the world."[2] On the other hand, he had not a good word to say about the Turks. "You cannot trust them," he observed to a friend, "and they are a decadent race."[3] He subscribed to Venizelos's view that "the most important result for humanity of the great war was not the dissolution of the Austro-Hungarian Empire, not the dissolution of the German, but the disappearance of the Turkish Empire."[4]

Balfour, Curzon, and the Foreign Office too were pro-Greek oriented. Characteristic was a memorandum by Harold Nicolson, a member of the Central European Department of the Foreign Office, the son of Sir Arthur Nicolson. The memorandum was written in response to the proposition expressed by Aristide Briand, who on January 12, 1921, became president of the French Council and minister for foreign affairs. Briand maintained that it would be necessary to revise the Treaty of Sèvres and reach an arrangement with Mustafa Kemal. Nicolson doubted whether such a proposition would be acceptable to Greece and particularly to King Constantine, who may be "roused into definite hostility to the Allies and embark upon some extravagant Nationalist crusade." There was, moreover, a far more vital objection to any revision of the treaty.

> Greece constitutes a very positive asset in British imperial policy and so long as we have an Empire, our policy is bound to be imperial. We now propose to surrender this asset in deference to the French. . . . I do not see why, because of the very vivid jealousy of French we should throw away a factor which is of definite defensive value to the Empire . . .
>
> The revision of the Treaty of Sèvres will face us with a discontented and possibly an actively recalcitrant Greece. . . . A compromise on the question will not either please Greece, placate Turkey or be loyally subscribed to by the French. . . . We are not prepared to follow the French in a policy which is the negation of our war policy and which entails the sacrifice of a former ally for the benefit of a former enemy.[5]

Nicolson seemed oblivious that the period of empire building was over and, was subsequently to discover, that Greece had become a burden rather than an asset. In the final analysis, it was Briand that was right, not the British policymakers.

The French were a war-weary nation, and they had no interest in supporting Greek adventurers, whom, in any case, they regarded as British clients. Their positive dislike of Greece deepened following the accession of Constantine to the throne in January 1921. During the war, he had been pro-German and behaved treacherously toward the Allies. Although popular among the Greek royalist party, he brought misfortune upon his people. An imperialist, he endeavored to outdo Venizelos (who lost the elections) in his pan-Hellenic dreams. He was obdurate and unbending. Colonel Repington, former military correspondent of *The Times* got the impression of a king that was "stupid but honest."[6] The French made no secret of their ill-feeling toward him. French eyes were set on Syria, not on Turkey, and their overriding interest was to get their garrison out of Cilicia unscathed. Hence, it was imperative for them to reach an accommodation with Mustafa Kemal.

In December 1920, General Papoulas, the newly appointed Greek commander in Asia Minor, was ordered to attack and capture the Turkish strongholds in Afion-Karahissar and Eskishehir. The Greeks enjoyed marked superiority—both in man power and armaments. They had 110,000 soldiers with 243 heavy guns compared to 60,000 Turks, still underequipped. The Greek offensive began on January 6, 1920, but victory eluded them. Ismet Pasha, the Turkish field commander, launched a sudden and devastating attack on the Greek troops, inflicting six thousand casualties and forcing them to withdraw to their original lines. This fateful battle took place in a valley at Inönü in the neighborhood of Eskishehir.[7]

In Constantinople, newspapers, sympathetic to the Nationalist cause, made no secret of their gratification. Marquis Garroni, the Italian commissioner, who was in touch with the Nationalists, passed on to Rumbold information that the Nationalists were ready to sign a military, political, and economical treaty with the Allied powers, provided hat the Turkish rights of "complete independence in the boundaries laid down by the national covenant was recognized. This was a reference to the pact, which had been drawn up by the Nationalist Congress in Sivas (September 4–13, 1919) and confirmed on February 17, 1920, by the Parliament of Constantinople, in which the Nationalists were represented.[8]

Earlier in the month, Bekir Sami Bey, Mustafa Kemal's foreign minister, told Colonel Bodrevo, an Italian officer, when they met at Tiflis, that the Nationalists wished to make peace with the entente and "must have it. But they must stand out for Turkish frontiers of 1914 in Europe and for elimination of foreign territorial rights, etc., in Asia Minor, although they would agree to a special regime for Smyrna."[9]

Impressed, Rumbold advised Curzon that it was "useless to regard Mustapha Kemal any longer as 'a brigand chief.'" Angora government has a tight grip on the whole of Asia Minor. It exercises all functions of government. Bulk of population had recognized its authority without demur. The Muslim element, in particular, supports it strongly, being convinced that its serves the best Turkish interests. "It would [be] most unwise to count upon collapse of Kemal in the near future."

Whatever their difficulties [Rumbold went on] leaders of Nationalist movement are now elated and self-confident, their pronouncements show them to be intensely hostile to Allies with exception of Italy. . . . They are especially hostile to Great Britain. That is their chief common ground with Bolsheviks. . . . [Though] some of them would like to revert to traditional friendship with Great Britain if only Great Britain would transfer her affiliation from Greece to Turkey but even these would now regard retention of whole "Turkey proper" with complete sovereign rights [as sine qua non].

Moreover, Rumbold warned, it would be a mistake to regard the present Constantinople government to be submissive to Allies' point of view. Its sympathies are with the Nationalists, and they are determined "to give nothing away." The Treaty of Sèvres made the Turkish situation "almost inextricable." It was the Allies that had imported the Greeks into Asia Minor. Now, to liquidate "the Greek complications" would be difficult. It beholds, therefore, the Allies to find a solution "if only to avoid the alternative of being compelled . . . to recognize Kemal government to which it is certainly not desirable that victorious Allies should go as suitors for peace."[10]

It was in order to settle the Eastern question, particularly the Greco-Turkish conflict, that the supreme council of the Allied powers decided on January 25, 1921 to convene a conference on February 21 due to take place in London. In addition to Allied representatives, Turkish and Greek governments were also invited; the Turkish delegation was to include Mustafa Kemal or a qualified representative of the Angora government. The Treaty of Sèvres was to serve as the basis of the conference.[11]

Initially, Curzon evinced "strong moral objections" to the idea of "purchasing peace with Turkish Nationalists at exclusive expense of Greeks."[12] But apparently under Briand's pressure, gave away.

The Greek government, while accepting the invitation, expressed surprise that Kemal had been invited too, particularly as in the previous month the British prime minister had declared in the Parliament that it was "not possible to negotiate with Kemal, who was a rebel." The Greek government was convinced that Kemal was "a mere bogey."[13] In event, Kemal himself preferred to delegate his authority to his foreign minister, Bekir Sami, but insisted that the Angora government should be regarded as the "sole representative of Turkey."[14]

Rumbold lost no time and on January 29 sounded out Sefa Bey, the foreign minister of the government in Constantinople, on Turkey's position. Turkey, Sefa maintained, expected the Allies to eliminate the principle of sphere of influence and wondered why Turkey should be treated with greater harshness than the other defeated powers. She had been sufficiently punished by losing what he described as nine-tenths of her territory; moreover, the notion prevalent among British statesmen that Turkey constituted a potential danger in the future was mistaken. "If properly handled, Turkey could be of considerable use to England in the future."

Responding to Rumbold's criticism about Turkey's conduct, Sefa Bey admitted "the folly," which had brought Turkey into the war on the side of the Central Powers, but this was caused by a few politicians, but the country as a whole should not be blamed. "He sincerely regretted the Armenian massacres," but the Armenians too were perpetuating atrocities against the Turks. In the past, Turkey had been very liberal toward Christians of every denomination, but over centuries, Tsarist Russia were using them, the Armenians in particular, as "agents pro-vocateurs to the detriment of Turkish sovereignty."[15]

Several days later, Rumbold reported that Izzet Pasha, who suc-ceeded Sefa as foreign minister, was in sympathy with the Kemalists and that the Constantinople government had made considerable efforts to effect rapprochement with Angora and demonstrated much tact and skill in its discussions with Mustafa Kemal.[16] The concomitant result was that Tewfik Pasha, the grand vizier, was able to tell Cur-zon, during the Allied Conference in London, that the sentiments of Bekir Sami Bey, the Angoran foreign minister, toward the British are "identical with his own. This, indeed," Tewfik added, "was the feeling of the entire Turkish people."[17]

Throughout the conference, Bekir Sami Bey displayed a very con-ciliatory spirit and acted in close cooperation with Tewfik Pasha—friendlier than one would have imagined. The "wild cats of Angora," according to Tewfik's admission to Curzon, "had become quite tame under his fatherly care."[18]

The proceedings of the conference of the supreme council of the Al-lied powers began on February 21 and lasted until March 17, 1921. The meetings took place in London. M. Kalogeropoulos, the Greek prime minister, also in charge of foreign affairs, arrived earlier on February 18, and Lloyd George, greeting him, declared unequivocally that he was "a true friend of Greece and . . . intended to remain a friend." Yet, he doubted, whether Greece was capable of defending her possessions in Asia Minor, to which Kalogeropoulos responded that the Greek army could easily scatter the Kemalist forces. He thought that the Allies were mistaken "in allowing themselves to be bluffed by Mustapha Kemal." With regard to the maintenance of the Greek possessions in Smyrna and Thrace, "Greece was absolutely one and united." He rejected the idea of any constitutional concessions such as making Smyrna an autonomous province with a Christian governor appointed by the Allies, following the model of Eastern Roumellia.[19] The Greek government in Athens endorsed Kalegoropoulos's statements.[20]

When, on February 21, the first Allied Conference opened, Lloyd George had the unsavory task of announcing the delegates that he found Kalegoropoulos to be "very obstinate and unbending" and that he had come to the conclusion that the Constantinists would be very much more difficult to deal with than the Venizelists. Moreover, the Greek government nourishes the greatest confidence in their army and in their power to defeat the Kemalists; it enjoyed the support of all the Greek people. All the signs indicate that the Greek government intends "to fight and to reject any compromise." Lloyd George commented that if the Greeks prove to be unreasonable, he would turn against them; the same would apply toward the Turks. Lord Curzon also got the impression that the Greek government was "determined to reembark upon hostilities."[21]

During the following meeting on the same day Kalogeropoulos revealed that the Greek army, facing Mustafa Kemal, consists of 121,000 soldiers, combatants and non-combatants, and was confident that it would be able to annihilate Kemal's forces within three months. The morale of the Greek army was "excellent" and the Greek soldiers were only "too anxious to continue to fights". He unhesitatingly affirmed that the Kemalists were in fact "not regular soldiers; they merely constituted a rabble worthy of little or no consideration." His confidence in the Greek troops was "absolute, and their courage was undoubted."

Count Sforza, the Italian delegate, remarked that should the Kemal forces retire deep into the country, a very serious situation would be created similar to that which caused to "the downfall of a great army led by one of the world's greatest generals." Sforza had in mind the hapless Moscow campaign of Napoleon in 1812.

Aristide Briand did not question the patriotism of the Greek people and "their desire and will to give expression to it in a striking manner at Smyrna" but sharply disagreed with Kalegoropoulos's opinion about the military value of the Turkish troops. France had maintained in

238

Cilicia a force of sixty thousand men, courageous, well-trained, and perfectly equipped. They were facing the Turks, for over a year, who had inflicted on the French forces cruel losses. The Turks were "full of pluck," fighting savagely, contesting every inch of ground. They were not a "rabble band," which the Greek prime minister despised.

General Gouraud followed his premier. Gouraud was a brilliant general, noted for his achievements on the Western front. He fought against the Turks in Gallipoli and Cilicia. Weighing his words carefully, he warned that Turks were "dangerous adversaries and not to be lightly despised." Under his command, in Cilicia, there were fifty thousand French troops of excellent quality. And yet the defense of Aintab was a very difficult and arduous task, which was likened to the siege of Verdun. The Greek army, he warned, would face a dangerous enemy. Moreover, the distance of six hundred kilometers from Smyrna to Angora constituted a serious impediment. Angora is situated in a mountainous terrain fifteen hundred meters high. It is an impregnable fortress. He recalled Marshall Foch's estimate that a force of twenty-seven divisions would be required to pacify Anatolia. Unlike on the French front, where the soldiers were protected by trenches, in Anatolia, Gouraud emphasized, an invading army would have to fight in the open and at a very considerable distance from the base of supplies.

Colonel Georges added that the Kemalists have about forty thousand men in training camps; numerous officers were constantly joining him from Constantinople, and they were also recruiting Russian officers. He doubted whether the Greek resources in men and money were sufficient to undertake an operation of such hazardous character.

The Greek delegation was not convinced, and Colonel Sariyannis brought up a number of instances when the Greek troops easily had repulsed the Turks. Moreover, the Greek troops, he said, "were fighting to relieve their oppressed brethren, the recollection of whose wrongs filled them with ardour and enthusiasm."[22]

Since the occupation of Smyrna, Arnold Toynbee, reported, Greek Nationalism "has welled up strong and compelling."[23] Toynbee was at that time the correspondent of the *Manchester Guardian* and was in a position to observe the events from close quarters. Indeed, so overpowering was the newly found nationalism in the Greeks that it blurred the distinction between the desirable and the possible. Their claim that they "were fighting to relieve their oppressed brethren" masked their undisguised imperial Hellenic ambitions.

Turkish nationalism was just as fierce. The Turks of all denominations resented the invasion of foreign powers and stubbornly fought for restoration of their sovereignty over Turkey proper. This, in their conception, embraced also Smyrna and Thrace. The clash between Greek and Turkish aspirations was absolute.

The first meeting between the Allies and the Turkish delegation took place on February 23, 1921. It included also the representatives of the Angora government. For Angora it was a no mean achievement since the powers for the first time acknowledged its legitimacy. The Nationalists, however, refused to be considered as adjuncts to the government of Constantinople. On the day before the conference, the Angora delegation made it clear that they regarded themselves as the only persons who could speak for Turkey "and that delegation from Constantinople in any respect should not be considered as 'representative of Turkish opinion.'" Ultimately some modus vivendi between the factions was reached,[24] but the leading voice was that of the Nationalists.

Questioned by Lloyd George, Bekir Sami, the Angora foreign minister, presented his case clearly and eloquently. He assured the conferees that the Grand National Assembly sincerely desired "to secure the restoration of a lasting and just peace in the East." He hoped that steps would be taken to enable Turkey to exist as an "independent nation . . . and maintain her national honor." This would not be possible so long as the Treaty of Sèvres was being implemented; it spelled "doom of the economic and political life of Turkey." Bekir Sami referred specifically to Smyrna and Thrace, which, according to the treaty, had been allocated to Greece. Turkey's claim to these territories was based on principles of nationality, as well as on economic interests.

Bekir Sami went on elucidating that 95 percent of the landowners of the town and vilayet of Smyrna were Turks. During their occupation, the Greek administration forced three hundred thousand Turks to flee and abandon their homes in Smyrna; but before these events, the population had been absolutely Muslim. Moreover, the Greeks inhabiting these territories were not Hellenic Greeks but Ottoman Greeks. A great number had been recently imported from Greece in order to change the demographic balance. His statistics, Bekir Sami maintained that, were accurate and based on the work of M. Puymet, a recognized French authority, who had collected the data in 1896 in connection with the Ottoman Public Department and published them in a Yellow Book. Moreover,

> Smyrna was tied by three lines of railway to the centre of Asia Minor ... and it was the only outlet to the coast for all the trade from the interior territories. Consequently, the town of Smyrna was of vital necessity for the economic life of Turkey in Asia. ... The presence of foreign troops, or the attribution of Smyrna to a foreign Power would indubitably constitute a constant source of friction and disturbance, and would be a permanent menace to the world peace.

In the past, the Greeks settled along the coast of the Ottoman Empire, chiefly as navigators and traders. In contrast, the Turks were cultivators and attached to the land. In world history, traders never succeeded in evicting the farmers from the land. For all these reasons Smyrna and the vilayet should remain Turkish. Its allocation to a foreign power would bring to Anatolia economic ruin.

The principle of nationality applied also to Thrace, where the Turkish population predominated. For historical, political, and economic reasons, it should fall under Turkish sovereignty.

In their memoranda, the delegation of the Nationalists made it unequivocally clear, among others, the following:

1. The Grand National Assembly of Turkey, constituted "the only legal representative of the Turkish people."
2. Smyrna and all territories in Asia Minor occupied by the Greeks should be evacuated and restored to the sovereignty of Turkey.
3. Turkey's frontier in Europe should follow the Treaty of Constantinople of September 16/29, 1913 between Turkey and Bulgaria; that is to say, all Eastern Thrace should be evacuated and restored to Turkey.
4. Turkey would adhere to the principle of freedom of navigation of the straits for flags of all nations on a footing of equality without affecting the security of Constantinople and with due respect to the Turkish sovereignty.
5. Turkey would not object to the demilitarization of the straits and to an institution of an international commission of supervision, in which Turkey would be represented.
6. The protection of racial, religious, and ethnic minorities shall be assured as provided in the Treaties of Saint-Germain, Neuilly, and Trianon.[25]

With hindsight it could be said that, had the Allied powers accepted the demands of the Turkish National delegation, the tragedy that befell the Greek population in Smyrna could have been avoided. The Allies, however, had neither the foresight, nor the will to force the Greek army to evacuate the captured territories in Turkey.

The nature of the difficulty that had confronted the Allies became evident during the conference in February 24 during which the Greek delegation presented its case. Demetrious Gounaris, the new prime minister, disputed the statistics, which had been presented by the delegation of the Angora government. The Greek data, Gounarakis claimed, had been prepared before 1912–3 by reliable authorities; they had been presented by M. Venizelos, his predecessor, before the signing of the Sèvres Treaty and accepted by the supreme council of the Allied powers. These statistics showed that in the Aidin area, which had been allocated to Greece by the Sèvres Treaty, there existed 548,194 Greeks, as opposed to 300,921 Turks. In 1914 and during the war, the Turkish government expelled 140,889 Greeks, who took refuge in Greece, and deported 50,319 Greeks to the interior of Asia Minor; about 25,000 of them died in deprivation.

In addition to the Greeks, there were in Smyrna 18,647 Armenians, 31,346 Jews, and almost 20,000 foreigners and others, making the total of nearly 70,000. In Thrace, Gounaris went on, there were 365,278 Greeks, 345,198 Turks, 24,100 Armenians, and 30,000 Bulgarians, or people of Slavonic tongue, making the total of 764,576 inhabitants. The number of Greeks that had been deported before and during the war amounted to 250,878.

The Greek delegation implored the conference not to reopen the question or give way to Turkish representations. They pointed to the "sacrifices" that Greece had made during the war for the Allied cause. The strongest argument, however, which prime minister Gounarakis made was when pointing out that the Greek presence long antedated the Turkish conquest in 1453. For many centuries prior to that date

> the district had been Greek. Since 1453 the Greek population had diminished owing to Turkish misrule, but the fact that Greek ideals and culture had survived, in spite of Ottoman oppression, indicated how strongly and vigorously Greek sentiment and sympathies had permeated the district.[26]

The Greeks definitely had a case. In retrospect, had they concentrated their claims on Smyrna and Eastern Thrace alone, a compromise solution with the Turks could perhaps have been found. The Greeks, however, nourished wider ambitions: their aim was to smash the Kemalists and found a Hellenic Empire. This objective proved unattainable and eventually rebounded on the Greeks themselves. It also ran counter to the proclaimed principles of the Allies.

The conflicting statistics placed the Allies in a dilemma. Thereupon, Lloyd George suggested that "a full and impartial investigation into the facts respecting the populations of Eastern Thrace and Smyrna" be submitted to an International Commission in order to enable to the powers to decide "justly and fairly between the parties." He stipulated, however, his proposal on an understanding that the remaining clauses of the Treaty of Sèvres should remain unaltered.

The Turkish National delegation, headed by Bekir Sami, accepted the proposal, provided that the supreme council obtained, from the Greek government, reliable guarantees as to the protection of life and property of the Turkish population inhabiting the regions occupied by Greek forces, whose "methods of extermination have already entailed the loss of many lives and much property upon the wretched inhabitants." This claim was particularly justifiable because the Grand National Assembly, from its creation, "have scrupulously applied the necessary measures to ensure public order and the security of national minorities" in the territories under its control. Bekir Sami added succinctly that Turkey was asking "for the right to live as free community, just as every other state would ask in similar conditions."

In contrast, the Greek delegation was by far less responsible. M. Kalegoropoulos, the foreign minister, was displeased that his government was being asked "to nullify a title deed that bore the signatures of the Great Powers." Moreover, the Greek army was ready to take the offensive; now, were it suddenly stopped in its "victorious progress," much irritation would be created, which could probably lead to "regrettable incidents."[27] On March 1, 1921, the Greek Parliament unanimously rejected the proposal of sending the international commission of inquiry to Thrace and Asia Minor. Revision of the Treaty of Sèvres was unacceptable. Representatives of all the parties expressed their "unanimous feeling of the Greek nation to persevere in the light for the realization of the national destinies for which she declares herself ready to make new sacrifices."

Lloyd George responded bluntly. He told Kalegoropoulos, who delivered the message, that the Greek people should not delude themselves into thinking that they themselves had emancipated Thrace and Smyrna. It was mainly because of the gigantic effort made by the Allies, mainly by Great Britain, that Greece had expanded her territory. It had cost Britain over £1,000,000,000 to defeat Turkey, and her casualties amounted to two hundred thousand—a figure approximate to the total Greek army. In view of their sacrifices, the Allies had "a great right in trying to establish peace in the Near East and give advice to Greece."

Lloyd George pointed out to Kalegoropoulos that the diplomatic position of Greece was weak. Italy sympathized with Angora, while

France's attitude changed considerably. She was anxious to make peace with Turks in Cilicia, and the recall of Constantine to the throne had affected French public opinion very deeply. Even the British nourished bitter feeling about King Constantine; he had surrendered Fort Ruppel and the whole Greek division to the Bulgarians and the Germans in "a very critical moment of the war." Britain was, therefore, not in such a strong position to help Greece as she had been. The Turks had declared their willingness to accept the Allies' proposals. If the Greek simply stated a non possumus, "trouble would certainly ensue. Not only would the conference be turned against the Greeks but public opinion too." It was therefore essential that the Greek government accepted a fair compromise.

The kind of compromise that Lloyd George had in mind was that the Turks should be given formal sovereignty over Smyrna, while the Greeks would be in control of its administration. Such a solution in his view would make peace possible. It would enable Greece to demobilize her army and put her finances in order.[28]

On the same day, Lloyd George received Bekir Sami Bey. Although admittedly not a trained diplomat by his own admission—something of a parvenue in diplomacy—his presentation was anything but that of an accomplished diplomat. He declared that, in order for Turkey to exist independently as a nation and be useful to humanity, it was necessary that it should be guided by Great Britain. Turkey was determined to regenerate itself, and she preferred the British to serve as guides and mentors. He thought that the Turkish nation was of "great importance to Great Britain . . . a trump card in England's hands." Turkey could be more beneficial to British interests than those expected from Greece. The perennial question that concerned Britain was freedom of navigation through the straits. Provided that Constantinople and its hinterland were not menaced by a coup de main from its turbulent neighbors and Turkish sovereignty guaranteed, Turkey was quite ready to accept whatever conditions Great Britain laid down it deems necessary for its security. Moreover, Turkey would be willing to cede to the British the islands at the mouth of the straits.

Bekir Sami suggested that both the British and the Turks should concentrate on building the future, rather than dwell on iniquities of the past. The Angora government abandoned the idea of Pan-Turanism, as it turned its back on Pan-Islam. Both Pan-Turanian policy and Pan-Islam led to Turkey's disaster. Instead, Bekir Sami unveiled his grand design. The plan centered on the Caucasus, which could serve as a barrier against the danger from the north, whether it was from the Bolsheviks, the Mensheviks, or the Tsarist government. In northern Caucasus, there were abut three million inhabitants, which included Daghestan, Tchetchnia, and Circasia, while in Transcaucasia, which comprised of Georgia, Azerbaijan, and Armenia, there lived from seven million to eight million inhabitants. They could maintain an army of two hundred thousand and possibly even three hundred thousand on a war footing. They were good soldiers, who had proved themselves in their struggle against Tsarist invasion during the nineteenth century.

Sami himself was of Caucasian origin and was familiar with the aspirations of the inhabitants to emancipate themselves from Bolshevik domination. They sympathized with Great Britain. Hence, if the British government availed itself of this force, a barrier would be provided both for Turkey and Britain against Russia, and consequently, the Russian march into Central Asia would be checked. An independent Caucasian confederation would be an asset for Britain. Strategic value apart, there were economic benefits too. In Baku, and elsewhere in the Caucasus, there were rich deposits of oil, whereas in the region between the river Don and Terek, there was a great granary. While Britain would benefit from an alliance with the Caucasian confederation, the Bolshevik regime would be deprived of these natural resources. Moreover, Bekir Sami went on, Turkey would harness the caliphate to counter Bolshevism in Central Asia, in Bokhara, Khiva, Turkestan, and Afghanistan. Such a role, Greece would not be able to fulfill. The number of Greeks does not exceed the figure of five million; they are mercantile-minded and of "no great military value."

It should be recalled that Bekir Sami Bey was the Nationalists' foreign minister who, negotiated with the Bolshevik government on behalf of the Angora government. That he could have expounded before Lloyd George a definite anti-Bolshevik orientation shows that the Nationalists' agreement with Moscow was merely a marriage of convenience, dictated by an existential necessity. It also shows that, given Britain's positive response, the Nationalists essentially preferred an alliance with Britain than with any other power. This fact is unknown in historiography. It stands to reason that such a far-reaching statement of policy could not have been done without Mustafa Kemal's knowledge, let alone inspiration.

Lloyd George was impressed. He complimented Bekir Sami for his "statesmanlike" presentation that deserved "careful consideration." He fully agreed with his statement, notably with regard to the barrier in the Caucasus. Personally, he was concerned more with the revival of Russia's imperialist designs, rather than with Bolshevism per se; and there were indications that Bolshevism was "gradually slipping back into the imperialistic idea." This was a great menace to Turkey, as well as to Great Britain. From this point of view, "it was perfectly true that . . . the interests of the two countries were identical."

Lloyd George went on and declared that

> [h]e himself had always been a strong advocate of leaving Turkey with an independence worthy of her dignity, and independence within the territories remaining to her after the war. He was opposed to anything which tended to keep a country in bondage. No nation could continue its independence while remaining in servitude. As an old Nationalist he was a firm believer in liberty and independence. . . . He was more than delighted at the prospect of restoring the old friendship between Turkey and Great Britain, and that the wild advisers who had been the cause of Turkey's troubles [the Young Turks], were not likely to be restored.

Not all statements of Lloyd George conformed to the truth. He despised the Turks; he reneged on his vow made in his celebrated Trade Union speech on January 5, 1918, and his support of the Greeks against Nationalist Turkey proved disastrous. It seems, however, that Bekir Sami opened his eyes to see Turkey in a different light. The transformation in Lloyd George's weltanschauung was short of remarkable, albeit it was incomplete.

The first priority was Smyrna. If the Turks insisted that the Greeks vacated it, there would be war. It would be almost impossible for any Greek king to order the troops out without sacrificing his dynasty. The Greek government would have to choose between war and revolutions: they "would choose war." Lloyd George brought up his plan of Smyrna remaining under Turkish sovereignty, while its administration would be placed in Greek hands.

Sami rejected the proposal out of hand. If the Greeks remained in occupation, it would be tantamount to Smyrna becoming Greek within two years; it would be a repetition of what had happened in Crete, where before the war, after Turkey renounced all claim to Crete, the Greeks returned to the island and took it over. In any case, the Turkish National Assembly would not accept such a proposal. It considers Smyrna "absolutely essential to the existence of Turkey. To take it out was like pulling out their heart. Without it they could not exist."

Sami agreed with Lloyd George that the Allies had invited the Greeks to go to Smyrna and could not compel them to withdraw by force. He did not want Greece to be humiliated in front of the world; all that Turkey expected from the Allies was "to perform an act of justice: Smyrna was necessary for [Turkey's] very existence."[29]

The impasse was absolute. Lloyd George was in a dilemma. His newly found sympathy for Turkish national aspirations was genuine. It was a remarkable volte-face in his outlook. He also concurred with Sami's argument about the benefit likely to accrue to Britain from a strategic alliance with Turkey. By logic, this line of thought should have made him admit his mistake of tacitly encouraging the Greeks against the Turks, in which case, the obvious conclusion would have been to ask the Greeks to withdraw from Anatolia and place Smyrna under international trusteeship. Thus, the chief bone of contention between the Greeks and the Turks would have been removed and the well-being of Smyrna's inhabitants assured.

News about atrocities committed by the Greeks against civilian population in Thrace should have prompted Lloyd George to decide quickly and act. One of the telegrams from Constantinople, dated March 1, 1921, read as follows:

> The Greeks under the pretext of looking for arms, are committing freely unheard acts of violence and excesses against Mussulman villages of Eastern Thrace. These villagers are terror-stricken, and seek to save themselves by abandoning their villages. At Adrianople and some other towns wholesale arrests of prominent and wealthy personages began some days ago and are still continuing, they number already many hundreds. The Mufti of Serai, a man of 75 years, has been arrested also.

Other telegrams indicated that the purpose of the Greek measures was to force the Turkish inhabitants to leave the country in order to secure a Greek majority. The cables were sent by Ghalib Kemali Bey, president of the Turkish delegation of Thrace and a former ambassador, to the Allied Conference in London, appealing for help.[30]

The events in Thrace—which incidentally were a mere replica of what had happened in Smyrna—were not discussed. Graver issues, those of war and peace were occupying the minds of the Allies. On March 9, Lord Curzon met Bekir Sami Bey and warned him that the Greeks "were anxious to fight. If hostilities ensued, all prospects of peace in Asia Minor were at an end and all prospects of peace between the Turks and the Allies." He asked Bekir Sami to consider whether something could not be done. Sami expressed himself with ability, clearness, and courtesy and stated that the desire of the Turks was "to resume friendly relations with the principal powers of the West." However, with regard to Smyrna, "nothing could be done. The Turks had defeated the Greeks before and they would do so again. . . . [Eventually] the Turks would resume complete occupation of Smyrna." Sami repeated the same during a conversation with Count Sforza.

The Greeks were equally uncompromising. "The Greeks would rather fight," Lloyd George concluded. "Evacuation of Smyrna meant the fall of the dynasty, and heaven knew what would happen then."[31] On the following day, Gounaris made it perfectly clear that the Greeks were not in a position to compromise with regard to Smyrna. Greece was determined to "complete her mission." The Greek people, irrespective of opinion, were ready to make any sacrifice for this end. He was confident that the military operation "would surely bring about the dissolution of the Kemalist forces in a short time, which he estimated at about three months."

Lloyd George got the impression that the Greeks were as much convinced that their army could defeat Mustafa Kemal as Bekir Sami was convinced that Mustafa Kemal could beat the Turks. He "had never seen two combatants who were so confident of being able to beat each other."[32]

Lloyd George was powerless to control the situation. The drift toward war was inevitable.

Notes

1. Winston S. Churchill, *The World Crisis*, Vol. IV ("The Aftermath") (New York, 1929), 391.
2. Harold Temperley, *A History of the Peace Conference of Paris*, Vol. VI (London, 1924), 32.
3. *Lord Riddell's Intimate Diary of the Peace Conference and After: 1918–1923* (New York, 1934), 208.
4. Michael, L. Smith, *Ionian Vision: Greece in Asia Minor, 1919–1922* (New York, 1973), 184.
5. *Documents on British Foreign Policy 1919–1939* (thereafter *DBFP*) eds. W. W. Medlicott and Douglas Dakin, First Series, Vol. XVII (London: HMSO, 1970), No. 12, Memorandum by H. Nicolson on the Revision of the Treaty of Sèvres, January 18, 1921, pp. 13–6.
6. Ibid., No. 15, Cited in Granville (British Minister in Athens) to Curzon, January 21, 1921, pp. 24–5.
7. Howard M. Sachar, *The Emergence of the Middle East, 1914–1924* (New York, 1969; London 1970), 419.

8. *DBFP*, Vol. XVII, No. 13, Rumbold to Curzon, January 19, 1921, pp. 20–1. It would be recalled that the Nationalist Deputies to the Parliament in Constantinople were thereafter deported by the British authorities to Malta. The Turkish National Pact (in English) appears in E. G. Mears, *Modern Turkey* (New York, 1924), 629–31; also in Helen Miller Davis, *Constitutions, Electoral Laws, Treaties of the States in the Near and Middle East*, 2nd ed. (Durham, NC, 1953), 465–6.

9. Ibid., No. 4, Rumbold to Curzon, January 6, 1921, 3.

10. Ibid., No. 14, Rumbold to Curzon, January 20, 1921, 21–4.

11. Ibid., No. 20, Hardinge (Paris) to Curzon, January 26, 1921.

12. Ibid., No. 19, Hardinge to Tyrell, Paris, January 26, 1921, 28.

13. Ibid., No. 23, Granville (Athens) to Curzon, January 27, 1921, 31. Lloyd George's speech in the House of Commons took place on December 22, 1920 (see *H.C.*, Vol. 136, Dec. 5 S.J. cols. 1893–901).

14. Ibid., No. 29, note 1, where gist of Mustafa Kemal note to the grand vizier is quoted (p. 38). For the full version, see enclosure in No. 34, 49–50.

15. Ibid., No. 29, Rumbold to Curzon, January 29, 1921, 38–42.

16. Ibid., No. 32, Rumbold to Curzon, February 6, 1921, 44–6.

17. Ibid., No. 46, Curzon to Rumbold, March 2, 1921.

18. Ibid., No. 50, Curzon to Rumbold, March 15, 1921, 72–3.

19. *DBFP*, I, vol. XV, ed. by Rohan Buttler and J. P. T. Bury (London, H.M.S.O., 1967). No. 13, pp. 125–6, 129. By the Treaty of Berlin of 1878, Eastern Roumelia had been established as an autonomous province within the Turkish Empire; a Christian governor was to be nominated by the sultan with the assent of the Great Powers.

20. Ibid., App. I + II to No. 15, 132–5, February 21, 1921.

21. Ibid., No. 16, Allied Conference on February 21, 1921, 137–40.

22. Ibid., No. 17, meeting dated February 21, 1921 at 4:00 p.m., 147–59.

23. Arnold J. Toynbee, *The Western Question in Turkey and Greece* (London, 1923), 125.

24. *DBFP*, XV, No. 18, Notes of an Allied Conference, February 22, 1921, 160.

25. Ibid., Nos. 19, 20, and Appendices, Allied Conference on February 23 and 24, 1921, 168–81. For statistics, see also M. Cuinet, *La Turquie d'Asie*, 4 vols. (Paris 1890–5). Cuinet served as a dragoman in the French embassy at Constantinople. For the treaties referred to in paragraph (f), see *British and Foreign State Papers*, London 1920, Vol. 112, 353–5, 794–6 and vol. 113, 512–4.

26. *DBFP*, XV, No. 21, Allied Conference, London, February 24, 1921, 181–8.

27. Ibid., Nos. 23, 24, 25, Allied Conferences, London, February 25, 1921, 194–207.

28. Ibid., No. 32, Interviews between the prime minister and M. Kalegoropoulos, March 21, 1921, 265–9.

29. Ibid., No. 33, Notes on a meeting between Lloyd George and Bekir Sami Bey, March 4, 1921, 269–78.

30. Ibid., Appendix to No. 36, 285–6.

31. Ibid., No. 51, Notes of an Allied Conference, London, March 9, 1921.

32. Ibid., Nos. 52, 53, Allied Conferences held on March 10, 1921.

11

Great Britain, the Allies, and the Greco-Turkish War, 1921–1922

From their perspective the Greeks felt confident that they could defeat the Turks. Their army was much better equipped; it was highly motivated and imbued with a sense of purpose or rather a mission. The Greek people were highly patriotic and supportive.

However, carried away by enthusiasm, they were oblivious of the dangers: Anatolia's vast territories, long lines of communication, Angora's impregnable strategic position, the financial shortcomings of the Greek treasury, and above all, the toughness of the Turkish peasant/soldier who was fighting for the survival of his country against an invading enemy. It was for these reasons that General Metaxac, an outstanding Greek military commander, refused to accept Prime Minister Gounaris's offer to lead an offensive in Anatolia in April 1921. In his estimate, a war against the Turks could not be won. The Turks were intensely nationalistic

> and they mean to fight for their freedom and independence. . . . They realize that Asia Minor is their country and that we are invaders. For them . . . the historical rights on which we base our claims have no influence. Whether they are right or wrong is another question. What matters is how they feel.[1]

The Turks were fortunate to have an outstanding leader in the person of Mustafa Kemal.[2] Lieutenant Colonel Rowlinson, the British control officer, who met Kemal, was impressed by his striking personality, his strength of character, patriotism, and complete and wide-ranging knowledge. Rowlinson described him as a "great Turk" who was "European rather than Asiatic type."[3] Sir Horace Rumbold, the British high commissioner at Constantinople, in his annual report for 1920, praised Mustafa Kemal's "administrative capacity, political ability, and determination." His speeches "show considerable skill in handling people and situations. He is spectacular and domineering, [and] there is no reason to accuse him in lack of patriotism . . . or of personal dishonesty."[4] Arnold Toynbee thought that by personal example Kemal had proved that "a Turk can be his own master in Anatolia . . . and under his inspiration, the National Movement sprang to life."[5] Mango, Kemal's biographer, pointed out his rare qualities as "a superb organizer, with a clear grasp of priorities."[6] The Greeks had no leader of comparable stature.

Assuming for argument's sake that the Greeks had been successful in defeating the Turks, the question arises—how did they expect to control such a vast country as Turkey? They did not possess sufficient manpower, nor the material resources for such an undertaking. The method which they employed was ethnic cleansing deportations and, as Toynbee described it, a "war of extermination." Immediately after the occupation of Smyrna,

> [t]he soldiers . . . attacked any civilian wearing a fez, Greeks, Armenians and Jews. . . . The killings went on for two days. . . . The looting lasted a fortnight, and probably more of this was done by Ottoman Greek civilians than by soldiers. Not only in Smyrna but in villages within six mile radius of the city, local Greeks—suddenly possessed of arms—raided their Turkish neighbours' houses, stripped of their furniture, and lifted their cattle. This was allowed to go on by the occupying authorities.[7]

Hearing of what had happened at Smyrna, the able-bodied Turks in the neighboring town of Aidin took revenge and wiped out the Greek quarter. Women and children were hunted like rats from house to house, and civilians caught alive were slaughtered in batches—shot or knifed or hurled over a cliff. Houses and public buildings were plundered, and the whole Greek quarter finally was burned to the ground. Toynbee, a living witness, described these mutual atrocities in great detail and commented thus:

> The beast had come spontaneously in Turk and Greek, and acted after this kind.

Aided and abetted by the army, the Greeks had the upper hand in committing untold atrocities. The Greek authorities, far from discouraging brigands, so-called Chettés, organized them and gave them a free hand to accomplish their infamous task. Toynbee gained the impression that the invading Greeks had embarked on a systematic "war of extermination."[8]

This was a far cry from their self-proclaimed *mission civilisatrice*. Unlike Alexander the Macedonian, who won the hearts of the conquered people in Anatolia and the Near East by acts of friendship and by spreading enlightenment, the contemporary Greeks were bent on instituting a reign of terror.

In March 1921, when the Greek government decided to launch a new offensive against the Turks, they felt that they enjoyed the tacit approval of the British prime minister. On March 18 and 19, when Gounaris and Foreign Minister Calegoropoulos met Lloyd George, they found him very supportive. He told them that "[i]t was imperative to Greece to make it quite clear to the Western Powers, and particularly to the people of England, that responsibility for bloodshed and strife rested with the Turks and not with the Greeks." And that "[i]f the Greek army thought it necessary to take steps to provide for the safety in view of the increase of Mustafa Kemal's forces, the conference [of Allied Powers] would not take responsibility for forbidding them." He hoped that Greece would be "strengthened from the ordeal because Great Britain always had a warm corner in her heart for the Greek people . . . and looked forward to a . . . revived glory in Greece." Lloyd George had prefaced this overt encouragement by stating earlier that he intended to tell both Tewfik Pasha and Bekir Sami Bey that "[t]he Greeks were free to attack the Turks, and, vice versa, and the conference made no arrangement to prevent such an attack."[9] This sounded like an open invitation for war between the two belligerent parties.

Elated, Gounaris and Calegoropoulos briefed Athens on their successful meeting with the British prime minister who encouraged them also to raise money in England and had arranged for them to meet with the Chancellor of the Exchequer. In contrast, Lord Granville, the British minister in Athens, was anxious:

> If Greeks succeeded, as they say . . . in smashing Kemal very quickly well and good, but . . . if a success is not crushing and rapid, it means long and ruinous warfare for both parties which His Majesty's Government may be accused of having encouraged or at least of having acquiesced in. Also unsuccessful war might lead to revolution, civil war and anarchy in Greece.

Granville also observed that the Turks were better prepared and presumably were being encouraged, if not armed, by the Italians and French.[10]

Arnold Toynbee, who accompanied the Greek army as a reporter for the *Manchester Guardian*, was even more skeptical than Lord Granville. "I began to realise [he wrote] of how narrow a margin the Greeks had gambled for a military decision in Anatolia, and how adverse were the circumstances under which they were playing for victory over Kemal."[11]

Lloyd George thought differently. He asked Maurice Hankey, the secretary to the war cabinet, to tell the Greek military, who were still in London, that if they felt impelled to attack Kemal's forces, he would not stand in their way.[12] The Greek government took this advice as license to resume the war and launched a new offensive on March 23, 1921. Initial success at Afion Karahissar and the expected capture of Eskishehir whetted the Greek appetite for further expansion, but joy in Greece was short-lived. When it became known that, in fact, a desperate battle that incurred very heavy losses was raging, disappointment followed. The Greek press scathingly accused the Italians of supplying arms and ammunition to the Turks.[13]

General Ismet, chief of the General Staff of the Nationalist forces and commander of Turkish troops in Western Anatolia, had been lying in wait. On March 31, he repulsed the Greek army and the following day cabled to Mustafa Kemal, "The enemy has abandoned the battlefield to our arms, leaving thousands of dead behind." Kemal replied in style as follows:

> Few commanders in the whole history of the world have faced a task as difficult as that which you undertook in the pitched battles of Inönü. The independent life of our nation was entrusted to the heart-felt care of your commanders and comrades-in-arms, who have honourably discharged their duty under your brilliant direction. It was not only the enemy you defeated, but fate itself—the ill-starred fate of our nation.[14]

The victory was proof of the newly-gained military strength and the moral fervor of the Nationalists. Ismet emerged as a hero and in 1938, when elected president of Turkey, was given the name of Inönü.

Lloyd George was watching the battle of Inönü intensely. He felt that his political reputation depended a great deal on the outcome of this battle. If the Greek attack should fail, he would be proved wrong. On the other hand, if the Greek succeeded, his policy would be vindicated, and Turkish rule would be at an end. Consequently, "a new Greek Empire will be founded, friendly to Britain, and it will help [British] interests in the East." His secretary recorded that "[h]e is perfectly convinced that he is right over this, and is willing to stake everything on it."[15]

The battle did not turn out as Lloyd George had expected. Consequently, he felt it prudent to tone down his partisan stance on Greece.

The morale of the Greek army was deteriorating. The military debacle should have prompted the Greek government to do some soul-searching with regard to its policy. Instead, the Greek forces chose to take revenge on the Turkish population in the area under their occupation. In their report of May 23, 1921, the Inter-Allied Commission, which investigated the atrocities, stated that in less than two months in the Kāzas of Yalova and Guemlek, all the Muslim villages were destroyed, and its population had been forced to evacuate. In the opinion of the commission, there was "a systematic plan of destruction of Turkish villages and extinction of the Moslem population." The plan had been carried out by Greek and Armenian bands, which operated "under Greek instructions and sometimes even with the assistance of regular troops." These atrocities, the commission asserted, "are unworthy of a civilized government and the Greek authorities alone bore the responsibility."[16]

M. Gehri, the representative of the Geneva International Red Cross, who accompanied the Inter-Allied Commission and consequently the Ottoman Red Crescent, reached a similar conclusion.

> For the last two months the Greek army of occupation has been employed in the extermination of the Moslem population of the [Yalova-Gemlik] peninsula.
> The facts established—burning of villages, massacres, terrorizing of inhabitants . . . leave no room for doubt in regard to this. The atrocities which we have seen, or of which we have material evidence, were the work of irregular bands of armed civilians (*tcheti*) and of organised units of the regular army . . . the bands have been assisted in their activities and have collaborated hand in hand with organised units of regulars.[17]

Toynbee's own observations at Yalova and elsewhere corroborated Gehri's report, as well as findings of the Inter-Allied Commission.

On June 29, 1921, Toynbee and his wife witnessed Greek troops in uniform, committing arson without provocation along the south coast of Ismid. The Toynbees used a conveyance of the Red Cross and were accompanied by a representative of the Allied high commissioners. En route to the village Ulashly Iskelesi, they saw how Greek soldiers were setting fire to Turkish houses.

Everywhere else, they noted, "The destruction had been malicious and systematic . . . Turkish towns and villages had been burnt in cold blood, without provocation." The survivors told them gruesome stories about their ordeal.[18]

The atrocities were not confined to the Yalova-Gemlik-Ismid districts. Toynbee claimed to possess detailed accounts of raids and massacres that had been committed by soldiers in collaboration with Chettés. Thus, in the Aidin district, the deportees' houses were looted and their women folk violated; the deportees themselves were often murdered by their escorts. The policy of the Greek authorities was to remove the Turkish upper class first, in the hope that, without them, it would be easier for the Greeks to control the peasantry and working class.[19]

Toynbee compiled a list of fifteen villages in the Yalova district in which all the houses were burnt and destroyed. To this he added another list of six districts in which homes in 210 villages were totally destroyed. Had it not been for the Greek landing at Smyrna, he commented, these atrocities would have not occurred.[20]

During debates in the House of Commons in 1920, the British government three times refused to publish the report of the Smyrna Commission: on March 2 by Bonar Law, the leader of the Conservative party, and on March 10 and 22 by Lloyd George.[21] However, they could not prevent publication of the Inter-Allied Commission of Inquiry (1921). On April 7, 1921, Curzon dispatched a letter of reprimand to the Greek chargé d'affaires complaining about persecutions of Muslims by Greek authorities in the area under their occupation. He wrote thus:

> It is asserted that, in order to increase the preponderance of the Greek population, the Greeks are causing the disappearance of the Turks by every possible means. Educated classes are being annihilated; land-owners and merchants are being driven under threat, from their property. . . . In the last weeks the allegation is made that one thousand five hundred Turkish notables have been arrested and their goods have been pillaged. Young Moslem women and girls have

committed suicide to escape the persecution of the Greek troops . . . Turkish prisoners at Smyrna and in Greece are condemned in a starving condition to forced labour and as a result there is great mortality.[22]

Earlier the Greek *chargé d'affaires* was advised that their campaign in Anatolia was being waged on their own responsibility and without any mandate from the Allied powers. Ergo, the Greek move had not been approved by the Allies.[23] This was a marked departure from Lloyd George's policy.

In addition to the Greco-Turkish War, the British government had to contend with its allies, who tried to chart an independent policy. On January 7, 1921, M. de Fleuriau, the French chargé d'affaires, revealed to Sir Eyre Crowe, the permanent undersecretary for foreign affairs, that "[t]here was no doubt that Italian agents were in direct communication with Kemal systematically."

The move had been initiated by Count Sforza, now foreign minister, who maintained that direct contact with Kemal would enable the Italian government to influence the Turkish nationalists to be more amenable with regard to the Treaty of Sèvres. The Italian agent, he added, would act not merely on behalf of Italian interests but also "to take due account of the interests and wishes of the Allies, and notably those of Great Britain."[24]

The British government disapproved of this kind of procedure. Curzon, in a strongly worded message, objected that the Italian government "had entered into separate negotiations with an enemy government behind the back of the conference. Were such a procedure to be generally adopted, it would be useless to hold further conferences." Count Sforza admitted the force of this argument. However, when on April 12 *Le Temps* published a summary of the Turco-Italian agreement, it fell like a bombshell at Whitehall. In this agreement, in addition to economic provisions, the Italian government undertook to persuade Great Britain and France to support all the Turkish political demands, particularly "the restitution of Smyrna and Thrace" to Turkey. This version of the agreement was corroborated by secret information from an unimpeachable Turkish source. Curzon regarded it as "an indefensible breach of faith with an ally", adding that "Count Sforza has either distorted the facts or has been himself the victim of imposture."[25]

Contarini, the secretary-general of the Italian Foreign Ministry, protested at the "false interpretation" of the alleged agreement; his government had been engaged in supporting Turkey's claims only within the supreme council. He admitted, however, that Italy "had always been in favour of restoring Thrace and Smyrna to Turkey" and would continue to press its view with regard to revision of the Treaty of Sèvres on allied governments. Subsequently, however, Contarini disclosed to Sir George Buchanan confidentially the terms of the agreement. It confirmed (clause 4) the information that had appeared in *Le Temps*.[26]

On May 20, ambassador de Martino told Sir Eyre Crowe that Italy had definitely renounced all her territorial ambitions in Asia Minor and had decided to withdraw from Turkey altogether. "Italy would not now take Smyrna even if it was offered as a free gift, [hence] there was no longer any ground for antagonism between Italy and Greece." Crowe welcomed this development wholeheartedly.[27] Ten days later, Count Sforza declared frankly to Sir George Buchanan that he had always advocated that the allies come to terms with the Nationalists.[28] Sforza sympathized with the Nationalists, but his suggestion did not suit Curzon's book.

Curzon was dissatisfied also with France's conduct. Taking advantage of the presence of the Angora delegation in London, France had negotiated a separate agreement with them outside the conference. Nor had the French taken the trouble to brief their British counterparts on this. This conduct was difficult to reconcile "with the ordinary cannons of loyal cooperation" and augured ill for the future relationship between allies, Curzon complained. Lord Hardinge, the newly appointed ambassador, lodged a strong protest and showed M. Berthelot, the secretary-general of the Quai d'Orsay, a copy of *L'Europe Nouvelle*, a magazine, where the full text of the agreement with the Nationals had been published, while the British government had been kept completely in the dark. Berthelot apologized for the "misunderstanding" with the ensuing "misconception as to complete loyalty of the French Government towards the Allied powers in connection with the Franco-Turkish negotiations."[29]

Italy's loyalty to the Allied cause was dubious, but their appreciation of Turkey was more realistic than that of their British counterparts. They realized that the Treaty of Sèvres was unworkable and that the Nationalists would eventually emerge victorious. Politically, the National movement was going from strength to strength. Mustafa Kemal was elected its president and was mobilizing as many elements as possible to support the national pact as it had been laid down by the Erzerum Conference.[30]

Militarily too the scales were now tilting toward the Kemalists. Memoranda by the chief of the Imperial General Staff, by the General Staff, by General Harrington, as well as by the secretary of state for war, circulated to the cabinet pointed to the "grave" dangers to the British positions in the East, resulting from the Greco-Turkish War. Withdrawal of all British troops from the Dardanelles, as well as from the Bosphorus, would be tantamount to "military disaster." Sir Eyre Crowe became alarmed. He wrote as follows:

> The Turk re-established, as a result of military victory on his part, and the flight of the allies, means the loss of practically the whole fruits of our victorious campaign in which Turkey was completely defeated. The political consequences of such a consummation can hardly be overestimated.

He went on

> The present alliance between Angora and Moscow . . . is kept alive by the common desire to bring down our Indian Empire. With the Russians overrunning Persia . . . and having a foot in Afghanistan, and, with a reconstituted strong Turkey holding Constantinople and the Straits, the danger to India is formidable.

Crowe feared that eventually the Turks would drive the Greeks from Anatolia. If the Greeks refused to face the facts, they would most likely land themselves "in complete disaster; the fate of the Christians in Anatolia and especially in Smyrna will not be enviable." In these circumstances, what kind of assistance could Britain expect from her allies? Crower asked rhetorically.

> Italy may be ruled out. But what about France? It is to be feared that France may look with equanimity if not with satisfaction on the complete restoration of the Turkish Empire . . .
> If they would pose as friends of Turkey, as against England's hostility, they would . . . enhance their own prestige in the Mahommetan world at our expense.

To resolve the dilemma, Crowe hit on an ingenious solution: since it would not be possible to rely on Greek support, "French co-operation would become indispensable" and there was no way of obtaining French co-operation except at a price. "If we want France to stand by

259

us and support our policy in the East, I am afraid we must bargain and pay."[31]

Hard-pressed Crowe advocated the renewal of the British-Franco *entente*, which had been the late Sir Mark Sykes' standard policy. The inescapable question, however, was whether revival of the cordiality of the *entente* was still feasible.

William Rattigan, who acted as high commissioner during Rumbold's absence on leave, was very pessimistic. "Military circles here are unanimously of opinion that, without some support, Greeks must eventually collapse, in which case, we shall have to reckon with triumph of Nationalists, who will probably stick at nothing in their hostility to Great Britain." He added that the French military authorities had formed a very poor estimate of Greek fighting ability and think they are likely to prove "a broken reed." In desperation, Rattigan thought that the sooner the British intervened to impose a solution favorable to nationalist demands the better. And on the following day he warned, "Support of Greeks would land us in another Wrangel fiasco."[32]

Curzon too was perturbed. If the Greek army was defeated, the British position in Constantinople would become vulnerable. Turkey's success would enhance its prestige, would fortify its alliance with Russia, and would nullify any possibility of settlement in Asia Minor. "Turkish success would jeopardize every allied gain in the war and remove all prospects of peaceful reconstruction in the Middle East." To avert such a "catastrophe" Curzon did not venture as far as Rattigan. Instead, he hoped to find a solution that would satisfy both the Greeks and the Turks. Britain was bound "by honour and friendship to the Greeks, as they desire to maintain a friendly and helpful relations . . . with the Turks."[33]

Well-meaning as Curzon was, his suggestion had practically no chance of getting support either from the Greeks or from the nationalists. Izzet Pasha, the minister for foreign affairs in Constantinople, who entertained pronationalist sympathies, also took exception to the Greek garrison in Smyrna and to maintaining the Treaty of Sèvres; to the British compromise proposal he turned a cold shoulder.[34] Practically, Constantinople and Angora were now acting in unison. In due course, they would become one single international and juridical unit. Moreover, the majority of the leading Turkish newspapers in Constantinople were openly espousing the nationalist cause.[35]

The only friend that had remained pro-British was the sultan-caliph. His primary concern, however, was to solicit British protection to ensure his personal safety and the survival of his throne. Distressed, he invited Sir Horace Rumbold for a meeting that lasted two and a half hours. From copies of correspondence that passed between Mustafa Kemal and Tewfik Pasha, the grand vizier, the sultan deduced that there was a plot afoot to compromise the throne and to reduce its authority. "The Sultanate and the Caliphate [he stated] are two complementary parts of a single whole. The Caliphate was not like the Papacy. Temporal power was an adjunct essential to its completeness. . . . The removal of the Caliphate from Constantinople [to Angora] would be fraught with disastrous consequences."[36]

It was pathetic that the sultan, as the head of the Islamic world, should have asked for the protection of an infidel power. His apprehension was groundless. Kemal Atatürk, though personally a secularist, was enough of a statesman to realize that irreverence, let alone offence to the sultanate, would be counterproductive to his cause.

By contrast, the sultan poured scorn and venom against the Nationalists.

> The Angora leaders [he declared] were men without any real stake in this country. . . . Moustafa Kemal was a Macedonian revolutionary of unknown origin. His blood might be anything, Bulgarian, Greek or Serbian. . . . Bekir Sami was a Circasian. . . . There was not a real Turk among them. He [the Sultan] and his Government were nevertheless powerless before them. . . . These brigands were the men who sought his submission. They looked for external support, and found them in the Bolsheviks. . . . Bolshevism was incompatible with Moslem religion.

Finally, the sultan admitted that his position was one of "complete helplessness and isolation," but Rumbold was able to give him little comfort.[37]

Curzon intervened. He assured the sultan of the British government's "friendly interest in the maintenance of [his] position as sovereign of Turkey and Moslem Khalif" and urged him to make every effort "to establish harmony between political parties in his dominion. . . . To remain inactive and retire before forces of disorder and disintegration," Curzon warned, "would not only be confession to personal failure, but would . . . undermine altogether the position of the Turkish State and the Khalifat."[38]

However, Sultan Mehmet V was palpably unfit to play the role of unifying factor for the Turkish people. He was a weakling, and the fact that he chose to shelter under the wing of "unbelievers" disqualified him a priori in the eyes of his Muslim followers.

On May 23, when Rumbold paid him a courtesy visit before leaving, the sultan complained bitterly against the Greeks who were pursuing "a policy of extermination," while the Angora leaders, "bent on personal aims, were sustaining disturbance." As a result, the innocent people were the victims of both. Bolshevism constituted a menace not only for Turkey but for the peace of the world.[39]

In the meantime, Greece was getting tired of the war. Lord Granville detected that throughout the country there was a growing feeling of revulsion, even hostility to the government and even to the king that *Greece was led as a slave into the war*. Certain papers advocated cutting losses and coming to terms with Mustafa Kemal. In government circles an idea was circulating that Greece should first achieve a military success, however unimportant, and thereafter get the best possible terms from the Turks.[40]

In contrast, the army was confident that they could beat the Turks in the next round provided they forestalled the nationalists in resupplying themselves with arms, ammunition, and transport facilities. The time element was crucial. This was the opinion aired by General Palles, the chief of the Greek general staff, as well as of his deputy Colonel Saryannis. The strength of the Greek army in Asia Minor amounted to 160,000 men, which could be increased to 175,000; the total fighting force was 100,000, as opposed to 60,000 Turks. Prime Minister Gounaris was equally upbeat. He declared that the Greeks were "champions of Europe against Bolshevism; that . . . complete victory is possible; and that unity of Greece had already been attained."[41]

The Nationalists were not sitting idle. They were getting arms from both the Bolsheviks and the Italians. Italian firms were reported to be selling arms and ammunition on "a large scale."[42] Italian agreement with the nationalists went far beyond that of a simple economic convention. In fact, they had undertaken to assist Turkey to recover Smyrna and Thrace.[43]

The Italian high commissioner in Constantinople was in close touch with the Nationalists and gained the impression that they were prepared to accept the Allied's terms except those relating to Smyrna, where "they will not tolerate presence of a single Greek soldier." They will be prepared to accept a mixed allied administration of Smyrna but "so long as the Greeks are in occupation of Smyrna, that town will be a centre of irridenta and a base for organisation of bands of Greek comitadj'is."[44]

With hindsight, it might be said that, had the Greek government accepted the terms of the Nationalists, the destruction of the Greek community in Smyrna and environs would have been averted.

The Greeks, however, would not even dream of abandoning Anatolia. Quite the contrary, on May 17, Athens issued a communiqué repudiating the idea of Allied intervention and proclaimed its desire "to see their enterprise in Asia Minor through to the end." In the meantime, so testified the Commission of Enquiry, irregular bands, organized by the Greek regular troops, were committing serious excesses against the Muslim population; "in some cases the Greek regular troops have been a party to them. The outcome is," Rumbold commented, "that the hatred as between Mussulmans and Christians in this part of the world is greater than ever."[45]

In view of the impending hostilities, first the French, and later, the British, declared a strict neutrality. The Greeks complained that neutrality was "unfair" to them, whereas the Turks considered it a farce. They ridiculed British declarations and believed that the Greek offensive "was planned in London." A month later, Rattigan confirmed that "[t]he vast majority of Turks, and everyone at Angora, believed with some justification that we had encouraged the Greeks to launch this offensive in the hope that they would crush the Kemalists and thus cut the Gordian knot."[46]

The renewed Greek offensive began on July 10, 1921. This time the Greek army had learned from the mistakes it committed in January and March and launched a brilliant three-pronged operation. It was singularly successful and was crowned with the capture of Eskishehir, a rail center and a strategic key to western Anatolia. The Turks were outflanked and were forced to evacuate. On July 21, Ismet launched a furious counterattack but was repelled.

Lloyd George followed the news with absorbing interest. Writing to his war minister, he described the events to be of "first importance":

> The future of the East will very largely be determined by this struggle, and yet the War Office has not taken the slightest trouble to find out what has happened. . . . The staff have displayed the most amazing slovenliness in this matter. Their information about the respective strength and quality of the two Armies turned out to be hopelessly wrong.[47]

Colonel Meinertzhagen sharply disagreed with Lloyd George's policy. He appreciated that past services of Lloyd George were of "incalculable value" to Britain and, though he had been the "main factor in the political arena during the war, he was gone far to lose the peace."[48] This sounded almost prophetic, but in July, it looked that fortune favored the Greeks.

When the position of the Turkish army seemed to be desperate, Kemal arrived on the scene. There is no way of knowing whether he was familiar with Napoleon's ill-fated war against Russia in 1812. However, he employed the same tactics as General Kutuzov had done: to save his army from destruction Atatürk ordered a general retreat behind the great bend of the Sakkaria River, fifty miles west of Ankara. Exultant at the prospect of a massive victory, Prime Minister Gounaris pressed the Greek army to cross the Sakkaria and occupy Ankara. The military leaders angrily opposed it, but King Constantine decided to cast the dice in favor of the attack.[49]

On August 14, 1921, the Greek army attacked. The chief of the supplies warned that due to the long line of communication, there was danger of a breakdown in transportation but his army colleagues, confident that they would be able to crush the Turks, paid no heed to his warning.[50]

In the meantime, the Grand National Assembly granted Mustafa Kemal the position of commander in chief with full martial powers. For Kemal, it was a moment of truth. With unbounded energy he embarked on a nationwide mobilization and material requisitions. The people responded magnificently. Minister Fevzi Pasha performed Herculean feats of reequipping the army which, although ragged and badly mauled, was still intact. Haldad Edib, the writer, made an apt remark:

> I knew that this was going to be the turning point in the hardest ordeal Anatolia had as yet undergone.[51]

Lord Granville was bewildered. On the eve of the Greek offensive, he confessed thus:

> My sympathy for the Greeks is not great—they are not very trust-worthy, they have behaved abominably and they have shown in their treatment of the Turks at Yalova etc. most lamentable incapacity to govern alien minorities, but what about Turks who were after all amongst our worst enemies? . . . a Turk always looks on concessions

and even politeness as sign of weakness and is only impressed by show of strength and firmness.[52]

Four days later, he changed his mind drastically. Impressed by the arguments propounded by the Greek government, he confessed that

> Greece and her army are at the present moment the only bulwark of Europe against Pan-Islamism and Bolshevism that Mustapha Kemal's arrogance, already insurmountable, is largely owing to the encouragement received from the French and Italians . . . [hence] the only possible means of arriving at a pacification of the Near East is the crushing of the Nationalists by military force.

Granville concluded that "[f]rom the point of view of the Allies and of Europe it was most desirable, nay essential, that the Greeks should win a really decisive victory over Kemal."[53]

These were strong words. Future developments showed how wrong Granville's assessment was.

Reports by the Inter-Allied Commission about excesses committed by the Greek troops against the Muslim population in Ismid made Lord Granville pause. The report revealed "numerous cases of murder and atrocities" as well as fires that had been set in villages. The Greek authorities, however, "took no proper steps to prevent these occurrences and their responsibility is established beyond question."[54]

Curzon lodged a strong protest with Athens, but its effect was tarnished when some alarming reports arrived about "a deliberate policy of deportation and extermination of Christians in Asia Minor," particularly in Pontus, which had been committed by the Kemalists. The latter were reprimanded by the British foreign minister.[55]

The Greeks, carried away by their enthusiasm, believed that a "complete break up of Kemalists movement was imminent." However, victory eluded them. They failed to encircle and trap the Nationalists' army, which remained intact. General Harington opined that the Greeks had not inflicted the decisive success they anticipated, while Premier Briand expressed doubts about the "permanence of Greek success, which, if it did not become decisive soon, might become dangerous to Greeks."[56]

Events proved Briand right. On August 10, the Greek army launched their frontal attack on the center, where the Turks were entrenched in unexpected strength. The battle raged for twenty-two days. It was the longest pitched battle in modern history. It was a ferocious struggle.

The Greeks had lost eighteen thousand men and the Turks nearly that many. It was, as Howard Sachar aptly described, "a primeval contest of extermination." The Turkish army was skillfully conducted by Kemal Atatürk. He managed to disrupt the Greek supply services leaving his adversaries at the mercy of the malevolent sun and succeeded in breaking through the Greek defenses. Overwhelmed, their units lost their nerve and began collapsing like rows of dominos. King Constantine, who had stayed at Smyrna, as well as at the supreme headquarters, returned to Athens with little honor.[57]

On September 23, Lord Granville reported that Athens "is thoroughly depressed and inclined to be very pessimistic," while Prime Minister Gounaris looked worn-out with anxiety and depression. The Turks, he understood from Rumbold's telegram, had won a great victory and were preparing "a great encircling movement which led to a complete Greek disaster."[58]

On his return to Angora, the Grand National Assembly conferred on Mustafa Kemal Pasha the rank of *mushir* (field-marshal) and the title of *Ghazi* (the victorious). In his speech to the assembly, Mustafa Kemal declared that "[t]he army would not lay down its arms while a single Greek soldier remained within the national frontiers." Izzet Pasha, the foreign minister of the Constantinople government, Tewfik Pasha, the grand vizier, and practically all the members of the cabinet demanded that Smyrna, as well as Thrace, should be restored to Turkey. They emphasized that it was essential to also achieve economic independence and abolish the system of capitulations.[59]

Turkey thus spoke in one voice and was united as never before. Atatürk emerged as Turkey's undisputed leader. In his person, he combined the supreme military command with almost dictatorial civilian powers. However, he was not a dictator. He bowed to democratic principles.

While the war was still raging, Kemal Atatürk, assisted by his crew, conducted intensive diplomatic activity with three objectives in mind:

1. To liberate Turkey from foreign invaders.
2. To achieve political and economic independence.
3. To win the good will, even friendship, of West-European Powers, England in particular.

That Kemal should be eager to reach a *rapprochement* with England looks strange. The Turks hated England. She was the power considered to be responsible for the Greek occupation of Smyrna and for the subsequent assault in Anatolia, which was offensive not only for Turkey but for the Muslim world in general. However, Kemal was first and foremost a statesman guided by interests and not only by sentiments. His long-range objective was to divorce Turkey from Pan-Islam and Pan-Turanism and to convert it into a Western-oriented country. In this respect, Western assistance (by Britain in particular) would be of incalculable value.

On June 8, Rattigan opined that the Kemalists were believed to be "ready to drop the Bolsheviks, if they can obtain satisfaction from the *Entente.*" Three days later, Sefa Bey, the Constantinople foreign minister, at Angora's request, assured Rattigan that the extremism attributed to Angora had been greatly exaggerated. Mustafa Kemal and his party, he maintained, were

> in reality moderate men, who had only been forced into contact with the Bolsheviks by [British] harshness towards Turkey. Bolshevik doctrines and ideas were utterly repugnant to them, and they had only accepted the aid provided from this quarter because they had no one else to whom they could look to support their just aspirations. If Great Britain even now showed the slightest sign of wishing to meet them half way they would drop the Bolsheviks at once.

The Greeks had laid the country waste, and Sefa questioned what had been the advantage to Britain in supporting them. Turkey's desire was to end the strife with the Greeks and to reestablish Turkey as a healthy state. Rattigan deduced that Sefa had been requested by Angora "to hold out a tentative olive branch."[60]

Nonetheless, Rattigan was not fully convinced. "Obvious policy of Angora at present is to thrust Great Britain and France apart and to appease us both to deter either from taking direct action against Kemalists or helping Greeks." This was a rather cynical observation. Two days later, Sefa Bey pressed again assuring that the Kemalists "sincerely desired to turn over a new leaf." Later he added that, if the allies declared that Smyrna "ought to belong to the Turks," the Kemalists would certainly abandon the Bolsheviks. "Smyrna was absolutely essential, though he believed Kemalists would accept plebiscite." On June 23, Angora declared that they were ready to enter into negotiations with the British.[61]

Since the British did not respond, Angora dispatched Bekir Sami in an unofficial capacity (he resigned earlier as foreign minister) to the

Allied capitals to prepare the ground for friendly understandings with the object of freeing Turkey from Greek invaders. If Britain helped, "there would be an end to all Bolshevik influence." Soon thereafter, Izzet Pasha, Constantinople's new foreign minister, confirmed that the Kemalists, and particularly Kemal himself, wished to reach "a good understanding with Great Britain." To prove their bona fides, the Kemalist forces were ordered to distance themselves from British positions and to take care not to violate the neutral zone.[62]

Early in July, Mustafa Kemal sent a message to General Harington proposing to present his case before him. Hamid Bey, the vice president of the Red Crescent, acted as Angora's agent. Hamid elucidated that Kemal's scheme was identical to the national pact that had been adopted at the congress at Erzerum. The memorandum, which Hamid submitted, was more specific. The main points were as follows:

1. Smyrna and Eastern Thrace to revert to Turkey.
2. Abrogation of capitulations.
3. Freedom of navigation in the straits provided that security of Constantinople was guaranteed.
4. Rights of minorities to be safeguarded similar to the stipulations made in other treaties by the European powers.

Rattigan commented sarcastically, "These were more terms of victor than of vanquished." He told, later, Izzet Pasha in Hamid's presence that the Kemalist claim to recognize the principle of complete independence of Turkey within its national frontiers before entering into any pourparlers was "preposterous." And to Curzon he wrote, "I do not believe anything short of complete capitulation by us will be considered by Angora." He placed little hope in Mustafa Kemal's supposed moderation.[63]

Sir Horace Rumbold, who, in the meantime, returned from his leave to Constantinople, was equally harsh. When Izzet Pasha, accompanied by Hamid Bey, called on him, he asked them point-blank whether the program of the "national pact" was still feasible in view of recent Greek military successes. Hamid replied that Angora would certainly stick to that program. Rumbold responded that he "was not looking facts in the face."[64]

The Nationalists persisted in their campaign. When R. M. Hodgson, the head of the British Commercial Mission to Russia, paid a visit to Chicherin, the Soviet Commissar for foreign affairs, Ali Fuad Pasha, the Angora ambassador in Moscow, invited Hodgson to his house and handed him a memorandum. During the conversation, he spoke eloquently about the unjust treatment meted out to Turkey at the conclusion of the armistice, that the Allies reneged on their solemn declarations made by President Wilson, as well as Prime Minister Lloyd George, and that Turkey, having laid down her arms, felt that "she had been tricked into a position of impotence."

Ali Fuad went on with a litany of complaints, emphasizing that Britain in particular had been "the initiator of repressive measures and had played largely an executive role." She treated the Angora government with "relentless hostility." Angora was the expression of Turkish national feeling whose only object was to achieve Turkey's independence within her ethnographical boundaries. "Surely, it was not to the interest of Great Britain, with her great interest in the Mussulman world, to follow a policy of oppression towards a Nationalist Turkey." Nor should she rely on the government in Constantinople. "Angora alone is the embodiment of national sentiment." Ali Fuad impressed Hodgson with his straightforwardness and distinctly attractive manners.[65] However, his arguments struck no chord in Whitehall.

French policy diverged sharply from that of the British. On July 15, Briand gave his blessing to the projected meeting between Mustafa Kemal and General Harrington, emphasizing that it was imperative "to seek all opportunities for making peace in the East and that it would be a political mistake to neglect any such opportunity."[66] Since Kemalists' démarche proved abortive, the French elected to chart an independent course. However, the way they carried it out did not conform to the normal etiquette customary among allies. It caused a dissolution of the alliance vis-à-vis the Turks and an irreparable blow to the Treaty of Sèvres.

In June, Rattigan detected strong influences at work that were influencing French policy veering toward with Angora. Indicative was the arrival of M. Franklin Bouillon in Angora, the former chairman of the deputies' commission on foreign affairs and Briand's personal friend. Ostensibly, he was dealing with exchange of prisoners but, as Rumbold found out, his mission had wider objectives, i.e., in return for some unspecified concessions, the French, on evacuating Cilicia, were to surrender to the Kemalists the military stores and munitions sufficient to equip two divisions.[67] During the subsequent week, Rumbold was in a position to elucidate as follows:

> The French are honestly anxious to come to a settlement with the Nationalists about the Cilician question and to effect the release of

the French prisoners of war. Inspired also possibly with the hope of counteracting our influence at Constantinople, besides being actuated by a real dislike of the Greeks, they are undoubtedly helping the Nationalists as far as they can . . . they look with sympathy on the Nationalist cause and they have done their best to convince the Turks both at Constantinople and the Nationalists that they are their friends. [In return] they will endeavour to obtain the exclusive organisation of the future gendarmerie in Anatolia besides a concession for the constructions of all future railways in that region.[68]

Curzon was furious. Briand had assured him that Franklin Bouillon was a private person, "rather a busybody" and had no official mission, but in fact, his agreement concluded with Angora was of a much more serious and far-reaching nature. It bore the appearance of "a treaty concluded with an enemy by one of the Allies without knowledge of the others" and was "tantamount to recognition of Angora National Assembly as government of Turkey." Curzon reminded the French ambassador bluntly that the Franco-British agreement of September 5, 1914, as well as the London pact of November 30, 1915, stipulated that the allies would not conclude peace with any enemy power, except by common agreement. The French government had reneged on these agreements, while Mustafa Kemal "could claim that they had received recognition from one of the most powerful of the European Allies." Other articles in Franklin Bouillon's agreement also traveled "far beyond the spirit of the Tripartite Agreement . . . and were in direct conflict with it."[69]

With such a drastic about-face by the French, the Treaty of Sèvres became obsolete. In fact, this treaty had never come into force. The French and the Italians had explicitly declined to ratify it, as did the Turks; both the governments in Constantinople and Angora also declined to put their signatures to it. Per force, Lloyd George reached the inescapable conclusion that the Treaty of Sèvres "had been practically torn up."[70]

Subsequently, Rumbold also discovered that the Franco-Nationalists' agreement had surrendered the allied position with regard to protection of minorities and recognized the National pact.[71]

The Kemalists, for their part, were greatly elated by concluding this agreement, which, in addition to the agreement that had been signed with the Italians, tended to weaken the allies' position vis-à-vis the Greco-Turkish conflict and, conversely, it hardened the Nationalists' bargaining strength.

Rumbold was bitter. The French move, he complained, "has undermined the whole position of the allies vis-à-vis the Nationalists and . . . , I can characterise French independent action in this matter as dishonourable, and as having greatly increased our difficulties." Curzon was fully aware that French agreement with Angora would aggravate the situation, while the Kemalists would endeavor to isolate Great Britain and compel her to be "the last suitor for their favours."[72]

Embarrassed, the French chargé d'affaires called on the Foreign Office and presented a formal reply to British complaints. He dwelt at length on the "unshaken determination of the French government to uphold the Entente with England in every part of the world," and assured that British fears about the consequences of France's separate understanding with Kemal were "groundless"; British anxieties were based on a "misunderstanding." He denied that France was supplying arms and war material to the Kemalists. In Paris, Briand tried to mollify Ambassador Hardinge, stating that the sole aim of the agreement with Angora was to secure an undisturbed evacuation of French troops; there was no formal agreement, only an exchange of letters. He emphasized that France was determined to act in "complete unity" with the British in Near Eastern affairs.[73]

The French needed British support in Europe vis-à-vis Germany, and they were therefore careful not to unduly overstrain their relations with the British on Eastern affairs.

During the conference with Curzon on October 21, the Greek Prime Minister Gounaris and his Foreign Minister Baltatzzis heard their host quoting Lloyd George's statement that the Treaty of Sèvres had been practically torn up. Its demise undermined the juridical basis —if there was any at all—of the Greek war in Turkey. The Greek ministers should have taken heed of this new situation. They were also aware that both Italy and France sympathized with the nationalists, while Britain found refuge in the self-imposed "strict neutrality." Practically, this development boded ill for Greece.

Although the Greek army was still strong, it was unable to defeat the Nationalists. It was, therefore, condemned to a stalemate, which in Anatolian winter conditions had a debilitating and demoralizing effect. Hence, prudence dictated a drastic revision of policy, i.e., to abandon the imperial Hellenic dream and concentrate on measures to safeguard the survival of the Greek community in Asia Minor.

And yet in Athens different considerations prevailed. Late in October, Gounaris and his foreign minister had a long conversation with

Briand. Briand found their attitude "intractable." The Greek government, they told Briand, proposed to establish Greek civil administration in the occupied areas of Anatolia and dismissed the idea of peace with Turkey. Briand strongly tried to dissuade them from their intention. Establishment of civil administration would imply annexation; the powers would not admit it. He warned them that if they continued in their course, "it will only lead to their eventual disaster." Curzon separately admonished that it would be "ill-advised . . . to take steps having the appearance of permanent occupation."[74]

At this juncture the French government conceived the idea of forming of a competent international gendarmerie to replace the Greek army and to safeguard the safety of the Greek communities in Smyrna and Thrace. However, those familiar with the mood of the Greeks, surrender of Smyrna, as well as Thrace, would be a too "bitter pill to swallow."[75]

Officially, as well as in the press, there was strong opposition to the idea of relinquishing Asia Minor, although "many Greeks," Granville attested, "say in private conversations that that would be the right solution." Should it happen, however, it would cause the fall of the government and possibly resignation of the king. Since formal annexation was not feasible, the Greek authorities embarked on a new wave of atrocities against the Muslim population in Anatolia, making hundred thousand inhabitants homeless and destitute. Youssouf Kemal, who replaced Bekir Sami Bey as the nationalist foreign minister, complained bitterly to Rumbold and wondered why Britain remained indifferent to Greek excesses.[76] Greek cruelties against the civilian Muslim population reflected badly on Britain's reputation. The Greeks had exceeded their brief and lost their credibility. It was high time for the British government to protest and to advise the Greek government strongly that, for their own benefit, they should vacate Asia Minor and be assured that the Allied powers would raise an international gendarmerie to protect the non-Muslim communities in Asia Minor, in Smyrna, and in Thrace in particular.

Instead, on September 30, 1921, Curzon proposed both to Paris and Rome to adopt a revised Treaty of Sèvres. A great amount of work was invested in preparation of a most detailed plan,[77] but it turned out to be an unwanted commodity. The Greeks refused to vacate the occupied territories, whereas the Nationalists were adamant on insisting that the Greek army withdraw completely. The positions between the belligerents were irreconcilable. Another round of a military contest was inevitable.

Colonel Richard Meinertzhagen, seasoned observer that he was, noted in his *Diary* thus:

> Our policy in the Middle East is rapidly leading us into position whence it will be difficult to withdraw . . .
>
> The problem resolves itself into this. We must make friends with the Turk and drop out our pro-Greek policy; or we must run the risk if being driven out of Constantinople . . . Consistently, since 1919 in Paris, I have preached against Greek occupation of any part of Asia Minor. We shall never get peace with Turkey as long as a single Greek soldier remains on Turkish territory.[78]

Notes

1. Michael Lewellyn Smith, *Ionian Vision: Greece in Asia Minor 1919–1922* (New York, 1973), 203.
2. On whom see above, pp. 35–43.
3. Cited in Andrew Mango, *Ataturk* (London, 1999), 238.
4. Martin Gilbert, *Sir Horace Rumbold. Portrait of a Diplomat 1869–1941* (London, 1973), 240.
5. Arnold J. Toynbee, *The Western Question in Greece and Turkey*, 2nd edition (London, 1923), 179.
6. Mango, *Ataturk*, 310.
7. Anrold J. Toynbee, *The Western Question in Greece and Turkey* (London, 1923), 272–3.
8. Ibid., 240, 274–8.
9. *Documents on British Foreign Policy 1919–1939*, eds. Rohan Butler and J. P. T. Bury, I series vol. XV (London, HMSO, 1967), No. 69, meeting in London, March 18, 1921, 447–452. Henceforth referred to as *DBFP*.
10. Ibid., I, vol. XVII, edited by W. N. Medlicott, D. Dakin, and M. E. Lambert, No. 67, Granville to Curzon, March 23, 1921 (London, HMSO, 1970), 86–7.
11. Toynbee, *The Western Question in Greece and Turkey*, 247.
12. Stephen Roskill, *Hankey: Man of Secrets*, vol. 2 (London, 1972), 199.
13. *DBFP*, I, vol. XVII, No. 78, Granville to Curzon, March 31, 1921, 99–102.
14. Cited in Mango, *Ataturk*, 311; also in Gilbert, *Sir Horace Rumbold*, 237–8.
15. Smith, *Ionian Vision*, 226.
16. Cmd. 1478 (1921), 11, quoted in Toynbee, *The Western Question*, 283–4.
17. Cited ibid., 284–5; also Gehri's account, 285–6.
18. Toynbee, *The Western Question*, 287–8.
19. Ibid., 288–91.
20. Ibid., 287–319.
21. Ibid., 366–7.
22. *DBFP*, I, vol. XII, No. 98, Curzon to Greek chargé d'affairs, April 1, 1921, 112–8.

23. Ibid., No. 71, Oliphant to the Greek chargé d'affairs, March 24, 1921; and No. 88, Rumbold to Curzon, April 5, 1921, 110–1.
24. Ibid., No. 6. Record of a conversation, January 1, 1921, 5–7; No. 31, conversation of Sir E. Crowe with de Martino, the Italian ambassador, February 5, 1921, 43–4; No. 41, conversation of Crowe with de Martino, the succeeding Italian ambassador, March 2, 1921, 69–70.
25. Ibid., No. 81, Buchanan (Rome) to Curzon, April 4, 1921, 103–4; Nos. 107, 108, Curzon to Buchanan, April 15, 1921, two cables, secret, 126.
26. Ibid., No. 114, Buchanan to Curzon, April 16, 1921, 131–2.
27. Ibid., No. 177, Conversation between Crowe and de Martino, May 20, 1921, 186.
28. Ibid., No. 200, Buchanan to Curzon, May 20, 1921, 206.
29. Ibid., Nos. 76, 84, Curzon to Hardinge (Paris), March 29; Hardinge to Curzon, April 2, 1921, 97–8, 106–7.
30. Ibid., No. 187, Rumbold to Curzon, May 25, 1921, 195–6. On the Congress at Erzerum see pp. 38–9.
31. Ibid., No. 201, memorandum by Sir Eyre Crowe, May 30, 1921, 207–11.
32. Ibid., Nos. 202, 204, Rattigan to Curzon, May 31, June 1, 1921, 212–4.
33. Ibid., No. 229, Curzon to Hardinge, June 14, 1921, 244–8.
34. Ibid., No. 99, Rumbold to Curzon, April 9, 1921, 118–20.
35. Ibid., No. 105, Rumbold to Curzon, April 13, 1921, 123–4.
36. Ibid., No. 68, Rumbold to Curzon, March 23, 1921, 87–91.
37. Ibid.
38. Ibid., No. 74, Curzon to Rumbold, March 29, 1921, 96.
39. Ibid., No. 186, Rumbold to Curzon, May 25, 1921, 192–5.
40. Ibid., No. 153, Granville to Curzon, May 6, 1921, 168–71.
41. Ibid., No. 213, Lamb (Smyrna) to Curzon, June 7, 1921, 221–3; No. 216, Granville to Curzon, June 8, 1921, 224.
42. Ibid., No. 54, Crowe to Italian ambassador, March 18, 1921, 15–6.
43. Ibid., No. 114, Buchanan to Curzon, April 16, 1921, 131–2.
44. Ibid., No. 110, Rumbold to Curzon, April 16, 1921, 128–9.
45. Ibid., No. 172, Rumbold to Curzon, May 18, 1921, 183.
46. Ibid., No. 149, 223, Rumbold to Curzon, May 4, 233–5, Rattigan to Curzon, June 11, 1921, 165–6.
47. Smith, *Ionian Vision*, 226.
48. Colonel R. Meinertzhagen, *Middle East Diary, 1917–1956* (London, 1959), entry July 5, 1921, 102.
49. Howard Morley Sachar, *The Emergence of the Middle East: 1914–1924* (New York, 1969), 422–3.
50. Smith, *Ionian Vision*, 228–9.
51. Sachar, *The Emergence*, 422–4.
52. *DBFP*, I, vol. XVII, No. 252, Granville to Curzon, June 22, 1921, 269–70.
53. Ibid., No. 266, Granville to Curzon, June 27, 1921, 280–2.
54. Ibid., No. 283, Rattigan to Curzon, July 5, 1921, 295–6. Repeated to Athens.
55. Ibid., No. 323, Curzon to Rattigan, July 28, 1921, 331–2.
56. Ibid., Nos. 313, 331, 345, Granville to Curzon, July 21; Rumbold to Curzon, August 4; Curzon to Rumbold, August 12, 1921, 323–4, 342–3, 352–3.
57. Sachar, *The Emergence*, 424–5.

58. *DBFP*, I, vol. XVII, No. 392, Granville to Curzon, September 23, 1921, 401–2.
59. Ibid., No. 396, Rumbold to Curzon, September 28, 1921, 406–7.
60. Ibid., No. 218, Rattigan to Curzon, June 8, 1921, 225–6; No. 223, Rattigan to Curzon, June 11, 1921, *Very confidential*, 233–5.
61. Ibid., Nos. 228, 236, 259, 269, Rattigan to Curzon, June 14, 16, 21, 24, 1921, 242–4, 252, 268, 271–2.
62. Ibid., No. 263, Buchanan to Curzon, June 26; No. 274, Rattigan to Curzon, July 1, 1921, 278–9, 288–9.
63. Ibid., Nos. 285, 288, 294, Rattigan to Curzon, July 5, 6, 8, 1921, 297–9, 300–1, 307.
64. Ibid., No. 238, Rumbold to Curzon, August 3, 1921, 339.
65. Ibid., No. 379, Hodgson to Curzon, September 6, 1921, 383–6.
66. Ibid., No. 228, Rattigan to Curzon, June 15; No. 388, Rumbold to Curzon, September 20, 1921, confidential; 242–4, 395–6.
67. Ibid.
68. Ibid., No. 395, Rumbold to Curzon, September 27, 1921, 404–5.
69. Ibid., Nos. 432, 434, Curzon to Hardinge, November 3 and to Buchanan, November 8, 1921, 461–6, 467.
70. Ibid., No. 425, Minutes of meetings between Curzon and Greek representatives, October 27, 1921, 452–7.
71. Ibid., No. 437, Rumbold to Curzon, November 9, 1921, 470–1.
72. Ibid., Nos. 440, 465, Rumbold to Curzon, November 11, 1921; Curzon to Hardinge, December 1, 1921, 499–503.
73. Ibid., Nos. 447, 471, Conversation between Sir E. Crowe and the French chargé d'affairs, November 18, 1921; Hardinge to Curzon, December 6, 1921, 480–2, 508–10.
74. Ibid., Nos. 417, 425, Hardinge to Curzon, October 21; meeting between Curzon and Greek ministers, October 27, 1921, 444–6, 452–7.
75. Ibid., No. 471, Bentrink (Athens) to Curzon, December 9, 1921, 517.
76. Ibid., Nos. 416, 464, Granville to Curzon, October 21; Rumbold to Curzon, December 1, 1921, 443, 498–9.
77. Ibid., No. 496, Curzon to Hardinge and to Graham, December 30, 1921 and Enclosure "Memorandum for Discussion", 535–56.
78. Meinertzhagen, *Middle East Diary*, entry September 26, 1921, 109–10.

12

Heading toward Disaster

The year 1922 was a fateful year—a year at the crossroads. Greece took the wrong turning, which ended in a disaster. On the other hand, Atatürk calculated his moves wisely, though brutally, and emerged victorious in his struggle for independence. The Allied powers were divided and Britain remained isolated. British policymakers were short-sighted and proved impotent. They were driven by events rather than shaping them. Ironically, although victorious in World War I Britain emerged a much weaker power. This was particularly the case vis-à-vis Turkey, where Britain forfeited her mastery.

Early in 1922, the scales began to tilt in the Nationalists' favor. Signor Tuozzi, the Italian emissary, returning from Angora, briefed Sir Horace Rumbold about his impressions. Mustafa Kemal's position, he told Rumbold, "is stronger than ever. As president of the national assembly and commander in chief of Nationalist forces, his power is that of a dictator." He intends to establish the future capital of Turkey in Angora, leaving the sultanate in Constantinople. Symbolism apart, a capital in Angora would be more immune from external and internal pressures. Kemal is being assisted by Fethi Bey, minister of the interior, and his personal friend.

The Nationalists' policy was to make separate agreements with the three allied powers, thus leaving the Greeks isolated. They were immensely elated by the Franklin-Bouillon Agreement and counted on the French to support them at the forthcoming peace conference. They expected Italy to follow suit, but Italy declined to go as far as the French had and negotiations broke down.

Signor Tuozzi thought that the Nationalists were aiming to achieve the complete territorial, economic, and financial independence of Anatolia and that no compromise with them would be possible on this score, particularly with regard to Smyrna. On Thrace, however, they would be more flexible. They had given up the idea of recovering former Arab dominions, but they wished to recover Mosul, which they considered to be a Turkish town. They were very bitter with King Hussein.

The economic situation, Tuozzi went on, was bad. He found the country completely deserted and ruined. Flocks of sheep, which formerly were in abundance had been driven up to the front to feed the army. Agricultural production had almost ceased. And yet, in spite of deprivation, Tuozzi discounted any chance of the Greek army being able to inflict a decisive military defeat on the Kemalists.

Minorities were treated with the utmost severity. Tuozzi saw groups of Christians being formed into labor battalions transported to the interior; "outlook for these people is hopeless." Eight hundred women whose male relatives were hiding in the mountains were taken into custody and kept as pawns until their relatives came out of hiding. The Nationalists claim that the minorities "have caused unending trouble to them in the past and the only way of [solving the problem] was to get rid of minorities. They want Anatolia for Turks." In Signor Tuozzi's opinion, "Evacuation of Smyrna and its district by the Greeks would be a deathblow in that region."

The Nationalists hated England and held her responsible for the Greek invasion. The Malta deportees, in particular, on their return to Anatolia, were indulged in violent anti-British propaganda. The Turks, however, regarded England as a "weak power" and pointed out to her setbacks in Egypt, Mesopotamia, as well as in Ireland.[1]

F. O. Lindley, who succeeded Lord Granville with the rank of minister, warned the Greek Prime Minister Gounaris and Foreign Minister Baltazzi, that "[n]o settlement with the Turks was possible so long as the Greeks remained in Asia Minor." He advised them, therefore, "to get accustomed to the idea of a withdrawal." To their question of what would happen to the Christian populations of the district, Lindley answered laconically that he presumed that the powers would make the necessary arrangements.

Lindley deliberately made no mention of Thrace since loss of both Smyrna and Thrace "would produce consequences of the utmost gravity in Greece and would, in all probability, compromise its whole future existence."[2]

Gounaris and Baltazzi heard the same advice from the British prime minister. In the presence of Lord Curzon, Sir Edward Grigg, and Robert Vansittart, Lloyd George told his Greek opposite numbers that no peace would be possible unless Greek forces were withdrawn from Anatolia and Smyrna. "The only alternative would be for the

Greeks to fight it out. Did M. Gounaris contemplate that?" He added that in the event of Greek withdrawal, "steps would be taken to protect the Christian population." Lloyd George did not specify what kind of steps would be taken to protect the Christian population but tried to console the Greek leaders that "an old-standing sentiment in England for Greece had not changed at all, although there was also a certain antagonism to the existing Greek" policy.[3] This was a dramatic reversal of British policy. It shocked the Greek people.

The position described by Tuozzi was confirmed by Rumbold. Kemal would reject any Allied offer falling short of the National Pact. The Nationalists aimed not merely to recover Smyrna and Thrace; "They are against real safeguards for minorities, capitulations, and any form of control, financial and otherwise." In his recent speech, Mustafa Kemal insisted on the right of the Turks to manage their own affairs. Several days later, the Constantinople undersecretary for foreign affairs opined that not even the most moderate Turk could accept a frontier that would leave a large portion of the northern shore of the Sea of Marmora in Greek hands. The Turks were ready to give Britain only guarantees to the effect that "[t]he Straits should remain absolutely free and unfortified. These guarantees would not be paper guarantees but material ones."[4]

The Nationalists' desiderata were presented officially by Yussuf Kemal, Angora's foreign minister. Accompanied by Hamid Bey, he called on Rumbold on February 17. Throughout the interview (which lasted two hours) he spoke with studied moderation and made (on his host) "a good impression." He was on a mission of exploration to allied capitals and had a mandate from the National Assembly. He pointed out that

> [n]ationalists not only sought a lasting peace with allies but also with Greeks. They would have need of Greeks in the future just as Greeks would have need of them. Greeks are merchants, Turks are peasants, each had needed help of the other. In order to attain a lasting peace it was necessary to eliminate all questions which might keep alive hostilities between the two races and give rise to conflicts in the future.

Among the controversial questions that Yussuf Kemal mentioned was Adrianople. It was essential that Adrianople, together with Eastern Thrace, be restored to Turkey. In response to Rumbold's query about the straits, Yussuf Kemal stated that Turkey recognized that

[i]t was in the interests not only of western powers, but of all states bordering on the Black Sea, that the Straits should remain open. It was impossible to conceive that Turkey at any time in the future could close the Straits in the teeth of the whole world. Turks were mainly concerned about the safety of Constantinople.

He suggested that an international commission be formed to supervise the freedom of navigation.

Kemal then turned to the question of capitulations; he pointed out that Germany and Austria had abolished the system during the war, the Russians had followed suit, and Italy, under the Treaty of Lausanne, also agreed to give it up. There remained only Great Britain, France, and America. The Nationalists were ready to offer guarantees for equitable administration and invite neutral powers "to strengthen their courts."

Finally, Yussuf dwelt on the vexed question of minorities, assuring that the guarantees would be modeled on the pattern of the treaties made with Poland, Romania, and other countries. Turkey would not object to supervision by the League of Nations and, if the minorities would desist from looking to foreign powers for support of the subversive activities, "the question of minorities would cease to exist." Finally, he declared that both the Nationalists and the government in Constantinople recognized that the nature of the regime of the old Ottoman Empire, composed of heterogeneous elements, should disappear. "A new Turkey had arisen; it repudiated bad traditions of the former Ottoman Empire."[5]

During the interview, Rumbold alluded to the situation in the Pontine region. According to information submitted by the Ecumenical Patriarchate to the three Allied high commissioners, the Nationalist government intended to deport into the interior all the women and children who had survived persecution. The patriarchate appealed to the commissioners to intervene and prevent these deportations.

Responding, Yussuf Kemal pointed his accusing finger at the "armed Greek bands," as he termed them, in the Samsoun region that endeavored to engineer "an open rebellion against the Nationalist government and to stab the latter in the back at the moment it was engaged in the struggle with the Greek army." He commented that there had been no deportations of the Ottoman Greeks into the interior prior to the bombardment of Samsoun by the Greek warships. The commissioners, however, were at a loss to establish what really happened.[6]

On March 16, Kemal met Curzon. He stated that the Turks "were not making war for war's sake: they desired a just and a durable peace." Their claims corresponded to Prime Minister Lloyd George's speech on January 5, 1918. In this speech Lloyd George stated inter alia, "Nor are we fighting . . . to deprive Turkey of its capital, or of the rich and renowned lands of Asia Minor, which are predominantly Turkish in race . . . ." This statement, in Yussuf Kemal's opinion, reflected "the principles for which the Great War had been fought." He went on as follows:

> The Turks desired to live like other nations. They considered that there was no incompatibility between the vital interests of Turkey and those of the British Empire. On the contrary, there was a great conformity between them. The solution of the Eastern question and the ensuing peace would serve the economic restoration of Europe.

This was a very able presentation. Demonstrating that there existed an identity of interests between Turkey and the British Empire, Yussuf Kemal skillfully undermined the prevalent notion among British officials that Turkey was still an enemy. Curzon, who heretofore despised, even loathed, the Nationalists, especially its leader, Mustafa Kemal, now evinced some respect toward his opposite number. The only thing that disturbed him was the alliance between Angora and the Soviet government.

Here again Yussuf Kemal's diplomatic skills excelled. He emphasized that the Russo-Turkish Agreement

> should not be interpreted as hostile to the British Government. It was not a treaty of alliance but of friendship. The Soviet Government had recognized the legitimate aspirations of the Turkish Government, but there was no aggressive article directed against anyone. It was a political treaty but Turkish economic and social principles had not been sacrificed. . . .. There was no limitation on [Turkey] to making treaties with any other Power. This proved that the Treaty was in no way directed against Great Britain.

Curzon continued to probe, but Kemal had a ready answer: "The Turks were waging a war of defence [and] it was natural that to defend their national existence they should use [all] means at their disposal." When their legitimate aspirations were satisfied, "these means [will] no longer be used." Curzon concluded that the first step for the Turkish government was "to declare its willingness for an armistice."[7]

Earlier, on the same day, Curzon received Izzet Pasha, the foreign minister of the Constantinople government, toward whom he was much more sympathetic than to Yussuf Kemal. Curzon assured him that the British government nourished no feeling of hostility toward the Turkish government, the Turkish people, or for Islam in general. However, the British could not forget that Turkey had been dragged into the war, which caused the British the loss of many millions of pounds and hundreds of thousands of lives. The Allies were entitled to take steps to prevent recurrence of such events. Otherwise, the British wished the Turks to reestablish themselves as an independent and strong nation, which could play a considerable part in Eastern politics on friendly terms with Great Britain.

Izzet Pasha was touched by Curzon's expression of friendship and admitted that Turkey had committed a "grave political error by entering the war; she had been driven by fear of Russia"; she had already paid the price by the loss of two-thirds of the Turkish Empire. Now, Izzet stated, "Turkey desired to link up again with England." With regard to minorities, "Turkey had no desire to hurt them. Protective measures could be taken, but not of character injurious to Turkish independence." As to the straits, the second question that concerned Curzon, Turkey was ready to neutralize them provided the Greeks vacated Marmora; the Turks could never live in safety in Constantinople if the Greeks were there.[8]

Two days later Curzon conferred with Yussuf Kemal again. Straight away Kemal declared that

> the Angora government was strongly in favour of a solution that would satisfy world opinion and ensure tranquillity of its own country. They were ready to accept the idea of an exchange of populations between the Greeks in Asia Minor and the Moslems in Greece.

He pointed to an agreement to this effect that had been concluded on July 5, 1914. Moreover, Turkey would be ready to subscribe to any arrangement made by the powers in other treaties for the protection of minorities. Curzon, however, was quick to point out the difficulty: The Greek population in Asia Minor was somewhere near half a million. "For physical reasons such a large number could not be entirely transported and, for agricultural and commercial reasons many of them would be unwilling to go. The same would apply to the Moslem population in Greece."

Kemal insisted that the first decision to be taken at the forthcoming conference in Paris should be the evacuation of Asia Minor by the Greeks, to which Curzon responded that "an armistice was obviously a preliminary necessity," for how one could effect an evacuation when the armies recommenced fighting?[9]

In the meantime, the position of Greece was becoming precarious. Prime Minister Gounaris had failed to raise a loan in England and other countries. "The complete exhaustion of our financial resources," he wrote to Athens, "has made the position of maintaining the Army in Asia Minor problematic. In addition to this, shortage of war-material must necessarily expose the Army to grave danger." Lindley, on his part, warned Curzon that, unless the Greeks received financial support, they would not be able to remain in Asia Minor. Curzon replied that there was little prospect of Greece being able to raise a substantial loan and advised Lindley confidentially to prepare the Greeks mentally to the idea of an "immediate evacuation of Anatolia by arrangement with Angora."[10]

On March 10, 1922, Harry Lamb, the high commission representative and consul general of Smyrna, reported that the morale of Greek troops was bad. They appeared to be disheartened, and he feared that, if the Nationalists would ever to be in position to attack, the Greek army "will crumble." Rumbold too pointed to the "possibility of internal trouble in the Greek army in Asia Minor."[11]

Between March 22 and 26, there were nine successive meetings of the Allied powers in Paris. The French delegation was led by Raymond Poincaré, prime minister and minister for foreign affairs (between 1913 and 1920 he served as president of the republic); the British delegation was led by Lord Curzon and the Italian, by Carlo Schanzer, foreign minister. The leading voice was that of Curzon. He emphasized that there must be an immediate cessation of all hostilities followed by the reduction of Greek forces in successive stages during at least eight months. The Greek population would require security, i.e., that it would not be molested by the Turks. However, Poincaré was doubtful whether the Turks would accept the armistice, to which Curzon commented that the Turks were aware that an armistice "was intended to be preliminary to a peaceful evacuation of Anatolia by the Greeks."

Curzon pointed out that, according to the American prewar figures, there were in Western Asia Minor about five hundred thousand Greeks and possibly not all would be repatriated. Hence, a scheme should be devised, while not prejudicing Turkish sovereignty, to afford protection to the non-Turkish population. Signor Schanzer agreed with Curzon but Poincaré disagreed: French public opinion, he stated, would object to granting "special favors shown to the Greeks." Moreover, the Turks "were in a state of violent patriotic exultation, and if any proposal was made touching their sovereignty in Asia, it would be rejected."

During the second meeting, Curzon reminded his colleagues that some intervention was necessary. He recalled how Armenians had been massacred following French evacuation of Cilicia, of Greeks at Isnik, and of Armenians at Zeitun and Marsivan. He quoted Colonel Rawlinson who saw the wholesale deportation of Greeks, the outrageous maltreatment of women and children, and men dying of starvation and exposure.

> The old Turkish plan of massacre and deportation to get rid of minorities he went on, was still in full operation. This was a moral responsibility of the Allies on all the Allies, and public opinion would not tolerate that they should not try to secure serious, and so far as possible, adequate protection for these unhappy minorities.

In Signor Tuozzi's opinion, Curzon went on, the Turks adopted a policy of extermination as "the only solution of the minorities problem." He suggested that the newly constituted League of Nations be empowered to serve as "the special protector of Moslem minorities in Europe and non-Turkish minorities in Turkey."

During the third meeting, Curzon broached the idea of forming a gendarmerie under foreign officers, but Poincaré retorted that this idea was "useless." The Turks were absolutely "intransigent on this point." However, during the fifth meeting (April 3), Poincaré had some second thoughts; he pointed out that the League of Nations had no troops. During the early stages of the Peace Conference, he suggested that creation of an international force to be at the League's disposal, but President Wilson objected. Since the idea had failed, Poincaré proposed that the three Allied powers occupy the western shore of Asia Minor "until the day when the League of Nations was ready to take over."

It was an excellent idea. The presence of Allied troops in the areas inhabited by the Greeks would enable the Greek army to withdraw peacefully in the knowledge that the safety of the Greek population in Smyrna and elsewhere would be safeguarded. The idea, however, was not taken up. The Italians claimed that they were overcommitted, whereas Curzon, it seems, could not emancipate himself from an outdated doctrine. "The Greeks were our Allies; the Turks were our enemies and had caused enormous sacrifices [by] all the Allies. The Greeks really deserved some consideration. Were we really to accept the dictates of Mustapha Kemal?" he declared.

Instead, it was decided that

> it should be the duty of the Powers to secure special guarantees for the protection of the Christian minorities in the Turkish dominions in Asia; of the Moslem minorities in Europe.
> The League of Nations would be invited, after consulting with the governments in Greece and Turkey, to appoint special commissioners for the supervision of the minority clauses in the new treaty both in Europe and in Asia.

After further discussions, it was decided unanimously at the ninth meeting to propose a scheme for the peaceful solution of the conflict to both the Greek and Turkish governments. First, the Allied powers expressed their desire "to re-establish the Turkish nation and the Turkish dominion in the areas which may be legitimately regarded as their own, with the historic and renowned capital of Constantinople." They desired also to secure "full and fair treatment to the followers of Islam and maintain the secular and religious authority of the sultan of Turkey." On the other hand, they wished to compensate the Greek nation for "the great sacrifices," which they had made during the war in the Allied cause. They desired also to provide for the protection and security of the various minorities, whether Muslim or Christian. From this purpose, the League of Nations would be invited to supervise the execution of the provisions of the treaties. Above all, they desired "to prevent the recurrence of armed conflict between the Turkish nation and the European powers."

Finally, if the proposal was accepted by the parties concerned and, assuming that the Greek army withdrew from Asia Minor, Turkish sovereignty in Asia Minor would "exist unimpaired" from the borders of Trans-Caucasia and Persia to Mesopotamia.[12]

These were the main points of the proposal. The Allied ministers endeavored to present an impartial document, though it undeniably tilted in favor of the Turks. It would hardly have satisfied the Greeks. The greatest drawback of the proposal, however, was that they expected the newly-pledged League of Nations to undertake the role of supervision. The league was an impotent body and its moral influence was yet untested. It behooved the powers, Britain in particular, who were responsible for the Greco-Turkish conflict, to back the league with military force. The absence of a military presence inevitably invited the failure of the whole scheme.

The response of the belligerents was quite predictable: the Turks accepted the allied proposal, whereas the Greeks rejected it. Both the Greek prime minister and minister for foreign affairs told Lindley that the guarantees for protection of Christian minorities were insufficient. They feared that, as soon as the proposal was known at Smyrna, panic would ensue followed by a general exodus of frenzied inhabitants with disastrous consequences for Greece. Prime Minister Gounaris was particularly bitter at the proposal to place the Greek and Turkish minorities on the same level. Whereas there were hundreds of thousands of Turks in European Greece, none of whom had suffered during the war, whereas the Turks "had committed the wholesale massacre of millions of Greeks. By placing the two nations on the same footing, the Allies had dishonored Greece." His government could not leave the Christian population in Smyrna and elsewhere "to their fate merely by throwing responsibility on the powers." Lindley, describing the debate in the Greek Parliament on April 1, commented as follows:

> I much fear that no Greek Government will be able to begin evacuation before they can persuade the public here that this population can remain secure in their homes after the Greek troops leave.[13]

Gounaris, upon returning to Athens from a conference in Genoa, declared that "[t]here was no question of the Powers forcing the Greeks to evacuate." He believed that the Greek forces could be considerably strengthened both in men and money by the resources of the local Greeks in Asia Minor. The latter had already formed a committee for National Defense. The atmosphere, however, was gloomy. Patriarch Meletios was despondent. He told Andrew Ryan, political officer at the British high commission, that the guarantees of the powers were useless. "If the Greek army left, the Christian population would be found trooping after them to the west." He quoted an appeal he had received from Panderma, in which the people said that "their choice lay not between life and death, but between different kinds of death."[14]

In sharp contrast, the Grand National Assembly in Angora welcomed the Paris proposal. It accepted in principle the Allies' request for an armistice on condition that the Greek evacuation followed suit. This was a sine qua non. Since the occupation of Smyrna, the invading Greek army had caused "loss of countless Moslem lives and incalculable devastation." This had recently intensified, "taking the form of wholesale massacre, destruction, and rape." They set a limit of four months for the Greek army to evacuate. The war office, however, thought that this period was not long enough to clear the depots and transfer a huge mass of equipment and men.[15]

Angora continued to press, and on April 22, Yussuf Kemal Bey sent a note to the three Allied ministers, stating that the Greek army was daily adding "new arson and devastation to previous crimes and increase[ing] the number of innocent Moslems massacred . . . Ruin of Turkish territory and atrocities . . . Greek occupation is attested by all neutral foreigners, including Red Cross delegates." On May 6, the Angora government lodged a formal protest against a new wave of atrocities committed by the Greeks in the occupied area.[16]

On February 27 from his vantage point at Smyrna, Sir Harry Lamb warned Rumbold that

> [t]he Greeks have realised that they have got to go, but they decided to leave a desert behind them, no matter whose interest may suffer thereby. . . . . Unless, [Lamb warned] the Allies were prepared to cover the Greek withdrawal from Smyrna, with adequate force, the fate of Anatolia will be settled by blood and fire alone.

On the same day Rumbold reiterated to the Foreign Office that

> [s]ystematic destruction carried out by the Greek army in its retreat from Sakaria River produced an effect on the Anatolian peasant who witnessed the destruction of villages etc. He is therefore willing to do everything possible to expel Greeks from Anatolia.[17]

This conduct had fortified the will of every Turk to fight. Revenge was soon to follow. Information obtained from American relief workers revealed "an appalling tale of barbarism and cruelty being practiced by Angora Turks as part of systematic policy of extermination of Christian Minorities in Asia Minor." Curzon thought that the British government should reconsider its attitude toward the peace proposals. "It is inconceivable," he noted, "that Europe should agree to hand back to Turkish rule, without the most stringent guarantees, communities who would be 'liable to be treated in the manner described by competent American witnesses, confirmed by independent information.'"[18]

Curzon's strongly worded message did not strike a chord in Paris. As di Martino, the Italian ambassador, told Sir Eyre Crowe, the French were acting hand in glove with Angora and that ever since the Franklin-Bouillon mission, they "had really been deceiving their Allies." de Martino added that Angora was determined to make no concessions and not to accept the peace settlement proposed by the Allies. He feared that mutual atrocities coupled with the inadequate protection of the minorities would cause a breakdown in the peace process.[19]

Crowe noted in resignation thus:

> France will continue to support Kemal directly or indirectly. Italy will talk ambiguous formulas.... Unless we were prepared to undertake a resumption of real war against Turkey—which seems unlikely if only for financial considerations—I see little chance of meeting Kemal by coercive measures, unless the League of Nations were able to raise such a storm of public opinion as would force France and Italy to participate. But this I doubt.[20]

Unwittingly, this statement was a declaration of impotence by a power that had won the war. The edifice of the peace proposal that the Allies were building so laboriously was crumbling.

On May 25, when Venizelos called on Crowe at the Foreign Office, he was in a gloomy mood, bordering on desperation. The situation that was rapidly developing in Anatolia was in his opinion "tragic." He was greatly worried about the fate of the Greek population. This was particularly so because, according to his information, the prospect of Angora accepting the Allied conditions of peace was "extremely slender." He foresaw a moment when the Allied powers would capitulate to Mustafa Kemal and agree to his terms. This would constitute an admission that "Turkey had won the war and not the Allies." The latter would be compelled to withdraw and "let Angora have its way." To Venizelos, it was clear: "The Greek army must retire from Smyrna . . . they must go. But what would follow? There was nothing that could stop Mustafa Kemal, after occupying Smyrna, from turning against the Allies . . . the Allies would have to evacuate Constantinople . . . and Turkish rule would be definitely reestablished over the Straits, with all that this implied."[21]

In Athens the mood was different. The Greek government claimed that, since the Turks rejected the armistice, the Greeks were under no obligation to accept the Paris peace proposals.[22] Inexplicably, on June 20 the Greeks ventured to bombard Samsun; they returned to

Constantinople, which was in the neutral zone, for resupply of ammunition, reentered the Black Sea, and after sinking several Turkish
crafts once more, returned to Constantinople. Angora's minister for
foreign affairs lodged a strong protest for Greek's unwarranted action
and for violating the zone of neutrality. Obliquely, he also criticized
the British for allowing this to happen. It made a bad impression not
only on the Turks, the minister stated, but on all Muslims. Moreover,
it prejudiced the prospects of peace. The Nationalists did not limit
themselves to words and retaliated by massive deportations of minorities in area under their control.[23]

The Turks had lost faith in the Allies. It was inconceivable, they
complained, that Constantinople served as a naval base for the Greek
fleet in spite of an inter-allied neutrality made the previous year. This
principle was repeated by the supreme council on August 10, 1922, and
reaffirmed by Lloyd George in the House of Commons on August 16.
The Turks were particularly averse toward the British; the Italians were
bowing out of the scene, whereas the French were now unequivocally
siding with the Kemalists.

French attitude was clearly demonstrated during the interview
between Colonel Mougin and Younous Nadi Bey, the editor of the
Angora paper *Yeni Guyr*. Early in June, Mougin was impressed by the
Turks' sincerity and "anticipated a constant strengthening of the relations between French and Turks," which had already been put on a firm
footing by the Franco-Kemalist agreement. Questioned regarding the
attitude of the French people toward Anatolia, Mougin replied that
in France there exists a great desire to see the peace reestablished in
general, and in the Near East in particular, and that Turkey's national
aspirations should be taken into account.[24]

While the Nationalists, under the leadership of Mustafa Kemal, were
gathering strength, both militarily and politically, the Greeks were in
a quandary. According to M. Sterghiades, the Greek high commissioner at Smyrna, without the help of the powers, the problem would
be "insolvable." Greece could neither evacuate nor continue the war
alone. Lindley, after a conversation with Mon. Baltazzi, the foreign
minister, got the impression that the Greek government was "unable
to take any decision however much they want to." Although officially
the Greeks claimed that the morale of the Greek army was "excellent,"
the morale of the population was less satisfactory; the people were
clamoring for peace, while the financial resources would be exhausted
by September.[25]

Finally, on July 14, a decision was taken. The minister for foreign affairs informed Lindley that the Greeks had decided that

1. no Greek forces [were] to be withdrawn from their present positions in Asia Minor; and
2. administration of the zone round Smyrna and Panderma, including the railway lines, [was] to be reorganized.

The Greek government felt obliged to bring matters to a head and intended to inform the Allied powers that "Greece must resume its liberty of action,"[26] which was tantamount to resumption of hostilities.

This was an unwise move as it was inopportune. Instead of insisting, even conditioning, the withdrawal of the Greek army on Allied military presence to protect the Christian minorities, the Greek government took a course that infuriated the Allies, the British in particular. Consequently, General Harrington, the general officer commander in chief, received orders to resist any attempt on the part of either of the belligerents to enter the neutral zone, particularly since a Greek move might provoke a corresponding move of Kemalists in Ismid peninsula.[27]

Athens remained belligerent. On July 27, the Greek minister for foreign affairs submitted a note to the Allied powers, stating that his government was not responsible for prolonging the war, adding that

> [m]assacres and deportations were threatening with extermination entire Christian populations of regions under Kemalists' occupation. In face of this situation, Greece was obliged to consider best measures for putting an end to conflict.

Two days later, the foreign minister declared that the Greek government had concluded that "only the occupation of Constantinople will bring about conclusion of peace."[28]

It seems that the Greek government was trying to force the Allies' hand. They overplayed it, however. General Harrington considered the more to be "directed against the allies" and asked the war office to initiate a joint action and warn Athens against the "folly of [the] step" that it appeared to contemplate. Henderson on his part, warned his opposite number against "madness of any precipitate action which would bring Greece into conflict with allied powers." Britain, in particular, "had no intention of permitting any violation of neutral zone." He added that if Greece tried to play her card "too early she would lose the game."

Rumbold, who, in the meantime, had returned from his leave, thought that the Greek menace to Constantinople was "50 percent bluff and 50 percent serious."[29]

It seems that Athens took the warning seriously. The Greek foreign minister told Bentinck that an urgent instruction had been sent to the Greek commander in chief to cancel any move and "to punish severely those responsible for the incident." After the meeting of the Greek cabinet, the minister of war rushed to the British legation and reiterated the foreign minister's message. "The troops," he assured, "were being withdrawn . . . behind the line."[30]

Lindley, since his appointment as minister to Athens, saw as his principal preoccupation to prevent the collapse of Greece and ensure a tolerable existence for the Christian minorities in Turkey. Late in June, he warned the British government that sands were running out quickly. Foreseeing the danger, he went to London to convey his conviction that, unless Greece received material and moral help from Britain, it would inevitably collapse by the autumn of this year. However, neither the prime minister, nor the acting secretary of state could find any way out of the Near Eastern deadlock.[31] Nonetheless, on August 4, Lloyd George felt the urge to make a speech in the House of Commons during which he stated as follows:

> I do not know of any army that would have gone as far as the Greeks have gone . . . . It was a very daring and a very dangerous military experiment. They established military superiority in every battle.[32]

As Lindley remarked, the speech contained "no promise that Greece would be allowed to retain any of the fruits of the campaign," but it raised a wave of enthusiasm in Greece and prompted an impressive demonstration in front of the British legation. Excerpts from the speech were circulated to the army as an order of the day. Ministers were most enthusiastic and saw in it a confirmation of sorts of the Greek's case.[33]

The Kemalists, however, saw the speech as a confirmation of their suspicion that Britain was siding with the Greeks and that the proclaimed Allies' neutrality was a sham. Aware of the weakness of the Greek army, the Kemalists decided to act.

In Greece, enthusiasm knew no bounds. The Greeks read into Lloyd George's speech what they wanted to read. On August 15, the Hellenic high commissioner at Smyrna, under Athens' instructions, issued a proclamation to the effect that "the autochthonal Hellenic element cannot return to the Turkish administration" and that "Greece is called upon to lay the foundation of a stable administration . . . under the liberating Hellenic army."[34]

This decision spelled out an annexation, at least of the Greek population to Greece. The presence of the Allied powers to this fait accompli was rather mute: they invited the governments of Athens, Constantinople, and Angora to an informal and preliminary conference to rediscuss the Paris Peace Proposal of March 1921. The initiative soon became irrelevant and was overtaken by events. At any rate, the Greeks looked upon France as an open enemy, and Italy, as only a secret one. All their faith and hope is still in England. The Greek army had been led to hope that assistance of some kind would be forthcoming, whereas a prophesy was in the air that "King Constantine and Queen Sophie may shortly be crowned emperor and empress of Byzantium at St. Sophia—thanks to the British lion!"[35]

Their enthusiasm, however, was misplaced. On August 31, Bentinck sent a disturbing message to Curzon as follows:

> Government circles are extremely depressed. Great indignation is expressed against [the] commander-in-chief who was taken completely by surprise and whose obstinate stupidity present disaster is attributed. . . . I am told that . . . Monsieur Gounaris wants entire evacuation . . .

On September 2, news which arrived from the front was "extremely grave." One of the two army corps had been cut off and driven north, with supplies and ammunition sufficient only for a few days. "Government," Bentinck urgently cabled to London, "are seriously alarmed . . . there is talk of abandoning Smyrna. Army seems to have lost morale . . . and can no longer oppose attacks of the enemy." The situation was so grave that the government instituted the commander in chief to ask for an armistice. The latter responded that it was impossible to defend Smyrna against Kemalist forces and that evacuation of Asia Minor "would be begun immediately . . . [the Greek] troops had practically ceased to fight."[36]

So what actually happened? Between the summer of 1921 and the summer of 1922, there was a lull in the fighting between the Greek army and the Nationalists. Nobody foresaw the impending disaster, least of all, Lloyd George. When Venizelos, overtaken by anxiety, came to see him, Lloyd George urged that Greece should stick to her policy. "This was a testing time for the Greek nation" and, if they persevered, "their future was assured. . . . Greece must go through the wilderness, she must live on manna . . . she must struggle through the stern trial of the present time."[37]

King Constantine was, however, overconfident. In a reckless move, he ordered the transfer of three regiments and two battalions from Anatolia to Thrace. Athens thereupon declared that Greece would occupy Constantinople, hoping that this would force the Allies' hand to terminate the Greco-Turkish war, presumably in a manner favorable to Greece. This was a fatal miscalculation. The Allies stood firm and foiled the Greek initiative, whereas the overextended line of the Greek front stretching over three hundred miles from the Sea of Marmora to Meander Valley weakened the Greek defenses. This Kemal Atatürk brilliantly exploited. Formerly, the Greek enjoyed a marked preponderance in manpower over the Turks. Now, in the last week of August, only fifteen thousand Greek soldiers faced a Turkish force of eighty thousand. The Greeks expected the assault in the north, where the terrain was flat, but Kemal chose the southern flank for attack. There, the mountain ridges of Afion Karahissar were practically invulnerable. The element of surprise was magnified manifold times.

The attack began on August 28 when Kemal issued his by-now-famous battle order: "Soldiers, your goal is the Mediterranean!" Imbued with patriotic fervor and stamina, the Turkish soldiers overcame the topographical obstacles and fortifications and by midmorning all the ridges were in Turkish hands. The citadel of Afion Karahissar fell like a ripe plum. The Greeks were stupefied. Several Greek divisions managed to evade the Turks and reached the Sea of Marmora (August 30), but the bulk of the Greek force was trapped at the mercy of the Turks. "The ensuing slaughter was of Armageddonic proportions. Within the next four days the entire Hellenic Army of Asia Minor was either destroyed or driven back to the sea."[38]

The retreating Greek units wreaked their revenge on innocent Turkish peasants, burning their villages, leaving behind heaps of ashes and angry and destitute Turks. It took a week for Kemal's army to reach Smyrna. Its Christian population—fifty thousand strong augmented by refugees from neighboring villages—was terrified at the thought of worse to come. The archbishop of Smyrna wrote to Venizelos on September 7 that

Hellenism in Asia Minor, the Greek state and the entire Greek Nation
are descending now to a Hell from which no power will be able to . . .
save them . . . it is a real question whether [when] your Excellency
reads this letter of mine we shall still be alive, destined as we are . . .
for sacrifice and martyrdom.[39]

Three days earlier, some friends of Greece appealed to Lloyd George to
do something for the Greeks. However, the prime minister admitted
the impossibility of doing anything. He severely criticized the action
of King Constantine and considered him responsible for the debacle.
Moreover, the king had appointed a most inefficient and unsuitable
general. Lloyd George deplored the situation but could do nothing.[40]

If Lloyd George was powerless, so was Venizelos, who could not
save the hapless archbishop. Several days after occupation of Izmir on
September 9/10, Nur-ud-Din, who became military commander
of Izmir, accused the archbishop of treason, pushed him out of his
residence, and invited a crowd of Muslims to deal with him. He was
lynched and mutilated, meeting the martyred death that he had fore-
seen. It was, as Andrew Mango described it, "an invitation to mob rule."
Attacks were directed mainly against the Armenians, as hatred against
them was intense. On September 13 a fire broke out in the Armenian
quarter, which spread quickly to other Christian neighborhoods to the
seafront. Three quarters of the city were entirely destroyed. Only the
Turkish quarter and the small Jewish quarter were spared.[41]

That the Jewish quarter was spared was not accidental. For generations, they had been the most loyal minority group devoid of territorial aspirations or links with foreign powers. They were industrious,
engaged in commerce and industry. Atatürk had a soft spot for them.
A Salonika man, he knew the Turkish Jews from close quarters and
appreciated their worth. Conflict with the Greek people made them
even more valuable to the economy.

In 1911, before the Turco-Italian war in Tripolitania, Mustafa Kemal,
then a young officer stationed in Jerusalem, met Itamar Ben-Avi, the
son of Eliezer Ben-Yehuda. Itamar suggested that Kemal introduce the
Latin script throughout the Ottoman Empire. The common alphabet,
Itamar Ben-Avi claimed, would serve as "a natural cultural bridge"
among the Ottoman peoples: the Turks, the Greeks, the Albanians,
the Jews, and others. The script in Arabic characters hindered, so
far, mutual understanding, whereas the Latin one would serve as a
"natural 'Esperanto'".[42]

Kemal also met Eliezer Ben-Yehuda and was favorably impressed by Palestinian Jews. He and other Turkish officers played soccer with members of Maccabi sports club.[43]

He was known to have a positive attitude toward Zionism and Jewish settlement in Palestine and distanced himself from Arab propaganda. He welcomed the arrival of German–Jewish physicians in Turkey during the Nazi persecutions in Germany.

Kemal Atatürk's victory was overwhelming. It was so swift—it took no more than six days—that the Greek army was unable to evacuate its stores and heavy armaments. The Greek generals and their monarch badly miscalculated and lost their nerve. The end result was that the native Greek population, in whose defense the Greek army had entered the war, was now left defenseless and destitute.

The Turks too suffered heavily. In their war against the Greeks, they lost thirteen thousand officers and soldiers, and suffered thirty-five thousand wounded. In their final offensive, the Turks lost thirteen thousand men, including the wounded. A huge amount of property was destroyed both in the Eastern part of Anatolia and in the Western provinces, the most prosperous parts of the country.

It is a moot question whether the destruction of the Greek community was a premeditated act. Left to the judgment of Kemal Atatürk, it is doubtful whether he would have gone so far, but neither he, nor Ismet or Fevzi, his lieutenants, were capable of restraining the vengeful Nurettin. Falih Rafki (Atay), the Turkish Nationalist journalist, who had come from Istanbul (formerly named Constantinople) down to Izmir to interview Mustafa Kemal commented, "I believe that but for Nur-ud-Din Pasha, known as a thorough fanatic and rabble-rousing demagogue, this tragedy would not have run its course." When contemplating the conflagration of Izmir, Kemal Atatürk would only say this: "Let it burn, let it crush down." It was, as Mango commented, "not an order; it was acceptance of the consummation of ethnic order." Two months later, criticizing Nurettin's readiness to exile and destroy the Greeks and Armenians in Anatolia, Mustafa Kemal described his conduct as "demagogy," which should have been avoided for fear of "damaging the national interest."[44]

Kemal Atatürk did not mention the fire in Izmir (Smyrna) and the ensuing destruction of the Greek and Armenian communities in his great speech of 1927 in the National Assembly. Nor did Turkish historians describe the sorry episode. However, contemporary journalists and observers left behind richly documented records.

Notes

1. W. W. Medlicott, Douglas Dakin, and M. E. Lambert, editors, *Documents on British Foreign Policy 1919–1939* I, vol. XVII (London: HMSO 1970) (hereafter *DBFP*) No. 501, Rumbold to Curzon, January 6, 1922, 560–3.
2. Ibid., No. 503, Lindley to Curzon, Athens, January 7, 1922, 569–71.
3. Ibid., No. 504, Note on conversation . . . at Cannes on Thursday, January 12, 1922, 572–3.
4. Ibid., No. 506, 510, Rumbold to Curzon, January 15, 26, 1922, 574–5, 583.
5. Ibid., No. 531, Rumbold to Curzon, February 17, 1922, 622–5. Hamid H. Bey served in 1921–2 as agent of the Angora government. On the guarantees for minorities in the treaties with Poland, Romania, etc., see: H. W. W. Temperley, *A History of the Peace Conference*, 1921, vol. V, App. IV. On the system of capitulations see Isaiah Friedman, *Germany, Turkey and Zionism, 1897–1918*, 2nd edition (Piscataway, NJ, and London: Transaction Publishers, 1998), with a new introduction by the author, 32–7.
6. Ibid., No. 535, Rumbold to Curzon, February 18, 1922, 631–3.
7. Ibid., No. 555, Memorandum of an Interview between Curzon and Yussuf Kemal Bey, March 16, 1922, 657–60. Lloyd George's speech appeared in the *The Times* on January 1, 1918, p. 1, and is quoted in Harold Nicolson, *Curzon: The Last Phase* (London, 1934), 99.
8. Ibid., No. 554, Memorandum on an Interview between Curzon and Izzet Pasha, March 16, 1922, 654–7.
9. Ibid., No. 556, Memorandum on an Interview between Curzon and Yussuf Kemal, March 18, 1922, 660–5. On exchange of population prior to World War I see D. Pentzopoulos, *The Balkan Exchange of Minorities and its Impact on Greece* (The Hague, 1962), 55–7.
10. *DBFP*, I, XXII, Nos. encl. to 544, 545, 548, Gounaris to Athens; Lindley to Curzon; Curzon to Lindley; February 27, March 6, 1922, 640–2, 645.
11. Ibid., No. 552, Rumbold to Curzon, March 13, 1922, 652–3.
12. Ibid., Nos. 560–8, Minutes of ten meetings of British, French, and Italian representatives in Paris, March 6–22, 1922, 668–754.
13. Ibid., Nos. 574–6, Rumbold to Curzon, March 28; Lindley to Curzon, March 29; and note 2, March 30, 1922, 766–8.
14. Ibid., Nos. 613, 618, Rumbold to Curzon, April 29, May 3, 1922, 801, 805.
15. Ibid., No. 583, Rumbold to Curzon, April 5, 1922, and a minute by the war office, 772–4.
16. Ibid., Nos. 603, 624, Rumbold to Curzon, April 23, May 6, 1922, 787–90, 811.
17. Cited in Gilbert, *Sir Horace Rumbold* (London, 1973), 251.
18. *DBFP*, I, Vol. XVII, No. 630, Curzon to Cheetham (Ambassador in Paris), May 15, 1922, 817–8.
19. Ibid., No. 632. A conversation of Sir E. Crowe with the Italian Ambassador, May 17, 1922, 821–4.
20. Ibid., Crowe's minute on No. 636, p. 829. Earlier, Rumbold complained that the French in Constantinople were "entirely unscrupulous in their attempts to curry favour with Nationalists and that their proceedings will greatly increase the difficulty of a settlement." No. 540, to Curzon, February 21, 1922, 637.

21. Ibid., No. 642, Record by Sir E. Crowe of a conversation with M. Venizelos, May 25, 1922, 836–41.
22. Ibid., No. 654, Lindley to Balfour, June 16, 1922, 854. Early in June Lord Balfour replaced Curzon temporarily.
23. Ibid., Nos. 662, 664 Rumbold to Balfour, June 24, 26, 1922, 861–4.
24. Ibid., No. 667, Rumbold (quoting from *Yeni Gyur* of June 11) to Balfour, June 27, 1922, 866–7.
25. Ibid., Nos. 674, 678, Lindley to Balfour, June 30, July 8, 1922, 872–4, 879.
26. Ibid., Nos. 685, 693, Lindley to Balfour, July 14, 23, 1922, 885, 890–1.
27. Ibid., No. 696, Henderson to Balfour, July 27, 1922, 893–4. Arthur Henderson acted as *chargé d'affairs* during Rumbold's absence.
28. Ibid., Nos. 697, 703, Bentinck to Balfour, July 27, 29, 1922, 894–5, 900–1. From July 25 to September 17, 1922 Bentinck was acting as *chargé d'affairs*.
29. Ibid., Nos. 708, 711, Henderson to Balfour, July 30, Rumbold to Balfour, July 31, 1922, 903–4, 906–7.
30. Ibid., No. 716, Bentinck to Balfour, August 2, 1922, 910–1.
31. Ibid., Lindley's Annual Report for 1922 in No. 727, note 2, 919.
32. House of Commons, Deb. 55, col. 1997–2006.
33. See Note 31 above, and No. 727, Bentinck to Balfour, August 7, 1922, 918–9.
34. Ibid., Note verbale, Athens, August 15, 1922, Encl. to No. 736, 926–7; also No. 732, Curzon to Bentinck, August 12, *Urgent*, 922–3.
35. Ibid., Encl. 3 in No. 737; N. 748, Bentinck to Curzon, August 29, 1922, *Confidential*, 939–41.
36. Ibid., Nos. 754, 755, 756. Three very urgent cables from Bentinck to Curzon on September 2, 1922, and note 3, 946–8.
37. Michael Llewellyn, *Smith, Ionian Vision: Greece in Asia Minor*, 1919–1922 (New York, 1973), 271.
38. Howard M. Sachar, *The Emergence of the Middle East*, 1914–1924 (New York, 1969), 434.
39. Smith, *Ionian Vision*, 232ff.
40. *Lord Riddell's Intimate Diary of the Peace Conference and after: 1918–1923* (New York, 1934), 385.
41. Andrew Mango, *Atatürk* (London, 1999), 345.
42. Jacob Landau, "Atatürk's Reforms in Turkey—Preliminary Notes . . . ," *Enstitu Yayin*, No. 5, 1975, 556. Professor Landau quotes from Itamar Avi's *Memoirs*.
43. Ibid.
44. Mango, *Atatürk*, 343–7.

13

Inferno in Smyrna

The Greek and Armenian communities in Smyrna were unfortunate indeed to have Nurettin as their governor. Nurettin was notorious for his brutal treatment of the prisoners of Kut. Vindictive by nature, he was a xenophobe who took delight in the cruelties meted out against his victims. He was the embodiment of an oriental satrap who knew no mercy.

Mrs. Birge, the headmistress of the girls' school, witnessed the entry of Nurettin's troops into the city. Dressed in black with Red Crescent and star, they proudly rode into the city calling to the terrified inhabitants: "Fear not, fear not!" but on the following day, they started the most terrible looting, raping, and killing. "Whole companies of soldiers broke into the stores . . . and swept them clean of their goods. . . . The city was systematically looted, and things were carried in carts down to the Turkish quarters. . . . When the sun set that evening dead bodies were lying all over the streets of that doomed city."[1]

During the first three days of the Turkish occupation, looting, murder, and outrage continued. "It was a massacre, with all its attendant atrocities." Turkish guards were stationed at all approaches to the Armenian quarter in order to prevent Europeans, as far as possible, from knowing what was going on. On the first day, the consuls of the various powers become alarmed and protested to Nurettin. The latter reassured them that order would be restored, but in fact, until the fire extinguished, "unspeakable scenes were taking place in the quarters inhabited by Armenians and Greeks. Hundreds of Greek and Armenian girls were placed in brothels for the delectation of the Turkish soldiery and massacre, rapine and pillage without stint and on a scale unequalled. These few instances were indicative of what was taking place."[2]

In their frenzy the Turkish soldiers did not bypass American institutions and property. Thus, the house of Dr. and Mrs. Birge near the American International Institute for boys at Paradise, a suburb of Smyrna, was thoroughly looted, although it had an American flag flying over it.

On September 11, the second day of occupation, Dr. Alexander McLachlan, director of the American International Institute for boys, learned that the college had been looted. He was stunned because his pro-Turkish sympathies were known. Accompanied by five American sailors, he set out to ascertain what had happened. Moreover, he was beaten and robbed by the Turkish soldiers. "I was left with scarcely any clothing—shoes, stockings, pants—an attempt to smash my right foot with a butt of a rifle resulting in the splitting open of my big toe only"—runs his story. The American sailors in uniform were fired upon, while the sergeant in charge was robbed and maltreated.[3]

The following day the horror escalated. Ms. Minnie Mills, the director of the American College for girls testified thus:

> Soon after lunch fire broke out very near the school, and spread rapidly. I saw with my own eyes a Turkish officer enter a house with small tins of petroleum or benzene, and in a few minutes the house was in flames. Our teachers and girls saw the Turks in regular soldiers' uniforms, and in several cases in officers' uniforms, using long sticks with rags at the end of which were dipped in a can of liquid, and carried out into houses which were soon burning. There was no one in the streets at that time, but bands of Turkish soldiers. While the fire started just across the street from our school, throughout the quarter (the Armenian quarter) every third or fifth house were set on fire.

Ms. Mills' testimony is borne out by numerous witnesses. Mr. Jaquith, director of the Near Eastern Relief, in his report to Admiral Bristol, the American high commissioner to Turkey, testified that he saw persons throwing oil on some buildings in the presence of Turkish soldiers. Major Davis of the Red Cross, in his report, confirmed it in his testimony. Ms. Birge provided an even more detailed testimony. From the tower of McLachlan Hall, she was able to see how Turkish troops were entering houses with tins of petrol in their hands, and a few minutes later, she saw the houses bursting into flames. The fire broke out almost simultaneously at four points of the Armenian quarter. It extended for two miles and consumed all the "infidel Smyrna," *Giraur Izmir*, as the Turks called it. The same pattern followed with regard to the Greek quarter. Only the Turkish and the Jewish quarters were spared the fire. The Turks, evidently, wished to make Izmir Christian-free.[4]

Contemporary journalists also provide us with vivid, albeit gruesome, descriptions. The *Daily Telegraph* (September 16, 1922), among others, wrote thus:

> Three-fifths of Smyrna is in ashes. More than 300,000 persons are homeless this morning as the fire burns itself out after destroying the entire Armenian, Greek and foreign quarters. The financial loss is close upon £40,000,000, of which between £2,000,000 and £3,000,000 is American. The loss of life is impossible to compute. Every Allied ship in the harbor volunteered its services in clearing the refugees, many of whom are badly wounded. The streets are littered with dead.
>
> All the foreign Consulates are destroyed, together with fine business buildings, banks and homes along the quays of the foreign quarter. Except for the squalid Turkish quarter, Smyrna has ceased to exist. Among the houses are the headquarters of Kemal Pasha. The problem of the minorities is here solved for all time. The refugees are being removed to other lands as fast as possible.
>
> No doubt remains as to the origin of the fire. *On the sworn testimony of the American staff of the Collegiate Institute, the torch was applied by Turkish regular soldiers.* Evidently it was a reprisal for the incalculable damage caused by the Greek army during the retreat.[5]

The conditions were described as "terrible" and the risk of the plague was imminent.

Mr. Roy Treloar, the son of Sir William Treloar, the director of Eastern Carpets, Ltd., Smyrna, declared that the scene at Smyrna was "indescribable"; one could not imagine such deeds of barbarity to be possible in this age. At a moderate estimate the damage done could be put at £20,000,000.

Ms. Mills told the *London Times* (September 15) that before the houses were set on fire, Turkish soldiers roamed in the deserted houses with the result that

> [l]ooting was most extensive. Carpets, clothes, jewelry and all articles easily portable were carried away, and the interior of houses was completely wrecked. The pillaging was evidently permitted officially. The estimate of the extent of the massacres varies considerably, the highest figure quoted being four hundred thousand, which, however, would mean the killing of half the population, which had recently been greatly swollen by refugees. All accounts, nevertheless, agree that Smyrna has been turned into a charnel-house. Several streets were so littered with mutilated bodies that it was impossible to pass for [the] sickening stench.

The killing was carried out systematically. Turkish regulars and irregulars are described as rounding up likely wealthy persons on the street, and after stripping them, killing them in batches. Many Christians who had taken refuge in the churches were burned to death in the buildings, which had been sent on fire.

As usual, the most beautiful girls were torn from their families and sent to the interior, and where resistance was offered by brothers and fathers they were murdered.

Messages from Athens through Reuters and other agencies, give further details on the scenes in doomed Smyrna. The *Daily Chronicle* of September 18 reported the following:

> Refugees say that the Kemalists spared nobody, except their co-religionists and Jews. Massacre and incendiarism were the order of the day and were carried out by groups headed by Turkish officers. Houses and stores were looted by soldiers and civilians and afterwards set on fire. Mutilated and burnt corpses were everywhere to be seen, and the atmosphere was poisoned with the smell of burnt flesh emanating from the ruins. Women and girls were taken to the outskirts of the town and massacred.
>
> Since Thursday no Armenians have been living in Smyrna. Some doubtless are in hiding, but it is feared that even infants have been massacred.
>
> The quay on which were concentrated the panic-stricken and trembling refugees presents the most tragic human spectacle imaginable. The groans and agonizing cries of the wounded and dying are heard on all sides, and all are suffering from hunger and thirst. Boats and lighters to carry the refugees to the available ships are insufficient, and many attempting to reach the ships by swimming were drowned, whilst others were shot from the quay. Several of the refugees, particularly the women, became insane. It is impossible to learn the number of lives lost, but the lowest estimate given by refugees places the total at 120,000. Large numbers of Greeks and Armenians were summarily shot on a charge of having helped the Greek Army or committed imaginary crimes.

The Rev. Charles Bobson, the heroic Smyrna Chaplain, gave sworn testimony that illustrates "the unbridled brutality" of the Turkish soldiers.[6]

In spite of such unimaginable catastrophe, the League of Nations, on whom the Allies pinned their hopes, was powerless to intervene. Nor did the Allied powers themselves show any eagerness to stop the atrocities. Britain, France, Italy, and the United States had warships in Smyrna harbor and could have used their force to protect the persecuted minorities. However, the French sympathized with the Kemalists and, to smaller degrees, also the Italians, whilst the United States was neutral. Great Britain, on the other hand, was divided, weak, and war-weary. Its fighting spirit had gone. During the war, the Allies pinned on their banner the slogan: Liberation of small nationalities and protection of minorities. These were now well forgotten. It was a bad omen for the postwar world. Concluding, one might say that, had the Allied warships at Smyrna been ordered by their home governments to act, there would have been no massacre, and Smyrna would not have been burned. The powers, however, made no attempt to restrain the Turks.

There was no one to protect the Greeks and the Armenians. Defenseless and panic-stricken, thousands upon thousands of refugees rushed to the harbor in the hope of being rescued by the warships. So tightly was the great throng packed on the quays that when one died he could not fall but continued to stand upright, supported perforce by his neighbors. All through the days and nights that followed, bands of Turks would make forays into the frightened crowd, seize ten or twenty women and either abscond with them or violate and assassinate them. The dealer of an American tobacco company gave the following testimony:

> I watched in Cortelo, a suburb of Smyrna, an Armenian family, husband, wife, and children, walk out of their beautiful home down to the sea and drown themselves. The Turkish officers requisitioned the homes of the Greeks and Armenians and English in Cortelo, and filled them full of the most beautiful of the Greek and Armenian girls whom they had captured. A Turkish officer said to me, "We have those houses filled with those girls, and they dance for us naked every night. If you want to see a fine show come over and see it."

Dr. Esther Lovejoy, a member of American Women's Hospital, gave an account which, in horror, surpassed perhaps all others. On September 24 she found the quay to be packed with people, and the unfortunates squatted as closely as they could and held their places because it was presumably the place of greatest safety. "At night it was possible for the warships in the harbor to throw on this group their searchlights when the women screamed for protection, as they did night after night.

> One could constantly hear the screams and moans and shrieks of those poor women and girls moving up and down that quay.... There

was no retreat from that position. If they had tried to go back to the ruins of the city they probably would have lost their lives.

The quay became a reeking sewer, and at last, the evacuation started on September 24, the very day I got there . . .

The Turkish airplanes had gone over these places and dropped down a proclamation saying that all were to be deported on September 30 to the interior, regardless of age or sex, women and children as well as men. All the men between fifteen and fifty were deported to the interior, anyway. And they all looked upon deportation to the interior as nothing less than a sentence of death. It is, in fact, worse than death, because it is preceded by slavery on the part of the men and even worse on the part of the girls and women.

On September 26, the nineteen ships began to evacuate the people of the city. The sight was indescribable. The great mass of miserable people pushed down toward the quay and the long railroad pier in order to get aboard the rescuing ships. Practically all of them had on their backs all their earthly possessions at that time. Many of them carried their sick and their infants on their back. And many of these people had lived in that city for years, and their families had lived in that city long before the coming of the Turks from Asia.

These poor unfortunates rushed along the quay, having in mind, doubtless, that they would be deported on September 30. They had four days to get away. . . . The great crowd surged down the line, and then met fences. There would be only one fence, I should say, two hundred or three hundred feet from the end of the quay and then another fence at the end of the railroad pier. And out of the pier three fences had been made with timbers. These fences were so constructed that everybody would be obliged to go down through those five gates and pass through a double line of Turkish soldiers for inspection. The point was that the Turkish authorities did not want any man to get away, and this plan afforded an opportunity to search and rob the women. The surging crowd would crush against the fence with terrible results, especially to the young, the old, and the weak. . . . Many were pushed into the water.

On account of the horrors of that city, with a population of 300,000, bereft of their homes and burned out, naturally there were among those people a large part of expectant mothers. . . . There were many premature maternity cases on account of this crushing and rushing. I was assigned to watch especially for those cases, and as I stood there, one poor woman in the agony of her labor was thrust through this gate just as her baby came into the world. But there were hundreds of cases occurring at that time.

A Turkish soldier would stand on either side of this line of women, and if they saw a prosperous looking woman, they would reach out, seize her, pull her aside, examine her—going over her body and lifting up her skirts and looking into her stockings to see whether she had any money they could take. Then another woman would pass, and they would seize and search her.

Then the men would come through. After being robbed and ill-treated, the man would finally find himself in the prison group. I saw one man at the first gate cut his own throat as a protest against being taken through.

Further on, down the line, I saw a young man with arms bound behind. They must have especially wanted him, so they bound him. He saw the possibility of suicide and made one jump overboard and drowned himself.

The feeding was a terrible thing because it frequently started great rushing and a great crush. In the agony of starvation, the people could not restrain themselves. And then, too, when the ships came in, they were provisioned. They were without food. The refugees were carried over to an island, and there they were dumped.

This was the most terrible thing on the quay. Families of five or six members had been together on the quay. Or it may have been man and wife, mother and son, brothers and sisters. At one of these gates, a soldier would seize the man, while his wife would cling to him and beg the soldier to let him go with her. The baby would hang to his mother as an attempt was made to separate them in driving the women to the ships. The soldiers were continually saying to them, "Get out; be gone." And the soldiers would beat the women and men with a bunch of straps or with the butts of their guns. In the mean-time, the soldiers would invariably separate families. In many cases, a mother would cling to her son of fifteen as she was being driven away, but the soldiers held all men between fifteen and fifty.

And now the women and children are on the islands of Greece. Many of them, I have no doubt, have died of pestilence and starvation, and the men have been sent away to the interior to death.[7]

According to the order, sanctioned by Kemal, all males, Greek and Armenian, between the ages of seventeen and forty-five, were to be deported into the interior to serve in Turkish "labor gangs." This meant simply a prolonged agony followed by death. The whole story of the 160,000 men who were separated from their families and deported will never be known. It was a revenge—a most cruel revenge—for what the Greek army had committed against the Turks during its occupation of Anatolia. Nonetheless, it was an inexcusable crime.

When the same pattern was followed in Anatolia, it became clear that the Angora government intended to embark on a policy of ex-termination of unwanted minorities. This is what was depicted by Ms. Ethel Thompson, a former worker of the Near East Relief, during 1921 and 1922.

The ghastly lines of gaunt, starving Greek women and children who staggered across Anatolia through the city of Harput, their glassy eyes fairly protruding from their heads, their bones merely covered with skin, skeleton babies tied to their backs, driven on without food, supplies or clothing until they dropped dead—Turkish gendarmes hurrying them on with their guns.

She continued thus:

Upon arriving in Harput, we entered a city full of starving, sick, wretched human wrecks—Greek women, children and men. These people were trying to make a soup of grass, and considered themselves fortunate when they could secure a sheep's ear to aid it—the ear being the only part of the animal thrown away in Anatolia. The Turks had given them no food on the 500-mile trips from Samsun. Those with money could bribe the guards for food or buy a little on the way until they were robbed. Those without money died by the wayside.

When a woman with a baby died, the baby was taken from her dead arms and handed to another woman, and the horrible march proceeded. Old blind men led by little children trudged along the road. The whole thing was like a march of corpses, a march of death across Anatolia, which continued during my entire summer.

The heaviest winter weather, when a howling blizzard was raging during a blinding snowfall, was the favorite time chosen by the Turks to drive the Greeks on. Thousands perished in the snow. The road from Harput to Bitlis was lined with bodies. I saw women with transparent lips who did not look human. They were like gaunt shadows. The roads over which women and children travelled were impassable for any kind of travel excepting pack mule.[8]

This testimony is verified by other reputable witnesses. The 1,150,000 refugees, who finally reached Greece, were fortunate, by comparison, to reach relative safety. Nonetheless, their position was inevitably precarious as described by Mr. Jaquith of the Near East Relief Association.

In the harbor, crowded with 21 warships of 7 different nations, are four refugee ships crammed with deportees from Asia Minor who have waited for days to be landed. . . . Ashore, earlier arrivals are huddled together in windowless, doorless, leaky buildings under conditions beyond description. Afloat and ashore smallpox, typhus, dysentery and pneumonia go unchecked . . . Sixty percent of those who live through the voyage on filthy, crowded ships are diseased on arrival here.

And Dr. Lovejoy, mentioned already, sent the following report:

> Refugee conditions are indescribable. People mostly women and children without a country. Rejected by all the world, herded and driven like animals from place to place, crowded in damp holes and hovels, wet, cold, hungry, sick. Shortage of food, water, bedding, no clothing, suffering very great. Mercy of immediate death withheld. Greece is willing but unable to cope with conditions and outlook here is hopeless.[9]

In truth, Greece was overwhelmed by such an enormous increase in population. Herself in financial straits and paralyzed by a political crisis, she was unable to cope with the situation. Greece had not the food, clothing, or shelter to give adequate protection to the vast crowd thrust upon her. The American Red Cross almost instantly rushed to help. It contributed the sum of $26,000,000 of its treasury. But it soon became apparent that this help, although magnificent, was inadequate.

The position became further aggravated when, following the Lausanne Conference in October 1922, Greece had to return Eastern Thrace to Turkey. W. T. Massey, the London *Times* correspondent, reported on October 23, 1922, that the evacuation of Christians had begun with terrible panic. Kemal's propagandists spread rumors calculated to inspire terror among civilians that Turkish gendarmeries were coming into Thrace within two days.

Immediately there was a sauve qui peut. Practically every Greek villager and farmer packed his possessions on ox-wagons and trekked coastward. Consequently, every port was choked with refugees, who were in hopeless confusion, living under deplorable conditions, without sufficient transport to carry them, and betraying the greatest fear that an avalanche of Turks would drive them into the sea. "The whole country is a sad picture of a broken-spirited people who have lost everything, and the statements of many that they would welcome death to relieve their suffering appear to be true."

Mr. Alford E. Brady, of the American Smyrna Disaster Committee, told the *Chicago Times* some vivid stories of the robbery and massacre of the fleeing Christians. The Turks, he stated, were interfering with the efforts to aid and rescue the panic-stricken Christian population. Whilst thousands of homeless were huddled on the beaches, the Turks fired on vessels flying the American and British flags that had come to the rescue. Brady commented that the majority of Greek and Armenian civilian men in Asia Minor have been deported to Angora, into what is tantamount to slavery, and the majority of women and children were exiled also. The object of Turkish campaign of massacre and terror was to wipe out the last surviving Christian communities one by one.

Hospitals on the Greek islands, he went on, were crowded with people who have been beaten and attacked by the Turks. In the hospital, at Chios, he saw a child who still lived, although shot through the face by a Turkish soldier who had killed his father and violated his mother. In the same hospital, there was a family of six orphan Armenians. The father, knowing the Turks were invading the district, collected his savings and sewed the money into the children's garments. The Turkish troops, after killing the parent, found the money sewed in the clothes, but being unable to find any money on the four-year-old baby, they beat the child with rifle-butts.[10]

William Klutz, of the American Relief Organization, filed the following report with the *Chicago Tribune* (October 16, 1922):

> Thracian refugees are already beginning to arrive in Salonika. The poorer peasants are filtering in afoot, plodding along the roads beside their donkeys, heaped high with pitiful possessions of household goods. The more prosperous Thracians have sold everything they possessed, and are arriving in autos heaped high with trunks and baggage. *Seventy thousand refugees from Asia are already in Salonika*; there is no place to receive them; they have to sleep in the streets, parks, churches. The staggering proportions of the tragedy are unrealizable, for the avalanche of Thracian migration had only just began.
>
> The earlier refugees were housed in four big camps on the outskirts of the city, which were built for the British Army during the thrust for Gallipoli. Seventy per cent of these people are stricken with malaria from the swamps about the city, and disease cannot be coped with, quinine being unavailable. The start of the rainy season is expected daily, when pneumonia will take a heavy toll, even if cholera and typhus can be staved off.[11]

Massey was particularly moved by the plight of refugees from Eastern Thracia. He witnessed

> the scene of one of the greatest human dramas in modern history, the trek of a people who, having had their land hunger satisfied under treaty, are now abandoning all profit gained by work and thrift, and are seeking, if possible, for some new outlet for their energies, where they will not again suffer a great betrayal.

It was a tragic journey—the picture, he observed, "beggared" description:

> All the way northwards, the road is cumbered with a vast amount of transport, which is continually being increased by arrivals along the tracks to the east and west of whole processions from the villages coming together, with a few men-folk under arms to protect the convoy from bandits and raiders. Unutterable misery is written in every face, and pain at leaving their homes and farmsteads is apparent everywhere. But fear of the Turks' approach overwhelms all sense of personal loss, and the terrified people press forward regardless of fatigue continually looking behind them for their mortal enemy.
>
> From Baba Eski the difficulties were increased by reason of the broken road bridges, but the volume of traffic had beaten down hard tracks greatly resembling the sun-baked mud roads used by mechanical transport in Lord Allenby's campaign in Palestine. From within twenty kilometers of Adrianople the roads presented the amazing spectacle of an absolutely continuous line of refugees, sometimes with wagons "two abreast," all except the aged and infants walking, mostly in bare feet. At places of hopeless congestion—points where the maneuvering of beasts on uneven ground slowed up this column of agonized humans, numbers pulled out to rest and formed camps as big as those occupied by a brigade of British artillery. The hapless people drank and washed in the dirty streams and rested their weary limbs on the banks, silent, uncomplaining, but broken-spirited. A few Greek priests tried to comfort them, but I am afraid their words of hope and cheer fell on deaf ears. Three miles from Adrianople there was a square mile of refugees, and I doubt if they will succeed in passing to the west of Maritza by daybreak, though the traffic was fairly well controlled by Greek gendarmerie and kept moving over the two river bridges that the poor folk believe lead to safety.

This was the only hope that kept them alive. However, Massey was aware of the bitter truth. "The wet season is approaching and the position . . . will become infinitely worse. It is feared that thousands who survive the hardships of migration will perish of starvation in the winter."[12]

The plight of the refugees of Eastern Thrace—180,000 strong—elicits particular compassion since they were in no way involved in hostilities. It was simply a merciless act of ethnic cleansing. The inhumane treatment of minorities in other parts of Turkey is equally unjustifiable and reflects badly on the newly borne Turkish nationalism, however appealing might be its cause. There were about 1,040,000 Greek, 100,000

Armenian, 1,000 Assyrian, and 9,000 Circassian refugees making the total of 1,150,000.

One cannot part from this terrible human tragedy without examining the question of responsibility. In our opinion the prime responsibility should be laid at the door of Eleutherios Venizelos for conceiving and piloting the idea of building a Hellenic Empire on the ruins of the defeated Turkey. It was a crazy idea that had no chance of succeeding. It went against the ideals for which the Allies were fighting, and it was morally wrong. Nonetheless, it was followed with even greater fervor by his successors. Prime Minister Gounaris was fully aware of the financial weakness of his country and of being involved in a war that could not be won, while King Constantine unwisely intervened in military strategy with disastrous consequences.

This Greek policy could not have been implemented had its proponents not found a ready ear in Lloyd George, the British prime minister. To him the idea of a Hellenic Empire had a strong appeal. It appealed both to his romantic and imperialistic instincts. He hated Turkey, and his motto was that Turkey *delenda est*. He miscalculated and had dearly paid for his mistake.

The Turks were the evil doers and made no effort to improve their behavior toward the minorities in their midst. To their credit, it must be said, however, that their policy, as propounded by their foreign ministers, was sound and statesman-like. It gave the promise of a peaceful and satisfactory solution. When, however, it struck no chord among the British counterparts, and when the Greek army refused to withdraw and instead, embarked on wanton destruction of Turkish country, passions were ignited for revenge. It was so excessive that it harmed Turkey's reputation.

The original sin, however, was the Greek invasion of Smyrna with Allied support, if not encouragement. Its repercussions were unforeseen. For this major miscalculation all the Allied powers were responsible, the United States not the least, since President Wilson gave his approval of the move.

After the catastrophe at Smyrna there was an inclination in Britain to blame other powers. The United States was accused of agreeing initially to accept the mandate and occupy Constantinople, the Dardanelles, and Armenia. However, America vacillated and eventually went back on her word. This unwittingly prolonged unduly the peacemaking. The results were dire.

The United States rejected this accusation. Secretary of State Hughes, in a conversation with the British ambassador, stated that he

> could not for a moment assent to the view that this Government was in any way responsible for the existing conditions. . . . The United States had not sought out spheres of influence in Anatolia; [it] had not engaged in intrigues in Constantinople; [it] was not responsible for the catastrophe of the Greek armies during the last year and a half . . . Diplomacy in Europe for the last year and a half was responsible for the late disaster. . . . The secretary continued, "What troubled the dreams of the British statesmen was their maintenance of their imperial power, the question of India, the question of Egypt, of the Suez Canal, and their relations to the Near East in connection with their vast imperial domain." He did not wish to criticize this attitude and was quite ready to admit that the British Empire was a supporter of civilization, but must point out that whatever these imperial ambitions and difficulties were, the American government was not associated with them.[13]

By pointing to the British imperial ambitions, Secretary Hughes put his finger on the primary cause of British miscalculation. The American position with regard to the Smyrna disaster had been explained by Secretary Hughes in a speech in Boston on October 30. He declared that

> [w]hile nothing can excuse in the slightest degree to palliate the barbaric cruelty of the Turks, no just appraisement can be made of the situation which fails to take account of the incursion of the Greek army into Anatolia, of the war waged, in the burning of towns, and general devastation and cruelties. There were those . . . who proposed that the United States should have actively intervened in Turkey. The situation in Turkey was the result of a war to which the United States was not a party, and if the Allies, who were close to the scene, did not choose to intervene, the American people would not shoulder the burden. It would also be futile to talk of going to war in Turkey at the present, when all the other powers were preparing for a peace conference. The United States had no connection with the political ambitions of the Allies there and did not propose to become involved with them.[14]

This assessment was sound. It was also true that America was not at war with Turkey and tried not to get involved in the controversies among the belligerents. However, Secretary Hughes was apparently oblivious of the fact that initially President Wilson agreed to the occupation of Smyrna by the Greek army. Had he objected, it is unlikely that the Allies would have embarked on the ill-advised adventure.

There is voluminous literature on the period after the Greco-Turkish war. It would be superfluous to recapitulate it. In the following pages our purpose is merely to sketch the salient points in order to round out the story.

In Greece, the repercussions of the debacle were far reaching. Athens was paralyzed. The dream of the Hellenic Empire vanished overnight. The destruction of Smyrna and the eviction of the surviving Greek community had a traumatic effect. On September 26 Prime Minister Gounaris resigned. King Constantine abdicated in favor of his son, George, and, heartbroken, in the following January, died in Palermo, Sicily. On September 28 a triumvirate of revolutionary officers captured the reins of power and, on November 13, arrested Gounaris and a number of ex-ministers. They were accused of high treason and blamed for causing a national catastrophe. Some of them were imprisoned for life, others, including Gounaris, were sentenced to death. They refused to be blindfolded and went to their death with their eyes open.[15]

Triumphant, Atatürk now aspired to take over Constantinople and Eastern Thrace. But here he encountered the firm and unbending opposition of the British government. The Sèvres Treaty had delineated the entire straits zone as a neutral area and on September 11, 1922, the Allied high commissioners in Constantinople issued a severe warning against violation of the neutral zone. The British fleet, now reinforced at Chanak on the Asian shore of the Dardanelles was a force to be reckoned with. Now Churchill, hitherto pro-Turkish, took the lead. "The line of deep water separating Asia from Europe," he declared, "was a line of a great significance, and we must make that line secure by every means within our power. If the Turks take the Gallipoli Peninsula and Constantinople, we shall have lost the whole fruits of our victory."[16]

Lloyd George fully agreed with Churchill.

> In no circumstances, [he said] could we allow the Gallipoli Peninsula to be held by the Turks. It was the most important strategic position in the world, and the closing of the Straits had prolonged the war by two years. It was inconceivable that we should allow the Turks to gain possession of the Gallipoli Peninsula and we should fight to prevent their doing so.[17]

However firm Churchill and Lloyd George were, they failed to carry the nation with them. The press was furious at the thought that Britain must be dragged into yet another war. The French took offence at not being consulted and withdrew their contingent from Chanak. The Italians followed suit. The cabinet was shocked to hear that, with the exception of New Zealand, the Dominions refused to send their troops. Diplomatically Britain was isolated.

The worst was still to come. Lloyd George was losing support of the Conservative party, his erstwhile partners. Granting independence to Ireland, recognizing Bolshevik Russia, an economic crisis at home coupled with mass unemployment, and a number of foreign policy failures culminating in the Chanak crisis diminished his stature in the eyes of his partners. Above all, they felt offended at not being consulted about Turkish policy. Traditionally, the Tory party was pro-Turk and they were alienated by Lloyd George's pronounced orientation toward Greece.

Concerned, lest Lloyd George became an electoral liability, the Conservatives no longer felt compelled to follow his leadership. Bonar Law, supported by Lord Beaverbrook, was the man chosen to bring down the coalition government and challenge Lloyd George. On October 11, Lord Beaverbrook commented thus:

> We are now in the throes of a political crisis. The failure of the Prime Minister's Greek policy has resulted in a complete collapse of his prestige with the Conservatives. . . . The immediate future will decide whether the Conservative Party is to remain intact, or whether the Prime Minister is strong enough to split it.[18]

In the event, it was the Conservative Party that remained intact, while the prime minister was defeated. In a coalition caucus he received only 87 votes, as opposed to 187. Lloyd George resigned immediately and soon afterward, Andrew Bonar Law replaced him as prime minister. The day of elections was set for November 15, during which Lloyd George suffered yet another defeat. The Conservatives won the majority of the seats in Parliament, whereas the Liberal Party, like its leader, lost its preeminent position. For the once all-powerful statesman, who, during World War I, had saved his country from defeat, it was a sad day.

Colonel Meinertzhagen was critical of Lloyd George's policy. He was sorry, however, that Winston Churchill too was a casualty. He had lost his seat in the Parliament, and Meinertzhagen regretfully jotted in his diary as follows:

> So Winston is gone. For many reasons I am sorry. He has a brilliant brain and is as quick as lightning. He acts almost entirely by instinct and is usually right, though easily led astray by some enthusiast [such as T. E. Lawrence]. He was a hard master to serve, working like a Trojan himself and expecting equally hard work from his staff.[19]

In his defense against criticism from the Conservatives, Lloyd George claimed that it was thanks to his and his government's firmness at Chanak that Kemal's army was halted. Meinertzhagen, as a keen observer, viewed matters differently.

> We certainly do not wish to fight, the country would not stand it. And I doubt if Turkey wishes to embark on a new war. She is bluffing. . . . I have never seen [a] government department so rattled as they have been during the past few weeks, and all because they have all made hideous mistakes.[20]

Indeed, Atatürk was too much of a statesman to risk a confrontation with an overwhelming Allied naval power over the straits, which was not even on the Nationalists' agenda. They aimed to reacquire Constantinople and Eastern Thrace but realized that the straits, as an international waterway, should be left open to the powers without discrimination.

The Turks, for their part, were quick to detect that the Allies were disinclined to hold on to Constantinople and Thrace. They were prepared to give these up honorably through negotiations. This suited the Turks. If one could retrieve Turkish territory at a conference table rather than on a battlefield, the choice was self-evident. This the Turks did, first at a preliminary conference at Mudania followed by the conference in Lausanne on November 21, 1922. Britain was represented by Lord Curzon, who joined the Bonar Law's government, whilst the Turkish delegation was led by Ismet Inönü. Curzon was an accomplished diplomat, whereas Ismet had made his name on the battlefield as an outstanding general. Curzon dominated the debate but Ismet stubbornly stood his ground. The encounter ended with Ismet's triumph. With the exception of Mosul, Turkey got practically all that it claimed. It obtained absolute sovereignty over her territory as stipulated in the National Pact. On August 24, the Grand National Assembly ratified the Lausanne Treaty of July 24, 1922, and on the following day, the Allies began their evacuation of Constantinople and the straits. Within two months, not one foreign soldier remained on Turkish soil.

This was an outstanding achievement since, unlike other vanquished powers, like Germany, Austria-Hungary, and Bulgaria, Turkey was the only power that emerged victorious both militarily and politically and in a position to dictate its peace terms.

One bright spot at the Lausanne Conference was an attempt to solve the refugee problem. The idea was borne in Venizelos' fertile mind. It was warmly supported by Dr. Fridtjoy Hansen, a Norwegian diplomat of international standing whom the League of Nations had commissioned to study the Middle East refugee question. Even before examination, Hansen realized that the flight of refugees was of such massive proportions that it was not reversible. He suggested, instead, that the exodus be treated as a fait accompli and that a mutual exchange of Greek and Turkish minorities be initiated under the supervision of the League of Nations. In concrete terms the Islamic population of Macedonia and other Greek regions—four hundred thousand strong— should emigrate to Turkey; their abandoned land and property was to be occupied by the Greek newcomers. Both Venizelos and Ankara gave their approval to the idea of exchange of populations, and on January 30, 1923, the convention for reciprocal migration of Greek and Turkish populations was later incorporated into the Lausanne Peace Treaty. As Howard Sachar characterized it, the exchange represented "the most daring and unprecedented solution of an endemic political problem ever to have been devised in modern history. . . . Both sides were prepared to bear the cost. . . . [Henceforth] Turkey and Greece would experience, at last, the incalculable and enduring blessing of ethnic homogeneity."[21]

Notes

1. Edward H. Bierstadt, *The Great Betrayal* (London, 1924), 26.
2. Ibid., 27–8, 31.
3. Ibid., 28–33.
4. Ibid., 33–6.
5. Ibid., 215–7.
6. Ibid., 224–6.
7. Ibid., 37–43.
8. Ibid., 56–7.
9. Ibid., 58–9.
10. Ibid., 228–31. Brady's report was reprinted in the *Daily Telegraph* and the *Manchester Guardian*.
11. Ibid., 231.
12. Ibid., 236–9.
13. Laurence Evans, *United States Policy and the Partition of Turkey, 1914–1924* (Baltimore, 1965), 375.

14.   Ibid., 373–4.
15.   Michael L. Smith, *Ionian Vision, Greece in Asia Minor1919–1922* (New York, 1973), 326–8.
16.   Martin Gilbert, *Winston S. Churchill: Companion Volume*, vol. 4, pt. April 3, 1921–November 1922 (Boston, 1978), 1980.
17.   Ibid.
18.   A. J. P. Taylor, *Beaverbrook* (New York, 1972), 197.
19.   Colonel R. Meinertzhagen, *Middle East Diary, 1917 to 1956* (London, 1959), 121–4.
20.   Ibid., entry October 5, 1922, 124.
21.   Howard M. Sachar, *The Emergence of a Middle East, 1914–1924* (New York, 1969), 446–8.

14

Was a Peaceful Coexistence between Arabs and Jews in Palestine Possible?

During the period of the mandate, the Arabs blamed the Balfour Declaration as a source of all their troubles. Elizabeth Monroe, in her book *Britain's Moment in the Middle East, 1914–1956*, published in 1963, stated that "[m]easured by British interests alone [the Balfour Declaration] was one of the greatest mistakes in our imperial history."[1] This was a *political*, not a historical, judgment. It reflected the view held at the Foreign Office during the late thirties and forties when relations with the Zionists had reached their nadir and the need to appease the Arabs was at its highest. It is instructive therefore to recall how the Balfour Declaration was considered by its makers, the contemporary press, and the public at large.[2]

Few pledges or statements of British Middle Eastern policy were so thoroughly examined at all administrative levels as the Balfour Declaration. It was not issued in haste or lightheartedly. It was made as a deliberate act of the British cabinet, as part of their general foreign policy and their war aims. As Lloyd George told the House of Commons on November 12, 1930, it was a "truly national [policy] in the sense that it represented the views of the three parties in the state." It had acquired international status since the principal Allies, Russia, France, Italy, and the United States, had given it their prior approval. It was reaffirmed by the principal allied powers at the San Remo conference in April 1920. When it was subsequently incorporated into the Mandate of Palestine and approved by the Council of the League of Nations on July 24, 1922, it became part of international law. The act coincided with the joint resolution of the United States Congress on June 30, 1922, approved by the president three months later.

Leopold Amery, one of the chief draftsmen of this document, regarded the Balfour Declaration as a "Charter to Zionism—one of the most momentous declarations that have been made in recent history," while General Smuts referred to it as "[t]he foundation of a great policy of international justice. The greatest, most ancient historic wrong has at last been undone." Lloyd George went so far as to state that the Balfour Declaration was "a contract with Jewry"; most likely he used it in a moral sense, which was not necessarily less binding. Lloyd George specifically pointed out that the Zionist leaders had given the British "a definite promise . . . to rally to the Allied cause Jewish support throughout the world," concluding that the Zionists "kept their word in the letter and the spirit," and the only question that remained was whether the British meant (in the late thirties) to honor theirs. Professor Temperley explained that the Balfour Declaration was a "pledge that in return for services to be rendered by Jewry, the British Government would 'use their best endeavors' to secure the execution of a certain definite policy in Palestine." David Hogarth, in his Introduction to Philip Graves's book *Palestine: The Land of Three Faiths*, wrote that the Balfour Declaration was "as binding [an] engagement as Great Britain had ever been committed to."

Sir Charles Webster thought that the Balfour Declaration was "the greatest act of diplomatic statesmanship of the First World War." There was no precedence for what the Zionists were asking. Unlike other small nationalities in physical possession of territories, whose demand for independence fit well within the doctrine of self-determination, the Jewish inhabitants of Palestine constituted only a minority of the population; the Zionists had therefore to go back nearly two thousand years to establish a claim to the country.

Sir Ronald MacNeil, a leading member of the parliament, in his masterly memorandum, stated that it would be "a glaring anomaly" if the Allies in the postwar settlement were to deny or ignore the claims of the people who had throughout history clung to their nationality more tenaciously than any other. One Briton, though not the only one who was sensitive to the "voice of Jewish history," was Balfour. He was a self-confessed Zionist, though he had no hand in drafting the declaration that bears his name. As records show, he was irresolute and cautious. He preferred to be pressed by the Foreign Office rather than lead it, and it was not before October 31, 1917, after being prodded by Sir Ronald Graham, assistant undersecretary for foreign affairs, that he threw all his weight on to the scales at the crucial cabinet meeting.

However, the Middle East policy was shaped by Lloyd George, and his responsibility for the declaration was greater. In day-to-day matters the prime minister's authority was delegated to the War Cabinet Secretariat, which was dominated by Sir Mark Sykes. Sykes considered Zionism an essential ingredient of the New Middle East Order.

However, the unacknowledged hero was Sir Ronald Graham. Seconded by Robert Cecil, Lord Hardinge, and Harold Nicolson, he pressed unremittingly for an early statement. It would, however, be true to say that the Balfour Declaration was the result of a collective effort, both Jewish and British, rather than the work of a single individual. The press almost unanimously supported the British policy enthusiastically.

For Britain, acquisition of Palestine was an irreducible strategic requirement. But even if the central powers were decisively defeated, a claim based on military conquest alone would have been inadmissible. It would have violated the principle of nonacquisition of territories by war enunciated by President Wilson and the provisional Russian government, and alienated world opinion. With annexation condemned, the only course open to the Western Allies, Britain in particular, was to link their war aims with the principle of self-determination. This was why Britain had to play the Nationalist card. It was also the raison d'être of the contract with Zionism. A British-oriented Jewish national home, it was thought, could be a major asset, and conversely an obstacle to German ambitions in that vital region.

Zionist wishes played directly into British hands, freeing them of any annexationist taint. Chaim Weizmann was rendering a singular service when he advised his friends in Russia and America that England's sole desire in protecting Palestine was "to give the Jews the possibility of getting on their feet and living independently." Sir Charles Webster, who during the war served in the political intelligence department, confirmed twenty-five years later that at the time it had been realized that a declaration on the Jewish national home would ease acceptance by other powers of Britain's position in Palestine, an assumption that events proved correct.

Undoubtedly there was a strong undercurrent of sympathy toward Zionism, which was reflected in the press. It was consistent with the encouragement to small and oppressed nationalities. But as the official records show, sentiment did not determine state policy. The declaration would hardly have been made unless it had been the considered judgment of the Foreign Office and the war cabinet that it was clearly in British interest to do so. There was a combination of motives rather than one that led to the final decision, but what determined was the desire for security.

In 1922, when the Balfour Declaration came under attack, Ormsby-Gore stated in the House of Commons (on July 4) that it would be "absolutely dishonorable" to go back on it. Neville Chamberlain was emphatic that Britain was "definitely pledged" and that he would oppose any proposal to renounce it, as did Sir John Simon, MP. Sir John Shuckburgh, head of the Middle East Department of the Colonial Office, recalled that the declaration was made at the time when the cause of the Allies was in extreme peril, and to throw the Zionists overboard when the peril was over would be shameful. And yet this was what happened.

It is instructive to examine Arab response to the Balfour Declaration. King Hussein, the sharif of Mecca, was fully aware that Palestine had been excluded from his understanding with the British high commissioner, Sir Henry McMahon. He was also aware that, according to the Muslim holy scriptures, Palestine belonged to the Jews. Palestine, therefore, was of little concern to him. When some Arab notables in the newly occupied Jerusalem appealed to him to protest against the Balfour Declaration, he seemed indifferent to their plea. The Palestinians, being under the impact of Turkish propaganda, feared that the Zionists bent on creation of a purely Jewish state would reacquire their land and evict them. Hussein brushed aside this argument and told Colonel C. E. Wilson, British representative in Jeddah, that he was "not in favor of such letters being written to him from Palestine."

Hussein's lack of concern over the Balfour Declaration and Zionist aims was clearly demonstrated early in January 1918 during his conversations with David Hogarth, the director of the Arab Bureau, who came to Jeddah especially to reassure the king. The Turks used the Balfour Declaration to discredit the British, claiming that Palestine would be given away to the Jews. Unperturbed, the king welcomed the British policy and agreed enthusiastically to Jewish settlement in Palestine.

About three months later, Hussein was instrumental in publishing an article in *al-Qibia* (March 23, 1918), his official mouthpiece. Palestine, the article attested, was "a sacred and beloved homeland . . . [of] its original sons [*abna' ihl-l-asliyum*]—the Jews. The resources of the country are still virgin soil, which could not provide a livelihood for the Palestinian native. But the Jewish immigrants would develop the country. Experience has proved their capacity to succeed in their energies and their labours. . . . The return of these exiles [*jaliya*] to their homeland will prove materially and spiritually an experimental school for their [Arab] brethren . . . in the fields, factories and trades. . . . One of the most amazing things," the article went on, "was that the Palestinian used to leave his country wandering over high seas in every direction" The article called upon the Arab population in Palestine to bear in mind that their sacred books and their traditions enjoined upon them the duties of hospitality and tolerance, and exhorted them to welcome the Jews as brethren and cooperate with them for the common welfare.

This was an extraordinary statement. The question that inescapably comes to our minds is how Hussein had conceived these ideas. There is no evidence to show that he ever met a Zionist personality or consulted Zionist literature. One could conclude with certainty that the source of his inspiration was the holy scriptures, as indeed he did admit in his article.

According to the Koran, God gave the land of Israel to the Jews and will restore them to it in the End of the Days. "Then We [Allah] would say to the Israelites 'Dwell in the land. When the promise of the hereafter comes to be fulfilled, We shall assemble you all 'together.'"[3] Elsewhere the Koran states, "Children of Israel, remember the favour that I bestowed upon you, and that I exalted you above the nations."[4]

Elsewhere one reads, "Bear in mind the words of Moses to his People. . . . Remember, my people the favour which God had bestowed upon you. . . . Enter, my people to Holy Land [Land of Israel] which God has assigned for you. Do not turn back and thus lose all."[5]

Here is an assortment of additional statements that appear in the Koran:

"We gave the persecuted people [children of Israel] dominion over the eastern and western lands [east and west banks of the Jordan River] which we had blessed. Thus was your Lord's gracious word fulfilled for the Israelites. Because they had endured with fortitude . . ."[6] Elsewhere one reads, "We settled the Israelites in a secure land [Land of Israel] and provided them with good things."[7] "We delivered him [Abraham] to the land [of Israel] which we had blessed for all mankind"[8] "We gave Moses the Book [Torah] and made it a guide for the Israelites"[9] We said to the Israelites, "Dwell in the land [of Israel]. When the promise of the hereafter comes to be fulfilled we shall assemble you [children of Israel] all together [in the Land of Israel]."[10]

This is a selection of statements penned by Prophet Muhammad, who was influenced by dictums of Jewish prophets and traditions. It seems that Hussein, who was a guardian of the holy places in Mecca and Medina, was deeply impressed by Mohammad's statements and did not limit himself to making his views known in *al-Qibia* but instructed Emir Feisal, his son, then near Akaba as follows:

> If you ever meet the Zionists . . . you should remember that it is our interest to preserve their comfort and their material rights which we should defend with our lives. Do not think that this is merely a chance or passing thought, for God willing the future will show it to be my firm resolve.

Indeed, in this matter Hussein remained consistent until the end of his life. In October 1919 Colonel Charles Vickery interviewed King Hussein, but not until 1939 did he publish his impressions.

> I can say most definitely that the whole of the King's demands were central around Syria, and only around Syria. Time after time he referred to that vineyard, to the exclusion of any other claim or interest. He stated most emphatically that he did not concern himself at all with Palestine and had no desire to have suzerainty over it for himself or his successors.

On January 27, 1924, in his meeting with Lt. Col. Frederick Kisch, the chairman of the Palestine Zionist Executive, King Hussein declared that "[h]is heart was open to the Jews and his lands also. He was ready to give land free to the Jews provided they would enter through the door and not make a breach in the walls. The future would prove his sincerity . . . and would show that the Jews had nothing to fear from the Arabs."

These words were said in Amman when Hussein visited his son Abdullah. Before the meeting, the king decorated chief rabbi Meir, a member of the delegation, with the grand cordon of the order of Istaklal as an act of appreciation.

During the dinner party, Emir Abdullah said that he appreciated the Jewish love for Palestine, adding that "provided the rights of the Arabs be safeguarded . . . they would welcome the presence of Jews not only in Palestine but also in other Arab countries." However, the duty of the mandatory power was to do "everything possible to facilitate an understanding" between Arabs and Jews. On the following day King Hussein reiterated his appreciation of "the depth of Jewish sentiment with regard to Palestine" and asked Colonel Kisch to submit definite proposals for cooperation.[11]

On February 10, 1931, accompanied by a high-level delegation, Kisch met King Hussein again in Amman. The king reiterated his sentiments, which he had expressed earlier in 1924, and promised to reject Hajj Amin Hussein's appeal to publish an anti-Zionist declaration. He kept his word. He assured Kisch of his amity toward the Jews and asked Abdullah to do his utmost to "establish friendly relations between the two peoples." Abdullah, on his part, stated that "[c]onflict between Arab and Jew could benefit neither. He recognized and appreciated the Jewish connection with Palestine, which was even written in the pages of the Koran, but a solution must be found that was not inconsistent with Arab aspirations for a united Arabia."[12]

Kisch also met other Arab statesmen and personalities. During his visit to Egypt between March 19 and 22, 1924, he met Dr. Abd el Malik, the Hedjaz minister in Egypt, and Hassan Sabri Bey. They suspected that the money raised ostensibly for the repair of the Mosque of Omar in Jerusalem was being used by the Palestinians for political purposes. He also met Aziz Bey al-Misri, the founder of *al-Ahd* society. A Circassian by birth, he was a leading Arab Nationalist. He impressed Kisch as a man of great strength of character, well educated, and speaking French and German fluently. His aim, he declared, was "to promote the real freedom of the Arab people. . . . He wants the Orient for the Oriental and regards the Jews as such." Kisch noted in his *Diary* on this somewhat remarkable group:

> Remarkable for the fact that these three men, of such different origins but all Moslems and true Orientals, were equally emphatic in their pro-Zionist declarations, these declarations moreover were sincere; there was no pretense of embracing Zionism *pour nos beaux yeux*, but each of the three, for a somewhat different reason, recognized that progress of Zionism might help to secure the development of a new Eastern civilization.[13]

The opinion of Aziz Bey al-Misri is particularly important since, in 1915/16 jointly with Muhammad al-Faruqi, he negotiated with Sir Henry McMahon on territorial Arab demands. His statements are additional proof that not only had Palestine been excluded from the deal, but the Arab negotiators avoided demanding it.

Colonel Kisch set himself the task of cultivating good relations with the Arab population in Palestine. On January 24, 1923, he visited the

Moslem National Club at Tiberias and found that the club had done a great deal to combat anti-Semitism. Its members, however, were bitterly against the Mandatory officials who displayed "nothing but hostility." The Muslim mayor of Tiberias invited Kisch to a reception. The general impression created by his visit was "most satisfactory. Here Jews, Moslems and Christians live in close contact with each other and not in separate quarters . . . the Arabs seem to be in terms of real friendship with the Jews."[14]

In April, while on a tour of Galilee with Baron Felix de Menasce of Alexandria, Kisch revisited Tiberias. The former mufti was exceedingly obliging, and the present one, after familiarizing himself with the Zionist program, stated that "[a]s a Moslem he could not deny the right of the Jews to return to Palestine, provided that the Arabs were respected." He also paid a courtesy visit to Husni Effendi, the mayor of Tiberias, known for his friendly relations with Jewish inhabitants. On his return he had a two-hour interview with Sheikh Assad Shoukair of Acre with whom he discussed the possibility of forming a popular party to support the mandate. Shoukair was a bitter enemy of Hajj Amin al-Husseini. He was working closely with Ragheb Nashishibi and Arif Pasha Dajani, and made some very sensible suggestions of how to effect a change in Arab opinion, provided the government "would give them some encouragement."[15]

Among the personalities who called on Kisch was Hassan Bey Shukry, former mayor of Haifa (1914–20), known to be moderate in his views. He led a delegation of about twelve Arab notables. More interesting was a visit from Said Kiamil Pasha of Acre, the son of the former Turkish Grand Vizier and himself once ADC to Sultan Abdul Hamid. He was contemptuous of the ultra laxity employed by the Palestine administration and that the Palestinian Arabs were "foolish not to realize that it is a marvelous stroke of fortune for Palestine that the Jews are interested in making the country prosperous."[16]

This blanket accusation was not fully justified because a great many Arabs did appreciate the benefits of Zionist colonization and welcomed Arab–Jewish cooperation. Thus, the sheikhs of Beisan, eager to cooperate, complained to Kisch that they were being persecuted by junior government officials. Complaints from other sources reached him to the effect that the subdistrict governor was doing all he could to resist Arab–Jewish rapprochement and the formation of the new Peasant Party. This was, Kisch thought, unwise, since those Arabs who were friendly toward Jews supported the policy of the mandate.[17]

Ragheb Nashashibi was clear about it: the government was doing nothing to facilitate cooperation between Jews and Arabs; on the contrary, it continued to support extremist elements. This was also the opinion of Riad el Sulk, a Syrian national leader.

Sir Wyndham Deedes, the civil secretary of the government, revealed to Kisch confidentially that High Commissioner Samuel followed the advice of Ernest Richmond. The latter "makes all cooperation with the Jews impossible." During a luncheon meeting with Kisch, Richmond made no secret of his opposition to Zionism. "I believe," Kisch noted in his *Diary*, that "a man with his views should not be employed as political adviser to the Government in Palestine."[18]

On May 8, 1923, a new colony called Gezer, near Ramle, was founded. Present at the ceremony was the high commissioner and a sprinkling of non-Jewish officials. It also included at least a hundred Arabs from neighboring villages. Kisch was gratified to see so many Arabs participating happily in such a ceremony under the shadow of the blue and white flag. "No better answer could be given," he noted, "to the constantly repeated charge that all Arabs are opposed to Zionist work. As a matter of fact, the fellaheen like having Jewish colonists as neighbours."[19]

Resentment against the self-assumed leadership of the Husseini family and its allies was on the increase, in the rural areas in particular. In 1924 farmers associations were founded in Nablus, Nazareth, Hebron, and elsewhere. Their avowed aim was to emancipate themselves from the oppressive exploitation of the large landowners and unscrupulous moneylenders. They were apolitical and dissociated themselves from the vocal propaganda of the extremists. Employment in Jewish farms and commercial intercourse benefited them, and they were eager to cooperate with the Jews. They welcomed the mandate and evinced no objections toward the Balfour Declaration.[20]

This was an important development, and Dr. Weizmann was not slow to act on it. When the Palestine Arab executive complained to the League of Nations that the Jewish colonists were dispossessing Arab farmers from their lands, Weizmann wrote to William Rappard, head of the Permanent Mandates Commission, and denied the allegation that there were "poor innocent Arabs who are being bled by the Jews."

> There is not an atom of truth in all this. The country is quiet and prospering. Arabs of Akko, of Gaza, have come to me with reproaches

for ignoring their districts, saying how sorry they are that Jews don't come there.

Nobody can point to a single case of an injustice done to an Arab peasant. These poor wretches have been bled white by the Effendis, the very agitators who write protests to the League. The peasants have been transformed into brutes by oppression, usury, and barbarism of every kind at the hands of the Effendis. The latter are constantly offering their land to us, while in their press they admonish the people to boycott the Jews.

We have no quarrel with the peasant, who is more likely to receive fair treatment at our hands than from the tender care of the Effendi politician.[21]

In 1928 the farmers associations ceased to exist. They were persecuted by the Effendis and harassed by administration officials. Hajj Amin al-Husseini was physically annihilating any Arab who collaborated with the Jews. The idea of Arab–Jewish cooperation was dead.

We must now return to the Sharifians. Like his father, Emir Feisal evinced innate sympathy toward Zionism. When Sir Mark Sykes tried to enlighten him on the merits of Zionism, he was preaching to the converted. He nourished a genuine admiration for Jews and welcomed a good understanding with them based on solidarity of interests. No wonder that the meeting between Feisal and Weizmann in May 1918 at Wadi Waheida, near Akaba, went off so successfully. Feisal alluded to the historical traditions of both races and pointed to the need for close cooperation between them. He accepted the possibility of future Jewish claims to Palestine.

In his utterances in London Feisal was even more emphatic. He met Weizmann again on December 11, with Lawrence acting as interpreter. He attributed the current unrest among the Palestine Arabs to Turkish propaganda and was confident that he and his followers would be able to convince them that the advent of the Jews into Palestine was for the good of the country and that the legitimate interests of the Arab peasants would in no way be interfered with. He did not think that there was any scarcity of land in Palestine. He assured Weizmann on his word of honor that he would do everything to support Jewish demands. This he did.

On the following day he made an unequivocal declaration to Reuters that the Arabs intend to give the Jews "fair play," and in a banquet given in his honor by Lord Rothschild on December 21, 1918, he emphasized the kinship between the Arabs and the Jews and pledged cooperation with them to the best of his ability.

On January 3, 1919, when Feisal signed his famous agreement with Weizmann, his mind was fixed that the Jewish national home and the Arab state were to be two separate entities. The agreement was a formal confirmation of what had been already agreed upon between these two leaders on December 11, 1918.

On February 6, when appearing before the Council of Five, during the Peace Conference, he demanded that the council recognized Arab independence and at the same time made it unmistakably clear that Palestine was excepted.

Feisal's statement to *le Matin* (March 1, 1919) was out of tune with his declared general line of policy. It was, however, a slip of the tongue, and Feisal took care to correct the impression. In his letter to Prof. Felix Frankfurter, a leading member of the American Zionist delegation, he reiterated his sympathy for the Zionist movement and regarded the Zionist proposals, which had been submitted to the Peace Conference, as "moderate and proper." Jewish and Arab national movements "complement one another . . . and neither can be a real success without the other." He was convinced that some misunderstandings would disappear in due course.

On April 15, in the spirit of his accord with the Zionists, Feisal received a delegation of the Palestinian Jewish community and addressed them as "brothers." He hoped, on his return to Syria, to be able to convince the Palestinians to cooperate with the Zionists and invited his visitors to see him in Damascus in the near future. On April 20, he received the Jewish delegation again, and it was decided to found a joint Arab–Jewish committee, the objective of which would be to prevent hostilities and create a "rapprochement and an entente" between the two communities in Palestine.

And yet, in spite of his good will, the plan did not materialize. So, what went wrong?

After his return to Damascus, Feisal hoped to be able to bring about an Arab–Jewish reconciliation and make Zionism acceptable to his fellow Arabs. He invited members of the Zionist Commission and leading Palestine Arabs with a view of rapprochement. However, he was taken aback by the vehement reaction of the Palestinians. They were clamoring for "independence"; others demanded Palestine's inclusion in the Syrian state, now named as "United Syria." They were organized into clubs, of which the most prominent were *al-Muntanda al-Arabi* and *al-Nadi al-Arabi*. The former was led by al-Nashashibis, and the latter by the al-Husseini family. The number of members did not exceed five hundred in each club. They were, however, unusually vocal and influential.

There was yet another factor that nipped Feisal's scheme in the bud. On May 15 both Feisal and the Zionists were advised that the commander-in-chief "does not consider it desirable that any conference should take place at present between Emir Feisal, the Zionist Commission, and Palestinian notables."

From its inception, the military administration was not particularly friendly toward the Zionists. Allenby suppressed publication of the Balfour Declaration in Palestine. His staff was ignorant about the aims of Zionism and was tinged with anti-Semitism rampant in British society after the war, among the military in particular. Nonetheless, in 1918 Allenby gave his blessing to the Weizmann–Feisal meeting in Akaba. But a year later the military administration became decidedly antagonistic and averse to the implementation of the Balfour Declaration. "There are," Dr. Eder wrote to Weizmann, "influences at work who do not wish to see the Arab–Jewish entente."

So what caused such a drastic change? In the spring of 1919 the military administration fell upon the idea of forming a union of Palestine, Syria, and Mesopotamia under one Muslim flag and under British protection—a *Pax Britanica* of sorts. At this juncture, the military authorities decided to "go slow" on Zionism, which was tantamount to a demise of the Zionist cause.

The scheme was an amplified variation of Lord Kitchener's scheme in 1915 (Kitchener excluded Palestine). It was rejected by Prime Minister Asquith and by the de Bunsen Committee. It was revived in 1919 without the knowledge of the British government, let alone approval. It was illegal and impinged on the prerogatives of the peace conference. It was a conspiracy by inexperienced amateurs dressed in the mantle of empire-builders. It caused tremendous damage to Franco-British relations; it was a blow to Zionism and exacerbated the Arab–Zionist conflict.

The primary objective of the military was to eliminate the French from Syria. They soon found common ground with Arab, particularly Palestinian, extremists, France's archenemies. For this purpose the idea of "United Syria" was conceived, with Feisal being crowned the king of Palestine, Syria, and Mesopotamia.

Feisal's attitude toward Zionism had now undergone a radical transformation. He put on the mantle of Pan-Arabism and Pan-Islam, and his former friendship toward Zionism disappeared. He was prepared to accept it but only within the framework of the Arab Empire. He became a tool of the military and paid dearly for it.

The antagonism of the military toward Zionism was increasing and, in their utterances, gave the impression that they would welcome an Arab onslaught against the Jews. Hajj Amin al-Husseini, returning from Damascus, confirmed that the British government would not oppose handing over Palestine to an Arab authority. It was he who, jointly with Aref-el-Aref, organized the anti-Jewish riots in Jerusalem in April 1920 during the el-Nabi Musa festivities, which coincided with Easter and the Jewish Passover. It was Colonel Meinertzhagen who uncovered the plot. He found that a leading officer had urged Hajj Amin al-Husseini

> to show the world that the Arabs of Palestine would not tolerate Jewish domination in Palestine; that Zionism was unpopular . . . and that if disturbances of sufficient violence occurred in Jerusalem on Easter, both General Bols and General Allenby would advocate the abandonment of the Jewish Home. [The officer concerned] explained that freedom could only be attained through violence.

The conspiracy failed. The general uprising on which the Nationalists had pinned their hopes did not occur. Following the riots, sheikhs of eighty-two villages in the neighborhoods of Jerusalem and Jaffa lodged protest with the administration against anti-Jewish demonstrations that had been organized by a "few individuals." They claimed to represent the majority of the population—about 70 percent, and declared that they saw "no danger" in the Zionist immigration.

Lloyd George and Curzon, then in San Remo, acted instantly on Meinertzhagen's advice. The military administration was to be terminated and replaced by civil administration, headed by Herbert Samuel.

However, the biggest blow administered to Allenby's prestige was the findings of the Palin Committee, which had been appointed by Allenby himself. "The chief culpability" for the riots in Jerusalem, the committee asserted, "lay with the Military Administration for failing to make adequate preparations to avert the disturbances . . . in spite of ample knowledge of what was afoot." The authors of the report admitted that the Balfour Declaration was a "solemnly declared policy" of the British government and that of the Allies. Had the Balfour Declaration been published in Palestine, as it had been in the rest of the world, the native population, the committee surmised, would have recognized "its finality and, trusting in the guarantees it contains, ceased to agitate or to feel alarm." Its suppression by the military administration, however, "created doubts as to whether the Balfour Declaration would have ever come into operation, not only in the minds of the public, but in those officials of the Government." This was aggravated by the aggressive propaganda for a United Syria. The committee questioned the wisdom of the military's decision and concluded that the "nonpublication of the Foreign Office declaration of policy . . . was an error."

Thereafter followed a statement that concluded as a warning:

> Closely interwoven with the United Syria movement is the Pan-Islamic agitation which seems to unite Islam from India to the Mediterranean. This again connects with the Pan-Turanian ideals [upheld by] their Turkish co-religionists. All these movements are now definitely anti-British and anti-Allied, and their combined efforts are directed to fan the flame lit by the discontented Palestinian population.

Sir Mark Sykes was the first to warn the British officers of their dangerous policy. During his visit to Syria and Palestine after the war, he realized that Arab nationalism was assuming a Pan-Arab and Pan-Islamic character. Islam was becoming the core of the Arab movement. The dominant trend was "complete independence from any form of foreign control." The Arab movement was assuming an anti-Western and anti-alien stance.

Major J. N. Clayton, the political officer in Damascus, stated that in the eyes of the vast majority of Muslim Arabs, Arab nationalism and Islamism were "synonymous terms . . . . The Islamic movement [he predicted] will inevitably lead to a rapprochement with the Turks and with Mustafa Kemal." However, the British officers, in their drive toward "empire building," were oblivious to the dangers and ignored the warnings. Ironically, they were supporting their own enemies.

> Palestine is largely inhabited by unreasonable people. It will always be so, and strong Government by a strong external Power is essential.

This statement was made by William Ormsby-Gore on March 1, 1923, then acting as undersecretary of state or colonies. During his service on Political Intelligence at the Arab Bureau in Cairo, Ormsby-Gore acquainted himself intimately with Middle Eastern affairs, and his judgment was sound.

When Herbert Samuel was appointed high commissioner for Palestine, to his credit stood his proven Zionist record, as well as his reputation as an efficient and honest administrator. Lloyd George, his primary proponent, was confident that Samuel would faithfully implement the Zionist policy. He also enjoyed Weizmann's support and warm approbation of representatives of the Jewish community in Palestine. By nature Samuel was courteous and considerate, and his memoranda were closely argued. However, he lacked the strength of character and consistency so essential for any administrator of Palestine.

In due course Weizmann concluded that Samuel was "weak, frightened and trembling when dealing with the Arabs." Lloyd George too complained that Samuel was "weak . . . and he has funked his position." Meinertzhagen concurred. Samuel "is weak . . . . The moment the Jaffa rioting broke out [in 1921] he . . . [has] been hypnotized by the danger and did everything to placate the Arabs." Moreover, Samuel had not been able to stand up to the solid block of anti-Zionist feeling among the military advisers and civil subordinates. His judgment in Middle Eastern matters was hopelessly defective. His excessive liberalism proved counterproductive. In consequence it invited failure. From this perspective his choice as high commissioner was a miscalculation. His administration, rather than impede, inadvertently stimulated the growth of Palestinian nationalism.

Samuel's first year of administration proved a success, and he won praise from both Jews and Arabs. But the unexpected riots in Jaffa in May 1921 gave him a shock. It affected his outlook for the duration of his term of office and caused a complete transformation of his policy. Instead of facilitating and encouraging the growth of the Jewish national home, now his primary preoccupation was to placate the Arabs. His first step, rather than punish the perpetrators as any governor would have done, decreed the cessation of immigration. It infuriated Churchill and angered the Zionists who saw in his move a submission to terror. It had the opposite effect on the Arabs, who were quick to learn that they could intimidate the government.

In an address delivered before the Jewish Historical Society of England on November 25, 1935, Samuel explained the raison d'être of his policy. He said thus:

> From the outset it was obvious to the Government at home and to its administration in Palestine that the Arab question was the predominant issue. There were over 600,000 Arabs in the country . . .

they were apprehensive as to the possibility of being supplanted by the incursion into Palestine of millions of Jews . . . It was necessary to show that these anxieties were unjustified and allay these fears. It was plain that the establishment of the Jewish National Home must be conditioned not only by safeguarding for the existing rights of the Arab population, but also by a constant and active care, on the part of the Mandatory Power, for their economic and cultural progress. No other policy was consistent with the principles that prevailed throughout the British Empire . . . No other policy would be approved by the House of Commons and British public opinion . . . .

This was a novel interpretation. At no time did the British government *condition* the growth of the Jewish national home on Arab consent and on their well-being. Such a condition never entered the mind of any British statesman who sponsored the Balfour Declaration; it would have a priori nullified the growth of the Jewish national home. Leopold Amery testified that the various provisos that he drafted "gave away nothing that was not self-evident . . . it served its immediate purpose" of overcoming opposition and easing the birth of the declaration without impairing its substance. The relevant clause circumscribed, but would not bar, the implementation of Zionist aspirations.

The British government was of course alive to the fact that the Jews were outnumbered in Palestine by the Arabic-speaking population, but arithmetic could not serve as the primary guide, since the right of the Jews outside Palestine had to be taken into account. The declaration was made to the Jewish people as a whole. Hence, the beneficiary was not only the actual Jewish population in Palestine, but the Jewish people at large. In this respect Balfour's statement made to Lloyd George, on February 19, 1919, is illuminating:

Our justification for our policy [he wrote] is that we regard Palestine as being absolutely exceptional; that we consider the question of the Jews outside Palestine as one of world importance, and that we conceive the Jews to have an historic claim to a home in their ancient land; provided that home can be given them without either dispossessing or oppressing the present inhabitants.

Balfour nourished no ill-feeling toward the Arabs but with regard to Palestine he was convinced that the Jewish claim was superior. Zionism, in his opinion, was "of far profounder import than the desires and prejudices of the 700,000 Arabs, who now inhabit that ancient land." In August 1919 Balfour told Justice Brandeis that Palestine presented "a unique situation . . . which inevitably excluded numerical self-determination. . . . We are dealing not with the wishes of an existing community but are consciously seeking to reconstitute a new community and definitely building for numerical majority in the future."

This view was shared by Prime Minister Lloyd George and President Wilson. This was also how the Intelligence section of the American delegation to the peace conference understood the problem:

> It is right that Palestine should become a Jewish state if the Jews be-ing given the full opportunity, make it such . . . At present however, the Jews form barely a sixth of the total population of 700,000 . . . . England as mandatory, can be relied on to give the Jews the privileged position they should have without sacrificing the rights of the non-Jews.

Samuel was misinterpreting or misapprehending British policy. Palestine was sui generis, but as is evident from his address, he treated it as a British colony.

This was not his mind-set before being appointed high commissioner. In a speech that he delivered on November 2, 1919, on the occasion of the second anniversary of the Balfour Declaration, he spoke about "active promotion of Jewish cultural development and the fullest measure of local self-government, in order that with the minimum of delay the country may become a purely self-governing commonwealth under the auspices of an established Jewish majority."

It would therefore not be too far-fetched to assume that the transformation in his thinking had developed from the kind of advice he was given by his staff.

Soon after assuming office, rather than make a clean sweep, he retained most of the staff from the military administration. They changed their clothes but not their views, which were unmistakably unfriendly to Zionism. A notable exception was Brigadier Sir Wyndham Deedes, whose Zionism was motivated both by ideological and religious convictions. He acted first as civil secretary and later as chief secretary of the government.

Another senior appointment was that of Ernest Richmond. An architect by profession and an expert on Muslim antiquities and institutions, he was a close friend of Ronald Storrs, who brought him to Jerusalem to take charge of restoration works at the Dome of the Rock. It was Storrs who recommended him to Samuel to act as a liaison with the Arab population as assistant civil secretary. Richmond believed that the Balfour Declaration and Zionism were evil "with a decidedly Communist bias" and that the Jews were interfering in Arab affairs with "a desire to disintegrate other communities."[22]

It was, however, Richmond who was interfering, not the Jews. Ragheb Nashashibi complained to Colonel Kisch that Richmond "makes all cooperation with the Jews impossible." This was confirmed by representatives of the Muslim national clubs from Jerusalem, Haifa, Nablus, and Jenin who met at Kisch's office. Kisch brought these facts to Deedes's knowledge, adding that Richmond was "definitely opposed to the policy of the Mandate." Kisch met separately with Richmond, who made no secret of his opposition to Zionism. "He is sincere, but . . . a man with his views should not be employed as political adviser to the Governor in Palestine."[23]

Weizmann was bitter. "The real difficulty [is] not so much the Arabs themselves, as their British advisers," he wrote to Deedes. "I know for a fact that the attitude of Richmond has stiffened the Arabs up very much."[24] Several months later, writing to a friend, Weizmann noted that there was a great number of anti-Semites and anti-Zionists among the officials, some of whom are "particularly malicious, as for instance the Political Secretary Richmond. He is an open, obvious, and apparently honest opponent. [He] is fanatical, bitter and malicious, and, as a result, we have a very sad state of affairs, . . . in the hands of an enemy."[25]

The colonial office too was highly disappointed. Gerard Clauson had this to say:

> I should not personally have one minute's regret if M. Richmond resigned . . . he is a declared enemy of the Zionist policy and almost as frankly declared an enemy of the Jewish policy of H.M.G . . . Indeed, I think that the government, so far from losing, would gain very greatly by excluding from [the] secretariat so very partisan a figure as Mr. Richmond and starting again on a strictly non-partisan basis.

In the event Richmond did not resign, Samuel objected on grounds that he was irreplaceable. When he did finally resign on March 13, 1924, he told Samuel that during his three-and-a-half years of service he became convinced that the Zionist Commission, the Middle East Department of the Colonial Office, as well as Samuel's own administration were dominated and inspired by a spirit that he regarded as "evil." His opposition to this policy was not merely political, but also moral, even religious. "He had tried to alter the machine, but had completely failed and now he had to go."[26]

What Richmond meant in his phrase "to alter the machine" is a matter of speculation. However, judging by his methodical attempts to frustrate official policy, there is only one plausible explanation: his endeavors to destroy the Zionist experiment had not succeeded.

It was Richmond who influenced Samuel to pardon Aref-al-Aref and Hajj Amin al-Husseini, both leaders of the April 1920 riots in Jerusalem and fugitives from justice. It was also Richmond who pressed for the appointment of Hajj Amin as the grand mufti of Jerusalem while his stepbrother Kiamil was on his deathbed. Colonel Kisch expressed serious reservations, but his advice was ignored. Both Deedes and Norman Bentwich, the legal adviser, protested, but Samuel overruled them. More forceful language was used by Colonel Meinertzhagen. He thought that the appointment of Hajj Amin to such an exalted office was "sheer madness . . . he can do untold harm to Zionism and to the British; he hates both Jews and the British." Meinertzhagen knew Amin well. Hajj Amin "is a strong character . . . he is very ambitious, quite unscrupulous and grossly dishonest; sooner or later his appointment will be bitterly regretted by us."[27]

Hajj Amin was known neither for his scholarship nor for his piety. The fact that Sheikh Hassan al-Din Jarallah was elected by a concord of Muslim divines, notables, and Beduin sheikhs speaks for itself. Hajj Amin was elected only fourth in the list, but Samuel prevailed upon Sheikh al-Din Jarallah to withdraw his candidature, and on May 8 Hajj Amin was nominated for the position as grand mufti. This was a gross interference in internal Muslim religious affairs.

Samuel disregarded the warnings of the authoritative persons and trusted the word of Hajj Amin. On April 11, in Storrs's presence, Hajj Amin declared his earnest desire to cooperate with the government and his belief in the good intentions of the British government toward the Arabs.

> He gave assurances that the influence of his family and himself would be devoted to maintaining tranquility in Jerusalem, and he felt sure that no disturbances need be feared this year. He said that the riots last year were spontaneous and unpremeditated.[28]

Hajj Amin's appointment was not gazetted; nor was there any definition of the conditions and tenure of his appointment. This allowed Amin to usurp the power of the leader of the Arab community in Palestine and to emerge as its spokesman.

The establishment of the Husseini dominance over Arab Palestine was facilitated by the creation of the Supreme Muslim Council. This institution was meant, inter alia, to balance the Zionist Committee that became a focus of suspicion and a "proof" of the government's favor toward the Jewish community.

The Supreme Muslim Council was to have unfettered control over the management of religious endowments, appointment of all shari'a and wakf officials, as well as of all qadis. This bestowed enormous powers in the hands of the council, which was totally exempt from official inspection and control. On January 9, 1922, by forty votes out of fifty-six, Hajj Amin was chosen Rais al-Ulema, that is, president of the council. It was a life appointment with a salary of £100,000. The juridical powers of the council were so wide, as Harry Luke, assistant governor of Jerusalem, expressed himself, amounted to "almost an abdication by the Administration of Palestine of responsibilities normally incumbent upon a Government." And vis-à-vis the Palestinian community, the council assumed sheer despotism. In 1937 it was disbanded by the government.[29]

It was Hajj Amin who instituted the regime of despotism. Although meant as a religious body dealing with social affairs, Hajj Amin turned it into a *political* instrument. He misused religion for political purposes. Moreover, it became a center of terror against both Jews and Arabs. He instigated the riots of 1929 and again in 1936–39, his promise to Samuel notwithstanding. On September 26, 1937, when L. Y. Andrews, the acting district commissioner for Galilee, was assassinated together with his police escort, the government sought Hussein's arrest, but he managed to escape in disguise to Lebanon. From there, and thereafter from Iraq, he continued to conspire against the British government. In 1941 he fled Iraq and found refuge in Berlin under the wing of Nazi Germany. He met Hitler and on several occasions also Adolf Eichmann, the bureaucrat responsible for implementing the plan to wipe out European Jewry. Mufti and the Muslim SS divisions in Bosnia were willing accessories to the "Final Solution." Amin al-Husseini's dream was to become governor of Palestine free of Jews and of the British under German Nazi protection.[30]

Samuel never expressed regrets for promoting Hussein to such an exalted position. On the contrary, in a speech in the House of Lords on December 8, 1938, Viscount Samuel vigorously defended his decision. It elicited a sharp retort from Lord Harlech, formerly

Ormsby-Gore, who had been colonial secretary during 1936–37. Hajj Amin al-Husseini, Lord Harlech declared, had shown himself as an implacable enemy of the Jews, as he was an implacable enemy of the British. He had been bitterly hostile to the Sharifian family, to King Feisal, as well as to Emir Abdullah, whose position he sought to undermine. He had no qualms about murdering Palestinian Arab leaders who stood in the way of his ambitions. A high-ranking Turkish officer described him as "the blackest hearted man in the Middle East."

In September 1937 the Permanent Mandates Commission censured the government for having failed to declare martial law at an earlier stage of the riots. Ormsby-Gore pointed his accusing finger at the mufti:

> I still feel that we shall never get on top of this murder campaign . . . until we have eliminated the Mufti and his gang. He was the *fons et origo* of the murders in 1929, and as long as he appears to funk dealing with this black-hearted villain and allows him to disseminate anti-British propaganda throughout the Islamic world, and organize terrorism on any Arabs in Palestine not subservient to him and his Supreme Moslem, we cannot hope to maintain law and order or even be *de facto* government in Palestine.[31]

General Dill, the general officer commander, Palestine, regarded the mufti as the "main instigator" of the riots and that until he was removed from his position law and order would not be restored in Palestine. Arthur Wauchope, the high commissioner, thought the same.[32]

In 1938 Colonel Kisch's *Palestine Diary* was published. It contains abundant evidence not only of persistent efforts made by the Zionist Executive to reach an understanding with the Arabs but also of the fact that there existed "a large body of moderate Arab opinion which would have been ready to follow a lead from the Mandatory Government in coming to an understanding with Jews on the basis of the policy embodied in the Mandate." However, that lead was not given, to the contrary. Samuel's government never ceased to uphold the authority and power of the Arab extremist group, headed by the mufti of Jerusalem, Hajj Amin al-Husseini:

> I have no doubt whatever [Kisch concluded] that had it not been for the Mufti's abuse of his immense power and the toleration of that abuse by the Government over a period of fifteen years, an Arab–Jewish understanding within the framework of the Mandate would long since have been reached.[33]

Had Samuel followed Kisch's example, he would have found scores of Palestinian notables and sheikhs knocking at his door. They all desired to cooperate with the government, as well as with the Zionists. Kisch's pleas to this effect fell on deaf ears. Samuel turned his ear to Richmond and his likes instead and tried to placate the implacable. The extremists remained as obdurate as ever. From their perspective concessions demonstrated weakness and had the opposite effect. Appeasement proved a short-sighted policy. It infuriated the Zionists but did not win the consent, let alone the friendship, of the extremists among the Arabs.

Samuel's speech on June 3, 1921, was a case in point. In it he stated among other things that for the happiness of the people of Palestine, the British government as the trustee under terms of the mandate "would never impose upon them a policy which that people had reason to think was contrary to their religious, their political, and their economic interests."[34]

Here was another misinterpretation of the Balfour Declaration and the terms of the mandate. The Zionists were outraged and regarded Samuel's speech as betrayal. On July 18 Weizmann wrote to Samuel, "It seems that everything in Palestine life is now revolving round one central problem—how to satisfy and 'pacify' the Arabs. Zionism is being gradually, systematically, and relentlessly 'reduced.'"[35]

On July 22 at a meeting at Balfour's home, at which Lloyd George, Churchill, Sir Maurice Hankey, and Edward Russell were present, Weizmann gave vent to his fury. He stated, "The Declaration means ultimate Jewish majority," but the implication of Samuel's speech "would never permit such a majority to eventuate. It was a negation of the Balfour Declaration." Lloyd George and Balfour responded that "by the Declaration they always meant an eventual Jewish state."

Both Churchill and Shuckburgh were of the opinion that Samuel had been influenced "not only by the Arabs but also by British officials who were not in sympathy with Zionist policy." It fell to Hubert Young, in charge of the Middle East desk at the Foreign Office, to prepare a memorandum for the cabinet. The term "National Home," he emphasized, "implied no less than full statehood for the Jews of Palestine and there could be no halfway house between a Jewish State and a total abandonment of the Zionist program." An identical interpretation reached Forbes Adam, in a memorandum dated December 30, 1919, with which neither Vansitrat nor Curzon disagreed.

For some reason these statements of policy were not communicated to Samuel. So without specific instructions Samuel continued to plough his own furrow.

However, Churchill was very firm when he confronted the Palestinian delegation in London on August 1921. They arrived there due to some thoughtless permission by Samuel to plead their case.

Assisted by some British advisers, the delegation demanded the creation of a national Palestinian government according to the "treaty" that had been concluded between King Hussein and Sir Henry McMahon on October 24, 1915, adding that during the war they fought side by side with the Allies. Churchill, accompanied by Young, had no difficulty in demolishing the Palestinians' claims and in defending the validity of the Balfour Declaration. It was a policy of the imperial government, he declared, and rested on the Allied decision. He had neither the power nor the authority to alter it and urged the Palestinians to cooperate with the Zionists for the benefit of the country as a whole. Churchill reminded the delegation that they were not an official body, nor were they representative.

In spite of two successive meetings, the Palestinians remained uncompromising. The Balfour Declaration, they maintained, was "at the root of all our trouble." However, all attempts to persuade the delegation failed. "Experience has shown," Shuckburgh commented, "that they are a hopeless body to deal with." The difficulty was compounded by the fact that they were being guided by some British advisors, "whose real object is to defeat our whole policy, and whose primary concern is to strengthen the Arab resistance, if not to encourage actual resort to measures of violence."

To resolve the impasse, Samuel suggested that Weizmann issue a statement formally renouncing the Zionist aspirations to create a Jewish state in Palestine. Weizmann rejected the idea out of hand. Thereupon, on March 9, 1922, Samuel sent Churchill a confidential dispatch in which he insisted that, in order to set Arab fears at rest, it was imperative that the government issue an official interpretation of the Balfour Declaration. It formed the basis of the white paper. Both Churchill and Shuckburgh entertained strong reservations to publication of this document, but Samuel managed to convert them to his point of view. What tipped the scales in his favor was the argument that he had been consistently hammering home, that is, if the Palestine Arab delegation returned home empty-handed, a renewed wave of violence was bound to occur. The statement was published

over Churchill's signature in June 1922. However, its author and driving force was Samuel. It formed the basis of British policy in Palestine
for almost a decade.

The white paper imposed two limitations on the growth of the
Jewish National Home: one geographical—this was the meaning of
the phrase "in Palestine"—and the other on immigration, which was
circumscribed to the economic absorptive capacity of the country.

The white paper failed to achieve its major purpose, that is, to reconcile the Palestinians. The delegation rejected it instantly. The delegation
too failed to achieve its purpose, however. British commitment to the
Balfour Declaration—albeit watered down—remained as firm as ever,
and all Arab claims were unequivocally rejected. On July 24, 1922, the
Council of the League of Nations confirmed the mandate. It included in
its preamble the text of the Balfour Declaration, which thereby became
a recognized and binding document by international law.

The delegation returned to Palestine empty-handed. Yet despite all
Samuel's dire predictions, no rioting occurred. The premise on which
he had built his policy, and which he had used so effectively to convince
Shuckburgh and Churchill, was devoid of any foundation. He was a
victim of his unfounded fears—fears on which some of his staff played
skillfully in order to neutralize, if not nullify, the Zionist policy.

The deeper reasons why riots did not take place was because the
delegation, and the Executive in general, was not a representative
body and commanded only limited following. Businessmen as well
as educated people dissociated themselves from the militant and aggressive stance adopted by the extremists. More telling were cables
dispatched to the colonial secretary by dozens of town and village
notables, sheikhs, and mukhtars during the early summer of 1922 protesting the behavior of the Palestine Arab delegation, then in London.
The statements of the delegation were not authorized by the people
of Palestine. "We are convinced that progress and prosperity lie in the
path of brotherhood" with the Jews.

The representatives of the National Islamic Society of Nazareth
and environs also protested against the delegation, which "had been
elected by a minority and had no right to speak on their behalf. They
declared that

> the Arab people are not opposed to the realization of the hope of
> the Jewish people and we particularly request that the organized
> Jewish immigration be given full encouragement. . . . [We hope]

that under the British Mandate we shall be finally delivered from the machinations of the instigators of trouble and discord who are leading the country to ruin.

A variant of the telegram was sent by inhabitants and elders of Beisan, Haifa, as well as other towns in the north, while the organizations of the farmers complained of the methods of intimidation employed by the Palestine Executive. "The Jews are our brothers and Palestine can never thrive without their financial and cultural help."

However, the cables arrived at the colonial office too late to reverse the white paper policy, while the government in Palestine completely ignored them.

Notes

1. Elizabeth Monroe, *Britain's Moment in the Middle East, 1914–1915* (London, 1963), 43.
2. What follows is based on excerpts from Isaiah Friedman's books: *The Question of Palestine, 1914–1918: British–Jewish–Arab Relations*, a second expanded edition (New Brunswick, NJ: Transaction Publishers, 1992); *Palestine: A Twice Promised Land? The British, the Arabs, and Zionism, 1915–1920* (New Brunswick, NJ: Transaction Publishers, 2000); *British Pan-Arab Policy, 1915–1922. A Critical Appraisal* (New Brunswick, NJ: Transaction Publishers, 2010), unless quoted otherwise.
3. Koran, Sura 17, "The Night Journey", verse 104.
4. Ibid., Sura 2, "The Cow", verse 47.
5. Ibid., Sura 5, "The Table", verse 20.
6. Ibid., Sura 7, "The Heights", verse 159.
7. Ibid., Sura 10, "Jonah", verse 93.
8. Ibid., Sura 21, "The Prophets", verses 70–1.
9. Ibid., Sura 17, "The Night Journey", verse 2.
10. Ibid., Sura 17, "The Night Journey", verses 100–60.
11. Lt. Col. F. H. Kisch, *Palestine Diary* (London, 1938), 93–8.
12. Ibid., 386–7.
13. Ibid., 109–10.
14. Ibid., 26–7 and 48–9.
15. Ibid., 49–50.
16. Ibid., 101–2.
17. Ibid., 126, 142.
18. Ibid., 34–5, 46–7, 135.
19. Ibid., 54.
20. Yehoshua Porath, *The Emergence of the Palestinian Arab National Movement, 1918–1929* (Jerusalem: Routledge, 1971), 185–7 [Hebrew].
21. *Weizmann Letters*, vol. XII, no. 197, Weizmann to Rappard, November 15, 1924 (Translation Books and Israel University, Jerusalem, 1977), 261–7.
22. Bernard Wasserstein, *The British in Palestine: The Mandatory Government and the Arab–Jewish Conflict, 1917–1929* (London, 1978), 144–5.
23. Kisch, *Diary*, February 21, 22, 1923, 34–5.

24. *Weizmann Letters*, XI, A, Weizmann to Deedes, February 4, 1922, 26–9, My very dear friend.

25. Ibid., Weizmann (Jerusalem) to Naiditch (Paris), December 11, 1922, 219–22.

26. Elie Kedourie, *The Chatham House Version: And other Middle Eastern Studies.* (Hannover and London, 1984), 65; Wasserstein, *The British in Palestine*, 145–6.

27. Meinertzhagen, *Diary*, 97.

28. Wasserstein, 98, an abbreviated version in Kedourie, *The Chatham House*, 62. The matter is fully researched in Porath, *The Emergence of the Palestinian-Arab National Movement*, 149–58 [Hebrew].

29. Kedourie, *The Chatham House*, 70–3; Porath, *The Emergence of the Palestinian-Arab National Movement*, 158–68; Wasserstein, 131–5.

30. On this issue, see Klaus Michael Mallmann and Martin Cüppers, *Nazi Palestine: The Plans for the Extermination of Jews in Palestine* (New York, 2010).

31. Cited in Michael J. Cohen, *Palestine: Retreat from the Mandate* (London, 1978), 53.

32. Ibid., 50, 52.

33. Kisch, *Diary*, 19–20.

34. For the full text of Samuel's speech, see Central Zionist Archives, Jerusalem Z4/16055.

35. Ibid., Weizmann to Samuel, July 18, 1921.

Index

G